WELSH PONIES AND COBS

WELSH PONIES AND COBS

Wynne Davies

J. A. ALLEN & COMPANY LIMITED
London

British Library Cataloguing in Publication Data
A catalogue record for this book is available from
the British Library

ISBN 0 85131 361 2

Published in Great Britain by
J. A. Allen & Company Limited
1 Lower Grosvenor Place
London SW1W 0EL

First published 1990
Reprinted 1994

Printed in Hong Kong

Contents

WELSH PONIES

WELSH PONIES (COB TYPE) AND WELSH COBS

Note on the Illustrations

In any historical work an author is dependent for illustrations on widespread sources. This is the case with this book. Originals submitted for the author's consideration included negatives, printed handbills, stud cards, handwritten letters, fragments of posters, transparencies and so on. Most were of some age and a good many were damaged or marked in some way.

In making his choice for the book, the author has included subjects in the belief that a picture, even a damaged one, is what the reader will want to see when reading about a particular animal. This is especially so in the case of animals who are long dead. Most of the originals selected are owned by individuals and are of value and, in many cases, unique. Some have never been seen before by others outside their owner's immediate family and certainly a good many will never have been published before their appearance in this book. Retouching or repair of these originals has not been carried out and the author is indebted to those who so generously lent illustrations from their collections. Acknowledgements for illustrations are shown in the relevant captions throughout the book. Where no acknowledgement is given the subject is from the author's own collection or from other sources.

Preface

It is many years since Mr. J. A. Allen first wrote asking me to write a history of Welsh Ponies and Cobs but it seemed such a formidable task that I kept putting it off. Then I realised how much easier it would have been had I undertaken this history when the members of the previous generation of Pony and Cob breeders were still with us; many of them called and stayed at my home in my childhood days and my late father visited them in turn; these folk knew the Welsh Ponies and Cobs of the last century, with their passing any history is more difficult. To the next generation it would be more difficult still, so here is my contribution!

An interesting fact which came to light when researching into the pedigrees of Royal Welsh Show Champion Welsh Mountain Ponies and Cobs of the last twenty-five years is that one sees the same names cropping up time and time again e.g. Coed Coch Seren (foaled in 1925) and Vardra Charm (foaled in 1924) (and further back of course Dyoll Starlight) amongst the Mountain Ponies and Dewi Black Bess (foaled in 1926) and Ceitho Welsh Comet (foaled in 1913) amongst the Cobs. This, I found surprising in view of the total numbers of 20,000 registered stallions and 60,000 registered mares and 20,000 foundation stock mares to date; the greatest proportion of these registered families (and some of them being popular winners in the show ring) have long since faded into obscurity.

For this reason, I have presented the histories in "families". All sections of the *Welsh Stud Book* are inter-dependent and consequently some Cobs may appear with the Mountain Ponies in the earlier chapters; conversely some Mountain Ponies appear amongst Welsh Pony (Cob type) and Welsh Cob families.

Registration numbers which appear in the extended pedigrees refer to the *Welsh Stud Book*; other numbers which appear in the text are noted as such e.g. *Hackney Stud Book, Polo Pony Stud Book* etc.

Doubtless in a work of this magnitude there may be errors, I would be

ix

grateful to anyone discovering some to inform me of them; hopefully they are very few. Any views expressed herein are entirely my own and not those of any Society or Committee of which I am a member.

I have selected families which I consider to have had the greatest influence on the development of Welsh Ponies and Cobs, anyone else undertaking this work could well have selected other families. I am aware of many other families which deserve to be in this book and apologise for having to omit them at this stage.

Any work of this kind would not be possible without the help of many colleagues. For photographs I wish to thank the Welsh Pony and Cob Society (*Welsh Stud Book* and *Journal*), Mr. Gwyn Berry, Mrs. Binnie, Mr. Stephen Blythman, Mrs. Borthwick, Mr. Dai Davies, Mr. Mostyn Isaac, Mr. Cerdin Jones, Mr. Peter Jones, Mr. Ifor Lloyd, Mr. John Roderick Rees and Mr. David Reynolds.

The following have checked individual chapters for which I am very grateful: Mrs. Blandy, Mrs. Cuff, Mr. Emrys Griffiths, Mr. and Mrs. Cerdin Jones, Mr. S. D. Morgan, Mrs. Mountain, Mrs. Morfydd Davies, M.A., (University of Wales), Miss R. Philipson-Stow, Mr. George Preece, Miss Miriam Reader, Mr. John Roderick Rees, B.A., Mrs. Reeve-Reeves, Mr. H. Llewellyn Richards, Miss Pauline Taylor, Mr. D. E. Williams (National Library of Wales).

A special note of thanks must go to Messrs. Rowlands Harris who allowed me to borrow their collection of stud cards.

Finally thanks to anyone else who contributed towards this treatise and especially to the members of my family for their encouragement.

WYNNE DAVIES *1980*

GWREICHION,

Gweld yn ei lygad ar Ddydd Llun y Preimim gynt
Golyn o fellten hen gobiau gwibiog y gwynt
Pan oedd lladdwr o frenin yn eu herlid o'u hynt.

Hen yw y gwres yn y gwaed o dafodau'r fflam
Wedi enhuddo mewn cnawd ac yn gaeth i'w llam
Yn burdan a lusg mewn osgo a cheinder cam.

A thyr drwy'i synhwyrau heddiw y gwreichion rhydd
A'i hysbarduna ymlaen o'r tanau cudd
Yn seren ym mhaladiwm meirch y dydd.

Vernon Jones

Eisteddfod Genedlaethol Aberteifi 1976.

(Cyflwynedig i Wynne Davies a'r diweddar E. S. Davies.)

Poem dedicated to Wynne Davies and the late E. S. Davies Royal
National Eisteddfod of Wales, Cardigan 1976.

1
Early History

1. Early History

The origin of the native breeds found in the United Kingdom has long been a matter for conjecture. Researchers learned in the art of deducing theories from ancient bones and pre-historic relics have failed to offer a wholly satisfactory solution of the mystery. One school of thought suggests that horse life of some kind, both large and small has existed here since the Ice Age (i.e. to about 10,000 B.C.); others have been equally satisfied that these regions were not included in the zone of possible Ice Age migrations and that all such life became totally extinct in subsequent Neolithic times (i.e. about 4,000 to 1,000 B.C.).

A large collection of fragments of harness and chariots dating from the Bronze Age (i.e. about 1,500 to 500 B.C.) found in North Wales (Llyn Cerrig Bach hoard) suggest from the dimensions of the harness that ponies, rather than horses were used for harness work. The lengths of the bits were under 3 ins suggesting that the harness ponies were under 12 hands.

Julius Caesar during his visit to Britain in 55 B.C. was amazed at the competence of the British charioteer and stated that the "Britons were masters over their horses and chariots".

Hywel Dda (Howell the Good) was a ruler of Deheubarth (who eventually gained sovereignty over the whole of Wales) and his probable codification of the laws[1] in the tenth century formed the basis .of Welsh law for six centuries.

The laws describe three types of horses: (i) Palfrey which was the riding horse or riding pony, (ii) Rowny or Sumpter, the pack horse and (iii) the working horse "equus operarius" the light, able-bodied working horse which pulled the sledge ("car llusg") or small gambo. This classification was similar to that existing throughout Britain during the Middle Ages.

From the fifteenth-century manuscript of Lydgate's Siege of Thebes[2] it was seen that the British knight and his horse (destrier) as the basic fighting unit of the medieval army, needed a minimum of three other horses to keep them in action day after day. Preferably there should be a second destrier because the Great Horse, despite its virtues, was rather soft and was ridden only in action. There must be a palfrey for the knight to ride when not in action and a Cob or rouncy (runcinus) for the

---

[1] *The Laws of Hywel Dda.* National Library of Wales, Aberystwyth.
[2] *The Foals of Epona*, pp. 89. A. Dent and D. Machin Goodall.

3

squire to ride while leading the destrier, also a pack-horse to carry the knight's armour. The rouncy had to travel at a trot because the war-horse which the squire led was a natural trotter. The palfrey, on the other hand, paced or ambled and could thus be supplied from any of the native breeds which were predominantly non-trotting by nature. If a foal out of a palfrey mare grew up with trotting propensities, it would be schooled in hobbles until it did pace. The palfrey goes back in name and in blood to the Roman occupation (derived from "Paraveredus" relay-horse).

The laws of Hywel Dda continue by quoting values of horses. A foal until a fortnight old is worth fourpence. From the fifteenth day of his age until a year, 24 pence ($1\frac{3}{8}$ oz silver). When a year and one day old he was worth 49 pence and stood at that value till he began his third year when he was valued at 60 pence. In his third year he was broken in and his value depended on the work for which he was fitted: a palfrey or a sumpter was valued at 120 pence (8 oz silver) and a working horse to draw a cart or harrow 60 pence. It was not permissible to use horses, mares or cows for ploughing for fear of injury, oxen only might be used. Any entire male animal was worth three females; thus a wild stallion was worth ninescore pence to the mare's value of threescore pence.

The laws also specify the values of individual parts of the horse: the worth of his foot was equal to his full value. Every blemish was equiv-alent to one-third of the total worth, including his ears and tail, (possibly cropping and docking were in vogue). It was quoted that the worth of the tail of a filly for common work was the same as the total value of the animal, probably because a harrow was often secured to the tail.

The laws continue: "Any man who borrows a horse and frets the hair on his back has to pay fourpence; if the skin is broken to the flesh eightpence; and if the skin and flesh are broken to the bone sixteen-pence." Borrowing without the owner's permission fourpence for mounting, fourpence for each rhandir (league) he rode the horse. The unfortunate offender also had to pay a fine to the owner's lord.

It was apparently customary to fetter or clog the horses when they were turned out to graze. Trespass by day in corn by a clogged horse cost one penny and two by night. If the horse was kept free it cost only half. Stallions were free and there was no fine for his owner for any damage which he might do to the crops.

Many references to the horses are obtained from the medieval litera-ture of that period. The thirteenth-century *Book of Taliesin* contains a poem *Canu y Meirch* which probably derives from an earlier period.

Tri Thri nodet atcor ar henet:
A march Mayave, a march Genethave,
A march Karadavc, kymrvy teithiavc.
A march Gvythur, a march Gva(w)rdur,
A march Arthur, ehofyn rodi cur;
A march Taliessin, a march Lleu lletuegin,
A Phebyrillei llvynin, a Grei march Cunin;
Kornan kyneiwave (= kynelwawe?), Awyd awydave,
Du Moroed enwavc, march Brvyn bro(n) bradavc;
A'r tri carn aflav(c), nyt ant hynt hilav:
Kethin march Keidav, carn avarn arnav,
(r)scvydurith yscodic, gorvyd Llemenic,
March Ryderch rydic, Llvyt lliv elleic;
A Llamrei llavn (= llamm?) elwic, a Ffroenuoll gvirenhic,
(A) march Sadyrnin, a march Custenhin,
Ac ereill yn trin rac tir allgvin(in);
Henwyn mat dyduc kychwedyl o Hiraduc . . .

To the Famous Threes, a return to ancient times
Mayawg's horse, Genethawg's horse,
Karadawg's horse, a strong thoroughbred
Gwythur's horse, Gwawrddur's horse
And Arthur's horse, fearless in giving battle.
Taliesin's horse, the horse of half-reared Lleu
And splendid Dun the dejected,
And "Grey" horse of Cunin.
Kornan the reliable, Awyd the vigorous
The famous Black Moroedd, horse of Brwyn Wily Breast
And the three Cloven-hoofed ones
They do not go on a journey to procreate
"Roan" the horse of Ceidaw, a hard hoof on him,
"Shying Dappled Shoulder", horse of Llemenig,
The horse of Rhydderch the Giver,
"Grey Tawny-Colour".
And Llamrei of surpassing leap
and "Lively Full-Nostril".
And Sadyrnin's horse, and Custennin's horse,
and others in battle, before a dejected land.
Henwyn who brought good tidings from Hiraddug

5

Extracts (this and page opposite) *from the laws of Hywel Dda. (Courtesy of the National Library of Wales, Aberystwyth.)*

It is thought that much of the improvement and final type of Welsh Pony and Cob in the period 1100 to 1500 must be attributed to the influence of Arab stallions brought back to Wales and the Marches by the Crusaders and used extensively on the horses and ponies of Wales and finally that the native type became fixed on that of the Arab with more bone and height to serve the purpose of war and peace in that tempestuous period.

In the year 1188 the crusades were going very badly and, as part of a recruiting drive, Baldwin Archbishop of Canterbury set out on a tour of Wales accompanied by Giraldus Cambrensis, Archdeacon of Brecon. As a result of this tour, Giraldus (Gerallt Gymro) wrote his famous *Itinerary through Wales* and his *Description of Wales*.

In the mid-Wales area of Powys, Gerallt found "most excellent studs put apart for breeding and deriving their origin from some fine Spanish horses which Robert de Belesme, Count of Shrewsbury, brought into this country; on which account the horses sent from hence are remarkable for their majestic proportion and astonishing fleetness".

By the union of these Spanish stallions with the Welsh mountain mares, there was produced the "Powis horse" the Welsh Cob which was to provide so many remounts for English armies from the thirteenth-century onwards.[3]

The work of the fifteenth-century Welsh poets such as Guto'r Glyn describe a type of Welsh Cob which should still be the ideal as far as the present-day animal is concerned. We also find that the importance of pedigree is stressed.[4] Note the reference to the "Du Moroedd", the stallion quoted in the *Book of Taliesin*[5] two hundred years previously.

This poem is seen to refer to the "Powys horse" and also to the term "hackney". The term "hackney" in this respect bears no relationship to the present-day pedigree Stud Book Hackney;[6] it was derived from the "hakenay" which was the late medieval all-purpose animal – from the French "haquenee": a light saddle horse, other than a palfrey.

---

[3] *Dream of Rhonabwy*. Mary Giffin. Transactions of the Honourable Society of Cymmrodorion (1958) pp. 33–40.

[4] *Welsh Stud Book, Vol. XXXVIII*, pp. 6 (Moses Griffith, M.Sc.)

[5] *Trioedd Ynys Prydein*, Rachel Bromwich. University of Wales Press.

[6] *"The Foals of Epona"*, pp. 138.

ACHAU'R EBOL

(Allan o waith Guto'r Glyn—Tudalen 60)

Mab i'r Du, ymhob erw deg,
O Brydyn, o bai redeg;
Merch ei fam i'r march o Fon
Aeth i ddwyn wyth o ddynion.
Mae wyrion i Ddu'r Moroedd,
Gwn mai un onaddun oedd;
Mae yngo nai Myngwyn Ial
Ym Mhowys, nis rhwym hual;
Mae car i farch Ffwg Warin,
A'i gar a fal gwair a'i fin.
Ucha march ei achau ym Mon,
O baladr Talebolion.

Peddestr o eddestr addwyn,
Prior ffraeth yn pori'r ffrwyn.
O bwrw naid dros aber nant,
Ef yw'r trechaf o'r trychant.
March fal gwddw alarch yw fo,
O myn y ffroenwyn ffrwyno,
A'i fwnwgl yn addfwynwych
Fal bwa'r crwth, flew byr crych,
A'i fwng yn debig ddigon
I fargod tŷ, neu frig ton.
Llun ei gorff yn llawn o gig,
Llun o gwyr yn Llangurig,
Llygadrwth a lliw gwydraidd,
A llew yn ei flew neu flaidd.

Llyna farch a'm llaw'n ei fwng
Troellog a ddaw i'r Trallwng.
Nid eirch dy nai hacnai hen,
Ond erchi un diarchen.

Moes d'eboli i'w bedoli,
Moes dy blanc i'm ystabl i,
Moes orwydd grymus hiriell,
Moes farch, ac arch a fo gwell.

PEDIGREE OF A WELSH COB
By Guto'r Glyn (circa. 1445–1475)

He is a son of 'Du o Brydyn'
He would win the race in any fair field;
His mother was daughter to the stallion of
Anglesey which carried eight people,
They are descendants to Du'r Moroedd
And I know that he is one of them.
He is nephew to the Myngwyn Ial.
In Powys no fetter could hold him,
He is of the stock of Ffwg Warin's stallion,
And that stock grinds its fodder small
with its strong jaws.
He is a stallion of the highest pedigree
in Anglesey.
From the line of Talebolion.

A handsome stepping stallion,
A lively prior gnawing his bridle;
When he leaps over a stream's course
He is best of three hundred!
When you put a bridle on the white-nosed stallion
He curves his neck like a swan,
With his neck beautiful and splendid
Like the bow of a crowd, with short curly hair,
And his mane is indeed like
The eaves of a house, or the crest of a wave,
The frame of his body is full of flesh,
An image of wax in Llangurig!
His eyes are wide open, his colour gleams like glass,
[He stands] in his coat like a lion or wolf [?]

That is the stallion which will come to Welshpool
With my hand in his curly mane
Thy nephew does not ask for an aged hackney,
Rather he asks for one which has never been shod.
Give your colt to be shod [now],
Give your young horse to my stable,
Give a strong long-limbed brown horse,
Give a stallion, and ask for a better one yourself.

Tudur Aled of gentle birth (uchelwr) and a famous Welsh poet of the early sixteenth-century gives several descriptions of the stallions of those days in his poems; especially in one to the "Abbot of Aberconwy" and these are the points he makes:[7]

The stallion should have the outlook and poise of a stag; The face should be dished; The forehead wide; The nostrils wide and open like the muzzle of a gun; The eyes like two ripe pears, bulging and dancing in his head; The ears should be small and fine, restless, and like two sage leaves; His coat like new silk.

He again stresses poise and gait, like that of a stag. He can both trot and gallop, and when he trots on a stoned road, fire sparks from his shoes. He then describes the ability of the horse to jump, to swim, and to jump rivers, and further that his jump could be likened to that of a deer springing from an adder. Not only are the horses (described by these bards) fast at a gallop, and not only do they jump well, but they must be able to carry weight also. One horse is described as having carried eight men on its back. It is the first reference in literature to eight horse-power traction! How they fixed themselves there, I do not know! One point made in particular, is that the head should be small like that of a pony, with dished nose, *never* a Roman nose. A description is given of the length of rein; shoulders; quarters; forearm; straight hind leg; the fetlock and the hoof.

This is Tudur Aled's description:

Trem hydd, am gywydd, a gais,
Trwynbant, yn troi i'w unbais;
Ffriw yn dal ffrwyn, o daliwn,
Ffroen y sy gau, fal Ffrawns gwn;
Ffroen arth, a chyffro'n i en,
Ffrwyn a ddeil i ffriw'n ddolen.

Llygaid fel dwy ellygen
Llymion byw'n llamu'n i ben;
Dwy glust feinion aflonydd,
Dail saeds, uwch i dal y sydd;
Trwsio, fal goleuo glain,

---

[7] *Welsh Stud Book, Vol. XXXVIII*, pp. 8.

Y bu wydrwr i bedrain;
I flew fal sidan newydd,
A'i rawn o liw gwawn y gwydd;
Sidan ym mhais ehedydd,
Siamled yn hws am lwdn hydd.

Ail y carw, olwg gorwyllt,
A'i draed yn gweu drwy dan gwyllt;
Dylifo, heb ddwylo, 'dd oedd,
Neu weu sidan, nes ydoedd!
Ysturio cwrs y daran,
A thuthio pan fynno'n fan.

Bwrw i naid i'r wybr a wnai,
Ar hyder yr ehedai,
Cnyw praff yw yn cnoi priffordd,
Cloch y ffair, ciliwch o'r ffordd!
Sêr neu fellt o'r sarn a fydd
Ar godiad yr egwydydd;
Drythyll ar bedair wyth-hoel,
Gwreichionen yw pen pob hoel;
Dirynnwr fry draw'n y fron,
Deil i'r haul dalau'r hoelion;
Gwreichion a gaid ohonun,
Gwniwyd wyth bwyth ymhob un;
I arial a ddyfalwn
I elain coch ym mlaen cwn;
Yn i fryd, nofio'r ydoedd,
Nwyfawl iawn anifail oedd;
O gyrrir draw i'r gweirwellt,
Ni thyrr a'i garn wyth o'r gwellt!
Neidiwr dros afon ydoedd,
Naid yr iwrch rhag y neidr oedd;
Wynebai a fynnai fo,
Pe'r trawst, ef a'i praw trosto;
Nid rhaid, er peri neidio,
Dur fyth wrth i dorr efo,
Dan farchog bywiog, di bwl,
Ef a wyddiad i feddwl!

In exchange for a song he asks for a stallion
With a stag's sidelong glance and a dished nose,
A head to hold a bridle, should we catch him;
A nostril wide like a French cannon,
A bear's nostril, with a quivering jaw;
A bridle will hold his head in a loop,
Eyes like two pears,
Keen and lively, dancing in his head;
Two slim restless ears,
[Like] sage leaves, above his forehead;
A glazier has been furbishing his hooves
As if he were polishing a gem;
His coat like new silk,
And his mane (lit. horsehair) of the colour of wood-gossamer;
[There is] silk in the garment of this lark,
[There is] a chamlet as a covering for this young stag.

[He is] like the deer, with [his] fierce look,
And his feet, weaving through wildfire;
He would spin, [though] without hands,
Or weave silk . . .
He would pursue a thunderclap's course,
And, when he wished, trot with a high short step.

He would [sometimes] leap into the sky,
As if he were about to fly [?],
A sturdy colt devouring the roadway,
Hark, the alarm bell, clear out of his way!
Stars or lightning-flashes will rise from the street
At the rapping of his hooves;
A spirited one on his four eight-nailed [shoes],
Each nail-head is [as] a spark;
He twists about above there on the hill-side,
He holds to the sun the heads of the nails;
Sparks arose from them,
Eight stitches had been sown in each one;
I would compare his spirit
To that of a red deer [fleeing] before hounds;
If he had his will, he would be swimming;
He was the most vivacious of creatures;
If he is sent out into the hay meadow
He will not cut with his hooves even eight blades of grass.

13

He was a jumper of rivers,
His jump was like that of a roebuck from a snake;
He would face anything he wished,
Even if it were a roof-beam, he would attempt to clear it;
It is never necessary, to cause him to jump,
To put a steel [spur] to his belly;
Under a lively and skilful rider
He would read his mind!

Another event of great importance which occurred at this time was the legislation[8] passed in 1535 by King Henry VIII aimed to eliminate "nags of small stature". Owing to the great weight of the armour worn by the soldiers of that period, it was necessary to breed horses of considerable stature. A penalty of 40 shillings was to be imposed on anyone who used a stallion under 14 hands in height. This law was followed in 1541 by another prohibiting the use of "any stoned horse under 15 hands" and all "unprofitable beasts" (i.e. smaller ponies were to be caught and destroyed). Fortunately for Wales, many of the smaller ponies escaped into the hills evading being caught and possibly knowledge of the law never reached the land of Twm Sion Cati. The ponies which escaped survived the hardships of the Welsh uplands and consequently the survivors were the hardiest and most suitable types.

This law was annulled by Queen Elizabeth and in gratitude the *Welsh Stud Book* in its early days is full of Besses, Queen Besses, Lady Besses, etc., whilst there are no Henrys or Harrys!

An Act passed during the reign of George II in 1740 which banished "ponies" from the racecourse resulted in one such stallion called Merlin (a descendant of the Darley Arabian) being purchased by a member of the Williams-Wynn family and turned out on the Ruabon hills. This resulted in an improvement in the native ponies on these hills and descendants of Merlin were called "merlynnod" or "merliws" in Welsh; terms which are still in active use in North Wales.

By the middle of the seventeenth-century there must have been a use and therefore a sale for these wild ponies. Youatt[9] gives a long account of "Pony Hunting" as a favourite amusement amongst the Welsh

---

[8] *"The Foals of Epona"*, pp. 138.
[9] *"The Horse"*, pp. 104. William Youatt, Longmans (1831).

farmers at that time:

> The farmer set out in the morning with his lasso coiled round his waist, attended by two hardy dependants and their greyhounds. The lasso was then familiar to the Welshman. As the hunters climbed the mountain's brow the distant herd of ponies took alarm, sometimes galloping onwards, and then suddenly halting and wheeling round, snorting as if in defiance of the intruders, and furiously paving the ground. The hunters contrived to coop them up in a corner of the hills, where perpendicular rocks prevented their escape. Many of the three-year-olds had been known to break the legs of their pursuers and some had been dismounted and trampled to death.

Nimrod in his book *The Horse and the Hound*, published in 1842, gives some proofs of the power of these ponies of crossing a country:

> A pony was ridden ten miles in forty-seven minutes and taking thirty leaps in his course for a wager of 1,000 guineas, and that during the drawing of the Irish Lottery, the news was conveyed express from Holyhead to London chiefly by ponies at the rate of nearly 20 miles an hour.

In the latter years of the nineteenth-century, Welsh breeders used Hackney stallions on their native Cob mares to produce flashy carriage horses which could be sold for a high price. However, the Hackney of those days was an animal far removed from the slimmer "show-ground" Hackney in evidence these days. A surprising fact was that some of these sires "nicked" well with Cob mares (*see later chapters*) but unfortunately others produced "weeds". These "Hackney" sires are not to be confused with "Welsh" stallions registered in the *Hackney Stud Book*; animals which were Welsh withal but in pre *Welsh Stud Book* times (pre-1901) it was considered better to have their pedigrees registered somewhere (*Hackney Stud Book*, from *Vol. I* in 1884) rather than nowhere.

A fashion prevalent during those times also, alas producing much greater harm than the Hackney was the cross with the English "shire" horse to produce Colliery horses. The latter cross brought in the common head, the "Roman" nose, thick bone of poor quality and clumsiness.

Much information regarding the early pre-Stud Book stallions in Wales can be obtained from stud cards. Sometimes the information on the stud cards differs from what might have appeared later in the Stud

Book, in some cases presumably the stud card is correct, in others perhaps a certain amount of "camouflage" took place. I shall endeavour to give examples to illustrate these points:

(i) Eiddwen Flyer, one of the great tap-root Cob sires (and the only one which was taken to illustrate the breed in *Vol. I of the Welsh Stud Book*) was not registered until *Vol. X* (1911) (where he was registered as "now dead") and the genealogies describe him as having been foaled in 1880. His stud card (dated 1880) proves that he was standing at stud in 1880 and in fact, foaled in 1877.

18   80.

TO COVER THIS SEASON,

At One Pound each Mare,

And 2s. 6d. the Groom,

(The Groom's Fee to be paid at the first time of Covering, and the remainder on or before the 28th of June next,)

THAT SPLENDID CHESTNUT COB,

EIDDWEN FLYER

The Property of Mr. William Jones, Hafodglas, Llangwyryfon, Cardiganshire.

EIDDWEN FLYER is rising 3 years old, stands 14½ hands high, he was got by Welsh Flyer, which was the fastest trotter in Cardiganshire; Welsh Flyer by old Comet, old Comet by Flyer, Flyer out of Brown Bess, Brown Bess by Black Jack; Welsh Flyer's dam out of Trotting Nancy, by old Cymro Llwyd. Welsh Flyer won the prize at the Cardigan Agricultural Show in 1868, and at Llanwrtyd Entire Horse Show in 1875. EIDDWEN FLYER'S dam was got by Welsh Jack, the property of Mr. Thomas Daniel, Caecefnder, Pennant, Cardiganshire, out of Cymro Llwyd, both of which were excellent trotters. Cymro Llwyd was the successful Competitor at the Brecon Agricultural Shows in 1851, 1852, and 1853.

The Season Money to be paid for any Mare sold from under this Horse.

The Groom will specify the time and places of attendance.

PHILIP WILLIAMS, PRINTER, ABERYSTWITH.

(ii) Cymro Llwyd, foaled 1850, a stallion who had a great influence on the Welsh Cob breed (*chapter 18.6*) and to a lesser extent on the ponies of the Breconshire areas. From the researches of Mr. Charles

16

Coltman Rogers (who devoted endless time, labour and expense in the construction of genealogies in the first volumes of the *Welsh Stud Book*) it appears that Cymro Llwyd was sired by an imported Arab owned by Mr. Crawshay, an iron-master of Cyfarthfa Castle, Merthyr Tydfil. Two stud cards relating to Cymro Llwyd, dated 1855 (the property of Mr. D. D. Evans) and 1864 (the property of Mr. T. James) both quote the sire as Welsh Jack. Presumably this was an act of "camouflage" for an oriental sire; it cannot be an erroneous reference to Cymro Llwyd's most famous son, Welsh Jack since this latter Welsh Jack would not have been foaled in 1855. Whichever it was, the influence of Cymro Llwyd has permeated for well over 100 years and it is the proud boast of present-day breeders that their animals are descendants of Cymro Llwyd e.g. on the stud card of Llanarth Braint (*chapter 27.1*) it quotes that he has 13 crosses of Cymro Llwyd in his pedigree.

Confusion also arose from idol-worshipping a successful sire and naming the offspring after him; the earlier Stud Books are full of Flyers (twenty of them), Comets, Expresses etc. We find Trotting Comet, Welsh Comet, Cardigan Comet I, II and III, Young Trotting Comet (presumably he became Old Trotting Comet in after years?), Flying Comet, Young Comet, Cheltenham Comet and even a Comet Comet! From them came the Expresses, Express I, II, III and IV, Young Express I and II, Manest Express, Grand Express and Royal Express. Then the Flyers from Old Trotting Comet viz Welsh Flyer I, II, III and IV, Trotting Flyer, Young Flyer, Glanne Welsh Flyer, Eiddwen Flyer I, II and III, Llangurig Flyer, Young Eiddwen Flyer, Idloes Flyer, Trotting Brown Flyer, Trotting Flyer, King Flyer and Cardigan Flyer and so on.

With the exception of Cymro Llwyd (who was 50 per cent oriental anyway!) it seemed more fashionable to baptise these famous Welsh animals with English names. Congratulations to Professor Tom Parry (of Neuadd, Llwyndafydd and later Professor of Agriculture at the University College of Wales, Aberystwyth) for naming his ponies with the Welsh names: Olwen, Dwynwen, Brythonwen, Caronwen, Ceinwen, Teifwen, Ceridwen, Eiranwen, Cranogwen etc which appear in the early volumes of the *Welsh Stud Book*.

English name or Welsh name, the owners did not fail to wax eloquent about the virtues of their steeds.

Phenomenon III, Season 1892 (*chapter 17*):

He has the full physical development and vigorous character of a progenitor, with precise and imposing carriage; has a high and sagacious temperament, delighting to obey but scorning fear and rest.

Plynlimon Champion, Season 1912:

I am prepared to compete with Plynlimon Champion against any Welsh bred trotting horse in Wales by himself for £30 or with his offspring for £40. I shall also have a bunch of Plynlimon's offspring against the offspring of any Welsh-bred horse, prize to be an American gig, four-wheeler, cost £30. I can also make up a Tandem (2 or 3) against any Welsh-bred Stud, prize £20.

Pistyll Cob, Season 1919:

Strong enough to work on the farm, and swift enough to fetch the doctor in an emergency, or put to a cannon for artillery work and ride for cavalry work.

A popular travelling stallion would find free food and lodging to stay overnight whereas it was a difficult task to secure accommodation even with payment, for a second-rate horse.

A verse relating to the hard times experienced when travelling the not-so-good stallion went:

Dwy geiniog mewn cyfyngder
A ges gan Ianto Tinker
Gwell yw tred yr ambarel
Na dilyn cel Ty Tyler.

When I was in distress I received
Two pence from Ianto the Tinker
There is better trade in umbrellas
Than in leading the Ty Tyler stallion.

Even if the majority of the Welsh horses had English names, the language of the Welsh countryside in those times was predominantly Welsh and the English "handles" were rarely referred to, instead colloquial Welsh names were used: One such stallion was Cardigan Briton owned by the Rev. Owen of Taihirion, Blaenpennal, Tregaron. I knew well the Rev. Owen's nephew, Mr. O. D. Owen who farmed Berthlwyd (where his daughter now farms) at Talybont; he was a

A typical Welsh Mountain Pony of the last century i.e. prior to the influence of Dyoll Starlight.

founder member of the Welsh Pony and Cob Society in 1901. The Rev. Owen was in great demand as a judge of horses all over the United Kingdom, he was well-known for the fine stallions which he kept and he always drew large congregations to his preaching, it was suspected more to admire his mounts than listen to his sermons!

Cardigan Briton was never registered in the *Welsh Stud Book* although

Another view of the pony on the previous page. The original caption to this photograph reads: "Was reared by Mr. Owen, Garregwen, Lledrod and was sold as a sucker to Mr. J. Owen, Rhiwarthen Uchaf for £2-2s-6d. Was sold the following autumn to Mr. I. Jones, Ystumtuen for £11-2s-6d who again sold him to Mr. J. Oliver (the man in the photographs), Odynfach, Talybont for £20; who exhibited him in 1894–95 at Machynlleth and 1896 at Talybont Show where he took first prizes. Was sold to Mr. J. Jones of Llandudno (Dinarth Hall) for £72-10s who afterwards sold him to T. E. McConnell, Esq., Belfast for £120. Has been shown in all the leading and Royal Shows of the country and a prize-winner every time shown. And only 12 hands."

he was of Stud-Book era and his ancestors were registered e.g. his sire Briton Comet (Comet Bach Tynfron, foaled 1893 and owned by Thomas Rees, Cwmgwenin, Llangeitho: *chapter 23.8*) was registered, number 30 in the *Welsh Stud Book, Vol. I.*

Cardigan Briton was never referred to using these names; he was always known as "Ceffyl Pregethwr" (the horse owned by the Preacher) or simply "Pregethwr". References to "Pregethwr" would continue for many generations e.g. the 1919 stud card of Llwynog Y Dyffryn 882 *Welsh Stud Book* (foaled in 1912) (owned and bred by Thomas Jones, Troedrhiwrhwch, Llandyssul, Cardiganshire) who was the Radnorshire Board of Agriculture Premium stallion for that year, is quoted as sired by Briton Flyer 622 *Welsh Stud Book* by "Pregethwr".

Comet Bach, a son of Cardigan Briton was better known as "Pregethwr Yr Ail" (Preacher The Second) and his stud card is included to show a typical stud card of 70 years ago.

Many of the stallions (and also mares) were referred to using the names of the owners or the names of their farms or villages. The term "bach" (small) was often used, more in an affectionate capacity than as a reference to height. Examples of these would be:

Trotting Rattler: "Cel Melyn Llanrhystyd" (the chesnut horse of Llanrhystyd).

Wild Buck: "Derlwyn Fach."

Trotting Briton (foaled 1884) *Polo Pony Stud Book, Vol. I* (1894) (I have his stud card for 1890): "Cel Bach Y Login".

Ceitho Welsh Comet (*chapter 24.2*) "Cel du bach Lluestybroga".

Welsh Flyer III (foaled 1877) "Ceffyl Caebidwl" or "Ceffyl Dafydd Ellis" or "Ceffyl Cwmins" (*chapter 20.2*).

Satisfaction: "Hen geffyl gwyn bach Blaengorffen".

Eiddwen Flyer II: "Tyreithin" (*chapter 21.2*).

Trotting Flyer: "Aberhenwenfach" (*chapter 23.14*).

Briton Flyer: "Cefnlleithdre" (*chapter 23.10*).

Trotting Polly: "Poni felen Waunfawr".

King Jack: "Ceffyl Morgan Y Gors' (*chapter 23.9*).

Young Caradog: "Caerllugest".

King Flyer (35 *Welsh Stud Book*): "Cel Bach Glandulais" (*chapter 25.8*). In this latter case "bach" did not refer to small height since King Flyer stood at over 15 hands 2 in.

These famous names of the nineteenth-century belong to the Cobs, the proliferation of Comets, Flyers and Expresses, so what of the ponies? As already mentioned, the Williams-Wynn family turned out Merlin on the Ruabon hills in the mid-seventeen hundreds. It seems that about 50 years later Col. Vaughan of Nannau and his brother Sir Robert Vaughan of Rug, near Corwen imported some "Barb Arabs" one of whom sired "Apricot" from a "pure Welsh Pony mare".

Apricot was in great demand as a sire and very soon, Col. Vaughan's stud became the "best of its kind". In addition Apricot set up records at racecourses all over North Wales, at Harlech, Ruthin and Mold; indeed, at Mold, it is recorded that he won four races the same day! Mr. John Hill records in the introduction to the *Welsh Stud Book, Vol. I* that:

"When staying at Rug as a boy about 1850, I noticed two distinct types of Welsh Ponies around the 13 hands in height, the one 'old' type, thick set, well made carrying the shooting parties with wonder-

21

SEASON 1905.

TO SERVE MARES THIS SEASON

At £1 10s. each Mare, and 5s. the Groom.

(The Groom's Fee to be paid first time of service. Remainder on or before the
25th of June next, or 5s. extra for collecting.)

THAT HANDSOME AND WELL BRED COB STALLION

COMET ❈ BACH

(PREGETHWR YR AIL.)

The Property of Mr. John James, Ivy House, Tremain, Cardigan.

COMET BACH is of a beautiful black colour. He stands 15 hands high
on good sound feet and legs, with great power and substance. He is a
remarkably brilliant all round mover, and very fast, combined with fine
temper and splendid constitution. This horse contains the blood of them
noted sires—Cardigan Briton, Briton Comet, and Young Comet, which
sort are seldom found nowadays.

COMET BACH'S Sire, the renowned Cardigan Briton, better known as
Pregethwr, was one of the best and fastest all round cobs of his day;
sired most valuable cobs, which were sold at satisfactory prices.

COMET BACH'S Dam is by that noted stock producer, Young Comet,
that was bred by the late Mr Ellis Thomas, Talbot Hotel, Tregaron, and
was without a doubt one of the best mares ever bred in Wales.

COMET BACH has had a most successful show yard career, amongst
his winnings are- in 1898, Llanarth, 1st; Alltyrodyn Arms, 1st; Llandyssul, 1st; Newcastle-Emlyn, 1st; Cardigan, 1st, He has won several
first and special prizes on different occasions at New Inn, Rhydowen,
Newcastle-Emlyn, Cardigan, Haverfordwest, and Narberth.

COMET BACH is a most sure and impressive Sire, he is so widely
known that full comments are unnecessary, He has sired some of the
best cobs that ever went from Wales, and which have won prizes in keen
competitions, afterwards realizing high prices. and it may be further said
that his stock year after year demand a readier sale with advanced prices.
These are few of his Stock which have been sold from Farmers in this
Locality when three or four years old :—Tivyside, a dark brown mare, the
property of Mr. S. Evans, Penygraig, won 1st at Crewe Sale, June, 1901,
sold for 91 Guineas; Great Heart, bay gelding, the property of R.
England, Esq., Rumney Court, Cardiff, won 1st in his class at Wrexham
March Sale, 1905, out of 27 entries, sold for 80 Guineas (see the "Western
Mail" and "Daily News," April 2, 1905); Lady Ailsie, the property of
the late D. T. Lewis, Esq., Narberth, won 1st and Special Prizes at such
Shows as Bath and West of England at Cardiff, United Counties, Narberth, Tenby, and Pembroke, sold as a three-year-old for 85 Guineas;
Bay Gelding, bred by Mr. J. Phillips, Crynga Newydd. sold by Mr. T.
Griffiths, Pantybutler, at the North Wales Sales at Wrexham, for 75
Guineas; Mr. A. Lewis, Treprior, sold one for £50; a Two-year-old
made £35 in Ffynonwen Sale; Messrs. S. Morgan & Son, Cardigan, are
always purchasers of his Stock, and have disposed of many at prices
realizing from £55 to £85.

CERTIFICATE OF EXAMINATION.

Newcastle-Emlyn, April 2, 1904.

At the request of Mr. John James, Tremain, Cardigan, I have this day examined a Black Entire Cob (Comet Bach), in which I detect no unsoundness;
and I consider him sound, and free from hereditary disease.

(Signed), J. CLAYTON JONES, M.R.C.V.S.

Times and route will be specified by the Groom.

☞ All Mares tried by this Horse, served by another, dead, exchanged,
sold, or otherwise disposed of, will be charged the season's price.

M. M. AND W. R. THOMAS, STEAM PRINTERS, CARDIGAN.

ful ease and safety. The other type showed the influence of Apricot, lighter with more quality, they make excellent childrens ponies; the mares of this sort are exactly the ones to mate with either Thoroughbred or Arab stallions for breeding Polo Ponies."

These Welsh ponies soon built up a reputation for their performance feats. Sambo, standing only 11 hands 3 in high became the Champion jumping pony at Olympia in 1887. Owned by Dr. T. D. Harries of Aberystwyth, he was described as the "champion jumping pony of the world". At Olympia that day he beat Little Queen of Manchester winner of 274 first prizes, Tommy Dod winner of 24 prizes and Qui Vive the celebrated Aylesbury mare. To "show off" after this win his rider rode him under a bar, turned him around and then jumped over it!

Another pony who celebrated herself in another respect was "Old Stager", foaled 1865, height 13 hands, bred and owned by Miss Severn of The Hall, Penybont. When her story was recorded (1904) she was 39 years old, she had produced 34 foals (including one at foot in 1904) and it was recorded that she had always lived out on mountain land, summer and winter, with ten to twelve breeding mares, some rough hay being given them in the winter. I do not think that it was later recorded whether she produced any foals after this great age of 39 years.

And so it was in 1901, to quote the Preface of *Vol. I* of the *Welsh Stud Book*: "It had long been felt by those interested in the Welsh Mountain and other Ponies and Cobs for which the Principality has for so long been celebrated, that the establishment of a Breed Society similar to those which have done so much for other breeds was necessary."

A Preliminary Meeting was therefore called at Llandrindod Wells on the 25th April 1901; the conveners were Mr. H. Meuric Lloyd, Mr. E. Jones, Mr. W. S. Miller and Mr. O. Price. Mr. J. Marshall Dugdale presided, and there were also present Messrs. H. Meuric Lloyd, John Hill, E. Jones, J. Gwynne Holford, Delme Davies Evans, D. P. Evans, J. Jenkins, B. Davies, J. Campbell and James Hamer.

The feeling was unanimous that a Society should be established and arrangements were made to make the objects of the Society known throughout Wales. The Meeting was adjourned to Cardiff and was held in the Royal Show Yard when a large and influential body of gentlemen interested in the breeding of Welsh Ponies and Cobs attended.

The Preface continues with respect to the *Welsh Stud Book*: "It is not a jumble of all sorts and conditions of Cobs and Ponies into one Stud Book but, as it were, a distinct Stud Book for each, comprised in one volume. Each variety is so dependent on, and is so closely connected in its origin with the other, that breeders will doubtless from time to time take a dip into blood to be found in one or other of the sections as may suit their purpose."

The present-day sections of the *Welsh Stud Book* are labelled as follows:

Section "A" Welsh Mountain Ponies under 12 hands.
Section "B" Welsh Ponies, under 13 hands 2 in.
Section "C" Welsh Ponies (Cob type), under 13 hands 2 in.
Section "D" Welsh Cobs, over 13 hands 2 in.

In the chapters which follow the animals are not referred to as being in Sections "A", "B", "C" or "D" of the *Welsh Stud Book* since these letters over almost 80 years have referred to various types of animals and various heights.

In *Vols. I* to *IV* (1902–1905) Section "A" was allocated to Welsh Mountain ponies of up to 12 hands 2 in in height, Section "B" to ponies of Cob type standing between 12 hands and 2 in and 13 hands 2 in, "C" for Cobs between 13 hands 2 in and 14 hands 2 in and "D" for Cobs between 14 hands 2 in and 15 hands 2 in. This classification remained until 1907 when the upper height limit of 15 hands 2 in was dispensed with.

One alteration brought about in 1908 was the sub-division of Section "A" into two parts: A(i) up to 12 hands and A(ii) between 12 hands and 12 hands 2 in; otherwise the Section descriptions remained unchanged until 1927.

In the late 'twenties the need was realised for ponies suitable for children to ride and in 1927 the Foundation Stock (F.S.) register was established to record the pedigrees of animals of non-Welsh parentage and eventually up-grade them into the Stud Book by using three top-cross Welsh sires. Animals with 50 per cent registered blood went into the Stud Book proper at this time.

Also at this time, while Section "B" was meant to be for ponies of Cob type, with the advent of riding ponies for children, two stallions of Oriental parentage had been registered in the Welsh Book with the intention of breeding children's riding ponies. These were Tanybwlch Berwyn (*chapter 13.6*) by Sahara (Barb) registered in *Vol. XXVI* and Craven Cyrus (*chapter 14.13*) by King Cyrus (Arab) registered in *Vol. XXVIII*.

In *Vols. XXX* (1931–1934) and *XXXI* (1935–1938) the intention was to start a new Section for these ponies of riding type but unfortunately the inception of this new Section coincided with the combination of Sections "C" and "D" (for no obvious reasons?). This led into all sorts of confusion, Section "B" was labelled as "ponies of riding type" with no lower height limit but up to 13 hands 2 in whilst Section "C" was a combined Section for ponies of Cob type and Cobs and contained anything from little mares of 12 hands 2 in to the two big Cob mares Madeni Darling and her daughter Madeni Cymraes, both standing at over 16 hands.

The Section "B" got off to a very bad start in *Vol. XXX*: whilst the four stallions could broadly be called "of riding type", one had already been gelded and another had been exported. The twenty-four mares which were registered in Section "B" were a very mixed bunch, indeed three of them were over 20 years old and some were incidentally registered as "now dead". Very few of the remaining twenty-one entries could strictly be regarded as what the Section was set out to achieve. These twenty-one entries contained such mares as: Bryngwyn Gwen by Trotting Jack, Craven Bunny by Llwynog Flyer, Gwarcwm Gwenno (owned by Mrs. Parry of Taliesin, bridesmaid in my parents' wedding) by Tanrallt Fireboy (a National Hackney Show champion owned by the famous Tanrallt Stud where my sister now lives), Hafan Polly granddam of the influential Mathrafal (*chapter 28.4*), Hendre Gwen by Penllether Trotting Model, Hwylog Snowdrop by Cefncoch Country Swell, Lady Diana by Wild Buck and Myrtle Happy Girl by Royal Welsh Jack. These, I imagine, were all ponies of Cob type; some of them were exceptionally good specimens of Cob-type ponies and would have been better suited in another Section.

By *Vol. XXXII* (1939–1948) the intention of Section "B" was more apparent and only few Cob-type ponies crept into this Section. However Section "C" still contained anything from the two excellent pony of Cob-type stallions Teify Brightlight and Welsh Partriot (both later Royal Welsh Show Champions) to the three Blaenwaun stallions all standing at over 15 hands or the Gwenog and Madeni stallions who were also usually over the 15 hand mark.

The present-day Sections "A", "B", "C" and "D" came into force in 1949 whilst the Welsh Part-bred register was approved at the A.G.M. in January 1950. The "F.S." route has also now been closed, no more original F.S. animals have been accepted for almost 30 years, very few F.S.1. animals remain, eventually the "foundation stock" register will die out; it has served a very useful purpose but with its phasing out there should result a greater consistency of type within each particular Section.

25

2
Dyoll Starlight foaled 1894

1

Dyoll
Starlight 4

2

Dyoll
Glasallt 438

3

75 Dyoll
Moonlight

4

Flower of
Wales

5

bay mare

6

Glamorgan
shire
Mountain
Pony

8

Charlie

1. Dyoll Starlight
Registration number 4 in the *Welsh Stud Book,*
Vol. I (1902)
Registration number 167 in the *Polo Pony Stud Book,*
Vols. V and *VI*
Grey, height: 11 hands 2½ in, foaled 16 May 1894.
Breeder: H. Meuric Lloyd, Glanyrannell Park,
Llanwrda, Carmarthenshire. (Later of
Cynghordy, Llandovery)

Dyoll Starlight won prizes and these are listed:

1896 second, Mountain Pony stallion, Llandovery
first Mountain Pony two-years-old, Llandovery
1898 first Mountain Pony stallion, Royal Agricultural Society of England, Birmingham
1899 first Mountain Pony stallion, Royal Agricultural Society, Maidstone
1899 first and reserve Champion, Crystal Palace
1900 first Mountain or Moorland stallion, Royal Agricultural Society of England, York
1900 first and Champion, Crystal Palace
1901 first and Champion, Royal Agricultural Society of England, Cardiff
Retired from 1901 until 1912
1912 Special Parade, Royal Welsh Agricultural Society, Swansea
1913 first, National Pony Show
1913 second, Royal Agricultural Society of England
1914 first, Royal Lancashire

Mr. Meuric Lloyd was born in 1853 in the West Indies but the Lloyd family claims descent from a British King in the fourth-century and have played a very important part in the history of South Wales. It can safely be said that Dyoll Starlight revolutionised the Welsh Mountain Pony breed. Until he came on the scene, the ponies on the hills of Wales were almost 100 per cent browns, bays, blacks, duns or dark chesnut. According to an old Breconshire poem:

Y coch yw'r lliw i bara
Fe ddal y coch ei liw
Rhowch chware teg i'r coch
Mae'r coch yn siwr o fyw.

The bay is the best colour for hardiness
The bay colour persists for generations
Give the bay fair play
The bay is certain to survive.

Almost immediately about one half of the mountain ponies became greys! Also here was a pony with different blood-lines; his rivals e.g. Eiddwen Flyer III (*chapter 21.1*) who stood second to him at the 1901 Royal Agricultural Society of England Show at Cardiff, were mainly "Cob" bred and altogether of stockier build. Without doubt, when Dyoll Starlight was in his prime he was the most beautiful pony in the whole world, and he was progenitor of a whole new dynasty of beautiful ponies.

It was soon obvious to Mr. Lloyd that in Dyoll Starlight he had produced something out of the ordinary and he procured some very fashionable mares to join Starlight to form the Dyoll Stud. (Dyoll being "Lloyd" spelt backwards).

Amongst these mares (sixteen of which were registered in *Vol. I of the Welsh Stud Book*) were Dyoll Bala Gal, a brown mare of 11 hands purchased from Mr. John Williams, of Gwernhefin, Bala in North Wales and Dyoll Quicksilver (the most expensive of the mares bought at £25 since she had previously won 17 prizes!).

Bala Gal at Dyoll produced Dyoll Ballistite (sold for 36 guineas to Mrs. Greene who changed his name to Grove Ballistite and he became a great winner and a foundation sire at this famous Grove Stud), Dyoll Radium, Dyoll Rainbow etc.

Quicksilver produced eleven foals by Starlight, including Dyoll King Cole 197 (foaled in 1905, a black, like his mother) who also later became Grove King Cole (exported to the U.S.A. in 1912) and who sired in 1911: Grove King Cole II. Grove King Cole II in turn sired Caer Beris King Cole (bred at Grove from the same dam as the illustrious Grove Sprightly) a well-known Show stallion who also had a profound effect on the breeding of ponies in the Swansea area of South Wales.

Apart from mares of the Dyoll Stud, outside mares flocked from far and wide for the services of Dyoll Starlight producing e.g.

Bleddfa Shooting Star 73 in 1901 out of 572 Alveston Belle

Greylight 80 in 1900 out of 356 Myfanwy

Towy Model Starlight 748 in 1910 out of 2046 Lady Greylight (better known as Bwlch Quicksilver when in the ownership of Mrs. Pennell)

Stretton Torchlight 123 in 1902 out of 248 Star

Stanage Daylight 248 in 1905 out of 248 Star

Dyoll Starlight when owned by Mr. Meuric Lloyd. (Photograph courtesy of Mrs. Blandy.)

My Lord Pembroke 464 in 1909 out of Polly Pembroke
and many more.

Greylight bred by Mr. Evan Jones of Manoravon, Llandilo (who
with Mr. Meuric Lloyd, was one of the original Carmarthenshire
members of Council of the Welsh Pony & Cob Society) was an exceptionally beautiful pony winning so many prizes and championships
before being exported to Australia (Mr. Hordern) in 1911 for 1,000
guineas (equivalent to about £15,000 by today's standards).

It was Mr. Evan Jones who trained Dyoll Starlight for the show ring

31

Dyoll Starlight aged 28 years when owned by Lady Wentworth.

and Mr. Jones' groom who showed him up to about 1900 after which Mr. Lloyd's own groom always showed him. Starlight was not an extravagant mover but had a good stride and true and gave of his best when applauded from the ringside. His sons, Greylight and Bleddfa Shooting Star were trained to show more "action" and were usually shown in full stallion tackle. Mr. Evan Jones never showed Greylight against Starlight.

In 1919 Mr. Lloyd's health began to fail and Dyoll Starlight was sold to Lady Wentworth at 25 years of age on the understanding that he would never be sold and that, when he died, his skeleton would be presented to the British Museum in Mr. Lloyd's name.

Mr. Lloyd died in 1922 and when his daughter, Mrs. Raleigh Blandy returned from India in 1929, she failed to get Lady Wentworth to agree to let her see Dyoll Starlight. It later transpired (in a letter which Lady Wentworth wrote to the magazine *Riding* in 1943) that Dyoll Starlight was sold to Spain for £800 in 1925 (when 31 years old) and had died there in 1929.

Mrs. Blandy took Counsel's opinion on the fact that Lady Wentworth had sold Starlight contrary to her agreement but was informed that the agreement was between Lady Wentworth and Mr. Lloyd (and

Dyoll "Starlight". 167. P.P.S.B [Vol.V.] 4. W.S.B.

"Glasallt". { "Flower of Wales".
              { D.k: bay m.

"Flower of Wales". { "Charlie".

Flower of Wales. Iron grey, 12-0.
bought as yearling in Llandilo
Fair by Davies of Rhyblid who
sold it to Davies of Gwydre.
He came from Pantyffynon
nr. Hermon. Su 924. Adm. stud
Vol: III. W.S.B. "Eg. Traps" a roan, 12-1
, sold for 80 Gms.

"Charlie". Dk: bay. White forehead,
a shade
under 12-2. the pty of
John Jones, Bankcelwydd
Talley. It rough Welsh
Cob by bone, & thick set.

"Glasallt. Dam" was a Dk: bay mare
under 12-0. Bred by the Miners
Stores maskelyne, of Glanusk
Saunysbridge. "Breconshire".

Notes on the pedigree of Dyoll Starlight written by Mr. Meuric Lloyd.

33

Mr. Meuric Lloyd, breeder of Dyoll Starlight, photographed in 1905. (Photograph courtesy of Mrs. Blandy.)

should have been with Mr. Lloyd and his executors); therefore the agreement became invalid on the death of Mr. Lloyd in March 1922. Mrs. Blandy still has in her possession the agreement written in Lady Wentworth's own handwriting.

Dyoll Starlight sired some exceptional stock at Crabbet during the years 1919 to 1925 despite his great age (e.g. Champion Wentworth Springlight, foaled in 1920 out of 2046 Lady Greylight). The skull of Dyoll Starlight was presented by Lady Wentworth to the Natural History Museum in London in 1935. Originally it was labelled "Welsh Trotting Pony", this description being later corrected by Mrs. Blandy.

Three photographs of Dyoll Starlight appear in the *Welsh Stud Books*: *Vol. I (p. 5)*, *VII (p. 7)*, and *XIX (p. 57)*, the latter when in the ownership of Lady Wentworth.

34

2. Dyoll Glasallt
Registration number 438 in the *Welsh Stud Book,*
Vol. XI
Black, height: about 12 hands, foaled 1891
Breeder: Morgan Morgan, Glasallt, Myddfai,
Carmarthenshire

Glasallt was found by Mr. Lloyd as a yearling (still running with his
dam under the Carmarthen Van Mountains) and purchased him from
his breeder. Mr. Lloyd named him after the farm where he was foaled.

Mr. Lloyd described him as "dark brown/black with a strong loin
and the best of limbs, a little plain in the head and this was accentuated
by a big, white blaze". Glasallt was gelded after covering Moonlight
and was lost sight of.

3. Dyoll Moonlight
Registration number 75 in the *Welsh Stud Book, Vol. I*
Registration number 908 in the *Polo Pony Stud Book,*
Vols. V and *VI*

The story of how Mr. Lloyd purchased Moonlight is recorded in his
own words: "I went to see a Mr. Davies, Aberllech fach. It was on the
eve of the Fair held annually at Llanddeusant close to the Carmarthen
Van, our biggest mountain. He had some ponies gathered ready for the
Fair and I went to see them. On his way from his farm he rode
Moonlight up to where the others were. He said she was for sale too and

Dyoll Moonlight.

35

priced her at £13. I chose three others, the four came to £33. 15. o but I got them for £33. 1. o. Moonlight, I made out, had cost me £12."

Moonlight was bred by Mr. Thomas, Pentre, Talybont-on-Usk where Criban Biddy Bronze (*chapter 16.3*) was bred in 1950. Moonlight carried the "P" brand of the Pentre. It was thought that she was descended from the Crawshay Bailey Arab, sire of Cymro Llwyd (*chapter 18.6*) who had been turned out on the neighbouring Brecon Beacons around 1850.

She also possibly carried some of the blood of an Arab stallion which Mr. Morgan Williams of Aberpergwm had turned out on these same hills in 1840.

Mr. Llewellyn Richards states that the shepherds in that area referred to Moonlight, Gentle Mary (foaled 1885) and White Jenny (foaled 1875) as mares with "silk mane and tail". These mares all originated from the "Vaynor hill" area of the Brecon Beacons and their "silk mane and tail" suggest oriental descent rather than the coarser hair of the true hill pony. (Gentle Mary and White Jenny appear in the pedigrees of many of the original Criban ponies.)

Moonlight was described by Mr. Lloyd as a "miniature Arab, full of quality with a lovely head and good shoulder". Undoubtedly Dyoll Starlight inherited his Arab characteristics from her. Mrs. Lloyd drove Moonlight for several years until 1892 when the mare was savaged by some dogs and became unsafe for driving when it was decided to breed from her. Her first foal (her only filly) was by the Cilgwyn Cob. Between 1894 and 1902 she produced seven colts (Dyoll Starlight being the first) then in 1911, to everyone's surprise she produced Meteor, not having had a foal for nine years.

4. Flower of Wales
Iron grey or roan, height: 12 hands

He was sold for £80 which was a very big price for a pony in those days.

5.

The dam of Glasallt was a pretty little bay mare owned by the Misses Storey Maskerlyne who lived at Sennybridge.

8. Charley
Dark bay, white blaze, height: under 12 hands 2 in.
Owned by John Jones, Bankcelwydd, Talley
near Llandilo.

He was described by Mr. Lloyd as "thorough Welsh with a lot of bone and thick-set".

3

Bleddfa Tell Tale foaled 1896

Grove Peep O'Day foaled 1919

Tregoyd Starlight foaled 1935

1 Tregoyd Starlight 1577	**2** Grove Sprightly 1036	**4** Bleddfa Shooting Star 73
		8 Dyoll Starlight 4
		9 572 Alveston Belle
	5 4431 Grove Sprite II	**10** Grove Ballistite 200
		11 2531 Grove Fairy
3 6582 Grove Peep O'Day	**4** Bleddfa Shooting Star 73	**8** Dyoll Starlight 4
		9 572 Alveston Belle
	7 3017 Grove Twilight	**10** Grove Ballistite 200
		15 943 Bleddfa Tell Tale

1. Tregoyd Starlight
Registration number 1577 in the *Welsh Stud Book, Vol. XXXI*
Grey, blaze, white near hind sock, height (at two
years): 11 hands, foaled 1935
Breeder: The Hon. Mrs. Devereux, Hampton Green
Park, Leominster

The year that Tregoyd Starlight was foaled (1935) his dam was shown extensively so that he had his first taste of the show ring very early in life. Indeed he himself soon began his winning ways, since, as a foal he won a first prize at the Three Counties Show, and his photograph appeared in the press under the caption "The Hon. Mrs. Devereux with large horse".!

The following year, the Hon. Mrs. Devereux decided to disperse her stud and her twelve ponies were offered for sale at the end of the Craven Sale on 3rd October 1936. Included in the sale were Tregoyd Starlight, his full-brother the colt foal Tregoyd Nightlight, their dam, Grove Peep O'Day and her three-year-old son Tregoyd Morning Star by Criban Bumble Bee. Both Tregoyd Starlight and Tregoyd Morning Star fetched 14 guineas each, their dam fetching 24 guineas which was the highest price of the Tregoyd consignment. Tregoyd Starlight was purchased by Mr. Llewellyn Richards of the Criban Stud and Tregoyd Nightlight by Mrs. E. G. E. Griffith (who was then residing in Oxford).

Tregoyd Starlight did not stay long at Criban (Starlight was actually with Mr. Llewellyn Richards in Northants) since, on 7th May 1937, a sale was held of ninety ponies and Tregoyd Starlight was entered as lot 7 with a reserve figure of 50 guineas on him (since Mr. Richards was keen to use him at stud if he did not fetch a reasonable figure). The auctioneer thought the sale was going rather slowly, and thinking he might speed it up, ignored Mr. Richards' reserve and sold him to Mr. Emrys Griffiths for 10½ guineas (on behalf of Mr. T. N. Lewis who had bought his dam, Grove Peep O'Day at the Tregoyd Sale).

His stay at the Bolgoed Stud again was short-lived and in 1938 he found his way to the Shimdda Hir Stud at Llandudno, owned by Mr. J. B. Holden where the stud groom was Mr. Tom Thomas who had had such remarkable show ring successes at the Dinarth Hall Stud (dispersed on 27th October 1937). Mr. Holden also acquired Tregoyd Nightlight and at the 1939 Royal Welsh Show (Caernarfon), Tregoyd Starlight stood third and Nightlight fourth behind the invincible Grove Sprightly (then 21 years old) and Dinarth What Ho. Tregoyd Nightlight died during the winter of 1939.

Tregoyd Starlight with Mr. Tom Thomas.

After the war, Tregoyd Starlight's showing recommenced at the 1947 Shrewsbury Show. He won the stallion class from his son Shimdda Hir Sprightly Shot (foaled 1940, son of Vardra Sunflower) a stallion who was exported to Mr. Cuneo, Illinois in November 1947 and took the American harness classes by storm. At the 1947 United Kingdom Shows, Sprightly Shot was produced by Mr. Bob Black of Hackney fame for his owner, Mr. Tom Neal. Fifth in this class was Mr. T. Norman Lewis' Bolgoed Shot Star, full-brother to Sprightly Shot, foaled in 1942. Tregoyd Starlight was then awarded the Championship at this show. That year at the Royal Welsh Show he stood third to Dinarth What Ho and Whitehall Monarch.

In 1948 Tregoyd Starlight won at Shrewsbury, Cheshire, Timperley, and the Royal Agricultural Society of England at Lincoln.

In 1949, he gained the Championships at the Royal Agricultural Society of England at Shrewsbury, Royal Welsh Agricultural Society at Swansea (we stood Reserve Champion with the champion female Coed Coch Serliw), Three Counties and Bath and West. During 1950, Tregoyd Starlight made only two outings, he won at Chester in June then, after having been proclaimed Champion at the Royal Welsh Agricultural Society Show at Abergele, he was disqualified on veterinary grounds and that was the end of his show ring career.

It was 1950 also that saw virtually the end of his career at stud, although he lived on in peaceful retirement cared for by Miss Enid Holden at Shimdda Hir for many more years.

The first progeny of Tregoyd Starlight was Revel Rose, foaled in 1938, the next progeny being bred by Mr. Holden out of Vardra Sunflower, viz: Shimdda Hir Sprightly Shot (1940), Shimdda Hir Seren Ebrill (1950) and Shimdda Hir Seren Medi (1948) all three exported to the U.S.A.

Tregoyd Starlight with Mr. John Thomas at the Royal Welsh Show 1949.

Coed Coch Meilyr, Male Champion at the Royal Welsh Show 1950 son of Tregoyd Starlight. (Photograph courtesy of Lord Kenyon.)

The Coed Coch Stud was a firm supporter of Tregoyd Starlight. His progeny there included: Coed Coch Meilyr (winner of first prizes at the Bath and West and Royal Welsh Agricultural Society in 1949 and Champion Male at the 1950 Royal Welsh Show when his sire was disqualified, exported to Mr. Fernley of Pennsylvania in 1953 and winner of many American Grand Championships); Coed Coch Paun (foaled 1950); Coed Coch Pilan (foaled 1951); Coed Coch Seraph (foaled 1950 and exported to New Zealand); Coed Coch Serenllys foaled in 1947, the winner at the 1949 Royal Agricultural Society of England and second at the 1950 Royal Welsh Agricultural Society to Meilyr he was exported to Mrs. Mackay-Smith, Virginia in 1955 not however before laying his destination as grand-sire of two Royal Welsh Show Champions: the 1967, 1968 and 1970 Male Champion Treharne Tomboy (whose dam was Coed Coch Blodyn, daughter of Serenllys) and the 1968 Female Champion Ready Token Glen Bride (sired by Serenllys' son Coed Coch Bugail); the females Coed Coch Picil (foaled 1948, exported to Crefeld Farm, U.S.A.); Coed Coch Swynol (foaled in 1949 and also owned by Crefeld Farm); and finally perhaps the most important of the Coed Coch females, Coed Coch Pelen (foaled in 1948 and produced Coed Coch Planed, Pibydd, Pw and Prydus before leaving for Mrs. du Pont's Stud where she produced six colts and four fillies).

Miss Harrop of the Glascoed Stud was also a good supporter of Tregoyd Starlight, breeding Glascoed Lleuad, Llydaw, Merlin (Canada), Mervyn, Moonlight and Eira.

The colt foal with which we won at the 1949 Royal Welsh Show was Ceulan Stardust out of the 1949 Royal Welsh Champion mare Coed Coch Serliw; Stardust was not used at stud and was gelded and sold as a harness pony.

The only breeders to use Tregoyd Starlight after his disqualification were Mr. Campbell Moodie (Ankerwycke Sprightly in 1953 and Ankerwycke Starlight, also in 1953) and Lord Kenyon who bred what was probably the last by Tregoyd Starlight in Gredington Orinda (foaled in 1958). Orinda was exported to the Brays Island Plantation, U.S.A. who had previously bought her full sister Gredington Ennill, an extremely successful young show mare in the United Kingdom she had produced Gredington Melfed, and Lili and the most fashionable stallion Gredington Iolo before leaving the United Kingdom.

Thus it will be seen that although the lovely Tregoyd Starlight sired about thirty-five ponies in the period of about ten years, many of which were exceptionally successful in the show ring and at stud, very few of his blood-lines remain in the United Kingdom, the exceptions being Coed Coch Planed (sire of so many beautiful mares) and Gredington Iolo (Bengad Stud and Weald Stud).

2. Grove Sprightly (*chapter 5.1*)

3. Grove Peep O'Day

Registration number 6582 in the *Welsh Stud Book,
Vol. XX*
Light grey, blaze near hind white heel, height: 10
hands 2 in (as a yearling), foaled 1919
Breeder: Mrs. H. D. Greene, the Grove,
Craven Arms.
Re-registered: *Vol. XXIX page 40* to show ownership:
Mr. E. J. Reynolds, Blanche Stud, Dowlais,
Merthyr Tydfil
Re-registered: *Vol. XXX page 66* to show ownership:
The Hon. Mrs. Devereux, Hampton Green Park,
Leominster

There was a previous Grove Peep O'Day (brown mare) registration number 6038 registered in the *Welsh Stud Book Vol. XVIII* as foaled in 1917. However this was in error, a duplicate entry for 6037 Grove Firelight (full-sister to 6582 Grove Peep O'Day) and the entry for 6038 Grove Peep O'Day was subsequently cancelled in *Vol. XIX.*

Peep O'Day was purchased (as a three-year-old) at the Grove Sale on 6th September 1922 where the catalogue described her as "a mare of fine action and fast. Beautifully bred on both sides".

To breeders of today no doubt it seems unusual that none of Peep O'Days progeny was registered from 1922 until 1931 but it must be remembered that these were the years of the depression in the South Wales valleys and it was uneconomic to send a mare annually to a registered stallion and the price obtained for a registered foal differed very little from that of an un-registered one. The same situation applied generally throughout Wales; I got the same answer when I once asked my father why he bred only seven foals from Seren Ceulan (in this same era) during twenty-one years. It seems that the only establishments breeding regularly from their mountain pony mares in those days were those keeping their own stallions whether they were managed by the stud staff as at the Grove or running out on the Welsh mountains such as at Criban. Whether Peep O'Day bred un-registered animals during this period or not, no-one knows. However, if she may have been inactive in the stud, she was very active in the show ring especially during the late 'twenties when she won many first prizes, championships and Welsh Pony & Cob Society medals at such shows as Tredegar, Pengam, Pyle, Bedwellty, Abergavenny, Merthyr Tydfil, Blaina, and Nelson including three successive medals at Bedwellty.

Grove Peep O'Day, photographed at the Royal Welsh Show 1937. (Photograph courtesy of The University of Reading Museum of English Rural Life.)

After breeding two fillies (both by Criban Marksman) for Mr. Reynolds, Peep O'Day was sold in 1933 with a colt foal at foot (by Criban Bumble Bee) to the Hon. Mrs. Devereux. At the Tregoyd Stud she produced another two foals and her showing went further afield, when, despite advancing years she won first prizes at the National Pony Society Show at Islington in both 1935 and 1936 with second prizes at the Three Counties, Royal Welsh and Royal Agricultural Society of England only to be sold again at the Tregoyd Stud Dispersal on 3rd October 1936 along with her three sons. This time again it was Mr.

Bolgoed Atomic, driven by Mr. Tom Thomas. Son of Bolgoed Mighty Atom who was son of Grove Peep O'Day.

Reynolds who bought her back on behalf of Mr. Tom Norman Lewis of the Bolgoed Stud.

In the ownership of the Bolgoed Stud, Peep O'Day continued her winning ways all over South Wales until there were no more shows at the outbreak of war. At the 1937 Royal Welsh Show, Peep O'Day was placed first by Mr. Tom Jones Evans but was later disqualified because her shoes transgressed the regulations as to weight leaving Dinarth Stud's Criban Socks (*chapter 9.7*) as the winner. This was Peep O'Day's last appearance at a Royal Welsh Show but she continued breeding at the Bolgoed Stud right up to her death in 1944.

Her produce are appended below:

1931 Blanche Peep O'Dawn, filly, by Criban Marksman, a good breeder at the Blanche Stud including Blanche Dawn, Dewdrop, Bo Peep, Twilight, etc, several of which were sold for export.

1932 Bo Peep, filly, also by Criban Marksman, producer of Bolgoed Lady Grey who, in turn, produced Bolgoed Golden Arrow and the well-known Dutch Section "B" stallion Bolgoed Automation.

1933 Tregoyd Morning Star, colt (bred by Mr. Reynolds).

1935 Tregoyd Starlight, colt, by Grove Sprightly.

1936 Tregoyd Nightlight, colt, by Grove Sprightly.

1938 Bolgoed Squire, colt, he sired some good stock for the Revel, Criban and Cui Studs before being exported to Texas.

1939 Bolgoed Mighty Atom, colt (originally registered as Siwell Surprise), a good winner in hand and in harness in the United Kingdom before he was exported to Mr. Cuneo of Illinois in 1946. He became a phenomenal harness winner in the U.S.A. His best-known progeny in the United Kingdom was the big winner Bolgoed Atomic (also later exported).

1940 Bolgoed What Ho, colt, like Mighty Atom, he was also sired by Mathrafal Tuppence and exported in 1946 to Mr. Cuneo but then sold to Mr. Clifford of Ohio and again a big winner in harness.

1943 Bolgoed Peep O'Day, filly, by Criban Cockade, dam of many good stallions including Bolgoed Golden Glory, Mischief, Pippin.

1944 Bolgoed What Again, filly, by Bolgoed What Ho, exported to Mr. George Fernley of Pennsylvania.

4. Bleddfa Shooting Star (*chapter 4.1*)

5. Grove Sprite II (*chapter 5.2*)

7. Grove Twilight
Registration number 3017 in the *Welsh Stud Book, Vol. X*
Dark grey, height 11 hands 2 in, foaled 1909
Owner and Breeder: Mrs. H. D. Greene,
The Grove, Craven Arms.

Grove Twilight will be remembered, not as a show pony but as one of the most prolific breeders in the history of the Welsh Mountain Pony breed. It is significant that at the time of the dispersal of the famous Grove Stud (29th June 1927) out of the thirty-eight ponies remaining there after many "culling" sales, six were progeny of Grove Twilight. This shows the affection which their owner had for this remarkably successful family, and to get these numbers into the correct perspective, it must be remembered that over 300 ponies had passed through Mrs. Greene's hands during the years 1906–1927 in order to achieve her final thirty-eight favourites.

Grove Twilight did not appear very much in the show ring while in Mrs. Greene's ownership; perhaps she was considered too valuable to take out of the pasture. She did appear in the Novice mare class at the 1921 Shropshire and West Midland Show but was unplaced; the winners of that class have long since faded into oblivion. Indeed, her biggest show ring success was a second prize at the 1930 Shropshire Show in the ownership of Mr. Tom Jones Evans when she was twice as old as anything else in the class!

Listed below are her progeny. (It had not been appreciated that her earlier ones were such "gold mines" and they were not registered and sold on, these included the Islington Champion riding pony Pop Gun amongst many other good ones).

1917 Grove Firelight, filly, brown, sired by Bleddfa Shooting Star, described in the Sale Catalogue as "one of the most charming mares the breed has ever produced". Her photograph in *Welsh Stud Book, Vol. XXIII, page 10* certainly bears this out. Firelight was a prolific winner of Championships at Islington, Swansea, Chester, Royal Lancashire, Shropshire and West Midland, Bath and West etc; a truly exquisite mare. Her photograph also appeared in *Welsh Stud Book, Vol. XIX, page 49*. Firelight was purchased at the Dispersal Sale (along with her colt foal later registered as Tedstone Fireleaf) for 72 guineas by Captain Belville of Bromyard who showed her at the 1929 Shropshire Show (when she was not shown to best advantage) to stand fourth to her full-sister Dawn of Bryntirion.

1918 Dawn of Bryntirion, filly, grey, sired by Bleddfa Shooting Star. Sold as a yearling to Mr. William Taylor of Woolton, Lancs who registered her. In the ownership of Mr. Tom Jones Evans she was Supreme Champion at the 1929 Royal Welsh Show (beating the same owner's winning stallion Craven Master Shot), after which she was exported to Mrs. Hartley Dodge of New Jersey.

1919 Grove Peep O'Day, filly, sired by Bleddfa Shooting Star.

1920 Grove Nightshade, colt, sired by Bleddfa Shooting Star. Winner of many prizes in the ownership of Mrs. Green 1921–1923 such as first prizes at the Bath and West, Craven Arms and Welsh Pony & Cob Society Medal at Chester, then sold to Mr. H. J. Hughes of the Belgrave Stud, Shrewsbury (lot 183 at the 1922 Welsh Pony & Cob Society Sale).

1921 Grove Moonstone, filly, grey, sired by Bleddfa Shooting Star. Described in the sale catalogue as "a fine mover like all her family and considered by some of the best judges as the probable Champion Pony Brood mare of the future". This was the animal that topped the Grove Dispersal Sale at 141 guineas (more than the Champions Grove Sprightly and Grove King Cole II); she was purchased by Lady Wentworth. Her photograph appears in the *Welsh Stud Book, Vol. XXV, page 36.* Judging by photographs, Firelight, Peep O'Day and Dawn of Bryntirion were nicer mares, a view supported by the fact that one month later at the Royal Welsh Agricultural Society Show she stood only seventh in her class.

1923 Grove Will O'the Wisp, colt, grey, sired by Bleddfa Shooting Star. The photograph of Will O'the Wisp which appears in *Vol. XXXI Welsh Stud Book, page 25* depicts one of the most beautiful animals whose photograph has ever graced the pages of a *Welsh*

Grove Will O'the Wisp (foaled in 1923) with Mr. Tom Thomas. Will O'the Wisp, who is considered to be one of the most correctly proportioned Mountain ponies of all time, was a son of Grove Twilight. (Photograph courtesy of G. H. Parsons.)

51

Stud Book. Unbeaten as a yearling and two-year-old at Grove, he was turned out with mares at the time of the Grove Dispersal Sale when he was sold to Mr. Hamilton Crawford of Faaram, Killay, Swansea. For Mr. Crawford he won many prizes (ably produced and shown by Mr. Jack Havard) but was usually second or third to such brilliant animals as Craven Master Shot and Grove Sprightly. He was then purchased by Mr. Tom Jones Evans (who often exhibited both him and Sprightly in the same class, the owner himself handling Will O'the Wisp). His next owner was Mr. T. J. Jones of Dinarth Hall for whom he won first prize and Championship at the 1937 Royal Welsh Show after which he was exported to Italy.

1925 Grove Shadow, filly, grey, the last of seven registered progeny of Twilight by Bleddfa Shooting Star. Purchased by Lady Wentworth on the Grove Dispersal Sale for 10½ guineas, she does not seem to have bred any registered progeny at Crabbet.

1926 Grove Hoarfrost, filly, grey sired by Grove Sprightly, she topped the youngsters at the Grove Dispersal fetching 42 guineas from Captain Belville. Her dam was sold to the Craven Stud (before the Grove Dispersal) when she was a foal.

1929 Craven Twilight Shot, colt, chesnut, by Craven Master Shot.

1931 Craven Electric Light, colt, grey, by Craven Cyrus, exhibited extensively in the ownership of Miss Pauling of Thame.

1933 Craven Springlight, filly, black, by Grove Sprightly, won many prizes for Craven Stud but was sold at the Craven Stud Sale in October 1936 for 23 guineas to the Criban Stud who exported her to the U.S.A. in September 1937.

8. Dyoll Starlight (*chapter 2.1*)

9. Alveston Belle (*chapter 4.3*)

10. Grove Ballistite (*chapter 5.6*)

11. Grove Fairy (*chapter 5.7*)

12. Dyoll Starlight

13. Alveston Belle

14. Grove Ballistite

15. Bleddfa Tell Tale

Registration number 943 in the *Welsh Stud Book, Vol. III*
Dappled grey, height 11 hands 3 in, foaled 1896
Breeder: W. J. Roberts, Clive Avenue,
Church Stretton
Owners (in 1904) The Radnorshire Polo and Riding
Pony Company Ltd., Bleddfa, Radnorshire.
Sire: Tyrant, grey, 12 hands (foaled 1890, number 54
Polo Pony Stud Book, Vol. I)
Dam: Bleddfa Kocklani, dark bay, 12 hands, foaled
1888 (number 938 *Welsh Stud Book*)

Mr. Roberts, breeder of Bleddfa Tell Tale, was breeding ponies long before the inception of the Welsh Pony & Cob Society and it was largely due to his foresight and encouragement that the Longmynd Hill Pony Improvement Society was formed in 1890. In 1897, Mr. Roberts left the Church Stretton area to go to Newport in Shropshire and he left his ponies to be cared for by Mr. Harry Corfield who broke Tell Tale in to ride and it was here that the manager of the Bleddfa Stud saw Tell Tale and persuaded Mr. Roberts to exchange her (along with another four of his best mares including Tell-Tale's dam and half-sister Bleddfa Piegon) for shares in the Radnorshire Company Limited.

Before going to the Bleddfa Stud Tell Tale bred:
1901 Longmynd Lady Polo by Lord Polo (135 *Polo Pony Stud Book*)

Bleddfa Tell Tale with Mrs. D. H. Greene.

Whilst at Bleddfa she bred:

1902 Bleddfa Tom Tit by Shy Boy
1903 Bleddfa Tit Mouse by the good winning stallion Montgomery George
1904 Filly by His Lordship
1905 Picket Starlight 956 by Bleddfa Shooting Star

His Lordship was a thoroughbred by Welsh Pony, sired by Lord Polo from the Welsh Mountain pony mare 1209 Bahaillon Ruby and Lord Polo was by the beautiful small Thoroughbred Rosewater (also known as Johnnie Day) who sired Sir John Barker's phenomenally successful Polo Pony stallion Sandiway. Lord Polo's dam, Lady Florence was of unrecorded breeding but she was bought by Sir Humphrey de Trafford on the borders of Wales and is reputed to have been a Welsh Pony.

Alas for Mr. Roberts the shares of the Radnorshire Company proved to be worthless and Mr. Roberts lost his money and his ponies. The Bleddfa Stud was sold up in 1907 (when Mr. Roberts managed to buy back two of his mares) and Mrs. Greene wisely bought Tell Tale and her two fillies which she registered as Grove Gossip (foaled in 1906) and Grove Gwladys (foaled in 1907).

The story of Grove Gwladys is interesting to the extent of almost warranting a chapter all to herself! In 1914 she was sold (lot 28 at the first Grove Sale) along with a filly foal (lot 29) by Grove Arclight to Capt. T. A. Howson who was at that time a solicitor in Darwen in Lancashire (and "horse" correspondent to the *Livestock Journal* under the name of "Lancastrian". He kept Gwladys (along with another four top-class mares which he purchased at around the same time) on common land near Darwen. Capt. Howson then bred out of Grove Gwladys (all by the best stallions of the day, Grove Ballistite, Bleddfa Shooting Star etc) Blodyn Dewi, Send Silver Rays, H. E. Aurora, Ceiliog Ymladd and out of the daughters (again by top-class stallions) bred such as Gwenci Myndd, Scud Gwladys, Pluen Eira, King's Ale, Cwrw Da, Chwibanogl Y Mynydd etc. Indeed by the mid-'twenties, Capt. Howson was one of the largest breeders of Welsh Mountain ponies in the *Welsh Stud Book*. A photograph of a group of his mares which appeared in the *Welsh Stud Book* depicts a beautiful lot of mares with excellent foals. I was once told that when Capt. Howson was appointed Secretary of the Royal Welsh Agricultural Society (and later of the Welsh Pony and Cob Society) that he left all these good ponies on that common land and never went back there; what happened to them all is a matter for conjecture! I wish I had asked the Captain to confirm this fact since he often called at Talybont and left me an oil painting of a Hackney in harness when he died in February 1954. I am inclined to believe this account of the fate of his ponies since not one of them was ever transferred to another owner, nor was there any progeny registered out of them at a future date.

To return to the progeny of Bleddfa Tell Tale produced at the Grove:

1908 Grove Grenade, colt, by Grove Ballistite; he won several times when owned by Mrs. Greene and his photograph appeared in the *Welsh Stud Book, Vol. X, page 4.* He was exported to Dr. Nash P. Stead of Virginia, U.S.A. in 1911.

1909 Grove Twilight (*this chapter No. 7*).

1910 Grove Stallactite, colt, by Grove Ballistite. A very big winner he was sold (lot 48) at the 1914 Grove Sale (photographed in catalogue).

Grove Stallactite (foaled in 1910) son of Bleddfa Tell Tale.

1911 Grove King Cole II, colt, by Grove King Cole. Undoubtedly this is one of the most correctly proportioned stallions which has appeared; it so happens that he was also a very spectacular mover and when one looks at his photograph, one wonders whether the breed has progressed any in seventy years. Grove King Cole II was a Champion from the day he was born; as a yearling he won every time shown and was Reserve Champion

Grove King Cole II, son of Bleddfa Tell Tale. (Photograph courtesy of G. H. Parsons.)

at the Shropshire Show as a two-year-old winning the following year at Islington and the Royal Agricultural Society of England Show at Shrewsbury. For the next few years he mainly stood reserve champion to his stable-mates until 1920 when he won the Championship himself, and between this date and the Grove Dispersal Sale in 1927 he had won more first prizes and Championships at the National Pony Society Shows and Royal Agricultural Society of England Shows than any other pony of his breed. His photographs at the National Pony Society Shows in the winning groups appear in *Vol. XXIII of the Welsh Stud Book* on *pages 6, 8* and *10*. His individual photographs appear in *Vol. XII* (as a yearling) also as the frontispiece of *Vol. XIX*, an honour which he richly deserved. Grove King Cole II was the only animal to have a photograph in the Dispersal Sale Catalogue of 1927; he was the top-priced male going to Lady Wentworth at 130 guineas. He was used very little at stud at Crabbet; Grove Moonstone who produced Wentworth Moonstruck by him in 1928 was already in foal on the 1927 Sale; the only other which I can trace to be produced at Crabbet being Wentworth Glittering Star (foaled 1929) out of his maternal half-sister Grove Lightheart. I find this surprising since most of the best mares in the United Kingdom were at Crabbet at this time.

1912 colt (gelded) by Grove Starshine; he was offered for sale on the 1916 Sale described as "quiet to ride and drive, has been out with hounds and promises to make a good jumper." By then he was the property of Mr. G. Mildred having been bought from Grove (lot 68) at the 1914 Sale.

1913 Grove ap Tell Tale, colt, by Grove Arclight by Champion Greylight. This was a useful stallion who was awarded the Board of Agriculture's premium to run on the Eppynt hills during 1916.

1914 Grove Lightheart (*chapter 10.15*).

1916 Grove Woodbine, filly, by Grove Recruit. Woodbine was offered for sale at the 1922 Welsh Pony and Cob Society Sale (lot 108) but was withdrawn at 17½ guineas; she was later sold (lot 51) at the second Welsh Pony & Cob Society Sale (7th April 1923) at 13½ guineas.

1919 Un-named brown stallion, by Bleddfa Shooting Star, sold (lot 11) at the 1923 Welsh Pony & Cob Society Sale. This was probably her last foal.

Bleddfa Tell Tale will be remembered as an outstanding producer. Her blood-lines appear in so many present-day winners through Tregoyd Starlight, Coed Coch Madog, and Grove Peep O'Day. Not only was she a famous producer but she was also a good winner in the show ring starting with a first prize at the Bath and West Show in the ownership of her breeder. A photograph of her (when owned by the Radnorshire Company) held by a very unhappy-looking young lad is not very flattering and she did not do so well in the show ring when in this ownership winning only a few lowly prizes at Knighton Show until 1907 when she resumed her winning ways for Mrs. Greene winning at the Welsh National in 1908, Shropshire in 1909 and 1910 etc. In fact she was the "full back" for the Grove Show string for many years and was Mrs. Greene's favourite mare.

4
Bleddfa Shooting Star foaled 1901

1	2	4	
Bleddfa Shooting Star 73	Dyoll Starlight 4	Dyoll Glasallt 438_	
		5 75 Dyoll Moonlight	
	3 572 Alveston Belle	**6** Cymro	**12** Beaconsfield 27

1. Bleddfa Shooting Star

Registration number 73 in the *Welsh Stud Book,*
Vol. III (1904)
Very dark iron grey, height: 11 hands 2 in,
foaled 1901
Breeder: S. M. Wilmot, The Chalet, Alveston,
near Bristol.
Owners: The Radnorshire Polo and Riding Pony
Company Limited, The Farm, Bleddfa,
Llangunllo, Radnorshire.

Bleddfa Shooting Star was purchased by the Radnorshire (Bleddfa) Company from his breeder in 1903. Shortly afterwards this Company got into financial difficulties and Shooting Star was purchased for 200 guineas at the Bleddfa Sale by Sir Walter Gilbey who had a famous stud of Hackneys at Elsenham Hall in Essex. There was a large competent staff at Elsenham Hall and in 1906 Shooting Star appeared at the National Pony Show at Islington, sparkling like the proverbial new pin, tacked up with tight side-reins and over-check and moving with tremendous force and leverage off all fours. Lancastrian writing in the *Livestock Journal* said he was "one of the sensations of the Show-ring". Sir Walter Gilbey writing in his book *Thoroughbred and Other Ponies* published in 1910 said thus: "I am the happy possessor of one of these ponies 'Shooting Star' and though in height he is only 11 hands 2 in, I do not hesitate to say that he has the finest natural action of any animal that I have ever known in a long experience of horses". And Sir Walter should know since he had owned many famous Hackney Stallions such as Antonius, Flash Cadet and Royal Danegelt.

One of the early importers of Welsh ponies into the U.S.A. was Charles A. Stone of Boston, Mass who imported twenty-four registered ponies into the U.S.A. in 1911.

Mr. Stone commissioned Olive Tilford Dargan to write a book on Welsh ponies for him (which he printed privately on hand-made paper in 1913 with the title *The Welsh Pony*) and I quote from *page 5* of this delightful book.

Later, at the Olympia, during the International Horse Show, I spent a fatuously happy time in the stables. Many poor types were exhibited and nobly they represented their kind, but I found none so love-inspiring as the little conquerer from Cymric, "Shooting Star", owned by Sir Walter Gilbey. He is a dapple-grey, eleven hands high,

61

of perfect shape and brimful of spirit, not of the self-conscious kind, eager for gratuitous display, but unabashed, careful of the amenities and avowing with all the grace in him that he will be your friend if you choose to be his. If he has one defect it is a parsimony of tail, though I heard none of his thousands of admirers make that criticism; and he carries it up and out in true Arabian style. In the arena, when all of the horses came in for the general parade – the big Clydesdales first, followed by representatives of nearly every breed in the world, the procession ending with a wee Shetland whose owner is the little Princess Juliana of Holland – it was Shooting Star that received the most impulsive greeting – an applause of love evoked by his irresistible dearness, billowing where he passed until he completed the great circuit. I had the assurance of others who daily haunted the Show that this triumph was a feature of every general parade.

Towards the end of 1914 Sir Walter died and his famous Elsenham Stud was dispersed and despite the country being at war, Mrs. Greene of the Grove Stud bought Shooting Star for 280 guineas.

During the period 1905 to 1914, Shooting Star had not had a fair chance at Stud but had received a few mares from the Principality and some from the Grove Stud. However, during this period he managed to sire: Grove Starling winner at Chicago, Knighton and the Bath and West; Grove Gwladys; Gwyndy Twinkle Champion London and sold to America for £200; Grove Starshine; Hawddgar Piccadilly, first at the Royal; Spinaway first and medal winner at the Welsh National (the fore-runner of the Royal Welsh); Captain Hook third at London and the Royal; Grove Stella, Longmynd Star etc. Also during this period he

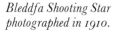

Bleddfa Shooting Star photographed in 1910.

Bleddfa Shooting Star on exhibition at the 1929 Royal Welsh Show when 28 years old. (Photograph courtesy of G. H. Parsons.)

had been leased for two seasons to Dafydd Evans, Llwyncadfor, Cardiganshire (whose son Tom Jones Evans later played such an important part in the history of the Welsh breeds in general and Shooting Star descendants in particular).

At the time of his purchase by Mrs. Greene in 1915, Shooting Star had already won innumerable first prizes and Championships, including five first prizes and Championships and four Reserve Championships London and six first prizes and Championships and one Reserve Championship at the Royal; in fact, Shooting Star had beaten every stallion about at that time including his great sire, Dyoll Starlight, and his almost equally great half-brother, the thousand-guinea Greylight.

It was in 1913 that Shooting Star and Dyoll Starlight had their great show ring battles; at the National Pony Show in March the judge, Mr. Roberts of Church Stretton could not decide between them; eventually he asked both handlers to remove their stallion tackle and Starlight, who wore only a light girth and one side-rein won the battle. The *Livestock Journal* was very indignant over the defeat of Shooting Star and a spate of letters from eminent judges (some favouring one and some the other) continued for a long time. Later that year, at the Royal, Starlight showed his age (20 years) and Shooting Star got his revenge. The report in the *Livestock Journal* described Shooting Star: "Full of vigour and vim using his knees and hocks, of course he is the fleetest, fastest and highest pony in Mother England."

Mrs. Greene with the help of her loyal groom Jimmy Wakefield, swept all before her during the years 1915 to 1927, winning not only the Welsh classes but often also beating all other native breed groups (which she did on four occasions at the National Pony Show with eleven different ponies). Most of her winning youngsters in those days were sired by Shooting Star and out of daughters of her former great champion Grove Ballistite.

In 1927, Mrs. Greene (at almost 70 years of age) decided to disperse her stud which she did on 29th June. The progeny of Shooting Star sold included Grove Fairy Queen (twice Champion London, Champion Royal Agricultural Society of England, first Royal Welsh etc) at 40 guineas, with filly foal, to Lady Wentworth; Grove Fairy Ring (dam of the American winner Grove Gas Ring) at 17 guineas with filly foal, to Hon. E. Mostyn; Grove Firelight (first London, first Swansea, Champion Chester, first Royal Agricultural Society of England, Champion Royal Lancs, Champion Shropshire and West Midland, first Bath and West etc) at 72 guineas with colt foal, to Capt.Belville; Grove Headlight at 16 guineas to the Duke of Newcastle; Grove Moonstone (first Shropshire and West Midland, Champion Royal Lancs etc) at 141 guineas to Lady Wentworth; Grove Pixie (full sister to Grove Sprightly) at 20 guineas; Grove Ladybird (Champion Shropshire and West Midland, Champion Royal Lancs, first Cheshire, second Royal Agricultural Society of England etc) at 50 guineas to Miss M. Dunne; Grove Sprightly (winner of 14 first prizes including London and Royal Championships) at 126 guineas jointly to Lady Wentworth and Tom Jones Evans; Grove Will O'The Wisp to Mr. Crawford, Swansea; yearling colt, later registered as Wentworth Sharpshooter (52 guineas to Lady Wentworth); and many others including Grove Nightfall (later owned by Mrs. Yeomans), Grove Blunderbus, Grove Shadow, Grove Gleam of Hope etc, all sired by Shooting Star.

Shooting Star (aged 26 years) was retained as a pensioner and lived on in honoured retirement for another four years making one last spectacular appearance in the show ring in 1929. At the special request of the Committee he led the parade of Mountain Ponies at the Royal Show and sensing that all eyes were upon him, he put up as great a "show" as ever in his successful life. Two years later, at thirty-one years and crippled with rheumatism, Mrs. Greene had him put down and buried at the Grove.

Many years later when the Grove house was demolished, Mrs. Meredith rescued Shooting Star's horse-shaped marble gravestone and placed it alongside the gravestone of his most famous son, Grove Sprightly, at Dinchope.

2. **Dyoll Starlight** (*chapter 2.1*)

3. **Alveston Belle**
Registration number 572 in the *Welsh Stud Book*,
Vol. II
Registration number 1086 in the *Polo Pony Stud Book*,
Vol. VI
Black mare, with white spot on forehead and nose,
height: 12 hands, foaled 1897
Breeder: S. R. Williams, Henllan, Pwllheli,
North Wales
Owner: S. M. Wilmot, The Chalet, Alveston,
Gloucestershire.

The above is all that was recorded in the *Welsh Stud Book* about Alveston Belle apart from the fact that she produced a bay filly named Alveston Beauty (by Little Reality) in 1900 and a dark grey colt Shooting Star (by Starlight) in 1901.

Such was the impact which Shooting Star had on the pony world that Lancastrian wrote in the *Livestock Journal* asking for more details about Alveston Belle and I have a reply (from a 1914 *Livestock Journal*) from O. G. Owen, Tanyfron, Penrhos, Pwllheli as follows:

I can well remember this little mare in my late father's possession. She was a typical specimen of the Welsh Pony, compact and thick-set, not in any way coarse, very dark brown in colour with quick, snappy action, which she no doubt inherited from her sire Cymro. She was about 12 hands high. Having been reared and kept on the open hills since a foal, with long, unkempt tail and mane, she had a wild fiery look and the unmistakable appearance of hardiness peculiar to Mountain Ponies. The sire Cymro was a smart, good-looking bright chesnut cob, 12 hands 2 in high, an extraordinary fine mover, and as a gelding in my father's hands won many prizes around here and afterwards under a new owner won first prize at the Royal Dublin Society's Show. Cymro's sire was a chesnut cob which came to travel this district from South Wales. I do not know his name or breeding but he was down here called "Southin" which was not his name but the Welsh for "South Walian", and I am told by those who have seen him that he was a smart one with good action and while in this district sired some very showy ponies.

Alveston Belle's dam was a Welsh Mountain Pony, dark brown, 11 hands high, but as few records of pedigrees were kept by farmers in those days I am unable to give the name of her sire or dam.

My father bought Alveston Belle when quite young from her breeder, Mr. Robert Williams, Henllan, near Pwllheli, a neighbouring farmer, and sold her to Mr. S. M. Wilmot, The Chalet, Alveston, Glos.

4. **Dyoll Glasallt** (*chapter 2.2*)

5. **Dyoll Moonlight** (*chapter 2.3*)

6. Cymro
Bright chesnut Cob stallion, 12 hands 2 in.

12. **Beaconsfield** (*chapter 22.1*)

5
Grove Ballistite foaled 1903
Grove Sprightly foaled 1918

1 Grove Sprightly 1036	**2** Bleddfa Shooting Star 73	**4** Dyoll Starlight 4	**8** Dyoll Glasallt 438
			9 75 Dyoll Moonlight
		5 572 Alveston Belle	**10** Cymro
	3 4431 Grove Sprite II	**6** Grove Ballistite 200	**12** Dyoll Starlight 4
			13 65 Dyoll Bala Gal
		7 2531 Grove Fairy	**14** Fairwood Mountain Pony
			15 Fairwood Mountain Pony

1. Grove Sprightly
Registration number 1036 in the *Welsh Stud Book,*
Vol. XX
Dark grey, blaze, foaled 1918, height: 11 hands
Owner and Breeder: Mrs. H. D. Greene, Grove,
Craven Arms, Salop.

Grove Sprightly was introduced to the show ring at an early age winning a first prize in the youngstock class at the Bath and West and a medal at the Royal Agricultural Society of England (Derby) in 1921. The following year he won a first prize and medal at the National Pony Society Show at Islington, London and another first prize at the Royal Agricultural Society of England (Cambridge). In 1922 also he was a member of the Champion group of Mountain and Moorland Ponies at the National Pony Society Show (along with Grove King Cole II, Grove Firelight and Grove Fairy Queen) and the group photograph published in the *Welsh Stud Book, Vol. XXIII* shows Sprightly as a very dark grey with a lighter grey face.

In 1923, Sprightly was once again a member of the Champion National Pony Society group and had another photograph in the *Welsh Stud Book.* Usually in the stallion class that year he stood second to his senior stable-mate King Cole II. During the years 1924 to 1927, Sprightly won four Championships at Shropshire and West Midland Shows; usually at other shows taking second place to Grove King Cole II but catching up and in movement he was superior to King Cole and the placings might have been reversed had they both not been in the same ownership.

On 29th June 1927 the Grove Stud was dispersed, Lady Wentworth buying King Cole II for 130 guineas and Lady Wentworth and Mr. Tom Jones Evans in partnership buying Sprightly for 126 guineas.

In 1930 Tom Jones Evans bought out Lady Wentworth's share in Grove Sprightly and he returned to Craven Arms, to Dinchope farm just "down the road" from the Grove.

Grove Sprightly appeared at the 1930 Royal Welsh Show at Caernarfon and swept all before him in hand and in harness and between this date and 1939 he won the Royal Welsh Show Championship nine times; in fact the only time that he was not present was in 1937 when, to give other exhibitors a chance, Tom Jones Evans was appointed to be the judge! On this occasion, Dinarth Hall was first, second and third with Grove Will O'the Wisp, Bowdler Brightlight and Dinarth What Ho.

Grove Sprightly when owned by Mr. Tom Jones Evans.

No other stallion has ever won nine Royal Welsh Show Champion-ships; the nearest to this record being Coed Coch Madog who won the Royal Welsh Male Championship on nine different occasions but never once succeeded in securing the overall award.

On Saturday, 3rd October 1936, Tom Jones Evans dispersed the Craven Stud with the exception of Sprightly. Prices were very low e.g. the lovely brown mare Craven Sunset, (dam of the well-known riding pony Craven Nell, dam also of the full-brothers Craven Sprightshot – from whence came the Twyford Gala family – and the big winner Craven Tit-Bit etc) fetched only 12 guineas, being purchased by Mrs. Pennell. The progeny of Sprightly sold rather better: e.g. Craven Franddu (already won at the Royal Welsh Show) 14 guineas to Tom Mathias; Craven Arddel, a fine moving filly, 17 guineas; Craven

Craven Tit Bit (foaled in 1938). Sire: Grove Sprightly. Dam: Craven Sunset by Craven Star Shot. G-dam: Lochtyn Tissie by Kismet. G-g-dam: Craven Tosca. (Photograph courtesy of Welsh Stud Book, Vol. 33.*)*

Grove Sprightly with Mrs. Lloyd Jones

Sprightlight a four-year-old black mare sold for 23 guineas to the Criban Stud from where she was exported to the U.S.A. in 1937; the three-year-old grey colt Craven Shooting Star 17 guineas, also to Criban Stud; and Craven Sprightshot, then a yearling colt, 11 guineas to Miss Pauline.

Sprightly's last progeny aptly named Craven Sprightly's Last was foaled in 1945 (out of Gwyndy Light). Sprightly's Last produced Craven Sprightly Light, winner at the Royal Agricultural Society of England for the Fayre Stud before being exported to the Fairway Stud, Australia; Dovey Dynamite three times Royal Welsh Agricultural Society winner before reaching the adult classes etc.

Grove Sprightly died in 1949 at thirty-one years of age (I feel very privileged to have seen him at Dinchope in 1948 when he still had a regal look about him despite his great age) and he was buried outside his stable at Dinchope.

Tom Jones Evans often admitted that, out of all the dozens of famous Cobs, Hackneys and ponies that he had owned, Sprightly was his favourite.

Craven Sprightly's Last photographed in 1954 with foal Dovey Dynamite (with Mr. Douglas Evans). Sprightly's Last was the last foal of Grove Sprightly.

Dovey Dynamite. (Photograph courtesy of Mr. G. C. Smith.)

One present-day stud where the influence of Grove Sprightly is profound is the Llanerch Stud of Mrs. P. A. M. Hambleton started by one mare Sunsprite (foaled in 1939) by Grove Sprightly and out of Craven Sunset (*chapter 7.11*). Every mare at the Llanerch Stud traces back to Sunsprite and one Sunsprite g-daugher, Llanerch Merrymaid sold for 1,000 guineas (September 1979).

73

3. Grove Sprite II
Registration number 4431 in the *Welsh Stud Book,*
Vol. XIII
Chesnut, foaled 1912.
Owner and Breeder: Mrs. H. D. Greene, Grove,
Craven Arms.

Sprite II had a full-sister Sprite I (one year older) and although her brothers and sisters, e.g. Grove Elfin, Grove Fairy Queen and Grove Fairy Ring were great winners in the show ring, Sprite and Sprite II are better known for what they produced.

Sprite II was lot 11 at the Grove Dispersal Sale on 29th June 1927 where she was purchased by Mr. Tom Jones Evans; she was also well represented at this Sale by having six of her progeny included:

Lot 9: Grove Pixie, chesnut mare, 6 years by Bleddfa Shooting Star (20 guineas)

Lot 15: Grove Sprightly, grey stallion, 9 years, by Bleddfa Shooting Star (126 guineas, Lady Wentworth and Mr. Tom Jones Evans)

Lot 18: Grove Catapult, grey colt, 3 years, full brother to Sprightly (Mrs. Philip Hunloke, Malmesbury)

Lot 25: Un-named chesnut yearling filly by Grove King Cole II (10 guineas to Mr. Ratcliffe, Stafford)

Lot 38: Grove Flutter, chesnut mare, 4 years by Longmynd Gambler

Lot 11a: Colt foal by Grove King Cole II (later named Craven Sprightly)

One of her progeny who had been sold prior to the sale (in fact he had been sold as a yearling in 1918) was a colt by Grove King Cole II who was registered as Pistyll King Cole (owned by David Davies of the successful Pistyll Stud, Blaenpistyll, Cardigan). This colt was later sold to the Lord Swansea who re-registered him as Caer Beris King Cole, and under this name he won very many prizes and Championships throughout the United Kingdom.

Grove Sprite II was in foal to Bleddfa Shooting Star when she was sold to the Craven Stud and duly produced Craven Sunflower in 1928; thereafter she went to the Craven stallions e.g. Craven Master Shot but did not afterwards produce anything quite so illustrious as the legendary Grove Sprightly, although Craven Master Sprite (by the

Champion Craven Master Shot) which she produced in 1930 went on to be Champion at the 1936 Australian Sydney Show and he also sired Craven Tosca (foaled 1933) before he left these shores.

4. **Dyoll Starlight** (*chapter 2.1*)

5. **Alveston Belle** (*chapter 4.3*)

6. Grove Ballistite
Registration number 200 in the *Welsh Stud Book,*
Vol. VI
(Previously registered as Dyoll Ballistite number 151
in *Vol. V*)
Also registered in *Vol. VII* (*p. 3*), *Vol. VIII* (*p. 5*), *Vol.*
IX (*p. 5*), *Vol. X* (*p. 5*) and *Vol. XI* (*p. 6*) to record
prizes won.
Dark grey, star, height: under 12 hands, foaled 1903
Owner and Breeder: Mr. H. Meuric Lloyd, Delfryn,
Llanwrda, Carmarthenshire.

Dyoll Ballistite was introduced to the show ring in 1906 at the Welsh National (now the Royal Welsh) Show. It was an any-age stallion class (judged by Mr. W. S. Miller, Forest Lodge, Brecon) and Ballistite

Grove Ballistite.
(Photograph courtesy
of F. Babbage.)

stood fifth (which was good for a three-year-old) behind the "big guns": Greylight, Montgomery George II, Gwyndy Cymro and Brigand (the latter also bred by Mr. Lloyd and was later to have a marked influence on the Church Stretton ponies). Ballistite was recorded in the Show Catalogue as being for sale for £100. Possibly this show result disappointed his owner since he was sold soon afterwards for 36 guineas to Mrs. Greene of the Grove Stud.

It was in 1907 that Ballistite, now re-named Grove Ballistite, started upon his long and successful show ring career with 1907 winnings including first prizes at Craven Arms, Ludlow, Church Stretton with third prizes at National Pony Society (Islington) and the Welsh National (behind his two famous half-brothers Greylight and Bleddfa Shooting Star). A photograph of the young Ballistite appears as the frontispiece of the *Welsh Stud Book, Vol. VII.*

In 1908, Ballistite won first prizes at the Shropshire and West Midland, Welsh National (my great-uncle John Thomas was fifth with Total), Craven Arms, Kington etc. Similarly a successful 1909 with some firsts and two thirds at Islington and the Royal Agricultural Society of England (Gloucester); 1910 with a Welsh Pony & Cob Society medal at Church Stretton etc, 1911 with a first prize at the Welsh National (now no longer at Aberystwyth but had started to move and in 1911 was held at Welshpool) with firsts also at Shropshire and Church Stretton. This successful career continued with many Championship awards until 1914 when Ballistite won at the Royal Lancashire Show and on *page 11* of *Vol. XVIII* of the *Welsh Stud Book* appears a stallion class photograph of which any present-day show ring could justifiably be extremely proud. Ballistite appears in all his magnificence in this photograph followed by Grove King Cole II, Grove Footlight, Hawddgar Mountain Chief, Gwyndy Comet and Stanage Daylight.

The younger Grove-bred stallions e.g. Grove King Cole II by now were catching up with Ballistite so it was decided to retire him from the show ring; also in 1915 Bleddfa Shooting Star was acquired by the Grove Stud and consequently Mrs. Greene, who was forever generous towards pony improvement societies, allowed Ballistite to go to South Wales where he sired some good ponies in the Brynamman area before returning to the Grove.

Ballistite by this time had not spent all his life in the show ring; he had built up quite a reputation for himself as a sire e.g. Grove Gunpowder, reserve Champion in the 1914 Royal Agricultural Society of England Show; Grove ap Ballistite from the good Grove Pansy by "Llew Llwyd" (Gwesyn Flyer) by Trotting Flyer 271 (*chapter 23.14*); Grove

76

Elfin, winner of the youngstock class two years in succession at Royal Agricultural Society of England Shows (1915 and 1916).

However, Ballistite (like Bleddfa Shooting Star) is better known as a sire of exceptional females such as Grove Sprite II (dam of Sprightly etc) and Grove Twilight (*chapter 3.7*) who produced the lovely brown Grove Firelight (foaled 1917) (Champion at National Pony Society, Swansea, Cheshire County, Bath and West, Royal Lancs, Shropshire etc), Grove Moonstone (foaled 1921) (the highest-priced pony on the 1927 Sale at 141 guineas to Lady Wentworth), Grove Will O'the Wisp (one of the most perfectly proportioned stallions of all time, owned successively by Mr. Hamilton Crawford, Faraam, Killay, Swansea; Mr. Tom Jones Evans and Dinarth Hall Stud before being exported to Italy); Grove Hoarfrost (foaled 1926) and Grove Shadow (foaled 1925) – all five of these sold on the 1927 Sale.

7. Grove Fairy

Registration number 2531 in the *Welsh Stud Book,*
Vol. IX
Chestnut, star, height: 11 hands, foaled 1905
Breeder: William Jones, Sandy Lane Farm,
Parkmill, Gower, Swansea
Owner: Mrs. H. D. Greene, Grove, Craven Arms

Grove Fairy was entered (lot 4) for the second Grove Stud Sale (August 1916) but must have been a favourite of Mrs. Greene's since she was withdrawn having not achieved her reserve price (all 81 ponies of the 81 offered were sold at the first Grove Sale held in 1914).

In the 1916 Catalogue she is described as "a wonderful little brood mare". By then she had bred Grove Elfin (winner of first prizes at the Royal Agricultural Society of England Shows in 1915 and 1916), Grove Sprite I (prize-winner and exported to the U.S.A. at a big figure) and Grove Sprite II (seldom shown, yet won a first prize at the 1915 Royal Agricultural Society of England Show).

Grove Elfin was later sold to Mr. Fitch-Mason of Killay, Swansea who won many prizes with him up to 1922 when he won a first prize at the Plymouth Bath and West Show and a first prize in harness at Pontardulais. After Mr. Fitch-Mason had no further use for his services he sold him (top price of the Sale 52 guineas) at the first Welsh Pony & Cob Society Sale at Craven Arms on 6th September 1922 (Mr. Fitch-Mason sold the well-known Bwlch Quicksilver at the same Sale for 35 guineas).

77

By the 1927 Dispersal Sale, Grove Fairy had produced more good Grove ponies: Grove Fairy Queen (lot 2) (Champion at National Pony Society, Royal Agricultural Society of England, Royal Welsh etc – 40 guineas to Lady Wentworth); Grove Fairy Ring (lot 3) (dam of Grove Gas Ring sold to the U.S.A. at a high figure, sold to the Hon. E. Mostyn at 17 guineas), in addition to Grove Sprite II (lot 11 to Mr. Tom Jones Evans).

8. Dyoll Glasallt (*chapter 2.2*)

9. Dyoll Moonlight (*chapter 2.3*)

10. Cymro (*Chapter 4.6*)

12. Dyoll Starlight (*chapter 2.1*)

13. Dyoll Bala Gal
Registration number 65 in the *Welsh Stud Book, Vol. I*
Brown, black points, tan muzzle, height: 11 hands,
foaled 1896
Breeder: John Williams, Gwernhefin, Bala,
North Wales
Owner: Mr. H. Meuric Lloyd, Glanyrannell,
Llanwrda, Carmarthenshire

Sired by one of the Pony stallions running on Gwastadrhos Hill, near Bala, her dam was a bay mare under 12 hands in height.

When mated to Dyoll Starlight, this mare produced a host of good ones: Dyoll Ballistite, Dyoll Breeze, Dyoll Radium, Dyoll Spark, Dyoll Rainbow (exported to the U.S.A. from the Grove), Longmynd Eclipse and Longmynd Favourite.

14. A Fairwood Mountain Pony stallion
Roan, height: 12 hands 1 in.

15. A Fairwood Mountain Pony mare
Chesnut, light mane and tail, height: 12 hands

6

Kilhendre Celtic Silverlight (foaled 1916)

Coed Coch Glyndwr (foaled 1935)

1	2	4	8
1 Coed Coch Glyndwr 1617	**2** Revolt 493	**4** Llwyn Tyrant 207	**8** Prince of Cardiff 84
			9 Florence
		5 145 Llwyn Flyaway	**10** Eiddwen Flyer I 421
			11 Llwyn Blaze
	3 8683 Dinarth Henol	**6** Llwyn Satan 1325	**12** Kilhendre Celtic Silverlight 953
			13 6086 Llwyn Tempter
		7 6350 Irfon Marvel	**14** Dyoll Starlight 4
			15 3502 Henallt Black

1. Coed Coch Glyndwr

Registration number 1617 in the *Welsh Stud Book,*
Vol. XXXI
Grey, height: 11 hands 1 in, foaled 1935
Owner and breeder: Miss M. Brodrick, Coed Coch, Abergele.

Every so often in the history of any breed a great progenitor is produced; it may only happen once every twenty years or perhaps forty years, but once it has happened the future of that breed is directed onto another course and will never be the same again.

With the breed of Welsh Mountain Ponies during Stud Book times it happened in 1894 with Dyoll Starlight and it happened again in 1935 with Coed Coch Glyndwr.

Glyndwr was born a weakly foal and were it not for the foresight of Shem Jones on his way home from school to Coed Coch in recognising that all was not well, then Coed Coch Glyndwr might never have survived to alter the course of the Welsh Mountain pony breed.

After the initial setback at birth, Glyndwr did not catch up with the other colts of his age for another two years, so during 1936 and 1937 it was his paternal half-brother Coed Coch Saturn (full-brother to Coed Coch Serliw) who kept the Coed Coch flag flying, winning at Shropshire Show in 1937.

On Saturday, 28th August 1937 Miss Brodrick held a sale at Coed Coch where eighteen Welsh Mountain Ponies and sixteen riding ponies went under the hammer (along with cattle, sheep, farm implements, etc.) Mr. S. Walton from Leeds bought thirty-one ponies (also most of the cattle, sheep etc), Coed Coch Serliw topping the sale at 63 guineas, Coed Coch Seon a dark grey yearling colt being top-priced male at 60 guineas followed by Glyndwr at 45 guineas.

It later transpired that Mr. Walton had no land on which to keep any animals and Miss Brodrick was persuaded to keep the animals at Coed Coch until a sale (for Mr. Walton) could be arranged.

The second sale took place on 11th September; Mr. Walton lost heavily on the ponies but gained on the cattle and sheep so that overall his experience did not prove too costly and he can claim to have been the owner of some of the most famous names in the *Welsh Stud Book* albeit for two weeks!

Serliw, who had topped the first sale was secured by my father and she remained with us at Ceulan until her death in June 1962, winning numerous important awards and starting a long line of influential animals (*chapter 10.11*). My father was also under-bidder on Glyndwr

Coed Coch Glyndwr. (Photograph courtesy of Welsh Stud Book, Vol. XXXII.)

(who was purchased back by Miss Brodrick at 30 guineas) and his description of Glyndwr at that time was that he was "the most spectacular and highest-stepping two-year-old that I have ever seen".

On 3rd May 1938 Miss Brodrick wrote to my father pointing out that he was under-bidder on Glyndwr at the Sale and enquiring whether he would be interested in buying him since with only two breeding mares retained after her sale, she did not think that her stud warranted keeping a stallion. With a Glyndwr son just born at Ceulan, my father turned down the offer, otherwise the course of the breed and of the Coed Coch Stud in particular would have been altered.

Glyndwr stayed on at Coed Coch until 1943 with the exception of 1939 when he was leased to the Criban Stud (in exchange for Mathrafal Tuppence) producing the influential Criban Winston (sire of Criban Victor (*chapter 13.2*) during his stay at Criban.

When Glyndwr arrived at Criban, Mr. Richards (senior) was not at all impressed thinking that here was a pony too "refined" for the South Wales hills and not possessing enough width across the chest. However Mr. Llewellyn Richards had faith in him and this faith paid dividends not only through Criban Victor but also through Criban Winston's other son, Criban Snowball a top sire at the Cui and Coedowen Studs. Criban Winston's daughter Revel Romance is the foundation of all the Turkdean ponies (Cob type).

It was during the period at Coed Coch up to 1943 that Glyndwr established himself amongst the "greats"; of the twenty-five male Royal

Welsh Show Champions and twenty-five female champions representing the years 1947–1972, twenty-one of the males and seventeen of the females are direct descendants of Glyndwr, some of them descended via various channels e.g. three of the four g-g-sires of Champions Coed Coch Planed, Coed Coch Siglen Las and Gredington Simwnt, both g-sires of the illustrious Coed Coch Madog and two separate strains in both Clan Pip (twice Champion) and Treharne Tomboy (thrice Champion).

In 1943 Coed Coch Glyndwr was sold to Lady Wentworth (for a reputed 400 guineas) leaving several of his beautiful daughters at Coed Coch including the five-times Royal Welsh Show Champion Coed Coch Siaradus, her equally beautiful full-sister Coed Coch Serog, the three sisters Pioden, Prydferth (dam of Champion Pelydrog) and Pansi (Pansi later followed Glyndwr to Crabbet but soon returned to North

Miss M. Brodrick (breeder of Coed Coch Glyndwr) with Coed Coch Siaradus (daughter of Coed Coch Glyndwr).

Wales only to go to the U.S.A. with Serog in January 1948), also the magnificent Coed Coch Mefusen (dam of Champions Madog and Meilyr).

Though Glyndwr went to Crabbet in 1943, Coed Coch mares continued to go to visit him resulting in such as Coed Coch Sidan (out of Seirian) in 1946, Coed Coch Sigldin in 1952, the Champion Coed Coch Anwyled in 1953 and Coed Coch Prydydd in 1955.

Quoting from Lady Wentworth's book *Ponies, Past, Present and Future* it seems that her Welsh Ponies were rather prone to wander and it was the "wrath of allotment holders, harassed policemen, nursery gardeners and farmers" which forced her to abandon her Welsh Mountain Pony Stud for the third, and last time.

Glyndwr and four mares went to Mr. McNaught's Clan Stud in 1949 or so; the four Wentworth mares were soon sold off but Glyndwr stayed there until 1953 and was widely used on the Clan mares and also on

Dinarth What Ho, Champion Royal Welsh Shows 1947 and 1952 with the author. Dam Dinarth Darling by Llwyn Satan.

Her Majesty the Queen and HRH Prince Philip admiring Mr. Emrys Griffiths' Owain Glyndwr (a son of Coed Coch Glyndwr) at the Brecon Bi-centenary Show. With them are Mr. H. Llewelyn Richards and Mr. de Winton (Show President).

Mrs. Mountain's mares (at that time under the Clan prefix until Mrs. Mountain married and used her own "Twyford" prefix). Noteable progeny from this period include Clan Dubail (of all he is the one bearing closest resemblance to his sire), Clan Tony, Clan Da, Clan Music, Twyford Moonshine, Twyford Gala, Twyford Gigi etc.

Glyndwr then became the property of Miss de Beaumont of the Shalbourne Stud, still siring some exceptional Welsh and Riding Ponies, and he stayed there until his death in 1959.

The last time that I saw Glyndwr was at the 1953 Royal Welsh Show at Cardiff when I showed Dinarth What Ho for my father to stand second to Coed Coch Madog followed by Bolgoed Atomic, Criban Bantam, Eryri Gwyndaf and Glyndwr in this order. By this time Glyndwr was showing signs of his age (though What Ho was three years older). He had lost one eye but he still had the look of greatness about him.

Glyndwr may not have been very successful in the show ring but he certainly put an indelible mark on the Welsh Mountain Pony breed.

85

2. Revolt

Registration number 493 in the *Welsh Stud Book,*
Vol. XI
Red roan, white star and hind fetlocks,
height: 11 hands 3 in, foaled 1909
Owner and Breeder: Miss Eurgain Lort, Castlemai,
Caernarfon, North Wales.

Revolt was introduced to the show ring at an early age, standing second in an any-age stallion class at the Shropshire and West Midland and fourth at the Welsh National Show when only two-years-old. The following year he travelled to the Royal Agricultural Hall, Islington (National Pony Show) but it seems that he had grown slightly over the 12 hands and was not allowed to compete in the stallion class won by Bleddfa Shooting Star (Sir Walter Gilbey), followed by Mrs. Greene's Grove Arclight and Grove Rushlight. However the *Livestock Journal* describes Revolt as "one of the smartest and best-actioned three-year-olds imaginable".

On 5th August 1913, Miss Lort held a reduction sale at Castlemai (the stud was started by her father in 1861) and Revolt was included in

Revolt.

the Sale Catalogue (lot 34). It was a truly remarkable catalogue including pens of Soa sheep, Manx sheep etc along with some of the most famous names in the *Hackney Stud Book*.

Revolt is described as "a regular rustic gentleman, having such majesty of bearing and perfect in harness".

Fortunately for the breed Miss Lort did not sell Revolt and continued showing her Welsh ponies and Hackneys all over the country. Her stud groom at that time was my father's great friend Ted Sowerby (previously stud groom at the famous Tanrallt Stud – where my sister now lives) and father often went to Castlemai before the Hackney Show (also held at Islington) to give Ted Sowerby a hand. My father described Revolt as having "a most impressive head and he was a spectacular mover".

Miss Lort dispersed her Castlemai Stud on 17th August 1926 and Revolt went to Mrs. Chadwick (Bryntirion Stud). It was during this ownership (1932) that Miss Brodrick sent Coed Coch Seren, Coed Coch Eirlys and Coed Coch Enid to him and also Dinarth Henol in 1934. It was this latter mating which produced Coed Coch Glyndwr. An interesting fact is that the sire and dam of Glyndwr belonged to different eras: whilst Dinarth Henol was only seven-years-old, Revolt was a grand old man of twenty-five!

There is no record of Revolt after 1934. When one appreciates the enormous influence which Revolt had on the breed after his twenty-third birthday, one realises what enormous possibilities were ignored by breeders during the previous twenty years.

3. Dinarth Henol
Registration number 8683 in the *Welsh Stud Book,*
Vol. XXVIII
Grey, blaze, foaled 1927
Owners and Breeders: John Jones and Sons,
Dinarth Hall, Colwyn Bay, North Wales

Very little is known about this little mare who had such an influence on the Welsh Mountain Pony breed. She does not seem to have produced anything before 1933 when she was selected for Miss Brodrick by her stud groom John Jones when the Coed Coch Stud was being built up. At Coed Coch, she was known as Dinarth Gwenol, she produced a filly Coed Coch Gwinc in 1934, Coed Coch Glyndwr in 1935, then she was sold (lot 24) at the first Coed Coch Sale (24th July 1936) with a colt foal at foot by Tanybwlch Rheiddol. It seems from that date that all

Llwyn Flyaway and foal Revolt photographed in 1909.

track of her was lost; she was never transferred through the Welsh Pony & Cob Society and nothing further out of her was ever registered.

It is strange that she was known as Gwenol at Coed Coch up until 1936 since *Volume XXVIII* of the *Welsh Stud Book* appeared in 1929. The only explanation I can think of is that Mr. Jones Dinarth Hall intended her to be called Gwenol and sold her to Coed Coch as such. Mr. Jones' hand-writing is very difficult to decipher (I have a large file of letters written by him to my father) and since no-one in the Secretariat at that time could speak Welsh, they probably interpreted it as Henol and the error was never rectified.

4. Llwyn Tyrant
Registration number 206 in the *Welsh Stud Book,*
Vol. VI
Roan, height: 11 hands 2 in, foaled 1905
Breeder: E. Edwards, Penygroes, Llanfihangel,
Borth, Cardiganshire
Owner: J. Marshall Dugdale, Llwyn Stud,
Llanfyllin, Montgomeryshire

Llwyn Tyrant appeared as a foal at foot of Florence at the 1905 Welsh National Show in the ownership of Mr. Edwards, a tailor from Llan-fihangel Genau'r Glyn (a friend of my father's, this Mr. Edwards died as a very old man in the 'sixties). The mare and foal were entered as "for sale at £100" and were bought by Mr. Marshall Dugdale (who was an exhibitor in the same class) and it was Mr. Dugdale who registered the foal as Llwyn Tyrant. It is interesting that Llwyn Flyaway, which Llwyn Tyrant was to serve three years later (to produce Revolt) was also a competitor at that show on that same day.

It is remarkable that Llwyn Tyrant had such a marked effect on the breed since as a three-year-old he was sold to Miss Kidstone, Lugton, Ayrshire and nothing further was heard of him.

5. Llwyn Flyaway
Registration number 145 in the *Welsh Stud Book, Vol. I*
Registration number 1101 in the *Polo Pony Stud Book*
Bay, small star, two white hind feet, height: 11 hands
2½ in, foaled 1897
Owner and Breeder: J. Marshall Dugdale, Llwyn
Stud, Llanfyllin, Montgomeryshire

This mare was surprisingly small in view of the fact that her sire was 14 hands 1 in; however the fact that she bred a foal as a two-year-old (named Llwyn Bobs) may account for her small size.

Flyaway was a good winner in the show ring, such as 1902: first prize at the Shropshire and West Midland, second Islington; 1903: silver medal Shrewsbury; 1905: first prizes at the Bath and West held at Swansea, second at the Welsh National (the show where Llwyn Tyrant was a foal), third prize Islington etc.

She was not shown in 1906 and 1907, Mr. Dugdale winning at most Shows with his Llwyn Snowdrop and Llwyn Nell. At the 1908 Shropshire and West Midland Show she won a large class judged by Mr. V. P. Lort beating such well-known animals as Mrs. Greene's Bleddfa Tell-Tale and Grove Starling, Mr. Cooke's Bleddfa Pigeon and Mr. Lloyd-Morgan's Lady Greylight (later a well-known Champion in the ownership of Lady Wentworth). Mr. Lort was so impressed with Llwyn Flyaway that day that he bought her for his daughter. Two months later at the Welsh National Show in the ownership of Miss Eurgain Lort, she did not do so well standing fifth in a class won by Bleddfa Tell-Tale. However her crowning achievement was producing Revolt the following year.

Flyaway later won many prizes for Miss Lort and was "one of the favourite brood mares, not on offer" at the time of the Castlemai Sale in 1913.

6. Llwyn Satan
Registration number 1325 in the *Welsh Stud Book*,
Vol. XXV
Dark grey, blaze, white near fore and both hind
fetlocks, height: 11 hands, foaled 1923
Owner and Breeder: Major W. Marshall Dugdale,
D.S.O., Llwyn Stud, Llanfyllin, Montgomeryshire
Photograph in *Welsh Stud Book, Vol. XXVII, page 28*,
and *Vol. XXVIII, page 14*

Llwyn Satan made an early entry to success by winning the colt class
at the Royal Welsh Show (Carmarthen) in 1925, a feat also achieved the
previous year at the Bridgend Show by his full-brother (a year older)
Llwyn Temptation.

By the Royal Welsh Show 1926 (Bangor) Llwyn Satan had become
the property of the Dinarth Hall Stud and he won the Open stallion
class judged by Mr. Tom Jones Evans of the Craven Stud. Satan with
Irfon Marvel, Llwyn Columba and Llwyn Pigeon won the "Group
award" for the Dinarth Stud; the latter two having been purchased at
the same time as Satan from Llwyn.

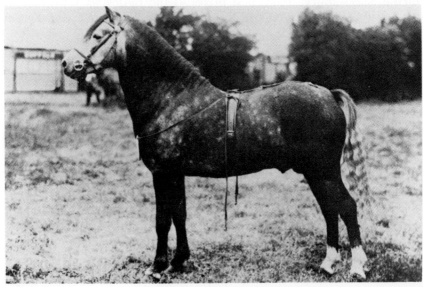

Llwyn Satan.

Photographed at the Royal Welsh Show 1926. Dinarth Hall winning group with owner Mr. T. J. Jones (white hat). Third from left is Irfon Marvel, fourth from left is Llwyn Satan with (in between them) the judge, Mr. Tom Jones Evans.

At the 1927 Royal Welsh Show (Swansea), Lady Wentworth won the stallion class with Grove King Cole II (purchased the previous month at the Grove Dispersal Sale for 130 guineas), Llwyn Satan was second, Llwyn Temptation third and Caerberis King Cole fourth. The following two years, Tom Jones Evans won the stallion class with Craven Master Shot; Llwyn Satan, Grove Will O' the Wisp and Caerberis King Cole occupied the other awards in various orders.

In 1929 Llwyn Satan was exported to the Argentine along with Brenin Cymru which was bred by my father and owned by my grandfather.

7. Irfon Marvel
Registration number 6350 in the *Welsh Stud Book, Vol. XIX*
Grey, height: 11 hands 3 in, foaled 1916
Breeder: Harvey N. Jones, Henallt, Builth Wells, Breconshire
Owner: T. B. Lewis, Bronallt, Llanwrtyd Wells
Photograph in the *Welsh Stud Book, Vol. XXVII page 28*

Mr. T. B. Lewis of the Irfon Stud owned many good show ponies including Irfon Talisman and Irfon Lady Twilight (later owned by the

Ness Stud), Cream of Eppynt (exported to Australia) and Irfon Lady Starlight (one of the foundation mares of the Vardra Stud). Irfon Marvel became the best-known of all the Irfon ponies, winning the Welsh Mountain Pony mare class at the Royal Welsh Show in 1925 and second prize-winner in both 1926 and 1928, these three wins when in the ownership of Dinarth Hall stud. A Royal Welsh Show journal describes her as "probably the best conformed pony in the show-ring of the day with elegant head and neck, good limbs, plenty of substance and a wealth of middle-piece; in movement she is not so good going very wide behind and is rather inclined to plod all round".

Irfon Marvel was sold for 8 guineas (at 21 years of age) at the Dinarth Hall Dispersal Sale (27th October 1937) to our good friend John Berry. She was thought to be in foal to Grove Will O'the Wisp but, despite several attempts, she did not breed again. Her yearling daughter Dinarth Wonderlight (*chapter 13.7*) (by Bowdler Brightlight) on the same sale also fetched 8 guineas to Lord Howard de Walden; she appears in many Section "B" pedigrees as the dam of Berwyn Beauty, in turn dam of Coed Coch Berwynfa, Coed Coch Blaen Lleuad, Brockwell Berwyn etc.

8. Prince of Cardiff
Registration number 84 in the *Welsh Stud Book,*
Vol. III
Re-entered in *Vol. VIII* to show prizes won.
Registration number 7226 in the *Hackney Stud Book,*
Vol. XVII (1900)
Dark chestnut, small star, white off hind fetlock,
height: 12 hands 2 in, foaled 1895
Breeder: James Howell, Green Farm, Cardiff
Owner in 1904: Charles Murless, Plaspower Farm,
Wrexham (purchased 21st August 1901)
Owner in 1909: W. Arthur Pughe, Gwyndy Stud,
Llanfyllin, Montgomeryshire
Sire: Hamlet Prince of Denmark 4085 *Hackney Stud
Book*
Dam: Welsh Wonder 1268 *F.S. (Hackney Stud Book)*
by Welsh Flyer 856 *(Hackney Stud Book) (chapter 18.1)*
Photograph *Welsh Stud Book, Vol. VIII, page 9*

In the ownership of Mr. Murless, Prince of Cardiff won first prizes at the Welsh National Shows in 1901 and 1902, also second prize at the

*Prince of Cardiff
(foaled in 1895).*

Royal Agricultural Society of England (Carlisle) in 1902. In 1904 he was Champion at the Denbigh and Flint Show and was Champion at Oswestry (winning the Challenge Cup outright) in 1903, 1904 and 1905.

It was in 1907 that Prince of Cardiff was sold to the Gwyndy Stud. He was advertised at stud in the 1910 *Welsh Stud Book* at a stud fee of 2 guineas and described as "the sire of Princess Cardiff who was third at the International Olympia Show, London in 1909 and sold for £1,600".

The Gwyndy Stud bred and owned many influential Welsh Cobs and Ponies over a long period. The greatest influence of Prince of Cardiff (apart from Coed Coch Glyndwr) on the Welsh breeds is through Gwyndy Limelight (died at Coed Coch in November 1951, having sired Coed Coch Purwen, Coed Coch Sws etc) and his g-g-daughter Gwyndy Light who produced Craven Sprightly's Last etc (*chapter 5*).

Prince of Cardiff blood was very popular in the U.S.A. *Vol. III* of the *American Welsh Stud Book* contains his sons Gwyndy Sparke and Pentre Prince whilst another son Gwyndy Brenin had so many progeny in the U.S.A. that another prefix (Gwindy's) was devised to have them all together in the records.

93

9. Florence

Registered in the "Provisional fillies" Section of the
Welsh Stud Book, Vol. I
Strawberry roan, blaze, two hind white socks, height:
12 hands, foaled 1898
Owner: Octavius Edmund Cooper, Cefngwyn,
Bontgoch, Talybont, Cardiganshire.

In *Vol. I* and *II* of the *Welsh Stud Book* a number of young Ponies and Cobs were accepted as provisional entries, free of charge, which could later be registered at half fees if their owners so wished. Mr. Cooper was an official at one of the lead mines which dotted the Talybont landscape and he left the area in 1903. Florence was sold to Mr. Owen Morris, Tynllechwedd, Llandre (Owen Morris and his two brothers John Morris, Penywern and William Morris, Brynowen were founder members of the Welsh Pony & Cob Society and various of their grand-children are breeding Ponies and Cobs at the present time. One grandson is a former Secretary of State for Wales and another is Professor of Agriculture at the University College of Wales).

Florence's next owner was Mr. E. Edwards of Penygroes, Llan-fihangel Geneu'r Glyn in whose ownership she produced Llwyn Tyrant. The only record of her breeding is in the Catalogue of the Welsh National Show, Aberystwyth, 1st August 1905 where her breeder was given as Mr. Jones, Nantstalwen, Tregaron and sired by Eiddwen Flyer III (*chapter 21.1*). The catalogue quotes her as being "For Sale: £100" and she was sold at that show to Mr. Marshall Dugdale of the Llwyn Stud who registered the foal as Llwyn Tyrant.

10. Eiddwen Flyer I (*chapter 21.4*)

12. Kilhendre Celtic Silverlight

Registration number 953 in the *Welsh Stud Book,
Vol. XVIII*
Light grey, height: 11 hands 2 in, foaled 1916
Owner and Breeder: Miss Beryl Chapman,
Kilhendre, Ellesmere, Salop.
Sire: Bleddfa Shooting Star (*chapter 4.1*)
Sire: Grove Apricot by Stretton Torchlight by Dyoll
Starlight (*chahpter 2.1*)

This is a stallion who, used at stud for four years only, had a great

94

Kilhendre Celtic Silverlight photographed in the U.S.A.

influence on very many studs throughout the United Kingdom. In 1920 Silverlight was sold to Maj. Dugdale of the Llwyn Stud for whom he won (in 1921) first prize at the Shropshire and West Midland Show, second at the Bath and West and the Royal Agricultural Society of England (Derby).

In 1922 he was shown only at Shrewsbury where he was beaten into second place by Mrs. Greene's Grove King Cole II who proved to be unbeatable that year. However in 1923 at the same Show, these placings were reversed and when it came to the Royal Welsh Show that year at Welshpool, King Cole II was kept away for fear of being beaten again by Silverlight. It so happened that Silverlight was not entered and Maj. Dugdale won the class with his second fiddle Llwyn Mighty Atom. During the years 1920 to 1924 Silverlight sired Kilhendre Celtic Silversand, Llwyn Brilliant, Llwyn Columba, Llwyn Mercury, Llwyn Redstart, Llwyn Satan, Llwyn Temptation (full-brothers), Llwyn Mona, Llwyn Moonbeam, Llwyn Roberta, Llwyn Silver, Llwyn Sparkle, Llwyn Venus, and Twilight of Dyffryn.

Five of these have had such a great influence on the Welsh Mountain Pony breed that today it is difficult to find any blood-line which does not trace back to one or more of them:

(i) Twilight of Dyffryn is dam of Mathrafal Tuppence used extensively at the Criban and Coed Coch Studs.

95

(ii) Llwyn Brilliant is sire of Ceulan Silverleaf who has a big influence on Welsh Mountain Ponies through her son Ceulan Revelry and on Welsh Ponies through her g-son Reeves Golden Lustre (*chapter 15.1*).

(iii) Llwyn Satan sired Dinarth Henol, dam of Coed Coch Glyndwr.

(iv) Llwyn Temptation sired Llwyn Tomtit who in turn sired Revel Spark, Revel Brightlight, Revel Dewdrop, Revel Hope, Revel Silva, Revel Sprig, Revel Vintage and many Llwyn ponies such as Llwyn Tinwen. Llwyn Tinwen was dam of Royal Agricultural Society of England winner Coed Coch Tlws and Coed Coch Trysor at Coed Coch before going to the Clan Stud where she produced (amongst others) Clan Tony, best known as sire of two Royal Welsh Show Champions Clan Pip and Clan Peggy.

(v) Kilhendre Celtic Silversand (foaled in 1923) sired Kilhendre Celtic King Cup (foaled in 1937) who in turn sired Kilhendre Celtic Silver Birch (foaled in 1947). The latter two stallions were used extensively at the Revel during the years 1951 to 1959, Silver Birch siring Skittle, Sunny Maid, Sultan, Sunny, Bow, Bridesmaid, Bride, and King Cup siring Breeze, Chirrup, Whist, Willow and Beryl (foundation mare of the Persie Stud).

From the same dam as Silverlight, Kilhendre Celtic Silverlight II was foaled in 1935 when the dam was twenty-six years old. Silverlight II and his son Kilhendre Celtic Chieftain also spent most of their lives at the Revel siring some fashionable stock including Chance, Pip, Roseann, Sloe, Sultanna, Rally, Relight, Rosa, Silverleaf etc.

Late in 1923 Kilhendre Celtic Silverlight was sold to Lady Wentworth for whom he won a second prize at Liverpool Show in that year followed the next year by a Silver medal at Islington.

The frontispiece to the 1967 Welsh Pony & Cob Society Journal is a very charming photograph of Lady Wentworth driving in her delightful miniature brougham behind Silverlight and Wentworth Windfall. There is no record of Silverlight siring anything at Crabbet and he was given in 1926 as a gift to the W. K. Kellogg Ranch at Pomona, U.S.A. Mr. Kellogg had bought several Arabs from Crabbet and Lady Wentworth wrote: "I have for Mrs. Kellogg my Champion Welsh Mountain Pony Silverlight who won four Championships and I am sure that Mrs. Kellogg will love this little fellow and they will become great friends".

From that date Silverlight never sired a pure-bred Welsh Pony and was given to the Los Angeles Boy Scouts in 1928 where he stayed for fifteen years until his death in 1943 at 27 years of age. During this period he appeared several times in "movies" making Boy Scout pictures.

13. Llwyn Tempter
Registration number 6086 in the *Welsh Stud Book,*
Vol. XVIII
Bay, star, near hind white pastern, height: 12 hands,
foaled 1915
Owner and Breeder: W. Marshall Dugdale, Llwyn
Stud, Llanfyllin, Mont.
Sire: Temptation by Total by Klondyke (*chapters 24.6*
and *24.12*)
Dam: Lady Lightfoot by Gwyndy Cymro

Temptation 527 *Welsh Stud Book* (foaled 1909), his sire Total 320 *Welsh Stud Book* (foaled 1904) and Klondyke 12 *Welsh Stud Book* (foaled 1894) were all owned by my mother's uncle, John Thomas, The Mill, Trerddol, Machynlleth, Montgomeryshire, all three were well-known winners in the show ring and later prolific sires e.g. Klondyke at Mr. W. S. Miller's Forest Lodge Stud. Temptation was exported to the U.S.A. in 1915.

Llwyn Tempter was a very versatile little mare, shown regularly in hand, under saddle and in harness and yet producing a foal every year from 1922 to 1935. My father remembered her at the 1923 Royal Welsh Show (where he showed the stallion Cream Bun for my grand-father) and Llwyn Tempter put up a very brave show in harness for a breeding mare to stand third behind the famous National Hackney Champion Olive Melbourne and another Welsh mare Brynhir Lightning (half-sister to the dam of Tanybwlch Berwyn). Tempter went on to win many important awards such as a first prize at the Royal Agricultural Society of England Show at Chester in 1925.

Llwyn Tempter will be best remembered as the dam of Llwyn Satan and Llwyn Temptation, both of which were prolific winners when owned by the Dinarth Stud and both were later exported.

14. Dyoll Starlight (*chapter 2.1*)

15. Henallt Black
Registration number 3502 in the *Welsh Stud Book, Vol. XI*
Black, star, height: 11 hands 3 in, foaled 1905
Breeder: W. George, The Lamb and Flag, Rhayader,
Radnorshire
Owner: Harvey M. Jones, Henallt, Llanddewi'r
Cwm, Builth Wells

This mare was sold to Harvey Jones in 1909 and it was Mr. Jones who registered her under his own prefix. She won several prizes for Mr. Jones such as a first prize and silver medal in hand at Builth Wells in 1913 along with a second prize under saddle and another second prize in harness.

Along with being successful in the show ring, Henallt Black was a consistent breeder of top quality foals being mated to the best stallions in the country e.g. Greylight in 1909, Dyoll Starlight in 1910, 1915 etc.

7

Bowdler Brightlight foaled 1923
Bowdler Blue Boy foaled 1933
Pendock Playboy foaled 1948
Revel Light foaled 1950
Brierwood Blue Boy foaled 1960

2 Pendock Playboy 1813	**4** Bowdler Blueboy 1571	**8** Bowdler Brightlight 1303
		9 7602 Cleveland Marine
	5 8912 Craven Tosca	**10** Craven Master Sprite 1544
		11 3546 Forest Tosca
3 9063 Winestead Larina	**6** Winestead Don Juan 1578	**12** Wentworth Springlight 1225
		13 7345 Grove Bright Spot
	7 4938 Grove Star of Hope	**14** Dyoll Starlight 4
		15 2047 Lady Starlight

1

Revel Light 1985

1. Revel Light

Registration number 1985 in the *Welsh Stud Book*,
Vol. XXXIV
Bay, blaze off fore and both hinds white, height: 11
hands 2 in, foaled 1950
Owner and Breeder: Emrys Griffiths, The Revel,
Talgarth, Breconshire

I first saw Revel Light during the summer of 1952 when I was staying at the Revel. I was very impressed by his rich bay colour and lovely head with large, expressive eyes and persuaded Mr. Griffiths to get him off the hills so that he could be got ready for the Breconshire Show. Light was very loath to leave his native hills and did not take too kindly to human interference since he had never been handled. However he was awarded a rosette at the show; as far as I know his one and only award. Mr. Griffiths would not sell Light at that time but told me that he would let me know if ever he did decide to sell and it took fifteen years of constant reminding before Revel Light came to Ceulan on the 10th September 1967!

Light was awarded premiums to run on the Breconshire Black Mountains from 1955 to 1957 and he sired so many good Revel ponies during the period 1953 to 1965. In 1952, Revel Light was mated to his two half-sisters Revel Fun and Revel Playtime (both sided by Pendock Playboy) the produce being Revel Frolic and Revel Pin-up which have had an immense influence on the breed. Pin-up also was Champion Welsh Mountain Pony at the 1955 Brecon Bi-Centenary Show when the award was presented to her by Her Majesty the Queen. Stallions by Light which appeared later at the Revel included Hop, Shell, Beagle, Sol-fa, Space and Wanderer. Possibly the stallions were out-shone by a lovely band of mares which included (at the Revel): Barmaid, Flinders, Sunspot, Selina (dam of the Fayre Oaks Sale topper Aston Garway etc), Be Good, Bush, Flair, Grey Goose (Hisland Stud), Guitar, Ladylike, Naomi, Oakleaf, Rosy Wings (out of Rosetta, daughter of the 1959 Royal Welsh Show Champion Revel Rosette), Sabrina, Siesta, Snow-light, So Shy, So Spry, Sugar Candy etc.

In 1959 Light was leased to the Bwlch Stud producing Bwlch Foam (Knighton Stud) Halo and Neon; then in 1965 he spent a season in Haslemere, where in 1966 his daughters Stoatley Fiesta, Gentian, Honeylight and Lightning appeared. He was also periodically lent to various South Wales breeders such as Mr. Les Evans of Nantybwch, Tredegar.

Revel Light in the snow.

Revel Light sired some exceptional stock at Ceulan during the period 1967 to 1973, then he was lent to the Wharley Stud where he continued as an outstanding sire until his death in 1975.

Of the most influential of Revel Light's daughters surely Revel Pin-Up has pride of place. One of her sons, Vardra Julius won many prizes for the Vardra Stud before being exported, another son of hers was Revel Pye, senior stallion at the Brierwood Stud where he sired, amongst many other good ones, the Brierwood Dispersal Sale topper Brierwood Victoria (at 2,000 guineas at the Fairway Stud, Australia), himself fetching 1,100 guineas at this same sale to go to the Weston Stud.

At the 1978 Weston Sale, fillies by Revel Pye were in great demand such as Weston Bridesmaid (900 guineas) and the same figure for an outstanding filly foal Hisland Pin Tuck.

Revel Pye was also successful when crossed with Persie mares producing e.g. the Royal Agricultural Society of England winner Persie Concord, later exported to Australia.

Whilst at the Revel, Revel Light produced best when bred back to his relatives e.g. his half-sisters by Pendock Playboy; his daughters seem to be crossing well with other Pendock Playboy families such as Twyford Sprig, son of Revel Springsong (daughter of Pendock Playboy).

A very lovely palomino-coloured mare of this breeding at the Revel (later at Belvoir and Rookery Studs) was Revel South Wind (foaled 1956); sired by Revel Frolic (by the Pendock Playboy son of Revel Light out of the Pendock Playboy daughter Revel Fun) her dam was Revel Springsong also by Pendock Playboy. Another Pendock Playboy line is introduced into this family in Revel Sirocco foaled in 1965 (g-son of Revel South Wind) in that his sire, Revel Society, is also a Revel Springsong son.

2. Pendock Playboy
Registration number 1813 in the *Welsh Stud Book*,
Vol. XXXII
Bay, blaze, off fore and both hind legs white,
foaled 1947
Owners and Breeders: Mr. and Mrs. Philipson Stow
and Miss E. Morley, Pendock Stud, Long Green,
Gloucester

Some animals enjoy a long life, they do the breed no good and very soon are lost into obscurity; Pendock Playboy lived only two years, he

Pendock Playboy (foal in front) with his dam Craven Tosca.

Mr. Emrys Griffiths of the Revel Stud with Revel Springsong Champion at the 1957 Royal Welsh Show and one of only four sired by Pendock Playboy. (Photograph courtesy of Miss Philipson-Stow.)

served only four mares and yet his influence on the Welsh Mountain Pony breed is profound.

The four foals born in 1950 sired by Pendock Playboy were:

(i) Revel Light.

(ii) Revel Playtime, whose dam Winestead Zenia was paternal half-sister to Winestead Larina, dam of Revel Light.

(iii) Revel Springsong, a lovely cream mare, Supreme Champion Welsh Mountain Pony at the 1957 Royal Welsh Show; she spent her last years at the Twyford stud.

(iv) Revel Fun, a dun daughter of Revel Fair Lady, whose other daughter Revel Fair Maid (by Ceulan Revolt) was originator of the best strain of Weston ponies: Weston Mink Muff and Weston Song.

3. Winestead Larina
Registration number 9063 in the *Welsh Stud Book, Vol. XXXII*
Grey, four white legs, height: 11 hands 3½ in,
foaled 1932
Owner and Breeder: William Hay, Winestead Hall,
Patrington, Yorkshire

As might be expected with a mare of such illustrious breeding,

Winestead Larina was a very lovely mare but she is best known for what she produced. Mr. Emrys Griffiths was very fortunate in securing Winestead Larina, Winestead Zenia and Winestead Teresa when Mr. Hay gave up breeding Welsh ponies. Apart from producing Teresa for Mr. Hay Larina produced the 1959 Royal Welsh Champion Revel Rosette (foaled 1948), the influential sire Revel Springlight (foaled 1942) and his full-sister Wentworth Silver Cream (foaled 1943). Larina died at the Revel in July 1952.

4. Bowdler Blue Boy
Registration number 1571 in the *Welsh Stud Book, Vol. XXXI*
Grey, star, near hind fetlock white; height: 11 hands, foaled 1933
Owners and Breeders: George Preece and Sons, Hope Bowdler, Church Stretton

The first time I saw Bowdler Blue Boy was at the Shropshire and West Midland Show on 25th July 1946. This was the first major show to be held after the war and most of the pre-war winners had either retired or died. In the stallion class my father placed Dinarth What Ho (which

Bowdler Blue Boy at Hope Bowdler. (Photograph courtesy of Mr. E. S. Davies.)

he later bought and with him won countless championships), Bolgoed Mighty Atom and Bowdler Blue Boy in that order. Of the latter my father wrote in the *Shropshire Journal*: "A nice quality pony with a grand 'front' but on the day hardly in show form".

Also present on that day were the mother and daughter Craven Tosca and Craven Toscanini owned by Mr. Tom Jones Evans and they were both sold that year (after being mated to Bowdler Blue Boy) to Mr. and Mrs. Philipson-Stow and Miss Morley of the Pendock Stud.

In 1947, Pendock Playboy (colt from Tosca) and Pendock Bluebell (filly from Toscanini) arrived. Playboy is a subject of this chapter; Bluebell went on to be one of the most successful producers ever creating a record by producing Pendock Phlox, dam of Pendock Pansy, dam of Pendock Pageant: all three having won the yearling class at Royal Welsh Shows! Another son of Bowdler Blue Boy foaled at the Craven Stud in 1947 was Craven Sir Horace, winner as a two-year-old at the Bath and West for Miss Blandy-Jenkins and leased for several seasons to the Revel Stud.

Bowdler Blue Boy was used mainly at the Bowdler Stud during the following five years his most noted progeny being the two full-brothers and full sister out of Bowdler Bess II: Bowdler Brewer (foaled 1949, premium stallion for the Breconshire Black Mountains in 1956 and Supreme Champion at the 1961 Royal Welsh Show and later exported to Holland), Bowdler Blighter (foaled 1950 and used for many seasons at South Wales Studs e.g. Revel and Gurnos and also premium stallion on the Aber Hills in North Wales during 1954 and 1955) and the lovely bay mare Bowdler Belle (foaled 1945 and well-known winner at major Shows 1955–1958). Bowdler Blue Boy himself served as Premium stallion at Church Stretton for 1936–1939 and also 1952–1954.

The next time I saw Bowdler Blue Boy, he was running out with the Gretton mares of Mr. Frank Preece. It was October 1955, just before the Gretton Dispersal Sale and we had been asked by Mr. Tolan from the U.S.A. to select two mares for him on the sale which was held on 29th October. For Mr. Tolan we got two good mares, the ten-year-old Gretton Sunset and the eight-year-old Gretton Suncloud (both out of Bowdler Butterfly). The daughters of Bowdler Blue Boy fetched the top prices that day, one lovely yearling daughter Gretton Charm going to the Pendock Stud where she became a well-known brood mare, Gretton Flashlight to the Revel, Gretton Moonsprite to Rhulan Stud, Gretton Moonshine to Tan Lan, Gretton Sunlight to Coed Coch and Gretton Sunray to Gredington; Miss Brodrick also purchasing the Blue Boy grand-daughters Gretton Flash and Gretton Sunbeam for Mrs.

Mackay-Smith and Mr. Fernley thus also spreading the blood to the U.S.A.

One of the most influential of all the Bowdler Blue Boy bloodlines was created when he was twenty-years old i.e. when he produced Brierwood Bluebird out of Brierwood Lollipop. When Bluebird was mated to Revel Pattern (son of Revel Playtime by Pendock Playboy by Bowdler Blue Boy: thus doubling up on the Bowdler Blue Boy line), Brierwood Blue Boy was foaled in 1960 and he created a very fashionable and successful line all of his own.

Another infusion of Bowdler Blue Boy blood (via his son Bowdler Brewer) occurred at Brierwood Stud in 1962 producing Brierwood Brewer, Carrie, Trinket and the 1971 Royal Welsh Show Supreme Champion (later exported to Fairway Stud, Australia) Brierwood Rosebud.

The blood of Bowdler Blue Boy continues through his Bowdler sons: Bandit, Barman, Beard, Beggar, Bitter, Blunderer, Booser, Bowler, Briton, Bradbury and Bugler and various grand-sons and female lines.

Brierwood Blue Boy is represented by the Brierwood Beechleaf, Fuzzy, Grumpy and Fusilier families (Fusilier also exported to Australia). Brierwood Blue Boy blood is also very strong in the Weston Stud where, from the original Weston Fair Lady he produced Mink Muff (1966), Carnival (1968), Fair (1970) and the next generation from Fair Lady (also by Brierwood Blue Boy) produced Harlequin (Penycwm and Bengad Studs), Fleur (1970), Pearly Necklace, Pearly Bangle etc.

It was a great loss to the breed when Brierwood Blue Boy died prematurely in September 1969 but the many successful channels of his blood ensures the prosperity of Bowdler Blue Boy for future generations.

5. Craven Tosca
Registration number 8912 in the *Welsh Stud Book,*
Vol. XXX
Chestnut, wide blaze, both fore and off hind white,
height: 11 hands, foaled 1933
Owner and Breeder: Tom Jones Evans, Dinchope,
Craven Arms

This was one of very few retained by Mr. Tom Jones Evans when he had his sale on 3rd October 1936, possibly retained because she was the last daughter of Forest Tosca (who had bred for him the double Royal

Craven Tosca (far side) with her daughter Craven Toscanini at the Shropshire and West Midland Show 1946.

Welsh Show Champion Craven Master Shot) and Craven Tosca's sire was a son of the same Craven Master Shot; therefore Craven Tosca was a double descendant of Forest Tosca who had served the Craven Stud so well. One daughter of Forest Tosca included on the Craven Sale was Craven Toss (foaled 1932) by Craven Cyrus (*chapter 14.13*) which Miss Brodrick bought for 22 guineas.

At the 1946 Shropshire and West Midland Show (where my father placed her daugher Craven Toscanini first in the youngstock class) Tosca showed her age (thirteen years) and stood third behind Miss Brodrick's Coed Coch Serog (full sister to the legendary Coed Coch Siaradus) and Mr. George Preece's Bowdler Blue Bess.

Tosca went to the Pendock Stud in 1946 and after Pendock Playboy she produced e.g. in 1951 Pendock Tosca which we sent to a very satisfied breeder in the U.S.A.

Her daughter Toscanini was also a very thriving breeder at Pendock producing e.g. the Royal Welsh Show winner Puccini which spent a successful time at the Ceulan Stud before he too, went to the U.S.A.

6. Winstead Don Juan
Registration number 1578 in the *Welsh Stud Book*,
Vol. XXXI
Grey, foaled 1929
Owner and Breeder: William Hay, Winestead Hall,
Patrington, Yorkshire

Mr. William Hay did not breed Welsh Ponies for very long but having started with three of the best mares in Great Britain at that time, Grove Star of Hope, Grove Bright Spot and Ness Thistle this stud, if it had continued would have been destined to great heights. Don Juan died in 1936 and his daughters Winestead Larina and Winestead Zenia fortunately went to the Revel Stud where these good blood-lines became available to breeders in Wales.

7. Grove Star of Hope (formerly Towy Lady Moonlight)
Registration number 4938 in the *Welsh Stud Book*,
Vol. XIV
White, height: 11 hands 1 in, foaled 1911
Breeder: J. Lloyd Morgan, Rhiwfelen, Abergwili,
Carmarthen
Owner: (as Grove Star of Hope): Mrs. Greene,
Grove Stud, Craven Arms

Whilst still in the ownership of Mr. Lloyd Morgan, Star of Hope won the Championship at the 1914 Royal Agricultural Society of England Show. She continued to win when shown from the Grove Stud e.g. she was second to her stable-mate Grove Lightheart at the 1921 National Pony Society Show at Islington and these two, along with the stallion Bleddfa Shooting Star and the colt Grove King Cole II won the best mountain and moorland group over all other breeds. The photograph of this group appears in the *Welsh Stud Book, Vol. XXIII, page 8* and Star of Hope is a grand-bodied, deep, "old-fashioned" little mare with an impressive Welsh expression. In her last years at the Grove she bred Ray of Hope (1919), Gleam of Hope (1920) and Hopeful (1922). Gleam of Hope was still at Grove at the time of the 1927 Dispersal Sale (lot 36),

Grove Stud winning group at the 1921 National Pony Show. From the left: Bleddfa Shooting Car, Grove King Cole II, Grove Star of Hope, Grove Lightheart.

the only other member of this family left at this time being a yearly filly out of Ray of Hope which Mr. Hughes of Shrewsbury bought for 5½ guineas.

It was in 1924 that Lady Wentworth bought Grove Star of Hope; she was the first Grove pony to go to Crabbet and was such a success there, that when the Grove Dispersal came along in 1927, Lady Wentworth seized upon the opportunity of buying the six best ponies in the sale.

It was Lady Wentworth who sold Star of Hope to Mr. William Hay (who had a major stud of Arabian horses).

8. Bowdler Brightlight
Registration number 1303 in the *Welsh Stud Book*, *Vol. XXV*
Grey, off fore and both hinds white, height:
11 hands, foaled 1923
Owner and Breeder: George Preece, Hope Bowdler, Church Stretton

The year that Bowdler Brightlight's best known son Bowdler Blue Boy was born (1933) Brightlight was sold to Mr. Tom Wood-Jones of

*Bowdler
Brightlight
photographed in
the U.S.A. in 1949.*

*Three winning
stallions at the 1933
Royal Welsh Show.
From the left:
Grove Will O'the
Wisp, Grove
Sprightly, Bowdler
Brightlight.
(Photograph
courtesy of
G. H. Parsons.)*

Aberystwyth (after a short period with Mr. Edgar Herbert who showed him at the 1933 Shropshire and West Midland Show) and Brightlight spent a lot of 1933 and 1934 at the Ceulan Stud where he sired some useful stock.

The Royal Welsh Show in 1933 was held at Aberystwyth and Brightlight stood second to Grove Sprightly in the stallion class with Grove Will O'the Wisp (then owned by Miss Mathieson) third.

Brightlight did not compete at the 1934 Royal Welsh Show and by 1935 he had become the property of the Dinarth Hall Stud and stood third to Sprightly and Will O'the Wisp (now both owned by Mr. Tom Jones Evans).

At the 1937 Royal Welsh Show, Mr. Tom Jones Evans was the judge and Dinarth Hall won all three stallion prizes with Will O'the Wisp, Brightlight and Dinarth What Ho.

One of the very rare occasions when Brightlight beat Will O'the Wisp (when both owned by Dinarth Hall) was at the National Pony Society Show in Islington on 13th March 1937 with Lt. Col. E. C. Loch judging. My father showed Brightlight into first place and Tom Thomas was not very pleased to be beaten by his "second string"!

Mr. Thomas John Jones of Dinarth Hall died very suddenly in September 1937 and the Dinarth Stud dispersal took place on 27th October 1937. Will O'the Wisp had been sold since the Royal Welsh Show to go to Italy with two mares from Ceulan (Ceulan Silver Belle and Ceulan Silver Gem), along with Bowdler Barbara and Craven Bywiog. Brightlight topped the sale at 45 guineas going to Mrs. Sivewright, of Lyndhurst, Hampshire (who also bought the famous Criban Socks for 41 guineas). One daughter of Brightlight which was included in the Dinarth Sale was the filly foal Coed Coch Sirius which Mr. Jones had only just bought (lot 25) on Mr. Walton's (Coed Coch) Sale. At the Dinarth Sale, Mr. Cyril Lewis bought her for 15½ guineas and of course from her later bred the illustrious Siaradus (in 1942).

Mrs. Sivewright stood third with Brightlight (to Sprightly and Mr. Holden's Coed Coch Erlewyn) with Coed Coch Glyndwr fourth at the 1938 Royal Welsh Show. She wrote to my father on 14th September 1938, presumably knowing that Bowdler Brightlight had been at Ceulan during 1933 and 1934, offering him for sale. One wonders why she bought him if she did not want him? The letter goes on: "As you know I paid 45 guineas for him and cannot sell him under £30 but if that is too much, make me an offer". Presumably my father did not make Mrs. Sivewright an offer, or if he did, the offer was not accepted.

Shortly afterwards Bowdler Brightlight was exported to Mrs. Mackay-Smith owner of the famous Farnley Farms, White Post, Virgina where he joined three lovely mares which were purchased the previous year: Bowdler Brownie, Criban Sunray and Coed Coch Seren (*chapter 10.11*).

From Criban Sunray, Brightlight produced three stallions which had an enormous influence on Welsh ponies in the U.S.A. viz Farnley Flyer, Farnley Sundial and Farnley Sunrise and three or more mares including the magnificent Farnley Sunshade whose name became legend in American pony circles.

Bowdler Brightlight was producing foals as late as 1949 when he passed away at Farnley Farms.

9. Cleveland Marine

Registration number 7602 in *Welsh Stud Book,*
Vol. XXIII
Bay, black points, height: 10 hands 2 in, foaled 1922
Breeder: Walter Hotchkiss, Cleveland Cottage,
All Stretton, Salop.

Very little is known about this little mare apart from the fact that she won a third prize (as a yearling) in an open class at Church Stretton Show in 1923. She was very well-bred, her dam being Penry Ruby by Brigand a Premium stallion that did much to improve the Church Stretton ponies before being exported.

The Hotchkiss family had been in the Longmynd Hills area since King John's time when it was known as the "Long Mountain Forest" and it is reputed that King John introduced a stallion onto this forest "to improve the local ponies".

Since Bowdler Brightlight did not particularly sire very short heads with tiny ears, it must be assumed that this particular head, for which Bowdler Brewer, Bowdler Blue Boy and Brierwood Blue Boy are so noted, originated with Cleveland Marine.

10. Craven Master Sprite

Registration number 1544 in the *Welsh Stud Book,*
Vol. XXX
Chesnut, blaze, near fore and both hind white,
foaled 1930
Breeder: Tom Jones Evans, Dinchope, Craven Arms
Sire: Craven Master Shot 1417
Dam: 4431 Grove Sprite II

Master Sprite won several prizes in the United Kingdom (e.g. first prizes at the Shropshire and West Midland and Craven Arms in 1932) before being exported in July 1935 to Mr. Edward Hirst, Springmead Farm, New South Wales, Australia. His sire Craven Master Shot (photograph in *Welsh Stud Book, Vol. XXVIII, p. 5*) was foaled in 1924 and won the Championship at the 1928 Royal Welsh Show. Master Shot was by the brown brilliant harness pony Craven Star Shot (who set the American harness world alight by his radiance) out of Forest Tosca.

Craven Star Shot was a son of the elegant harness winner Ness Sunflower. Sunflower's g-dam by Eiddwen Flyer III (*chapter 21.1*), Grove Sprite II, was also dam of Grove Sprightly (*chapter 5.1*).

Craven Master Shot (foaled in 1924) and sire of Craven Master Sprite. (From an oil painting by the courtesy of Mrs. M. Borthwick.)

Craven Star Shot (foaled in 1920) sire of Craven Master Shot.

Ness Sunflower (foaled in 1915) dam of Craven Star Shot.

It was in 1932 that the two-year-old Craven Master Sprite served his g-dam the twenty-three-year-old Forest Tosca to produce Craven Tosca.

A photograph of Master Sprite winning the Championship at the 1937 Royal Sydney Show appeared in the Royal Welsh Agricultural Show Journal of that year.

11. Forest Tosca

Registration number 3546 in the *Welsh Stud Book, Vol. XI*

Roan, height: 11 hands 3 in, foaled 1909
Breeder: W. S. Miller, Forest Lodge, Brecon
Owner in 1912: Evan Jones, Manorafon, Llandeilo
(breeder of Greylight)
Sire: Forest Ranger 288 (brown, foaled 1900)
Dam: 2511 Forest Roan Lark (roan, foaled 1901)

Forest Tosca was re-registered as Lochtyn Tosca with the same registration number. At the Lochtyn Stud she bred Lochtyn Tissie who was later dam of Craven Sunset (dam of the beautiful Craven Tit Bit). Tosca and Tissie both spent some years at the Craven Stud. Tosca was offered for sale at the 1922 Welsh Pony & Cob Society Sale but fortunately was not sold at 15 guineas; likewise Tissie was not sold for 24 guineas on the 1923 Sale.

12. Wentworth Springlight
Registration number 1225 in the *Welsh Stud Book*,
Vol. XIX
Light grey, height: 11 hands 2 in, foaled 1920
Owner and Breeder: Lady Wentworth, Crabbet
Park, Poundhill, Sussex
Sire: Dyoll Starlight (*chapter 2.1*)
Dam: 2046 Lady Greylight by Greylight 80

Lady Greylight was bred by Mr. Lloyd Morgan, Rhiwfelen, Abergwili, Carmarthen for whom she won Championships at the 1908 and 1909 United Counties Shows and three first prizes at the Welsh National Shows and for whom she bred Emlyn Grey Star (Grove Limelight) in 1908. She then passed into the ownership of Mr. Evan Jones (owner and breeder of Greylight) for whom she won a first prize and Championship medal at the 1913 National Pony Society Show. For Mr. Jones also she produced a filly in 1918 which was sold with her dam to Lady Wentworth, the filly being registered at Wentworth Grey Star,

Lady Wentworth with (left) Kilhendre Celtic Silverlight and Wentworth Springlight.

116

then followed a filly Wentworth Grey Night in 1919 and the colt Wentworth Springlight in 1920.

Wentworth Springlight was sired by Dyoll Starlight at a time when Dyoll Starlight had just arrived at Crabbet Park. Springlight was a special favourite of Lady Wentworth's; he was a very spectacular mover and appeared often in photographs being held by Lady Wentworth.

13. Grove Bright Spot

Registration number 7345 in the *Welsh Stud Book*,
Vol. XXII
Dappled grey, height: 11 hands 3 in, foaled 1916
Breeder: Gwilym Morgan, Arhosfa, Brynamman,
Carmarthen
Owner: Mrs. Greene, Grove, Craven Arms

Bright Spot was foaled in Brynamman at the time when Ballistite (*chapter 5.6*) had finished his show yard career and the ever generous Mrs. Greene allowed him to spend the season with the Brynamman Pony Improvement Society.

Bright Spot turned out to be a good show mare, she was third in the brood mare class at the National Pony Society Show Islington in 1923 and was a member of the first prize group; a photograph of which appears in the *Welsh Stud Book, Vol. XXIII, page 6*.

Bright Spot had been sold before the 1927 Grove Dispersal Sale, a yearling daughter of hers (lot 23) by Bleddfa Shooting Star fetching 15½ guineas, sold to Mr. Barnes.

14. Dyoll Starlight (*chapter 2.1*)

15. Lady Starlight

Registration number 2047 in the *Welsh Stud Book, Vol. VII*
Re-registered to show prizes won in *Vol. XIX, page 46*
Grey, star, height: 11 hands 3 in, foaled 1903
Breeder, J. Lloyd Morgan, Rhiwfelen, Abergwili,
Carmarthen
Owner: Lady Wentworth, Crabbet Park,
Poundhill, Sussex
Sire: Dyoll Starlight (*chapter 2.1*)
Dam: Lady White (foaled 1894)

Lady Starlight was bought by Lady Wentworth after she had won for

Lady Starlight photographed when she was Champion at the 1911 Royal Agricultural Society of England Show.

Mr. Lloyd Morgan a first prize at Cothi Bridge, two seconds at Shropshire and a third prize at Swansea in 1907, first prize at the Welsh National, first Lampeter and first Cothi Bridge in 1908, first and Welsh Pony & Cob Society medal Llandilo, first Narberth and first Cothi Bridge in 1909. The year 1911 was her crowning moment of glory when she was Supreme Champion Welsh Mountain Pony at the Royal Agricultural Society of England Show. This was also the year when she had her daughter Grove Star of Hope at foot. After winning another Welsh Pony & Cob Society medal at the 1914 Welsh National Show, she was sold to the Lady Wentworth.

Note

One fascinating aspect of this family is the dominance of the inheritance of white markings on the whole coloured (e.g. bay and chestnut) members of the family over a period of sixty years covering nine generations, all with three (rather than four) white legs.

(i)   Ness Sunflower, chestnut, foaled 1915, off fore and both hinds white;
(ii)   her son:
        Craven Star Shot, foaled 1920

brown little white on off fore and both hinds;
(iii)   his son:
Craven Master Shot, foaled 1924
chestnut, near fore and both hinds white;
(iv)   his son:
Craven Master Sprite, foaled 1930
chestnut, near fore and both hinds white;
(v)   his daughter:
Craven Tosca, foaled 1933
chestnut, both fore and off hinds white;
(vi)   her son:
Pendock Playboy, foaled 1947
bay, off fore and both hinds white;
(vii)   his son:
Revel Light, foaled 1950
bay, off fore and both hinds white;
(viii)   his daughter:
Revel Siesta, foaled 1961
bay, near fore and both hinds white;
(ix)   her daughter:
Ceulan Sprite, foaled 1964
bay, near fore and both hinds white;
(x)   her daughters:
Ceulan Sienna, foaled 1976
chestnut, off fore and both hinds white;
   and
Ceulan Sidan, foaled 1978
chestnut, off fore and both hinds white;
   and
Ceulan Seren Wyb, foaled 1979
bay, off fore and both hinds white.

8
Vardra Charm foaled 1924
Revel Choice foaled 1949

2	4	8
Vardra Sunstar 1832	Criban Pebble 1700	Criban Grey Grit 1699
		9 9060 Criban Martha
	3 8325 Vardra Charm	**6** Bleddfa Shooting Star 73
		7 6962 Nance o'r Bryn
3 8325 Vardra Charm	**6** Bleddfa Shooting Star 73	**12** Dyoll Starlight 4
		13 572 Alveston Belle
	7 6962 Nance o'r Bryn	**14** Ap Starlight 587
		15 Mountain Pony

1

9869 Revel Choice

1. Revel Choice
Registration number 9869 in the *Welsh Stud Book,*
Vol. XXXIV
Grey, blaze, height: 11 hands 2 in, foaled 1949
Breeder: the late Matthew Williams, Brynheulog,
Tonteg, Pontypridd
Owner: Emrys Griffiths, The Revel, Talgarth,
Breconshire.

Matthew Williams, a great lifelong friend of our family, died on 26th January 1951 and the Vardra Stud Dispersal Sale took place at Gowerton market on 16th April 1951.

Emrys Griffiths bought lot 8, a grey two-year-old filly for 32 guineas and she was duly registered later as Revel Choice. It was in 1953 that Revel Choice started as a prolific producer and her record is listed below:

1953 Revel Chancellor, colt, by Bowdler Brewer
1954 Revel Crusader, colt, by Bowdler Brewer
1955 Revel Cascade, filly, by Pendock Zenith
1957 Revel Caress, filly, by Revel Springlight
1958 Revel Copelia, filly, by Revel Springlight
1959 Revel Consul, colt, by Bowdler Blighter
1960 Revel Courtier, colt, by Revel Springlight
1962 Revel Capri, filly, by Rhydyfelin Syndod
1963 Revel Chip, colt, by Clan Pip
1964 Revel Cello, colt, by Clan Pip
1965 Revel Chase, filly, by Clan Pip
1966 Revel Cassino, colt, by Clan Pip
1967 Revel Chelsea, filly, by Clan Pip
1968 Revel Choosey, filly, by Twyford Sprig

These ponies have had a world-wide effect on the Welsh Mountain Pony breed. The first two full-brothers Chancellor and Crusader were used as successful sires at many other studs in addition to the Revel. One daughter of Crusader which I once owned, called Betws Nans, won for me the 1962 Royal Welsh Show cup award for the best Welsh pony under saddle. Cascade which followed was a small, stocky little sort with a super head like her dam; she won a very large yearling class at the 1956 Royal Welsh Show (Rhyl) under Mrs. Pennell and stood reserve Champion female to Brierwood Honey.

Of the females, Caress, the next in order, is the most famous; altogether bigger with more scope than her dam, yet with plenty of depth

Family group photographed in 1960 at the Revel. From left Revel Choice, her yearling son Revel Consul, her daughter Revel Caress, with Caress' foal Revel Carefree. (Photograph courtesy of Mr. Emrys Griffiths.)

Revel Cascade, foaled in 1955, daugther of Revel Choice. Photographed at the 1956 Royal Welsh Show.

Revel Caress, foaled in 1957, daughter of Revel Choice. Photographed when Champion Female at the 1963 Royal Welsh Show.

Revel Chip, foaled in 1963, son of Revel Choice. Photographed when Champion Premium stallion Glanusk 1972.

and powerful legs and quarters she was the female Champion at the first Royal Welsh Show to be held on the permanent site (1963). Caress has also the distinction of being grand-dam of a Royal Welsh Champion, her son Revel Carefree being sire of the 1975 Supreme Champion Springbourne Hyfryd.

Copeilia, foaled in 1958, was a full-sister to Caress, and her progeny have done useful work as Premium stallions e.g. the chesnut Revel Caesar (foaled in 1965) on the Preseli mountains.

Revel Consul, foaled in 1959 was a useful sire and was exported from Mr. Llewellyn Richards of the Criban Stud to David Coxhead of Timaru, New Zealand in March 1965.

Revel Courtier, foaled in 1960 is full-brother to Caress and Copeilia, and was an influential Premium stallion on the Breconshire Black Mountains from 1965 to 1968 when owned by Mr. E. T. Jenkins of the Vishon Stud, Llanthony. In fact several stallions of this family have been prestigious Premium stallions; during those same years 1965 to 1968, Mr. Baden Powell won Premiums on the Brecon Beacons with Revel Copyright a half-brother × half-sister cross (by Revel Crusader × Revel Caress, foaled 1959). I remember them both well since I was honoured to judge the Premium stallions in 1966 and 1967. Other brothers who have served their time as Premium stallions being Revel Chip (first Premium for both 1968 and 1972) and Revel Cassino (1970).

Choice did not have a foal in 1961 and spent the summer winning so many important awards including the female Championship at the Llandeilo Royal Welsh Show and Abergavenny Show (the latter being where the photograph which appeared in *Welsh Champions* was taken).

Revel Capri, foaled in 1962, is a very good producer at the Revel. Then followed five (three colts and two fillies) by the 1963 and 1964 Royal Welsh Champion Clan Pip; this was an ideal cross, Choice being small and typey with super head, huge eyes and tiny ears whilst Pip was big and "scopey" with tremendous length of rein and tail set right on top. Chip after (already mentioned) spending some time as Premium stallion is chief sire at the Six Oaks stud, Cello after winning the championship at Glanusk is a very successful sire at the Bengad Stud, having sired two Royal Welsh female Champions: B. Day Lily (1978) plus B. Love in the Mist (1974). Chase is a top brood mare at the Persie Stud producing such as Persie Concord Reserve Champion at the 1974 Royal Agricultural Society of England Show and then exported to Australia, Cassino Reserve Champion at the 1976 Royal Welsh Show and Champion the following year (altogether winning 270 Championships) and finally Chelsea already a producer of great note.

Revel Cassino, foaled in 1966, son of Revel Choice. Photographed when Champion at Glanusk Show 1978.

Choice's last foal was Choosey, foaled in 1968 and she also is producing creditable stock.

Apart from Chase at the Persie Stud, the other five daughters are at the Revel and keeping this magnificent line going well. Caress producing Carried (1970), Concorde (1971), Coy (1973), Carnation (1974) and Cover Girl (1975). Capri producing Calico (1973), Chapter (1974), Caprille (1975) and Chef (1976). Chelsea producing Chelsea Bun (1969), Chelsea Fan (1970), Chintz (1972), Chelsea Rose (1973), Centre (1974), Chelsea Cracker (1975), Curtsey (1978) and Choosey producing Chuckle (1972), Cinnamon (1973), Candytuft (1975).

2. Vardra Sunstar
Registration number 1832 in the *Welsh Stud Book,*
Vol. XXXII
Grey, blaze, little white on near hind fetlock, height:
11 hands 2 in, foaled 1945
Owner and Breeder: Matthew Williams,
Brynheulog, Tonteg, Pontypridd, Glamorgan.

Vardra Sunstar stood second to Coed Coch Madog at the 1951 Royal Welsh Show in the ownership of Mr. Llewellyn Richards of the old-established Criban Stud. Mr. Richards had bought him as a four-year-old since Mr. Williams was in failing health and could not cope with a stallion. He was then sold to Mr. Tom Parry of the Gurnos Stud (for 74 guineas, lot 2 on the Criban Sale, May 1952) acquiring a second Premium (to Owain Glyndwr owned by Mr. T. Norman Lewis) for the Penderyn Pony Improvement Society area during 1953.

By 1954, Owain Glyndwr had been sold to Mr. Emrys Griffiths and Vardra Sunstar gained first Premiums for Mr. Parry at the Penderyn area for 1954 and 1955 and also for the Dowlais and Twynrodyn area in 1956. There were many good ponies sired by Vardra Sunstar in these areas during this period.

Another successful Vardra Sunstar line is via his son Pendock Zenith (foaled in 1951) who sired some top-class mares such as the noted winner Twyford Mazurka. It is the striking head photograph of Pendock Zenith which has been adopted as the emblem of the Welsh Pony Societies of Australia and Belgium.

Vardra Sunstar was exported from Mr. Llewellyn Richards to Mr. William Marcus of the U.S.A. in June 1958 and his progeny appeared amongst the American winners consistently.

3. Vardra Charm
Registration number 8325 in the *Welsh Stud Book,*
Vol. XXV
Grey, snip on face, white hind fetlocks, height: 11
hands 2 in, foaled 1924
Owner and Breeder: Matthew Williams,
Brynheulog, Llantwit Fardre, Glam.

The year that Vardra Charm was born (1924) her dam was shown extensively and Charm won the first prize in the foal class at Llandeilo; a good start. In 1926 Charm went up to the National Pony Society Show

Vardra Charm photographed when winning at the 1938 Royal Welsh Show.

at Islington and won a first prize following it up the following year with a first prize at the Royal Welsh Show plus winning the gold medal at the Ferndale Show.

In adult classes, Charm won a third prize as a brood mare at the 1932 Royal Welsh Show; her half-sister the bay Vardra Sunflower (foaled 1929 and sired by Craven Master Shot) was second in the filly class. During the years 1932 to 1937, Charm was shown extensively in South Wales along with Sunflower and Charm's daughter Vardra Nance (foaled in 1927, sired by Criban Shot and died in 1950) winner of almost as many awards as her illustrious dam.

At the 1938 Royal Welsh Show with Capt. T. A. Howson judging, Charm won the brood mare class from Mr. Tom Jones Evans' Gates-heath Dainty (dam of Craven Bright Sprite etc) and Miss Brodrick's Grove Madcap (grand-dam of Coed Coch Madog) with Vardra Nance fourth. Charm also won a first prize and medal at the 1938 Royal Agricultural Society of England Show.

129

Vardra Sunflower, daughter of Nance o'r Bryn.

At the 1939 Show, Vardra Sunflower won for Mr. J. B. Holden. Then the war years intervened and Vardra Charm's showing career was interrupted; when the Royal Welsh Show started again in 1947, with Mr. D. O. Morgan judging Vardra Sunflower was first and Vardra Charm was second; however the Championships were judged by Mr. Morgan Evans who reversed these two placings and Vardra Charm was awarded the female championship. This was the last Royal Welsh Show appearance for both mares but their descendants have kept the flag flying by winning Royal Welsh Show Section "A" Championships in 1961 (filly), 1963 (filly), 1970 (filly), 1974 (filly), 1975 (filly), 1976 (colt), 1977 (Cassino and Heidi) and 1978 (Bengad Day Lily) as well as the Section "B" Championship of 1951.

Vardra Nance was very similar to her elegant dam, both had super heads, long, reachy necks, high withers and moderate bone. Revel Choice was altogether more stocky, smaller and possessing enormous bone and power whilst retaining a magnificent head.

Perhaps the best description of Vardra Charm can be obtained by quoting Capt. T. A. Howson who judged at the 1938 Royal Welsh Show and was the editor of the Royal Welsh Agricultural Society journal:

. . . she comes very near indeed to our conception of the perfect pony, for she has a very lovely head which is set gracefully upon a long and supple neck, good shoulders and a brood mare's middlepiece, a high-set tail and four good limbs. She walked into the ring majestically, with head and tail aloft and sailed along in sparkling Mountain pony style when asked to trot and, taken all in all, she justified her name and her claim to the female championship.

I consider this to be a very fitting tribute to one of the most beautiful ponies that ever I saw.

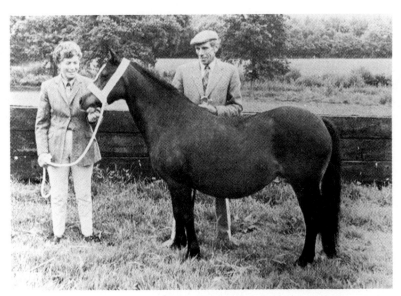

Royal Welsh Show 1975 Female Champion Springbourne Hyfryd with owners, Mr. and Mrs. David Reynolds. Sire: Revel Carefree (g-g-son of Vardra Charm. Dam: Cwmgarn Heidi (g-g-daughter of Vardra Sunflower. (Photograph courtesy of Stable Management.*)*

4. Criban Pebble
Registration number 1700 in the *Welsh Stud Book,*
Vol. XXXII
Dark grey, height: 11 hands 1 in, foaled 1942
Owners and Breeders: H. W. Richards and Sons,
Brynhyfryd, Talybont-on-Usk, Brecon

Criban Pebble was one of the "fashionable" stallions of South Wales at the end of the Second World War inasmuch as Mr. Matthew

Williams who used such famous stallions as Bleddfa Shooting Star (*chapter 4.1*) Criban Shot (*chapter 9.12*), Craven Master Shot (*chapter 7.10*) borrowed him for 1944. Other breeders also supported Criban Pebble with successful results such as Maj. W. P. L. Jones who took Ceulan Blue Vision to him on three successive occasions (and eventually bought him) producing Ty'r Sais Blue Marble in 1947, Ty'r Sais Carreg Lâs in 1948 and Ty'r Sais Blue Diamond in 1949 (three ponies which had a big influence on the breed in South Wales and in the U.S.A.) (Blue Marble was Grand Champion at the 1955 Timonium Show in the U.S.A.) Criban Pebble then exerted his influence as a Premium stallion, at Penderyn in the ownership of Mr. W. T. Davies during 1950–1952, on the Black Mountains for Mr. Roger Prosser in 1954 and 1955 and then back to Mr. W. T. Davies at Penderyn for 1956.

After this he was sold to Mrs. Cuff who lived at nearby Llanddeusant at this time and we shall hear more of him as sire of Downland Dauphin (*chapter 14.2*) etc in 1959.

6. Bleddfa Shooting Star (*chapter 4.1*)

7. Nance o'r Bryn
Registration number 6962 in the *Welsh Stud Book, Vol. XXI*
Grey, blaze, four white pasterns, height: 11 hands 3 in, foaled 1915
Breeder: Isaac Williams, Llandre, Pumpsaint, Llanwrda, Carmarthenshire
Owner: David Morgan, 3, Smithfield, Cwmllynfell, Swansea Valley

In 1922, Nance o'r Bryn was sold to Mr. Matthew Williams to establish the Vardra Stud along with three other top-class mares: Irfon Lady Daylight, Crossways Bohemian Girl and Vardra Sunshine.

Nance o'r Bryn immediately made her presence known in the South Wales show rings, in 1922 winning first prizes at Pontardulais, Palleg, Pyle and Bedwellty with a second and a third prize in saddle classes at Nelson (East Glamorgan Show) and Cardiff.

A very busy showing year for Nance o'r Bryn followed in 1923 since she won twenty-four prizes (in hand and under saddle) from as far afield as Llandeilo in the West to Knighton in the East.

In 1924, she did not visit so many shows but had now reached for greater heights winning fourteen prizes which included a first prize at the Royal Welsh Show (Bridgend), a Welsh Pony & Cob Society silver medal at Swansea Show and many other important awards including a National Pony Society medal. In 1925, Nance o'r Bryn won twelve prizes but by now her daughter Vardra Charm was taking over, especially for the further shows such as the 1925 Royal Welsh Show.

Nance o'r Bryn won her second Welsh Pony & Cob Society silver medal at the 1926 East Glamorgan Show with another six local prizes, Vardra Charm now going as far afield as the National Pony Society Show at Islington. Nance o'r Bryn continued winning in 1927 with another Welsh Pony & Cob Society medal at East Glamorgan and a third prize at the Bath and West Show (Bath) and another ten awards and again a Welsh Pony & Cob Society medal in 1928 at Llandeilo and another eleven awards. It might be thought of this busy show mare that she had no time to produce anything (especially since she was shown under saddle every year). However she produced the two magnificent mares Vardra Charm in 1924 and Vardra Sunflower in 1929 and various others such as the colt Vardra Sprig (in 1927) who was for some years stud stallion at Mrs. Alice Straker's Stagshaw Stud in Corbridge, Northumberland.

8. Criban Grey Grit
Registration number 1699 in the *Welsh Stud Book*,
Vol. XXXII
Grey, blaze, height: 11 hands 3 in, foaled 1939
Breeders: H. W. Richards and Sons, Brynhyfryd,
Talybont-on-Usk, Brecon
Owner: Emrys Griffiths, The Revel, Talgarth,
Breconshire (from 1944)

Criban Grey Grit was very highly thought of at the Criban stud and used extensively during 1941–1944 producing the stallions Criban D-Day, Criban Flag Day, Criban Marble, Criban Pebble, (*chapter 8.4*) Criban Pledge (*photograph in Welsh Stud Book, Vol. XXXV, page 29*, a big winner and a good sire at the Clan Stud), Criban Rocket and Criban Silver Sand (Premium winner for the Meredith Brothers Vaynor Stud, show-winner for Mr. A. D. Thomas). Amongst his daughters were Black Bonnet, Ensa and White Wings (both sold to Capt. Brierley at the November 1946 Criban Sale), Faith, Footlights, Red Chip (full-sister to Pledge and sold to Mrs. Pennell on the May 1952 Criban Sale) and Waaf (one of the first consignments to be exported to the U.S.A. after the war – photograph *Welsh Stud Book, Vol. XXXII, page 117*).

Two sons of Criban Grey Grit. Second from left Criban Flag Day (with Mr. Jim Eckley) and third from left Criban Silver Sand (Mr. Crad Meredith). Premium judging 1948 for the Vaynor area. This was a period when the judges would travel all over Wales to inspect the stallions in their respective areas (as distinct from the present-day procedure when all stallions travel to the same centre, e.g. Glanusk Show). People standing behind the ponies are, from left to right, Mr. E. J. Reynolds (wearing cap), Mr. H. Llewellyn Richards, Criban Stud (wearing hat), Mr. T. Edmunds (no hat) Landlord of the Pontsarn Hotel, Mr. A. R. McNaught, Clan Stud (wearing hat), judge Mr. David Meredith, Vaynor Stud with son, Mr. Tom Norman Lewis of the Bolgoed Stud and judge Miss Brodrick.

At the Revel he sired the stallions Blue Boy and Darkie and the mares Bliss, Grey Lady, Judith, Rosemond, Rosebud and Wisp up to the year 1949. Criban Grey Grit's pedigree is full of the old germane blood-lines: his sire Mathrafal Tuppence (*chapter 9.2*) was bred by Mr. Clement Davies, K.C., M.P. (for several years leader of the Liberal Party in

Wales) out of Twilight of Dyffryn by Kilhendre Celtic Silverlight (*chapter 6.12*). Grey Grit's dam was Criban Bay Leaf who goes back five generations (Criban all the way) to a mare called Twilight bred and owned by Mr. H. W. Richards in pre-Stud Book times by a stallion with the rather ignominious name of Black Dick!

Through the Premium scheme these good blood-lines have been of benefit throughout the hills of Wales, Grey Grit himself on the Black Mountains during 1944–1949 and later at Aberyscir, Flag Day and Rocket on Eppynt, Silver Sand at Vaynor and Dowlais and D-Day on the Denbigh Moors. Criban Silver Sand has the added distinction of being g-sire of the 1977 Royal Welsh Show Champion mare Cwmgarn Heidi, his daughter Cwmgarn Trixie being dam of Heidi.

9. Criban Martha

Registration number 9060 in the *Welsh Stud Book,*
Vol. XXXII
Black, height: 11 hands 3 in, foaled 1935
Owners and Breeders: H. W. Richards and Sons,
Brynhyfryd, Talybont-on-Usk, Brecon.

Criban Martha came from a very old Criban family, way back to pre-Stud Book times. Her sire Criban Marksman was by Criban Cracker by Bwlch Quicksilver (Mrs. Pennell). Bwlch Quicksilver was originally registered as Towy Valley Starlight, sired by Dyoll Starlight (*chapter 2.1*) out of Lady Greylight (also dam of Grove Limelight (*chapter 11.15*) and Wentworth Springlight, (*chapter 7.12*) by Greylight who was also, of course, by Dyoll Starlight. On her dam's side, Martha was out of Criban Charity (according to Mr. Richards, the best mare ever bred at Criban) (foaled 1932) out of Criban Mulberry (foaled 1924) out of Criban Raspberry (foaled 1920) out of Criban Duchess (foaled 1914) out of Roanie II (foaled 1900) out of one of the original registered Criban mares Vaynor Duchess (foaled 1896): Mr. Richards using the Vaynor, Ystrad and Criban prefixes up until around the beginning of this century according to upon which hill the pony grazed.

Thus Criban Martha was a typical Welsh Mountain Pony through and through.

12. Dyoll Starlight (*chapter 2.1*)

13. Alveston Belle (*chapter 4.3*)

135

14. Ap Starlight
Registration number 587 in the *Welsh Stud Book,*
Vol. XII
Black, blaze, silver eyes, four white socks, height:
11 hands 1 in, foaled 1911
Owner and Breeder: D. R. Williams, Brittyn,
Llanwrda, Carmarthen

Ap Starlight was a popular son of Dyoll Starlight (*chapter 2.1*). His dam, Mina (not registered) was a black mare with three white socks; his g-dam, was Dyoll Glitter a bay mare with four white socks.

15. Mountain Pony mare
Grey with white hind fetlocks, height: 11 hands 2 in
Sired by Dyoll Starlight.

9
Criban Socks foaled 1926
Criban Leading Lady foaled 1939

1 9247 Criban Leading Lady	2 Mathrafal Tuppence 1639	4 Mathrafal Vim 1481	8 Mathrafal Vulture 1480
			9 8756 Mathrafal Empress
		5 9058 Twilight of Dyffryn	10 Kilhendre Celtic Silverlight 953
			11 9057 Mary of Llanfechain
	3 8916 Criban Rally	6 Criban Bumble Bee 1394	12 Criban Shot 1276
			13 7963 Criban Busy Bee
		7 8703 Criban Socks	12 Criban Shot 1276
			15 8267 Criban Forest Lass

1. Criban Leading Lady

Registration number 9247 in the *Welsh Stud Book*,
Vol. XXXII

Bay, white face, silver eyes, four white legs, height:
11 hands 3 in, foaled 1939

Breeder: W. R. Richards, Pwllycalch, Brecon

I well remember seeing Criban Leading Lady for the first time. It was on 4th November 1946, the day before the Criban Sale and my father and I had gone to Brecon with our good friend John Berry of the Betws Stud to have a "preview" of the sale ponies. In addition to seeing the fifty or so ponies which were entered for the sale, we were invited onto the Criban hills and there, standing out amongst the group of mares and foals was this distinctively marked mare of magnificent rich bay colour. Unfortunately this bunch of ponies did not take too kindly to human interference and galloped away over the brow of the hill but Criban Leading Lady created such an impression on my memory that I cannot honestly say that I remember seeing anything else.

At the sale the following day, we bought her dam, the dun Criban Rally hoping that at fourteen years, she was in foal to Cwm Cream of Eppynt to produce another Leading Lady, but alas it was not to be. It

Criban Leading Lady. (Photograph courtesy of Ifor Lloyd.)

139

was also at this sale that John Berry bought Criban Golden Spray (*chapter 12.1*), a foal very similar in markings to Leading Lady, apart from being a dark chesnut, she too had silver eyes and four white legs.

At this time, Leading Lady had never been handled but by the following year she had been caught and was shown at a few Breconshire Shows. In 1948 she was chosen to represent the breed at a Parade of British Livestock at the International Horse Show at the White City, London, and the same year she was sold (in foal to Cui Squire) to Mr. Peter Jones of Gwalchmai who sold her with her filly foal (later registered as Glascoed Llyn) to Miss Harrop of the Glascoed Stud. At Glascoed, Leading Lady produced Glascoed Lleuad (1950), Glascoed Llydaw (1951), sire of some good ponies for Mr. J. Price of the Abbey, Craswall) and Glascoed Llinos in 1952. Miss Harrop also won quite a few big prizes with her at North Wales Shows.

Before leaving Criban, Leading Lady in 1945 had produced Criban Scilla (by Revel Wampus) another bay with silver eyes and white legs. Scilla won the Princess Margaret Cup at the National Pony Show at Roehampton in 1948 after which she was bought by Miss Brodrick for export to Canada. By 1948 Mr. W. R. Richards had adopted the "Cui" prefix and the foal which Leading Lady left behind when she went to Anglesey was christened as Cui Chorus Girl.

From 1953 to 1959, Leading Lady was owned by Mr. W. J. Jones of Gerynant, Lampeter and in this ownership she won literally dozens of prizes at shows all over mid-Wales; sometimes we would beat her with Ceulan Serenade (Dinarth What Ho × Coed Coch Serliw) sometimes she would beat us and then we would meet her again in the championships when we showed the stallions Dinarth What Ho and later, Clan Marshal.

Leading Lady was unplaced in the open class at the 1954 Royal Welsh Show at Machynlleth in a large class won by Coed Coch Siaradus, Ankerwycke Criban Snowdon (by Leading Lady's brother Criban Atom) and Wentworth Minilla, but she later won the local class.

When Leading Lady was sold to Mr. Roscoe Lloyd in 1959 (at twenty years old) it was thought that perhaps her breeding days were over but she had been served by Bolgoed Revelation and to her new owner's delight she duly produced a filly aptly named Derwen Delight. She went one stage further in 1960 and produced another filly named Derwen Fair Lady (by Brierwood Honeyway, which I later saw many times in Denmark) which was sold to the Count de Villegas de Clercamp of Belgium.

Derwen Delight, photographed when 19 years old. Daughter of Criban Leading Lady.
(Photograph courtesy of Ifor Lloyd.)

Derwen Delightful (left) daughter of Derwen Delight with her daughter Derwen Delilah.
(Photograph courtesy of Ifor Lloyd.)

141

Derwen Delight has many outstanding progeny at the Derwen Stud including a daughter (by Clan Gylen) named Derwen Delightful who is dam of the winning Derwen Delilah, and so this valuable bloodline is still permeating through several outlets in Welsh studs despite so many of the family having been exported in their prime.

2. Mathrafal Tuppence
Registration number 1639 in the *Welsh Stud Book*,
Vol. XXXII
Grey, two white hind fetlocks, height: 12 hands,
foaled 1932
Breeder: Clement Davies, K.C., M.P., Plas Dyffryn,
Meifod, Montgomeryshire

Mathrafal Tuppence won a few prizes (first prize at Knighton and a third at Chester) in the ownership of Mr. Meyrick Jones, Mathrafal. When he was a three-year-old and still at Mathrafal, Captain Brierley used him on Mathrafal Mistress (the first registered Welsh mare at the Brierwood Stud, purchased from Mr. Meyrick Jones in 1934). The result of this mating was Misty, the first registered foal to be born at this stud and what can truly be described as the "originator" of the Brierwood Stud. Misty goes down in history as dam of Brierwood Mistwyn, sire of the 1956 Royal Welsh Show Champion Brierwood Honey. Shortly afterwards Mathrafal Tuppence was sold to the Criban Stud.

At Criban he sired some very influential stock. Apart from Leading Lady he sired Criban Grey Grit (*chapter 8.8*) and a nice selection of mares including Criban Eve (foaled in 1939), Criban White Lark (foaled in 1939 and sold to Mrs. Cuff on the 1946 Sale), and Criban White Jane (foaled in 1939) whose daughter Criban White Wings produced some very good stock for Capt. Brierley, Tan Lan Stud e.g. Tan Lan Lili and Tan Lan Wennol (both well-known champions) and the Coed Coch Stud before being sold for export.

During 1939 Mathrafal Tuppence was exchanged (for Coed Coch Glyndwr) for the stud season to go to Coed Coch and he won a fourth prize at the Royal Welsh Show at Caernarvon. His 1940 progeny in North Wales included such good animals as Coed Coch Marchog, Coed Coch Serbysg and Eryri Gwyndaf. It is quite a coincidence that in 1947, Eryri Gwyndaf was our stud stallion, Criban Rally was put in foal to him and sold to the Whitehall Stud so the resulting foal, a very lovely mare, Whitehall Shonet was three-quarter sister to Criban Leading Lady.

Mathrafal Tuppence certainly did much to improve the standard of pony breeding on the Welsh hills, being a Premium stallion for the Breconshire Black Mountains Pony Association for 1941, 1944, 1945 and 1946, his progeny at the Revel during this period including Revel Russet, Revel Sugar, Revel Threepennybit and Revel Wild Rose.

3. Criban Rally

Registration number 8916 in the *Welsh Stud Book,*
Vol. XXX
Dun blaze, silver eyes, four white legs, height:
11 hands 2 in, foaled 1932
Breeder: H. W. Richards, Brynhyfryd, Talybont-on-Usk, Brecon.

Criban Rally was fourteen years old when we bought her on the Criban Sale in November 1946. She had been served that year by Cwm Cream of Eppynt but unfortunately proved barren.

Her first foal was Criban Parade (foaled 1936) by Ness Commander who sold for 7 guineas (as a yearling) on the Criban Sale in May 1937. After Leading Lady, there was Criban Atom; foaled in 1944 he was sired by Criban Winston. Sold to Maj. Careless for 28 guineas on the same sale at which we bought his dam, Atom changed hands many times leaving good stock behind him wherever he went. He was a very typical stallion, small and compact and a very spectacular mover. He has the great distinction of being grand-sire of Sinton Samite, the 12.2 hands riding pony who was Supreme Champion at the 1969 Ponies of Britain Show. When we bought Rally she had at foot a filly later registered as Cui Blue Rally by Bolgoed Squire.

We sold Rally to Mr. R. J. Jones of the Whitehall Stud in 1948. That year she produced Whitehall Shonet. Rally died in 1951 and her filly foal that year (by Craven Tit Bit) was named Whitehall Rally's Last.

4. Mathrafal Vim

Registration number 1481 in the *Welsh Stud Book,*
Vol. XXIX
Dark brown, no white, foaled 1925, height:
11 hands 3 in
Breeder: H. Meyrick Jones, Mathrafal, Meifod,
Montgomeryshire

The most important line from Mathrafal Vim was via his son Mathrafal Tuppence who was used extensively at Criban and also at Coed Coch when he was leased there for 1939 producing Coed Coch

Marchog, Coed Coch Serbysg, Eryri Gwyndaf etc. Another line recently to come to the fore is Dyfrdwy Midnight Moon (foaled in 1961); she is one of the many beautiful mares sired by Coed Coch Planed (*chapter 26.8*), she was female Champion at the 1972 Royal Welsh Show and her dam Betws Arian is by Mathrafal Finalist (son of Mathrafal Vim) and Mathrafal Silver (dam of Betws Arian) is by Mathrafal Tuppence; so Midnight Moon has two strains of Mathrafal Vim. Aston Superstar, son of Midnight Moon was Supreme Champion at the 1978 and 1979 Royal Welsh Shows amongst many other major awards won.

5. Twilight of Dyffryn
Registration number 9058 in the *Welsh Stud Book*,
Vol. XXXII
Grey, white hind socks, height: 12 hands, foaled 1924
Breeder: C. P. Owen, High Street, Llanfyllin,
Montgomeryshire

Twilight of Dyffryn was owned by Mr. Clement Davies, K.C., Liberal Member of Parliament for Montgomeryshire for many years. She was a well-known winner in her locality winning several first prizes at Welshpool and Llanfyllin Shows. She also won under saddle at Knighton Show and second and third prizes in saddle classes at the Royal Welsh.

6. Criban Bumble Bee
Registration number 1394 in the *Welsh Stud Book*,
Vol. XXVII
Bay, star and snip, height: 11 hands 3 in, foaled 1923
Breeder: H. W. Richards, Brynhyfryd,
Talybont-on-Usk, Brecon

Of all the dozens of stallions bred at Criban, Bumble Bee is singled out by Mrs. Pennell writing in the 1965 Welsh Pony & Cob Society Journal as one of the four most influential in the long history of this world-famous stud.

Bumble Bee does not seem to have been used at stud in his younger days; in middle age he produced some very influential Criban families: e.g.:

1932 Criban Charity, (g-g-g-dam of Solway Master Bronze, *chapter 16.1*) (dam also of Criban Gracie, dam of Criban Pep)

1932 Criban Blonde, (dam of Cui Mark, Cui Squire and Criban Winston, sire of Criban Victor, *chapter 13.2*)

1932 Criban Rally

1933 Criban Bay Leaf, dam of Criban Grey Grit (*chapter 8.8*) and Cribon Pilot (Premium stallion Eppynt 1950–1952 then at Church Stretton)

1933 The brown stallion Criban Crown (son of the Royal Welsh Show winner Criban Grey Swell) who was sold on the 1937 Criban Sale

1934 Criban Grey Bee, (full-sister to Bay Leaf)

1934 Criban Rachel, dam of Criban Ruth, Cui Mary, Cui Rachel, Cui Rose, Cui Sunset, Cui Emperor and Cui Spark.

7. Criban Socks
Registration number 8703 in the *Welsh Stud Book,*
Vol. XXVIII
Dark chestnut, blaze, four white socks, height:
11 hands 3 in, foaled 1926
Breeder: W. S. Miller, Forest Lodge, Brecon

Although Criban Socks was foaled whilst her dam was still in the ownership of Mr. Miller of Forest Lodge, the mare and foal spent more

Criban Socks.

145

Criban Socks (left) and Grove Will O'the Wisp when both were owned by the Dinarth Hall Stud. (Photograph courtesy of G. H. Parsons.)

time on the Criban side of the Brecon Beacons than on the Forest Lodge side so Mr. H. W. Richards very wisely bought them both and the foal was registered as Criban Socks.

Criban Socks had a very quiet life in the Criban Stud during her early days; she was not put into foal until 1932 when she produced Rally, she then produced Criban Sweetly (by Criban Marksman) in 1934, Criban Cavalier (full-brother to Rally) in 1935 and Criban Cockade (*chapter 12.6*) by Ness Commander in 1936.

It was while she had Criban Cockade at foot that Mr. Richards decided that she should compete at major shows. The Bath and West Show that year was held at Cardiff and Criban Socks won the brood mare class being immediately purchased by Tom Thomas, stud groom at Dinarth Hall on condition that Cockade returned to Criban at weaning.

In her new ownership Socks won at Chester, Merioneth and Anglesey that year whilst in 1937 she won first prizes at the Bath and West, Three Counties, Shropshire and West Midland and Royal Welsh (after a disqualification) (*chapter 3.3*).

Mr. T. J. Jones, owner of the Dinarth Hall Stud died in September 1937 and Criban Socks was lot 34 on the Dispersal Sale held on 27th October. It was in fact a photograph of Criban Socks (wearing the well-known Dinarth headcollar with the green brow-band which my father bought for £1 and which I often still use) which graced the cover of the sale catalogue and she fetched the second-highest figure of the sale at 41 guineas (Bowdler Brightlight fetching 45 guineas) going to Mrs. Sivewright (who also bought Brightlight).

Criban Socks did not stay long with Mrs. Sivewright being soon sold to Miss Calmady Hamlyn who kept mainly Dartmoor ponies but also had a few Welsh mares and the Welsh stallion Coed Coch Seronydd, son of Coed Coch Seren (*chapter 10.11*).

The following year war broke out and so many ponies were put down as part of the war effort, unfortunately Criban Socks was one of these; one of the most beautiful mares of all time and still in her prime at thirteen years.

Criban Socks belonged to a type that we do not find today, low and deep with plenty of bone and "feather" she still had the "look of the hills" about her; indeed, Tom Thomas often complained that she enjoyed her freedom too much, she was not too friendly in the stable and could use her heels to good effect! Unsuspectingly, we found the same was also true for Rally; ponies which have enjoyed the freedom of the hills for most of their lives often resent confinement.

Of the progeny of Criban Socks, Rally and her family are well represented in many studs today. Her full brother, Cavalier, was sold for 10 guineas on the 1937 Criban Sale and does not seem to have been kept as a stallion. Criban Sweetly was also sold on this sale, in colour and markings she was the most like her dam; she went to Mr. Moses Griffith of the Egryn Stud where she spent the next seven years (still not caught) breeding such as Egryn Criban by Coed Coch Erlewyn and Egryn Sweetly by the Cob, Gwenog Lad.

I remember seeing her on a very wet day in 1946 near Pontrhydy-groes in Cardiganshire when I went with Miss Brodrick and John Jones on one of their pony buying trips (my excuse for taking a day off school being that I would act as "navigator" along these narrow mid-Wales lanes!). Criban Sweetly was not to be tempted to come anywhere near us that day; shortly afterwards Mrs. Cuff went to view her with binoculars and she went to Downland where she produced among others, the influential Downland Serchog (*chapter 14.10*).

Within a very short time of going to Downland, Sweetly began winning many prizes in hand and under saddle at the Royal Agricultural Society of England, National Pony Shows and the Royal Welsh Shows. In fact at the 1951 Royal Welsh Show, Mrs. Cuff won all three ridden prizes with Criban Sweetly, Downland Dicon and Craven Brightsprite.

Sweetly was not the only progeny of Criban Socks to make a name under saddle since Peter Pan (produced at Vean Stud by Coed Coch Seronydd) won so many prizes ridden by Scarlett Rimell, daughter of the famous National Hunt trainer. Peter Pan certainly put the Welsh Pony on the map as a riding pony when he defeated all sizes for the ridden Championship at the International Show at the White City.

8. Mathrafal Vulture
Registration number 1480 in the *Welsh Stud Book*,
Vol. XXIX
Black, no white, height: 12 hands, foaled 1921
Breeder: H. Meyrick Jones, Mathrafal, Meifod,
Montgomeryshire
Sire: Mathrafal Wampus 1066
Dam: 7939 Mathrafal Ritaway (a well-known show
mare later in the ownership of Lord Swansea) (foaled
in 1912) by Mathrafal Cupid 646

The sire, Mathrafal Wampus was a dark brown stallion with black points used at Mathrafal until 1922 when he was sold on the Craven Arms Welsh Pony & Cob Society Sale for 39 guineas. Wampus during this period sired Mathrafal Cupid, Empress and Kit Kat but the best known of his progeny (full sister to Mathrafal Vulture) foaled in 1922 was sold as a youngster to Mrs. Greene and registered as Grove Wampa: a mare who has had a big influence on the breed, she was sold on the 1927 Grove Dispersal Sale to go to Dinarth Hall where she produced such good winners as Dinarth Lady Love (bought on the

Brierwood Honey, Champion of the 1956 Royal Welsh Show. G-g-sire Mathrafal Tuppence. G-g-dam (four times over) Mathrafal Mistress by Mathrafal Vulture. (Photograph courtesy of Capt. L. B. Brierley.)

Dinarth Dispersal Sale by my grandfather, Mr. L. O. Williams) then Wampa went to the Craven Stud, being purchased at the Craven Sale by Mrs. Pennell who showed her at the 1937 National Pony Society Show then sold her to Criban where she appeared at her third Stud Sale to go to Capt. Howson who bred Revel Wampus and Revel Bluebird out of her; two very influential stallions both in the United Kingdom and the U.S.A. Despite so many changes of ownership, Grove Wampa proved her worth at Stud and her blood and that of her brother

Mathrafal Vulture flows in the veins of many of our present-day best ponies (that of Vulture mainly through his daughter Mathrafal Mistress–Brierwood Stud).

9. Mathrafal Empress

Registration number 8576 in the *Welsh Stud Book,*
Vol. XXIX
Black, height: 12 hands, foaled 1919
Breeder: H. Meyrick Jones, Mathrafal, Meifod,
Montgomeryshire
Sire: Mathrafal Wampus 1066
Dam: 3528 Mathrafal Slippery Ann by Trannon
Hero 9

It will be seen that Empress was mated to her half-brother to produce Mathrafal Vim; nothing else was registered as being the progeny of Mathrafal Empress.

10. Kilhendre Celtic Silverlight (*chapter 6.12*)

11. Mary of Llanfechain

Registration number 9057 in the *Welsh Stud Book,*
Vol. XXXII
Bay, height: 12 hands, foaled 1914
Breeder: C. P. Owen, High Street, Llanfyllin,
Montgomeryshire

Mary of Llanfechain, although foaled in 1914 was not registered until *Vol. XXXII* of the *Welsh Stud Book (1939–1948)* by which time she was possibly dead, but nevertheless she was registered so that her progeny could be registered.

She was a winner of numerous prizes at Montgomeryshire shows, particularly in jumping classes!

Her sire, Prince of Cardiff (*chapter 6.8*) was also g-g-sire of Coed Coch Glyndwr; he was foaled in 1895 and was registered also (number 7226) in the *Hackney Stud Book.*

The dam of Mary of Llanfechain was 4222 Pentre Kitty, a brown mare foaled in 1910; both her parents having been foaled in 1897, her sire being George Horace (*Vol. I, Welsh Stud Book* and number 6755 *Hackney Stud Book*) owned by Mr. Forrester Addie of Powis Castle Park and bred by Sir Gilbert Greenall, Bart.

12. Criban Shot

Registration number 1276 in the *Welsh Stud Book,*
Vol. XXIV
Chesnut, star, three white socks, height: 12 hands
1 in, foaled 1920
Breeder: H. W. Richards, Brynhyfryd,
Talybont-on-Usk, Brecon

Criban Shot was sired by the blue roan Criban Kid who was by Criban Orion (brown, foaled 1912) described by Mrs. Pennell as having minute ears and enormous eyes. Criban Shot's dam was Criban Chesnut Swell (foaled in 1912) who was by Ystrad Klondyke by the noted Klondyke, (foaled in 1921) *Vol. I* of the *Welsh Stud Book* owned by my mother's uncle, John Thomas of Trerddol.

Criban Shot soon began winning prizes in the show ring including first prizes at Bedwellty and Devynock in 1921, and another first prize at Devynock in 1922. In 1924, Criban Shot won a first prize and the Welsh Pony & Cob Society medal at the Royal Welsh Show held at Bridgend and judged by Mr. W. Arthur Pughe of the Gwyndy Stud. The same year he won first prizes also at Talgarth, Devynock and Brecon.

Criban Shot's career at stud and in the show rings of Wales was cut

Criban Shot.

"Forest" ponies owned by Mr. W. S. Miller, Forest Lodge, Brecon, photographed about 1895. Photograph: Welsh Stud Book, Vol. I *(1902).*

short when he was exported to America in 1926. However he had been on the Welsh hills long enough to make his mark at stud, the Richards family saying that his best progeny was his chesnut son Criban Shot Again (foaled in 1924 out of Bwlch Starlight, again by Klondyke), who was sold to the Heyl Pony Farm of Illinois in 1930. Shot Again had a very great influence on the Welsh Pony of America siring such as Mr. John Tolan's Criban Monarch and Criban Grand Master.

13. Criban Busy Bee
Registration number 7963 in the *Welsh Stud Book, Vol. XXIV*
Brown, height: 12 hands 1 in, foaled 1920
Breeder: H. W. Richards, Brynhyfryd,
Talybont-on-Usk

Criban Busy Bee and Criban Shot had much in common: they were both foaled in 1920, they were both sired by Criban Kid and they both won first prizes at the 1921 Bedwellty Show. Therefore when they were mated in 1922, it followed that the progeny, Criban Bumble Bee had to be a good one!

Criban Baylight, dam of Busy Bee was foaled in 1914 and she was sired by Invincible Taffy who lived up to his name and became one of the most outstanding ponies of his day. Although under 12 hands, he was hunted by Mr. Dick Richards when a boy and he could jump like a stag, no day seemed too long for him. His name appears in the pedigrees of many of the well-known Criban riding pony champions.

15. Criban Forest Lass

Registration number 8267 in the *Welsh Stud Book*,
Vol. XXV
Bay, small star, height: 11 hands 3 in, foaled 1918
Breeder: W. S. Miller, Forest Lodge, Brecon

Mr. Miller had the largest pony stud in the United Kingdom around this time. Olive Tilford Dargan writing in the book *The Welsh Pony* (Boston, 1913) says: "At Forest Lodge I saw four hundred ponies freshly home from a winter sojourn on the hills near Aberystwyth".

Most ponies when turned out on the open hills (if reared on the same hills) will stick to their own areas. Forest Lass was prone to wander, presumably attracted to the smart Criban Shot and when she produced a foal by him in 1926, Mr. Richards bought her and her foal for the Criban Stud.

Forest Lass was of the best "Forest" blood. Her sire Forest Jehu sired some very good ponies in South Wales e.g. Blanche Black Bess and then went on the Bowdler Stud in Church Stretton where he proved a very valuable sire. His sire Forest Mountain Model had previously spent some years at Bowdler and when the stud had sufficient of his daughters, he was sold on at the 1922 Welsh Pony & Cob Society Craven Arms Sale (lot 23). Forest Lass's dam was called Forest Stranger Lass and she was a grand-daughter to the influential Forest Adbolton Sir Horace bred in 1900 by Mr. A. W. Hickling in Nottingham and registered also in the *Hackney Stud Book* (sired by the unbeaten Hackney Sir Horace).

10

Coed Coch Serliw foaled 1933
Coed Coch Seirian foaled 1937
Coed Coch Madog foaled 1947

1	2	4	8

	2	4	8
1	**2**	**4**	**8**
Coed Coch Madog 1981	Coed Coch Seryddwr 1716	Coed Coch Glyndwr 1617	Revolt 493
			9 8683 Dinarth Henol
		5 9047 Coed Coch Seirian	**10** Bowdler Baron II 1438
			11 8888 Coed Coch Serliw
3 9171 Coed Coch Mefusen		**4** Coed Coch Glyndwr	**8** Revolt 493
			9 8683 Dinarth Henol
		7 7347 Grove Madcap	**14** Bleddfa Shooting Star 73
			15 5159 Grove Lightheart

1. Coed Coch Madog
Registration number 1981 in the *Welsh Stud Book*,
Vol. XXXIV
Light grey, dark mane, tail and points, four white
legs, height: 11 hands 3 in, foaled 1947
Breeder: Miss M. Brodrick, Coed Coch, Abergele

Coed Coch Madog was not a particularly impressive foal; in fact he did not live up to expectations and was sold to Mr. Owen Ellis of the Hendre Stud. I first saw him with Mr. Ellis at the Caernarfon Show on 26th August 1950 where he stood last out of six stallions (class 20). We won the class with Dinarth What Ho but since What Ho was then eighteen years old, we were on the lookout for a younger stallion and were offered Madog for £25. Sadly to say, we were not impressed! His connections did not hold out much hope at that time for him either since he had not been registered (he was not registered until 1951, his registration number of 1981 was after such as Coed Coch Seraph 1959, foaled in 1950). Anyway he was bought back by Miss Brodrick, registered, and we were told that he was going for export. However, after returning to Coed Coch, he came on so well that it was decided to keep him for a while longer and he appeared at the Shropshire and West Midland Show on 23rd May 1951.

Mr. John Berry was the judge that day and Madog stood second to Mr. T. Norman Lewis' Eryri Gwyndaf (that we had had at Talybont for 1947/1948) followed by Lord Kenyon's Coed Coch Serenllys, Mr. T. Norman Lewis' second string Ceulan Revelry, Mr. R. T. Evans' Craven Daylight, Miss de Beaumont's Wentworth Golden Star, Mrs. Chadwick's Coed Coch Socyn and Mr. R. T. Evans again with Derwen Brightlight (in that order). Madog looked so magnificent that day that we immediately rushed off and offered Miss Brodrick £250 for him but alas he was not for sale!

After Shrewsbury that year, Madog won six first prizes at National Shows including the Championships at the Royal Agricultural Society of England and the Three Counties and the Male Championship and Reserve Supreme Championship (to his stable-mate Coed Coch Siaradus) at the Royal Welsh Show. For the next twelve years or so, Coed Coch Madog remained virtually unbeaten. We beat him into second place with Dinarth What Ho at the 1952 Royal Welsh Show; then the following year at Cardiff, Madog was first with What Ho second and What Ho died in 1953. From then on, his defeats were very rare; he was beaten once by Bolgoed Atomic at Shewsbury and once by

*Coed Coch Madog
in action.*

Royal Reveller at Cowbridge, his son Coed Coch Planed beat him for
the Male Championship at the 1954 Royal Welsh Show and he was
beaten into third place by Bowdler Brewer and Coed Coch Socyn at the
1961 Royal Welsh Show. Between 1951 and 1962, Coed Coch Madog
set up a record by winning the Royal Welsh Show Male Championship

The combined winnings during 1954 of Coed Coch Madog and Coed Coch Siaradus.

on no fewer than nine occasions; although he was invariably beaten by the females when it came to the Supreme award.

Altogether Coed Coch Madog amassed the enormous record of 139 first prizes, 63 Championships and 53 other cups and medals, including Championships at Shropshire and West Midland (four times), Three Counties (three times) Bath and West, Cheshire (twice), Royal Agricultural Society of England (ten times), Royal Welsh Male Champion (nine times) and National Pony Show (three times).

But it is not as a show winner that the name of Coed Coch Madog will go down in Welsh Mountain Pony history but as a sire of the calibre of Dyoll Starlight and Coed Coch Glyndwr; sires which unfortunately only appear four or five times in a century. An indication of the influence which he has had on the breed can be obtained from a study of the multitude of successes of his progeny at our major show i.e. the Royal Welsh Show.

As already quoted his son, Coed Coch Planed (*chapter 26.8*) owned by Lord Kenyon as a two-year-old won the Male Championship at the 1954 Machynlleth Show. His daughter Coed Coch Pelydrog, possibly

Coed Coch Siglen Las, Champion Stallion Royal Welsh Shows 1965 and 1966 with Mr. Jack Havard. Sire Coed Coch Madog. (Photograph courtesy of Photonews.)

the most elegantly beautiful of all Madog's progeny was Champion female in 1964 and 1965. In 1965 also the Male Champion was Madog's son, the small but very correct and spectacular moving Coed Coch Siglen Las who was Male Champion also in 1966. Coed Coch Pryd (son of Madog) was Male Champion at the 1969 Show; he was full-brother to Pelydrog but unfortunately died when still quite young.

Female Champion that year (1969) was the small but lovely Coed Coch Swyn, sired by Coed Coch Glyndwr (*chapter 6.1*) when he was twenty-three years old, from Coed Coch Siwan one of the best-known daughters of Coed Coch Madog. Siwan twice won first prizes at the Royal Welsh Show, she once was the Reserve for Frederick's Horse of the Year qualifier and twice won at the National Pony Show. Siwan was also dam of Coed Coch Shon (himself thrice winner at the Royal Welsh and sire of another Royal Welsh Champion Coed Coch Norman) which I saw in great shape in Denmark in 1977 and 1978. Coed Coch Swyn has really set the world alight with her progeny: Coed Coch Marli (sire of the many-times Champion Bengad Welsh Poppy), and the two Coed Coch Sale toppers: Coed Coch Bari and Coed Coch Saled.

An example of the usage of Coed Coch Madog on outside blood was the production of Rowfant Prima Ballerina, female Champion at the 1970 Show (later exported to Australia), her dam was bred by my uncle Evan Davies from his little mare Gwen Tafarn Jem by Shimdda Hir Sprightly Shot, son of Vardra Sunflower (*chapter 8.7*). Coed Coch Norman (above) was 1971 Male Champion before he too went to Australia (Owendale Stud). Gredington Simwnt, Male Champion in 1972 and 1973 was a half-brother × half-sister cross, being by Madog out of Coed Coch Symwl (female Champion in 1960 and another daughter of Coed Coch Seryddwr).

On these two occasions, Gredington Simwnt was accompanied for female championships by (1972) a Madog grand-daughter, Dyfrdwy

Gredington Simwnt, Champion Stallion Royal Welsh Shows 1972 and 1973, with Mr. Gordon Jones. Sire Coed Coch Madog. Dam: Coed Coch Symwl by Coed Coch Seryddwr.

161

Midnight Moon, daughter of Coed Coch Planed and in 1973 by a Madog daughter, the lovely Coed Coch Glenda who was purchased by the Hon. Mrs. Patterson at the Coed Coch Dispersal Sale.

Madog's g-son, Coed Coch Bari was 1974 Royal Welsh Champion and Reserve Lloyd's Bank Horse of the Year qualifier (as well that year he was first at West Midland stallion Show, Bath and West, Cheshire, and National Pony Society, with seven Championships in 1975, another seven in 1976 and three in 1977). He has gone down in history as setting the all-time record price when Lady Creswick paid 21,000 guineas for him at the memorable 1978 Dispersal Sale.

The 1974 Female Champion, Mrs. Gadsden's Bengad Love in the Mist is a Madog grand-daughter, her dam being Melai Melody by Madog. The Dutch-bred Rondeels Pengwyn was 1975 Male Champion, his sire, Twyford Thunder is a Madog grand-son and his dam Coed Coch Pwffiad is a Madog daughter. The 1976 Female Champion, Valley Lake Breeze (since exported to the Owendale Stud, Australia) has Madog as three grand-sires, her sire, Coed Coch Glynlws is by Salsbri out of Siwan and the dam Fieldcot Vivandiere is by Twyford Grenadier (by Madog).

Finally at the 1978 Show, the Male Champion Aston Super Star traces to Madog through his sire (Whatton Pennaeth, son of Melai Priscilla daughter of Madog) and through his dam (Dyfrdwy Midnight Moon, daughter of Planed). The Female Champion Bengad Day Lily is a daughter of Glenfield Dawn, daughter of Madog.

Two and three-year-old colts at the 1960 Royal Welsh Show. From the left Twyford Grenadier by Coed Coch Madog, Coed Coch Siglen Las by Coed Coch Madog, Twyford Mark and Coed Coch Salsbri by Coed Coch Madog.

It is thus seen that it is very difficult to find a champion who does not race back one way or another to the great Coed Coch Madog. He died in May 1978 at the age of thirty-one years but his blood is well-and-truly spread throughout the world; obviously extensively used at the Coed Coch Stud but also as an outcross into other studs e.g. Twyford Grenadier in Sussex, Pendock Puccini in mid-Wales and the U.S.A., Brierwood Fudge dam of the successful Brierwood Full-Back etc.

2. Coed Coch Seryddwr
Registration number 1716 in the *Welsh Stud Book,*
Vol. XXXII
Grey-roan, white near hind sock, height:
11 hands foaled 1943
Owner and Breeder: Miss M. Brodrick,
Coed Coch, Abergele

Seryddwr was not shown very extensively but in 1947 he won a second prize at the Bath and West, first at the Denbigh and Flint, a Welsh Pony & Cob Society medal at the Quorn Hunt Pony Club Show and a third prize at Chester. The last time I saw him was at the 1948 Shropshire and West Midland Show where, with Capt. T. A. Howson judging, he stood fourth in the stallion class to Mr. Holden's Tregoyd Starlight (*chapter 3.1*), Mr. R. J. Jones' Whitehall Monarch and Mr. T. Norman Lewis' Ceulan Revelry. It is interesting to note that (with Miss de Beaumont's Wentworth Golden Star standing fifth) his full-brother Coed Coch Sidi, in the ownership of Mrs. Cuff stood sixth. Sidi, unfortunately died very soon afterwards otherwise he could well have been the great success at Stud which Seryddwr was. Seryddwr's other prizes in 1948 being fourth at the Bath and West and a second at Chester. Unfortunately for the breed in the United Kingdom he was exported in October 1948 to Mrs. R. J. Lasbrey, Badgemore Farm, Cape Province, South Africa where we are told he had a profound effect on the pony breeding of that country; he died in 1965 at the age of twenty-two years.

Again unfortunately in the United Kingdom he was not used very extensively at stud, apart from Madog (foaled in 1947) there seems to be only Coed Coch Perl (1947 from Pioden), Symwl (1948 from Sensigl) and a Foundation stock mare Lucky F.S.1 from Periwinkle F.S. His full-brother, a year younger, Coed Coch Sidi, was sold by Miss Brodrick

Coed Coch Seryddwr photographed in South Africa in 1962 when 19 years old.

to the Lady Wentworth who sold him to Mr. Tom Jones Evans of the Craven Stud (who used him successfully and showed him a little) who then sold him to Mrs. Cuff of the Downland Stud where he was very influential e.g. sire of Downland Lavender.

3. Coed Coch Mefusen
Registration number 9171 in the *Welsh Stud Book,*
Vol. XXXII
Grey, four white fetlocks, height: 11 hands,
foaled 1943
Owner and Breeder: Miss M. Brodrick,
Coed Coch, Abergele

I first saw Coed Coch Mefusen at the 1946 Shropshire and West Midland Show where my father placed her second in a very large mixed youngstock class to Craven Toscanini (*chapter 7.5*). Writing in the *Shropshire Journal*, my father describes her as "a very nice filly" and he thought she would make a top-class show mare. Mefusen re-appeared the following year in the barren mare or gelding class at this show where she stood sixth to Craven Lymm, Gatesheath Moonlight, Capt. Brierley's Misty, the gelding Coed Coch Powys (later a famous riding

164

pony Champion), and Coed Coch Trysor but I see from my father's marking that he would have placed Misty first and Mefusen second.

This was the show where the legendary Coed Coch Siaradus appeared also; placed fourth in her class, my father thought she too was rather harshly treated!

Altogether in 1946, Mefusen won first prizes at the Denbigh and Flint, Llangefni (best light horse in Show), and Llanrwst, with second prize at Abergele and thirds at Bodedern and the Quorn.

Coed Coch Mefusen was exported to Mr. Frank Ross, Vancouver, British Columbia in November 1948 having produced only two colt foals in this country. When one realises that these two were Coed Coch Madog and the 1950 Royal Welsh Show Champion Coed Coch Meilyr, one wonders how many more Champions she might have produced had she stayed in the United Kingdom.

Meilyr followed his dam overseas in June 1953 when he went to Mr. George Fernley's well-known stud in Plymouth Meeting, Pennsylvania where he continued his winning ways.

4. Coed Coch Glyndwr (*chapter 6.1*)

5. Coed Coch Seirian
Registration number 9047 in *Welsh Stud Book, Vol. XXXI*
Grey, height: 11 hands 1 in, foaled 1937

Coed Coch Seirian was the first foal of her dam, Coed Coch Serliw and she remained at Coed Coch when her dam was sold (top of the Sale at 63 guineas) on the Coed Coch Sale in August 1937.

The next time that Seirian and Serliw met was at the 1949 Royal Welsh Show where Serliw stood first with Seirian second in an enormous brood mare class, brimful of many winners. In the absence of Serliw, Seirian was Champion at the 1948 Royal Agricultural Society of England Show at York as well as many other prizes and championships in the ownership of Miss Brodrick up until 1953 then many more prizes for Lord Kenyon. As an outstanding brood mare, Seirian produced three by Glyndwr: Seryddwr (1943), Sidi (1944) and Sidan (1946); two by Tanybwlch Berwyn: Samswn (1945) and the often-times Section "B" Champion Silian (1947), Seren Aur (by Wentworth Golden Star in 1952) and Siwan (by Madog in 1953; dam of Shon, and Swyn etc). Afterwards (1954, 1955 and 1961) Seirian produced another three by Madog viz Gredington Ianto, Gredington Llewellyn and Gredington

Coed Coch Seirian.

Seirion. Her other three foals being Gredington Meirydd and Oriana by Planed (1956 and 1958) and Gredington Rhinfawr (1960 by Revel Curio).

Gredington Ianto was a brilliant chesnut stallion who, after siring Criban Pep, Criban Clipper, Criban Columbus, Criban Crofter, Criban Idris, Criban Fay and Criban Feebee for Mr. Llewellyn Richards, was exported to the Kelvin Grove Stud in Oregon, U.S.A. Gredington Llewelyn sired some excellent stock for Mr. Tom Parry of the Gurnos Stud then for Messrs. Williams and Garrett at the Deri Stud. Seirion and Rhinfawr were also successful sires in South Wales. Meirydd followed Coed Coch Meilyr to the Crefeld Stud, U.S.A. Gredington Oriana is a very good mare for the Glenfield Stud producing Glenfield Silver Wings, Glenfield Monarch, Glenfield Oberon, Glenfield Giselle (dam of twice Lloyds Bank qualifier Glenfield Chocolate Soldier) etc. Sidan was also a very beautiful mare who followed her dam to Gredington and in addition to winning many important awards, produced excellent breeders, perhaps the most famous of which was Gredington Hynod.

Coed Coch Sidan, daughter of Coed Coch Seirian, with her owner Lord Kenyon

7. Grove Madcap
Registration number 7347 in the *Welsh Stud Book,*
Vol. XXII
Light grey, blaze, white off fore coronet and both
hind fetlocks, height: 10 hands 1 in, foaled 1921
Owner and Breeder: Mrs. H. D. Greene, The Grove,
Craven Arms

Grove Madcap had been sold before the 1927 Grove Dispersal Sale.

In the immediate pre-war years, she was the Coed Coch Show mare winning a third prize at the 1938 Royal Welsh Show behind Mr. Matthew Williams' Vardra Charm (*chapter 8.3*) and Mr. T. Jones Evans' Gatesheath Dainty (*chapter 14.14*). Capt. T. A. Howson who judged on this occasion wrote in the *Journal*: "Miss Brodrick's seventeen-year-old grey Grove Madcap is still a charming mare in many ways though age is telling on her now".

The following year with the Royal Welsh Show at Caernarfon, she was again third, this time to Mr. J. B. Holden's Vardra Sunflower (*chapter 8.7*) and Miss Clodagh Miller's Bowdler Boadicea.

Grove Madcap did not breed very many at Coed Coch considering the years that she spent there; apart from Mefusen (foaled 1943 by Coed Coch Glyndwr) there were only the mare Coed Coch Morwyf (foaled in 1937, by Coed Coch Emlyn) and the stallion Coed Coch Marchog (foaled 1940 by Mathrafal Tuppence) a stallion which was sold to Mr. Peter Jones in Anglesey but later spent the greater part of his life in the North of England, occasionally coming to compete at North Wales Shows.

8. Revolt (*chapter 6.2*)

9. Dinarth Henol (*chapter 6.3*)

10. Bowdler Baron II
Registration number 1438 in the *Welsh Stud Book,*
Vol. XXVIII
Grey, four white legs, height: 11 hands 2 in,
foaled 1924
Owner and Breeder: George Preece, Hope Bowdler,
Church Stretton

Bowdler Baron II was sired by Stanage Daylight (a member of that marvellous family of full-brothers and sisters by Dyoll Starlight out of Star I by Merlyn Myddfai; Merlyn Myddfai being one of the first stallions to be exported to Australia).

Bowdler Baron's dam was the brown mare Bowdler Birdie by Forest Mountain Model. Three Coed Coch mares were sent to Bowdler stallions in 1936, Coed Coch Seren to Bowdler Brightlight (*chapter 7.8*) producing Sirius, Seren's sister Coed Coch Ebrill, also to Brightlight (producing Eurliw Goch) and Seren's daughter Serliw to Bowdler Baron II (producing Seirian).

Bowdler Baron II won a third prize at the 1925 Church Stretton Show and a seventh premium at the 1928 Church Stretton Stallion show where the judges (Capt. J. D. D. Evans and Lt. Col. Loch) described him as "nice action but a rather small pony".

11. Coed Coch Serliw
Registration number 8888 in the *Welsh Stud Book*,
Vol. XXX
Red roan, two white hind socks, height: 11 hands
3½ in, foaled 1933
Breeder: Miss M. Brodrick, Coed Coch, Abergele
Photograph *Welsh Stud Book, Vol. XXXI, page 45*

It was a magnificent stroke of luck for the Welsh Mountain Pony breed that Miss Brodrick in the 'thirties decided to send some of her best mares to the aged Revolt to produce Ebrill (1933 from Eirlys), Eira (1933 from Enid), Rhyddid (1932 from Eiddwen), Serliw (1933 from Seren), Siwen (1934 from Shonet), Saturn (1935 from Seren), and Glyndwr (1935 from Dinarth Henol).

The dam of Serliw was the delightful brown mare Coed Coch Seren (Grove Sharp Shooter × Coed Coch Eirlys) who had won the Championship at the 1931 National Pony Society Show, the same year also first at the Royal Agricultural Society of England, Royal Welsh and Flint and Denbigh and again Champion at the National Pony Society Show in 1932 etc. Her photograph appears in the *Welsh Stud Book, Vol. XXX, page 39*. Coed Coch Eirlys, dam of Seren is described in the *Life Story of John Jones*, Coed Coch (1963 Welsh Pony & Cob Society Journal *page 45*) as "purchased by Miss Brodrick from a truckload of ponies in a siding at

Coed Coch Seren, photographed in 1931, dam of Coed Coch Serliw. (Photograph courtesy of G. H. Parsons.)

Coed Coch Serliw, with Mr. E. S. Davies.

Shrewsbury Station, she was a terrible mare. . . ." Looking up the original article written in the Welsh Language (Royal Welsh Agricultural Society journal, *Vol. XXX*) I see that it was not intended for her to be "a terrible mare" but "a very wild mare and difficult to break her in". In fact, Eirlys became one of the first of the Coed Coch show mares; her breeding being by Stretton Sweep and out of Brunslow.

Serliw was offered for sale on the Coed Coch Sale on 28th August 1937 having already won numerous prizes including first prizes at the 1935 Cheshire and Shropshire and West Midland Shows, and firsts at the 1936 Bath and West, Cheshire and Royal Welsh Shows. Serliw topped the sale at 63 guineas going to Mr. S. Walton of Leeds who also bought her dam Coed Coch Seren (lot 28), her sister Coed Coch Sirius (lot 25) her full-brother Coed Coch Saturn (lot 18) and half-brother Coed Coch Seon (lot 19) and her dam's sister Coed Coch Ebrill (lot 30) her paternal half-brother Coed Coch Glyndwr (lot 21) along with twenty-six others. It was fortunate for my father (who had failed to get to the first Sale on 28th August) that Mr. Walton had no land on which to keep any ponies (he had also bought cattle, implements etc) and father bought Serliw on Mr. Walton's Sale (held a fortnight later). My father was also under-bidder on Glyndwr and Ebrill, buying with Serliw a 14 hand riding pony gelding called Richard who had previously been shepherding with Mr. Llewellyn Richards on the Criban hills.

On the second sale Miss Brodrick bought back Coed Coch Glyndwr for herself and Coed Coch Seren for Mrs. Joan Mackay-Smith's famous Farnley Stud in Virginia, U.S.A. Both Seren and Serliw were in foal to Glyndwr, my father always proudly stating that he was the first to breed a pony sired by Glyndwr (Ceulan Revolt out of Serliw), Mrs. Mackay-Smith following very closely with Farnley Sirius (out of Seren) another magnificent red roan, champion over all breeds at the 1949 Timonium Show and sire of many champions including Farnley Gremlin, Farnley Sundance, Farnley Sunbeam etc. Coed Coch Sirius on the second sale was bought by Mr. T. J. Jones of Dinarth Hall who very suddenly passed away two days later and on the Dinarth Sale (on 27th October) Sirius was sold to Mr. Cyril Lewis (for 15½ guineas) later to produce the legendary Coed Coch Siaradus.

Almost as soon as Serliw came to Ceulan the war interrupted her showing career, but when it was over, her first major show was the 1948 Cheshire County Show (there was no Royal Welsh Show that year owing to petrol rationing) where (with Ceulan Serenader at foot) she

Royal Reveller, son of Coed Coch Serliw. Champion Mare at the 1949 Royal Welsh Show.

won the mare class with Mrs. Cuff's Craven Bright Sprite, Miss Brodrick's Coed Coch Mefusen (with Coed Coch Meilyr at foot) and seven others and eventually stood Reserve Champion to Mr. J. B. Holden's Tregoyd Starlight. She went one stage further at the 1949 Cheshire Show winning the Championship award, also best female and Reserve Championship (again to Tregoyd Starlight) at the Royal Welsh Show along with first prizes at Aberystwyth, Radnorshire, Montgomeryshire, Brecon, Pontardulais and other Mid-Wales Shows that year.

As regards the progeny of Coed Coch Serliw, Seirian (1937) and Ceulan Revolt (1938) have already been described. During the war years there were no Mountain Pony stallions available in mid-Wales; however, in 1942 Coed Coch Serliw was sent to Craven Arms to Craven Tit-Bit. This mating produced Ceulan Serene a nice, chesnut roan mare which was exported to Mrs. Illiff of Maryland, U.S.A. in January 1948. Her grey colt foal, Royal Reveller (sold to Maj. Careless of the "Royal" Stud (before he was registered) foaled in 1947 was by her grand-son Ceulan Revelry and he won many prizes for Maj. Careless and later at the major shows of the United Kingdom for the Penllyn Stud (Mrs. Homfray).

In 1948 and 1949 she produced two nice colt foals Ceulan Serenader and Ceulan Stardust by Eryri Gwyndaf and Tregoyd Starlight respectively, both good winners. For the following three years she was mated to Dinart What Ho producing Ceulan Serenade (winner of Championships), Ceulan Sonnet and Ceulan Shalimar all three of which unfortunately were exported to the U.S.A. but became well-known producers there. Serliw did not then produce anything until 1956 when she produced a riding pony stallion named Ceulan Golden Sovereign.

This family served well the premium scheme on the Welsh hills e.g. during 1955, Ceulan Revelry (Ceulan Revolt × Ceulan Silverleaf) won the first premium for Gower, his full-brother Ceulan Reveller won the first of eleven premiums for Eppynt with their sire Ceulan Revolt standing fourth (having previously won three premiums on the Black Mountains in the ownership of Mr. Emrys Griffiths) and Royal Reveller winning the first Premium for Llanafan and Llanwrthyl; four stallions which left their marks on their respective areas e.g. at the 1975 Royal Welsh Show both winning Mountain Pony mare and Champion Welsh Pony (Cob type) were foaled in the Gower area, both having Ceulan Revelry as grand-sire.

Serliw lived on as favourite of the family until she died at twenty-nine years old in June 1962; unfortunately too many of her progeny were exported but those that remained in the United Kingdom are proving their mettle, twenty-one of the fifty Royal Welsh Show Champions of the years 1947–1972 tracing back to her.

14. Bleddfa Shooting Star (*chapter 4.1*)

15. Grove Lightheart
Registration number 5159 in the *Welsh Stud Book*,
Vol. XV
Light grey, blaze, white near front pastern and
off fore coronet, height: 10 hands 2 in (as a year-
ling), foaled 1914
Owner and Breeder: Mrs. H. D. Greene,
The Grove, Craven Arms.
Sire: Dyoll Starlight
Dam: Bleddfa Tell Tale

Bleddfa Tell Tale (*chapter 3.15*) was one of Mrs. Greene's favourite mares (and one of the first to be purchased when the stud started in 1906). In 1913, Mrs. Greene was fortunate enough to be able to lease the great Dyoll Starlight himself (*chapter 2.1*) for four to five weeks and it was as a result of this short visit of Dyoll Starlight to the Grove, that Grove Lightheart was produced. Grove Lightheart was lot 1 of the Grove Dispersal Sale on 29th June 1927 where Capt. Dainty bought her (along with her filly foal by Bleddfa Shooting Star, later registered as Wentworth Flitaway) for 55 guineas for Lady Wentworth.

The Sale Catalogue lists the winnings of this great mare which include 1925: first and Champion National Pony Society Islington, second Royal Agricultural Society of England and first, medal and Challenge Cup beating all other breeds at the Royal Lancashire.

Mrs. Greene claimed Grove Lightheart to be "one of the most beautiful Pony Mares in existence".

11

**Touchstone of Sansaw foaled 1934
Dinas Moonstone foaled 1945**

1	2	4	8
9314 Dinas Moonstone	Coed Coch Glyndwr 1617	Revolt 493	Llwyn Tyrant 207
			9 — 145 Llwyn Flyaway
		5 — 8683 Dinarth Henol	10 — Llwyn Satan 1325
			11 — 6350 Irfon Marvel
	3 — 8962 Touchstone of Sansaw	6 — Grove Sprightly 1036	12 — Bleddfa Shooting Star 73
			13 — 4431 Grove Sprite II
		7 — 5782 Grove Limestone	12 — Bleddfa Sooting Star 73
			15 — 3002 Grove Limelight

1. Dinas Moonstone

Grey, height: 11 hands 3 in, foaled 1945
Breeder: Mrs. C. Armstrong-Jones, Coombe Place,
Lewes, Sussex
Owner: Miss Alison McNaught, East Mascalls,
Lindfield, Sussex (Mrs. Alison Mountain, Twyford
Farm, Horsted Keynes, Sussex)

Dinas Moonstone was bred by Mrs. Carol Armstrong-Jones (mother of Lord Snowdon) and was purchased by Mrs. Mountain as a yearling filly for £25. At the same time her father bought her dam Touchstone of Sansaw. Some mares go down in history for the prizes which they won; others are best remembered for what they produced. Dinas Moonstone was a very beautiful mare and, had she been shown extensively, I'm sure she would have made a name for herself in this field. However, it turned out that she had an in-born dislike for the show ring (on the one

Dinas Moonstone (right) with foal Twyford Mascot (foaled 1955) with (left) her son Twyford Moonshine (foaled in 1953) and (centre) her dam Touchstone of Sansaw.

177

Clan Marshall (foaled in 1949) son of Dinas Moonstone with the author.

occasion when she was persuaded to attend, she showed what she could do by winning a second prize in a very large class at the 1960 Royal Agricultural Society of England Show) and it was decided that the best place for her was in the home paddock where she produced a magnificent line of eight colts and eleven fillies!

Personally I have had great success with two sons of Dinas Moonstone and am proud to list her progeny below:

1949 Clan Marshall, colt, by Criban Pledge (Criban Pledge and his sire Criban Grey Grit *chapter 8.8*). Clan Marshall was sold to Mr. Llewellyn Richards of the Criban Stud from whom we bought him in 1953. During 1954 we won many prizes and Championships with him (including a second prize to Coed Coch Madog at the 1954 Royal Welsh Show at Machynlleth – a photograph of this class in *Welsh Champions, page 15*). Unfortunately at the end of the 1954 season we were persuaded to sell him to Mr. and Mrs. Canfield of the Merrie Mill Stud, Cobham, Virginia, U.S.A. along with a very good winning young mare Ceulan Serenade (Dinarth What Ho × Coed Coch Serliw) who was in foal to him. These two ponies became very well-known in the U.S.A., Serenade's 1955 foal being named Merrie Mill's Symphony and she was followed by another three full sisters who all became very influential in the American show ring and breeding circles.

1950 Clan Music, filly, by Coed Coch Glyndwr (*chapter 6.1*). Unfortunately Clan Music died of poisoning in 1963 but she was a very lovely mare and had won many prizes in hand and under saddle. She is represented at the Twyford Stud at present by her daughters Twyford Mazurka (a big winner foaled 1958 by Pendock Zenith) and Twyford Minuet (foaled 1960 by Twyford Grenadier) and Mazurka's two daughters: Twyford Magpie (a very elegant mare, winner of the novice brood mare class at the 1977 Royal Welsh Show, foaled 1970, sired by Twyford Gurkha), and Twyford Mazola (foaled 1975, sired by the young Twyford Buckle who is an outcross for the Twyford Stud being a son of Persie Buttons).

1952 Twyford Mistletoe, filly, by Clan Dana (Coed Coch Glyndwr × Wentworth Grey Dapples by Craven Cyrus – *chapter 14.13*). Clan Dana's bloodline has been very influential to the breed through his daughter, Clan Prue who produced the two Royal Welsh Show Champions Clan Pip and Clan Peggy. Clan Dana had an equally influential full-brother Clan Dubail

Clan Music (foaled in 1950), daughter of Dinas Moonstone.

Twyford Mazurka, daughter of Clan Music. (Photograph courtesy of Mrs. Alison Mountain.)

(Twyford, Llanerch, Escley Studs). Twyford Mistletoe was a very well-known winner in her younger days, amongst many good winnings being the Championship at the 1954 Bath and West Show. She lived all her life at Twyford, dying in 1975 and leaving behind at the Stud, her daughter Twyford Mica by Twyford Gamecock. She had 12 fillies and 3 colts and her offspring have gone all over the world.

1953 Twyford Moonshine, colt, by Coed Coch Glyndwr. Moonshine was for many years the senior Stud stallion at Twyford, then spent a few years at Mrs. Rimmington-Wilson's Rowfant Stud before being exported to Canada where he was very successful. He is still alive and well at the time of writing (1979).

1954 Twyford Myfanwy, filly, by Criban Pledge (*chapter 8.8 and photograph chapter 12*). This was another well-known show mare winning the Lord Arthur Cecil cup at the National Pony Show for the best female native pony of all breeds. One son of hers Twyford Mark (foaled 1957 by Twyford Moonshine) was a good winner in Wales when owned by Mr. Stephen Jones of the Dinas Stud, Aberystwyth and is now a popular sire in Holland where I saw him with Mr. Brugsma in 1979. Myfanwy died in 1976 but is represented at the Twyford Stud by her daughter Twyford Minerva (foaled 1962, sired by Twyford Grenadier).

1955 Twyford Mascot, colt, by Gredington Ffafryn.

1956 Twyford Mayfair, filly, by Dinarth Greylight. I was particularly interested in the Dinarth Greylight strain since he was sired by Ceulan Comet (*chapter 24.1*) out of Dinarth Darling who was also dam of Dinarth What Ho with which we had such enormous showing successes. It was gratifying to have some

Twyford Mistletoe (foaled in 1952) daughter of Dinas Moonstone photographed in 1973 with her foal Twyford Mica.

181

Twyford Moonshine (foaled in 1953) son of Dinas Moonstone.

well-known Australian breeders over in the United Kingdom during 1978 who were buying up all Dinarth Greylight descendants on the value which they placed on Ceulan Comet breeding. Twyford Mayfair was exported to Texas in 1957.

1958 Twyford Matador, colt. I first saw Matador as a little jet black colt foal with his mother at Twyford in 1958. When I bought him from Mrs. Matthews of the old-established Harford Stud in Devon on 7th May 1965 he had become a light grey. In 1968 we had his daughters of breeding age and sold him on the Fayre Oaks Sale to Mr. Charles Edwards of the Vyrnwy Stud at Llanfechain in Montgomeryshire. Of the three full-brothers and full-sister, Matador, Moonshine and Music, Matador was higher on the leg the other two being heavier in bone with all three being brimful of quality. Matador for us produced over 80 per cent fillies, usually dark greys but they lightened with age, they invariably had superb temperaments and many became outstanding children's riding ponies. I saw three of them being ridden in Denmark during the summer of 1978.

1960 Twyford Merlin, colt, sired by Coed Coch Socyn (one of the earliest sons of Coed Coch Glyndwr who was still going strong when he died in 1978 at thirty-four years old).

1961 Twyford Minx, filly, by Twyford Grenadier (Coed Coch Madog × Twyford Gala who was by Coed Coch Glyndwr from another of the original brood mares of Twyford: Wee Georgette who was still alive in 1978 at thirty). Twyford Minx was exported to Mr. Henderson of Australia.

1962 Twyford Mayday, filly, again by Twyford Grenadier. She was kept at Twyford until breeding age and was sold in-foal but unfortunately died as the result of an accident.

Twyford Mark, son of Twyford Myfanwy (foaled in 1954) daughter of Dinas Moonstone.

Twyford Matador (foaled in 1958), son of Dinas Moonstone.

1963 Twyford Moonlight, filly, by Clan Dubail (full-brother to Clan Dana). Moonlight was originally sold to the Isle of Wight but now bought back to keep the strain going at Twyford.

1964 Twyford Merrythought, filly, again by Clan Dubail, sold to Holland (to Mr. Brugsma in 1971) and winning and producing winners for him. I saw her there in 1979 and she is a very lovely mare.

1965 Twyford Monarch, colt, by Twyford Grenadier. Monarch had a successful showing season as a yearling (including a second prize at the 1966 Royal Welsh Show under Mr. Llewellyn Richards). He was then sold to Holland (where he did not find favour) later coming back to England only to be re-exported to Australia where he has been Champion Welsh Mountain Pony several times at major shows (owned by the Fairway Stud, in Victoria), and is a very successful sire.

1966 Twyford Magnum, colt, by Coed Coch Asa (Gredington Hynod × Coed Coch Anwyled by Coed Coch Glyndwr). Twyford Magnum returned to Wales where he is owned by Mr. J. James.

1967 Twyford Marquis, colt, again sired by Coed Coch Asa. Marquis was sold as a foal to New Zealand (to Mrs. Deans) and he has been a very influential sire there.

1968 Twyford Moonbeam, filly, by Twyford Gamecock (Twyford Grenadier × Wee Georgette). Moonbeam has been retained at Twyford and is one of their most valued brood mares.

1969 Twyford Monsoon, filly, by Twyford Gurkha (Twyford Puzzle × Twyford Gala; Twyford Puzzle being by Twyford Moonshine and out of Coed Coch Pwffiad by Coed Coch Madog). Monsoon is also retained at Twyford.

1970 Twyford Moorhen, filly, by Twyford Gamecock. Moorhen was sold as a foal to Mr. and Mrs. Hicks of the Valley Lake Stud which is quite near to Twyford, then sold to Mrs. Mather in

Twyford Merrythought (foaled in 1964), daughter of Dinas Moonstone. (Photograph courtesy of Ellen van Leeuwen [Holland].)

Cheshire. Moorhen was the last foal which Dinas Moonstone had. She had been a very healthy mare all her life but on the 17th March 1971 at the age of twenty-six she suffered a stroke and had to be put down. Looking through this long list of wonderful animals which she produced, she certainly deserves her place in this or any other book on the Welsh breeds. She produced nothing but grey foals, mostly born black and with few markings.

2. Coed Coch Glyndwr (*chapter 6.1*)

3. Touchstone of Sansaw
Registration number 8962 in the *Welsh Stud Book,
Vol. XXXI*, Photograph in *Welsh Stud Book,
Vol. XXXVIII, page 55*
Grey, height: 11 hands 2 in, foaled 1934
Breeder: Mrs. E. M. Campbell, Sansaw, Clive,
Shrewsbury
Owners: (1936) Miss M. Brodrick, Coed Coch,
Abergele
(1937) Mrs. Inge. The Plas, Tanybwlch, Merioneth
Later: Mrs. C. Armstrong-Jones, Coombe Place,
Lewes, Sussex

Touchstone of Sansaw was bred by Mrs. Campbell of the Sansaw Stud (who under her previous name of Mrs. Brian Bibby had been breeding and exhibiting Welsh Mountain Ponies since 1926 e.g. Kilhendre Celtic Myfanwy, Gatesheath Magic, Grove Limestone etc).

Mrs. Campbell sold Touchstone to Miss Brodrick who included her on the Coed Coch first Sale on 28th August 1937 (lot 31). Touchstone was one of only four out of the entire Sale (total of 35) not bought by Mr. Walton. Touchstone was purchased by Mrs. Inge for 34 guineas. Miss Brodrick described her as "a young mare with quite sensational action."

In 1946, when she was sold by Mrs. Armstrong-Jones to Mr. McNaught of the Clan Stud she had at foot a colt foal by Coed Coch Glyndwr which was sold to Mr. Emrys Griffiths of the Revel Stud and later registered as Revel Hailstone. Hailstone was an exceptionally successful sire at the Revel (siring e.g. the 1962 Royal Welsh Show Champion Revel Jewel) before being exported to Australia. Mr. McNaught then sold Touchstone of Sansaw to Miss Ann Lumsden where she produced Mountain Yaffel and Mountain Tess in 1952 and 1953 (both sired by Wee Cream Cupid=Criban Cockade × Cnewr Chestnut Lass) and Mountain Stone by Llanerch Squirrel in 1955. I took some photographs of Mountain Tess at the Revel, she was a particularly nice mare producing such as Revel Martina (1960), Revel Melba (1959, Mrs. Meecham-Jones), Revel Memo (1966), Revel Muslin (1958), Revel Mosaic (1965, Knighton Stud). Touchstone of Sansaw was exported to the U.S.A. by Miss Lumsden in 1955 when she was twenty-one years of age; so highly-prized did the Americans value her blood-lines.

As her photograph shows, Touchstone was a real "hill" type, low and deep with big, bold eyes. Her daughter, Dinas Moonstone and Moonstone's family were bigger, more "scopey" and sometimes lighter in bone, though of course this depended to what stallion Moonstone was put.

4. Revolt (*chapter 6.2*)

5. Dinarth Henol (*chapter 6.3*)

6. Grove Sprightly (*chapter 5.1*)

7. Grove Limestone
Registration number 5782 in the *Welsh Stud Book,*
Vol. XVII
Re-registered *Vol. XXIX, page 40*
Light grey, white near fore coronet and hind heel,
height: 10 hands 2 in, foaled 1916
Owner and Breeder: Mrs. H. D. Greene, Grove,
Craven Arms

Grove Limestone was kept on at the Grove Stud as a foal when her dam, the big winner Grove Limelight was sold on the August 1916 Grove Sale. At the 1925 Royal Welsh Show Limestone had changed her named to Pistyll Limestone and in the ownership of David Morgan, Trefwtial, Cardigan won a third prize to Irfon Marvel (*chapter 6.7*) and Bohemian Girl (Vardra Stud).

By 1927, she had reverted to her original name and was owned by Mrs. Brian Bibby of the Sansaw Stud and she won some good prizes in this ownership e.g. first prize at the 1929 Royal Agricultural Society of England Show at Harrogate.

Grove Limelight, photographed in 1912 with foal by Grove Starshine.

In addition to her winning ways, Limestone produced some influential progeny, Pumice Stone of Sansaw in 1929, Lodestone of Sansaw (by Faraam Mercury) in 1931, Touchstone of Sansaw in 1934 and Tywysfaen of Sansaw in 1935 (who was lot 23 at the 1937 Coed Coch Sale). Lodestone was a good Premium stallion in South Wales for many years e.g. Fairwood Common (Gower) 1935–1938 and Pengwern Common (Gower) 1939 and 1940. Touchstone and Tywysfaen were both sired by Grove Sprightly, in these cases, both sire and dam being sired by Bleddfa Shooting Star (*chapter 4.1*). Touchstone of Sansaw made her mark at the 1962 Royal Welsh Show when Revel Jewel sired by Revel Hailstone son of Touchstone won the Female Championship. Tywysfaen similarly made his mark at the 1954 Royal Welsh Show via his son Snowdon Tywysog sire of Ankerwycke Snowdon who was dam of the female Champion Ankerwycke Clan Snowdon. Tywysfaen was also sire of Snowdon Arian II who was dam of some of the most famous of the Coed Coch Ponies such as Coed Coch Brenin Arthur (Foxhunter

188

Stud) and Coed Coch Anwyled, winner of 10 Championships including Cheshire, Three Counties, Shrewsbury, Bath and West, Royal Agricultural Society of England, National Pony Show, and Frederick's Qualifier when Supreme Champion at the Ponies of Britain Show.

8. Llwyn Tyrant (*chapter 6.4*)

9. Llwyn Flyaway (*chapter 6.5*)

10. Llwyn Satan (*chapter 6.6*)

11. Irfon Marvel (*chapter 6.7*)

12. Bleddfa Shooting Star (*chapter 4.1*)

13. Grove Sprite II (*chapter 5.3*)

15. Grove Limelight
Registration number 3002 in the *Welsh Stud Book, Vol. XII*
(Originally registered as 3002 Emlyn Grey Star in the *Welsh Stud Book, Vol. X*)
Grey, white near fore and both hind legs, height: 11 hands 3½ in, foaled 1908
Breeder: J. Lloyd Morgan, Rhiwfelin, Abergwili, Carmarthenshire
Owner in 1911: David Evans and Sons, Llwyncadfor Stud Farm, Henllan, Cardiganshire
Owner in 1913: Mrs. H. D. Greene, The Grove, Craven Arms
Sire: Dyoll Starlight (*chapter 2.1*)
Dam: Lady Greylight (foaled 1903) by Greylight
G-dam: Puss (foaled 1896) by Honesty.

Grove Limelight followed into the winning ways of her dam Lady Greylight (dam also of Wentworth Springlight) by winning a first prize at the Shropshire Show, first at Penybont, first and Welsh Pony & Cob Society silver medal Llanwrtyd and first at the Swansea Welsh National Show in 1912; first prize and Welsh Pony & Cob Society silver medal at Llanwrtyd again in 1913 and a third prize at the Shrewsbury Royal Agricultural Society of England Show in 1914.

She was sold (lot 5) at the first Grove Sale on 12th August 1916. She was also represented at this sale by her yearling daughter (lot 21) sired by the Hackney pony Berkeley George and a four-year-old gelding (lot 33) also sired by Berkeley George. Grove Limestone which was her foal at the time of this sale was retained at the Grove.

12

Criban Golden Spray foaled 1946
Criban Old Gold foaled 1953

1	2	4	8

The pedigree chart is structured as follows:

1

7296 Criban Golden Spray

- **2** Bolgoed Squire 1681
  - **4** Grove Sprightly 1036
    - **8** Bleddfa Shooting Star 73
    - **9** 4431 Grove Sprite II
  - **5** 6582 Grove Peep O'Day
    - **8** Bleddfa Shooting Star 73
    - **11** 3017 Grove Twilight
- **3** 9132 Criban Brenda
  - **6** Criban Cockade 1627
    - **12** Ness Commander 1459
    - **13** 8703 Criban Socks
  - **7** 8612 Criban Ruby
    - **14** Criban Shot 1276
    - **15** 7965 Criban Chocolate Flake

1. Criban Golden Spray

Registration number 9296 in the *Welsh Stud Book,*
Vol. XXXII
Chesnut, blaze, silver eyes, four white legs, height:
11 hands 2 in, foaled 1946
Owners and breeders: H. W. Richards and Sons,
Criban Stud, Talybont-on-Usk, Breconshire

Criban Golden Spray was lot 38 on the Criban Sale on 5th November 1946 and was the top-priced foal, being bought by Mr. John Berry of Betws-y-Coed for 20 guineas. Criban Golden Spray deserves her place in the Welsh pony history via the outstanding stock which she bred at the Betws Stud where she remained until her death in 1975.

However, in her youth, she was also a consistent winner in the show ring, her moment of crowning glory being at the 1949 Royal Welsh Show where she won her class of ten two- or three-year-old-colts, fillies and geldings from such well-known names as Bolgoed Atomic, Coed Coch Sidan, Whitehall Bluebell, Whitehall Sunflower, Coed Coch

Criban Golden Spray with Mr. John Berry. (Photograph courtesy of Welsh Stud Book.)

Serenllys etc. Capt. Howson (the judge) writing of her in the Royal Welsh Agricultural Show journal quotes: "Criban Golden Spray earlier this year was fourth at the Bath and West and third at the Three Counties; she is a roomy, low-set, free-moving dark chesnut and having been deprived of some superfluous mane and forelock and generally smartened up since we judged her at Shrewsbury last year" (where she was beaten by Coed Coch Sidan).

A record of her progeny constitute a formidable list:

1951 Betws Seren, filly, by Gwyndy Limelight. Dam of Royal Agricultural Society of England Champion Betws Nia (foaled 1960) by Coed Coch Madog. Still alive at Betws Stud at 28 years of age.

1952 Betws Socks, filly, by Tregoyd Starlight. Dam of Betws Wiwer who is dam of Royal Agricultural Society of England and Royal Welsh Agricultural Society winner Bengad Welsh Poppy. Betws Socks is still alive in the U.S.A. (1979).

1954 Betws Rhian, filly, by Coed Coch Madog. A producer of noteable stock at Gredington and Polaris Studs and now at the Valley Lake Stud.

1955 Betws Hufen, filly, by Coed Coch Madog. A very pretty cream mare, shown successfully at the 1956 and 1957 Royal Welsh Shows.

1956 Betws Auryn, colt, by Coed Coch Madog. A chesnut stallion, very popular sire in Canada.

1957 Betws Eirian, filly, by Coed Coch Madog.

1958 Betws Mai, filly, by Coed Coch Madog. Mai won a second prize for Mrs. Ridgeway of the Sunrising Stud at the 1960 Royal Welsh Show and was later a good winner in South Wales.

1959 Betws Eurgain, filly, by Coed Coch Madog. A cream mare exported to the U.S.A.

1961 Betws Sion, colt, by Coed Coch Madog.

1962 Betws Cesar, colt, by Coed Coch Madog. Senior sire at the Eryl Stud for many years.

1963 Betws Seryddwr, colt, by Coed Coch Madog. A good-moving chesnut stallion who sired many winners and was sold to Mr. Charles Castle at the dispersal of the Deverell Stud.

1965 Betws Sian, filly, by Coed Coch Madog.

1967 Betws Glenys, filly, by Coed Coch Pryd. Retained at the Betws Stud.

Criban Golden Spray with her last foal. (Photograph courtesy of Mr. Gwyn Berry.)

Family group. From the right Criban Golden Spray, Betws Seren, daughter of Criban Golden Spray, Betws Valmai, daughter of Betws Seren, and Betws Wiwer (g-daughter of Criban Golden Spray). (Photograph courtesy of Mr. Gwyn Berry.)

1968 Betws Brenda, filly, by Coed Coch Salsbri. Sold to the Rookery Stud.

1969 Betws Ser-y-Bore, filly, by Coed Coch Shon. Owned by Mr. J. A. Russell, Scotland.

1971 Betws Robert, colt, by Coed Coch Saled. At stud in Scotland with Mrs. Baillie in Saltcoats, Ayrshire.

1973 Betws Siaradus, filly, by Coed Coch Saled.

1974 Betws Coch y Bonddu, colt, by Coed Coch Saled. Currently at Lyonshall, Herefordshire.

After producing eighteen such good foals for the Betws Stud, Golden Spray was put to rest at the stud in 1975. One of her descendants, her great-granddaughter Betws Mel (out of Betws Valmai, daughter of Betws Seren) really made her mark in the show ring during 1979 winning the Junior Championship at the Anglesey County Show and Reserve Supreme Champion at the Merioneth County Show.

2. Bolgoed Squire
Registration number 1681 in the *Welsh Stud Book*,
Vol. XXXII
Grey, height: 12 hands, foaled 1938
Breeder: Mrs. T. N. Lewis, Bolgoed Stud, Merthyr
Tydfil, Glamorganshire

Bolgoed Squire was a full-brother to Tregoyd Starlight (*chapter 3.1*) who had been foaled three years previously.

Bolgoed Squire won some prizes for his breeder around the Merthyr area e.g. first prize at Merthyr in 1941, first prizes at Merthyr, Cardiff, Porth and Mountain Ash in 1942 after which he was sold to Mrs. Sayer of Fairlight Place, Hastings.

However his stay in England was short-lived and he soon returned to the Criban and Cui studs where he sired some influential stallions, such as Criban Historical (Brierwood Stud), Criban Silver Link, Cui Squire etc.

The next owner was Mr. Emrys Griffiths of the Revel for whom he won Premiums for the Black Mountains for 1947 and 1948 and for Church Stretton in 1949, 1950 and 1951. At this time it was not usual for Mr. Griffiths to exhibit his ponies outside Breconshire, however on 19th September 1947 he ventured further afield with Bolgoed Squire to the Lampeter Agricultural Show and there won with him a third prize to Dinarth What Ho and Whitehall Monarch.

Bolgoed Squire's next owner was Mr. McTurk of the Cnewr Stud, Cray Breconshire and Squire sired some very good ponies there, mainly out of daughters of Criban Cockade (*chapter 12.6*). We once bought some very typical (and very wild!) Cnewr mares in foal to Bolgoed Squire and they produced some very good foals.

These famous old blood-lines were thought very highly of in overseas countries and at an age when most stallions would be pensioned off, especially stallions which have experienced the rigours of being a Premium stallion on the open hills, Bolgoed Squire was exported from Mr. McTurk in November 1955 to Mr. Goodrich of Forth Worth, Texas and his photographs appeared in the *American Pony* magazines for many more years.

3. Criban Brenda
Registration number 9132 in the *Welsh Stud Book*,
Vol. XXXII
Bay, blaze, wall eyes, four white legs, height:
11 hands 3 in, foaled 1940
Owners & Breeders: H. W. Richards and Sons,
Criban, Talybont-on-Usk.

Criban Brenda left her mark on the blood-lines of many Studs throughout the United Kingdom. One of her first sons was Criban D-Day (*chapter 16.12*) (foaled 1944, sired by Criban Grey Grit); D-Day was a very fine mover and was very highly thought of by Mr. Llewellyn Richards. However, he was of a rather dirty colour, not a bay and yet not a brown and many prospective purchasers were put off by this colour. D-Day eventually became a Premium stallion on the Denbigh Moors and sired very good stock.

One notable son was Criban Bantam (sired by Bolgoed Shot Star and foaled in 1947) who won many championships in the show ring when shown by Mr. David Reynolds. Bantam was sold to Mr. Gwyn Price of the Dyrin Stud (lot 1 of the Criban Sale held on 2nd May 1952) and died in the ownership of Mr. Price's daughter Mrs. Doreen Jones of the Synod Stud.

Brenda was sold for a few years to Mrs. Phelps Penry producing Criban Tirwaun Babette in this ownership in 1949, Babette was exported to the U.S.A., her twenty-four-year-old daughter Tregate Tra-La-La still producing good foals in the U.S.A. She was also shown during this period but disliked the show ring immensely and would never show to best advantage.

197

Criban Bantam, son of Criban Brenda. (Photograph courtesy of Les Mayall.)

On returning to Talybont-on-Usk she produced Cui Red Ronald in 1951 only to be sold again, this time to Mrs. P. Franks who bred three full-sisters out of her all by Potato (*General Stud Book*). One of the progeny of Potato and Brenda was Miss Crimpy Peek A Boo (foaled in 1955) a big winner under saddle.

Miss Crimpy Peek A Boo later became the foundation of the Section "B" ponies at the Weston Stud, producing Weston Romany (by Criban Victor) who later became dam of the Royal Welsh Champion Weston Mary Ann (one of the ponies taken to Australia when the Weston Stud went out there in 1979).

4. **Grove Sprightly** (*chapter 5.1*)

5. **Grove Peep O'Day** (*chapter 3.3*)

6. Criban Cockade
Registration number 1627 in the *Welsh Stud Book*,
Vol. XXXI
Dun, white face and muzzle, wall eyes, four white
socks.
Height: 11 hands 2 in, foaled 1936
Owners and Breeders: H. W. Richards & Sons,
Criban, Talybont-on-Usk, Breconshire

We have already learnt (*chapter 9.7*) how Criban Cockade accompanied his dam, the lovely Criban Socks to Dinarth Hall for the showing season 1936, then he returned to Criban at weaning time.

He soon began to influence the Criban Stud by siring particularly good mares such as Criban Posy in 1939 and Criban Dun Bee and Criban Fancy Lady both in 1940. There were several of his colts (foaled in 1943 and 1944) on the 1946 Criban Sale, but surprisingly nothing much became of his sons.

Cockade then spent the next five years (1944 to 1948) at the Cnewr Stud and again sired some very good mares. I remember attending one of the Cnewr Reduction Sales (4th November 1954) and admiring the high standard of the Cockade daughters; we ended up by buying three, grand quality mares but having never been touched and as wild as hawks!

Luckily, Cockade then returned to Criban and it was during this period that he had his greatest influence on the Criban ponies. Pride of place amongst the daughters of Criban Cockade must go to Criban Old Gold, foaled in 1953 out of Criban Mair. Old Gold was sold for export to the U.S.A. in 1956 on condition that her pregnancy test proved positive; Mr. Richards was convinced that she was in foal to Ceulan Revolt and was quite furious when it proved negative. Now fate often works in strange ways, Old Gold duly produced Rock Dove (she spent 12 years with me at Ceulan) in 1957 and from then until her death in 1978 produced one Champion after another, Champions who now cover eight different countries! Amongst the progeny of Old Gold are: Criban Gold Cockade (still siring foals in the U.S.A. at 24 years old), Old China (1962), Old Silver (U.S.A., 1958), Old Oak (Denmark, 1966), Old Pattern (1964), Old Print (1967), Old Memory (1968, bought back by Criban Stud in 1979), Old Story (1969, sold to Pendock Stud but then bought back and her progeny also are going all over the world), Old Treasure (1970), Old Melody (1971, Champion mare in Australia), Old Fashion (1972) and Old Vintage (1973).

7. Criban Ruby
Registration number 8612 in the *Welsh Stud Book,*
Vol. XXVII
Re-registered in *Vol. XXXII, page 120* (to show change
of ownership to Mrs. Pennell)
Chesnut, blaze, hind socks white, height: 11 hands
2 in, foaled in 1924
Owner and Breeder: H. W. Richards, Criban Stud,
Talybont-on-Usk, Brecon.

In addition to Criban Brenda (foaled in 1940), Ruby was a very good producer for the Criban Stud. Amongst her progeny were Criban Rachel (foaled in 1934 and dam of some of the best Cui ponies e.g. Cui Ripple) and the full-brother and sister Criban Pledge (foaled in 1944) and Red Chip (foaled in 1942).

Criban Pledge was an influential sire at the Clan Stud of Mr. A. R. McNaught (e.g. sire of Clan Marshall, *chapter 11.1*) and Red Chip was sold (in foal to Criban Cockade) to Mrs. Pennell at the 1952 Criban Sale. Red Chip was an extremely nice mare and would have made her name in the show ring had she not got far too fat on Mrs. Pennell's

Criban Pledge, son of Criban Ruby.

Ness King (foaled in 1920), sire of Ness Commander.

excellent land at Gloucester; however she also proved to be a valuable producer.

8. Bleddfa Shooting Star (*chapter 4.1*)

9. Grove Sprite II (*chapter 5.2*)

11. Grove Twilight (*chapter 3.7*)

12. Ness Commander
Registration number 1459 in the *Welsh Stud Book,
Vol. XXVIII*
Grey, blaze, white legs, height: 11 hands 3 in,
foaled in 1924
Breeder: Allan C. Lyell, Neston, Cheshire
Owner: W. V. Davies, Pentrenant, Churchstoke,
Montgomeryshire
Sire: Ness King 1182
Dam: 7360 Ness Violet by Llwyn Cymro 407

Ness Commander was shown by his breeder to win a second prize at the London National Pony Society Show in 1926 and a first prize and Welsh Pony & Cob Society medal at Knighton Show in 1928. He was then sold to Mr. Davies who sold him to the Criban Stud. Apart from Cockade the only other of his get to have a lasting influence on the Criban Stud was his daughter Criban Nesta (foaled in 1936).

Ness Commander was sold on the Criban Sale in May 1937 (lot 1 at 18 guineas) and he became a useful Premium stallion on the Gower (at Cefn Bryn) during the early war years. Surprisingly his sire Ness King (foaled in 1920 and bred by the Earl of Powis) also ended up as a Premium stallion on Fairwood Common during the same period.

13. Criban Socks (*chapter 9.7*)

14. Criban Shot (*chapter 9.12*)

15. Criban Chocolate Flake
Reigstration number 7965 in the *Welsh Stud Book, Vol. XXIV*
Chesnut, star, height: 11 hands 3 in, foaled 1921
Owner and Breeder: H. W. Richards, Criban,
Talybont-on-Usk
Sire: Criban Wild Wonder 1179
Dam: 3442 Chocolate Lass (foaled 1905)
G-dam: 213 Ystrad Jewel, one of the original Criban
mares, foaled in 1893

Criban Chocolate Flake does not seem to have stayed long at Criban; apart from Ruby the only other of her progeny to be registered was Criban Cocoa a chesnut daughter (foaled in 1926) sired by Criban Shot, who was sold (lot 15) for 9½ guineas at the 1937 Criban Sale. Chocolate Flake is descended from one of the oldest Criban families, Mr. Llewellyn Richards remembers walking Ystrad Jewel in 1907 over to Mr. Miller's Forest Lodge Stud to be served by Klondyke (*chapter 24.12*). One incident which stands out in Mr. Richards' mind about that journey in 1907 is that he had eaten all his sandwiches well before arriving at Forest Lodge and Mrs. Miller on seeing his hungry look made him some porridge on which (being a Scotswoman) she put salt!! Ystrad Jewel was a very good mare to which Mr. Miller had given a first prize at Bedwellty Show. The product of the mating with Klondyke was a colt Ystrad Klondyke which (although never registered due to a misunderstanding) appears in many pedigrees of the best Criban strains.

13

Tanybwlch Berwyn foaled 1924

Criban Victor foaled 1944

Coed Coch Berwynfa foaled 1951

Chirk Caradoc foaled 1958

Chirk Crogan foaled 1959

1 Coed Coch Blaen Lleuad 2222	**2** Criban Victor 1775	**4** Criban Winston 1705	**8** Coed Coch Glyndwr 1617
			9 8966 Criban Blonde
		5 9138 Criban Whalebone	**10** Mathrafal Broadcast 1502
			11 8611 Criban Mulberry
	3 9270 Berwyn Beauty	**6** Tanybwlch Berwyn 1383	**12** Sahara
			13 6974 Brynhir Black Star
		7 9269 Dinarth Wonderlight	**14** Bowdler Brightlight 1303
			15 6350 Irfon Marvel
16 Coed Coch Berwynfa 2114	**6** Tanybwlch Berwyn 1383	**12** Sahara	
		13 6974 Brynhir Black Star	**17** Bleddfa Shooting Star 73
			18 6884 Brynhir Flight
	3 9270 Berwyn Beauty	**6** Tanybwch Berwyn 1383	**12** Sahara
			13 6974 Brynhir Black Star
		7 9269 Dinarth Wonderlight	**14** Bowdler Brightlight 1303
			15 6350 Irfon Marvel

1. Coed Coch Blaen Lleuad
Registration number 2222 in the *Welsh Stud Book,*
Vol. XXXVII
Chestnut roan, star, dark hoofs, height 13 hands,
foaled 1953
Breeder: Miss M. Brodrick, Coed Coch, Abergele

For a stallion who spent only three mature years in this country before being exported to the U.S.A., Coed Coch Blaen Lleuad (Welsh for "new moon") had an enormous influence on the Welsh pony breed. His dam Berwyn Beauty (No. 3) was shown in brood mare classes in 1953 and Blaen Lleuad very soon hit the limelight when only a few months old by standing Reserve for the Warmore Cup (Champion foal) at the Ponies of British Show.

Blaen Lleuad was born at a time in the development of Welsh Ponies (Section "B") when there were insufficient numbers to warrant separate classes at shows for colts and in 1955, Blaen Lleuad was thrown in at the deep end into the any-age male class at the Royal Welsh Show to stand third to his half-brother (same age, same sire) Valiant who won and their sire, Criban Victor who stood second.

By the following year, Valiant had been exported to South Africa where he later became a very influential sire and at the Royal Welsh Show under Dr. Arwyn Williams, Blaen Lleuad stood second to his sire. The following year with Miss Morley judging he actually beat his Dad and stood Male Champion only to be beaten again by him in 1958 under Mrs. T. Price of the Mel Valley Stud (breeder of so many famous ponies when she was Mrs. Hepburn) in fact also beaten by Mrs. Yeoman's Kirby Cane Shuttlecock so Blaen Lleuad stood third and his son, the two-year-old Rhydyfelin Selwyn being fourth.

Blaen Lleuad was sold for 320 guineas (lot 122) at the 26th September 1959 Coed Coch Sale to Mr. and Mrs. Elliott Bonnie of the Glen Grove Stud, Ohio. He was described by Miss Brodrick as having the "most perfect temperament" and very soon after his arrival in the U.S.A. was ridden by the Bonnie daughter Gretchen. Blaen Lleuad soon sired some top class progeny from daughters of the two stallions which I had secured for Mr. and Mrs. Bonnie some years previously: Revel Starlight and Bolgoed Fashion. His full-brother Coed Coch Ballog (foaled in 1956) had already been sold for export. Later Ballog was owned by Heather de Young of Nova Scotia and proved a good harness pony.

Although his stay in this country was short-lived, his influence was long-lasting; this also despite so many of his offspring on the 1959 Coed Coch Sale being exported along with him.

Blaen Lleuad's progeny included on the sale were Coed Coch Bore (filly foal at 100 guineas to Mrs. Chambers, U.S.A.), Coed Coch Pala (grey filly foal, 150 guineas to Mrs. Illingworth, South Africa), Coed Coch Perfagl (four-year-old grey mare at 220 guineas to Lady Astor for whom she produced many well-known offspring including the five good stallions Wickenden Platignum, the American Wickenden Osprey, Hever Fiesta, Hever Lancelot and Hever Imperial), Coed Coch Bettrys

Coed Coch Blaen Lleuad photographed in the U.S.A.

(three-year-old grey filly sold for 180 guineas to Lady Astor, later producing Wickenden Partridge, Wickenden Bantam etc), Coed Coch Lafant (two-year-old red roan filly, 300 guineas to Mr. Campbell Moodie, Canada), Coed Coch Pefr (brown two-year-old filly at 80 guineas to Mrs. Bullock later to produce the British and Australian Champion Sinton Whirligig and Sinton Perl, dam of the Horse of the Year Champion Riding Pony Firby Fleur de Lis sired by Blaen Lleuad's son Chirk Caradoc of whom more anon), Coed Coch Perwyr (grey yearling filly, 160 guineas, Mrs. Reeves), Coed Coch Swynan (grey yearling filly, 250 guineas, Mrs. Bonnie, U.S.A.), Coed Coch Bugeiles (roan yearling filly, 210 guineas to Mr. Eckley, later to win second and third prizes in brood mare classes at the 1964 and 1965 Royal Welsh Shows for Mrs. Fawcett and prove a very successful breeding mare), Coed Coch Pawl (grey yearling colt at 55 guineas to Mr. Eckley, later to sire Cusop Hoity Toity, Male Champion at both 1965 and 1967 Royal Welsh Shows and also Cusop Blush, dam of the twice Royal Welsh Champion Cusop Banknote) and the good winning three-year-old colt Rhydyfelin Selwyn who fetched the same price as his sire to go to Sweden only to be re-imported later by Mrs. Alison Mountain of the Twyford Stud.

Luckily two of Blaen Lleuad's offspring were retained at Coed Coch at the time of the 1959 sale, namely Coed Coch Pannwl (foaled in 1958) (dam of Mynd Stud's noted sire Coed Coch Pedestr and the Coed Coch Stud's Coed Coch Gwenfron dam of the nine-times Champion Coed Coch Targed who topped the Section "B" males at the 1978 sale going to Holland at 3,000 guineas) and the diminutive beautifully proportioned Coed Coch Peioni (foaled in 1958 also and full-sister to Pefr) who was dam of Coed Coch Gala who was top-priced Section "B" female at the 1978 sale, fetching 3,800 guineas despite being fourteen-years-old and never been shown.

Blaen Lleuad also left some influential families at studs neighbouring to Coed Coch such as Mrs. Margaret Williams' Nefydd Stud. However the most influential of the stock left behind were the two full brothers Chirk Crogan and Chirk Caradoc who were the only progeny of Chirk Heather (since she died of strangles when five years old) bred by Lady Margaret Myddelton. Crogan stood as senior stud sire at the Weston Stud producing such as Weston Air Bell, Champion at the Ponies of Britain Show and Reserve at the Royal Welsh; Weston Vogue, first prize-winner at the Royal Agricultural Society of England in 1972 and 1974 and her full-brother Weston Paul etc. Crogan was sold to Miss Weston of Leicestershire for 850 guineas at the 1970 Fayre Oaks Sale.

Chirk Caradoc (foaled in 1958) was retained by Lady Margaret and is hale and hearty at the time of writing (1979); although his competition days are over he appeared in great form at the "personalities parade" at Malvern in September 1978. Caradoc has sired Champion Welsh ponies at the Royal, National Pony and Ponies of Britain Shows but probably his greatest influence has been on the Riding Pony world with animals such as Mrs. Mansfield's renowned Rotherwood Peepshow, Champion riding pony at the International Show before becoming a Champion brood mare, and the three sisters from the T.B. mare Kitty's Fancy: Chirk Caviar, Chirk Catmint and Chirk Cattleya. It was a wonderful day for Caradoc at the 1978 Ponies of Britain Show when Cattleya won the 14 hands 2 in brood mare class and Reserve Championship, Catmint won the 13 hands 2 in class and Championship and another Caradoc daughter, Mrs. Cooke's Nantcol Arbennig won the 12 hands 2 in class.

2. Criban Victor
Registration number 1775 in the *Welsh Stud Book*,
Vol. XXXII, page 59 and *page 62*
Roan, height: 13 hands, foaled 1944
Breeders: H. W. Richards and Son, Criban Stud,
Talybont-on-Usk, Brecon

Criban Victor was lot 4 on the Criban Sale on 5th November 1946 (where we bought Criban Rally) and was purchased by Mrs. Cuff of the Downland Stud at 40 guineas. In 1947 he was the only male representative of the Welsh Ponies (Section "B") at the Royal Welsh Show and shortly afterwards was sold to Lord Kenyon and he remained at Gredington until his death on 6th June 1973.

The first time that a Section "B" stallion class was held at the Royal Welsh Show was in 1950 and Victor stood second to Lord Kenyon's Coed Coch Siabod as was also the case in 1951, 1952 and 1953. Then Siabod was sold for export and Victor was Male Champion in 1954, his daughter the two-year-old Verity being Champion with her dam Coed Coch Silian (Tanybwlch Berwyn × Coed Coch Seirian) being Reserve Champion, the latter two being the property of Mrs. E. G. E. Griffith who also owned Valiant, full-brother to Verity who stood second to Victor. Victor was Champion in 1956, 1958, 1959 and 1960 then gave way for three years to the younger Solway Master Bronze but made a "come back" in 1964 winning the title for the last time.

In addition to Royal Welsh Shows, he was Champion at the Ponies of

Criban Victor with
Mr. Gordon Jones.

Britain Shows in 1959, 1962, 1965 and 1966 and the National Pony
Society Shows in 1956, 1959 and 1960. He left the show ring in a blaze of
glory in 1969 at twenty-five years of age when he won the Section "B"
Championship and was Reserve Supreme Champion of the whole Show
at Caernarfon.

Apart from the noteable Welsh (Section "B") progeny already

*Model for the 11p stamp, issued on 5th July 1978, Criban Victor Stamp designed by Patrick
Oxenham. (Reproduced by courtesy of The Post Office.)*

mentioned, Victor sired some exceptional part-bred ponies such as Henbury Sylvester, Henbury Limelight and Henbury Rebecca all bred by Mrs. Andrews; the well-known Gossip out of the famous Arden Tittle Tattle and Bwlch Melody out of Miss Minette. The head of Criban Victor has been preserved and surveys the Offices of the Welsh Pony & Cob Society at Aberystwyth.

3. Berwyn Beauty

Registration number 9270 in the *Welsh Stud Book,*
Vol. XXXII
Grey, height: 12 hands 2 in, foaled 1942
Breeder: Tudor E. Jones, Bryn Awel, Ruthin,
Denbighshire

Mr. Tudor Jones, breeder of Berwyn Beauty was the representative for Young's Sheep Dips in North Wales, a post which was taken over by Mr. John Berry of the Betws Stud on the retirement of Mr. Jones. Berwyn Beauty was then sold to Miss Brodrick of the Coed Coch Stud and she became the Section "B" show mare for the stud e.g. at the 1949 Royal Welsh Show she stood second to Mrs. Cuff's Criban Heather Belle (*chapter 14.11*) beating Craven Nell, Ceulan Silver Lustre and Craven Mona.

Berwyn Beauty's greatest value however was as a brood mare, producing very few fillies and several famous stallions:

1946 Berwyn Grey Lady, filly, by Tanybwlch Berwyn (sold to Downland Stud)
1950 Coed Coch Berwynedd, colt, by Tanybwlch Berwyn (exported)
1951 Coed Coch Berwynfa, colt, by Tanybwlch Berwyn (No. 16)
1953 Coed Coch Blaen Lleuad, colt, by Criban Victor (No. 1)
1954 Coed Coch Barwn, colt, by Criban Victor (exported to Sweden)
1956 Coed Coch Ballog, colt, by Criban Victor (exported to Nova Scotia)
1958 Coed Coch Berin, filly, by Coed Coch Sandde (sire exported to U.S.A.)
1960 Brockwell Berwyn, colt, by Rhydyfelin Selwyn (sire exported to Sweden)
1962 Brockwell Bertha, filly, by Brockwell Cobweb
1963 Brockwell Will O'the Wisp, colt, by Brockwell Cobweb (exported to South Africa)

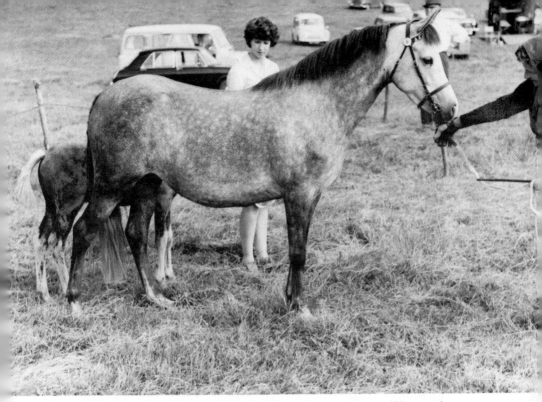

Brockwell Beauty Queen (foaled in 1964), daughter of Berwyn Beauty. (Photograph courtesy of Photonews.)

1964 Brockwell Beauty Queen, filly, by Brockwell Cobweb
1966 Brockwell Beetle, colt, by Brockwell Cobweb (stud stallion Mr.
      Manley's Bacton Stud).

Coed Coch Berin was included on the 1959 Coed Coch Sale (where Mrs. Binnie purchased Berwyn Beauty) and was sold to Mrs. Lorna Reynolds of the Springbourne Stud for 150 guineas. Her greatest influence on the breed was producing Springbourne Blueberry (by Brierwood Blue Boy) the stallion who headed his class at the 1971 Royal Welsh Show and was later a Champion in Australia.

When Mrs. Binnie purchased Berwyn Beauty she was in foal to her grand-son Rhydyfelin Selwyn and her 1960 foal was named Brockwell Berwyn who won many prizes in the youngstock classes for Mrs. Binnie and later was stud stallion at Mrs. Mountain's Twyford Stud, Lady Steon's Baylaurel Stud and Mrs. Courtauld's Cymbeline Stud.

Mrs. Binnie's pride and joy is the daughter Brockwell Beauty Queen who distinguished herself by producing the 1972 Supreme Champion Brockwell Chuckle (owned by Mrs. Margaret Williams, Nefydd Stud) as well as many other good ones for Mrs. Binnie; possibly her best being the 1978 colt by Downland Beechwood. Mrs. Binnie held Berwyn Beauty (since she did not allow anyone else to look after her) when she was put down on her farm in 1969 at 27 years.

4. **Criban Winston**
Registration number 1705 in the *Welsh Stud Book, Vol. XXXII*
Grey, height: 11 hands 2 in, foaled 1940
Breeders: H. W. Richards and Sons, Criban Stud,
Talybont-on-Usk, Brecon.

Criban Winston was used as stud stallion at Criban for seasons 1942 and 1943 after which he was sold to Mr. Emrys Griffiths of the Revel. His first daughter at Criban was Criban Vanity (foaled 1943) who was sold (lot 10) at the 1946 Criban Sale to Mr. Gwyn Price of the Dyrin Stud where she produced some very good ponies including Dyrin Boquet, Dyrin Doreen, Dyrin Flash, Dyrin Jennifer (noted brood mare at Valley Lake Stud), etc. Some of Criban Winston's sons bred at Criban spread his blood far and wide; apart from Criban Victor they included Criban Atom, Criban Nickle, Criban Pilot (for many years at Bowdler), Criban Snowball (Coedowen Stud) etc.

Thereafter Winston made his mark on the Revel Stud producing the useful stallions Revel Churchill, Revel Flag, Revel Popcorn, Revel Race etc. and the mares Revel Cheer, Revel Honeypot, Revel Honeyway, Revel Ring, Revel Romance (a Champion show mare of the Fayre Stud who later produced Supreme Champion Turkdean Cerdin), Revel Vanity, Revel Val (dam of Greenacres Cream Caramel) etc.

During his time at the Revel, Criban Winston also did sterling work as a Premium stallion on the hills of Wales, winning premiums for Eppynt in 1946, 1947 and 1948, Llanafan in 1950 and 1951 and the Black Mountains in 1949, 1952, 1953, 1955 and 1956.

5. **Criban Whalebone**
Registration number 9138 in the *Welsh Stud Book, Vol. XXXII*
Bay, height: 13 hands, foaled 1936
Breeders: H. W. Richards and Sons, Criban,
Talybont-on-Usk, Brecon

Criban Whalebone blood had an enormous influence on the Section

"B" Welsh pony through her son Criban Victor (No. 2) and through her other son Criban Gay Snip (*chapter 16.6*) who is grand-sire of Solway Master Bronze.

Whatever other virtue she passed on to her offspring, all this family are noted for their kind temperament, Criban Victor was regarded to be the kindest stallion at Gredington, Solway Master Bronze is a perfect gentleman and another brother of Whalebone's (son of Criban Mulberry) the 14 hands gelding called Spotless (foaled 1933) by Criban Lally (fifteen hands stallion, bred by Mrs. Pennell) sold at the 1937 Criban Sale for fifteen guineas; he spent several years at Ceulan where his super disposition made him very popular with all of us.

Funnily enough, Whalebone herself had a disposition which left something to be desired! When she was five years old and only broken to halter, the Richards brothers decided that she would make a good shepherding pony and endeavoured to break her to saddle in one day. Whalebone would have none of this; perhaps she realised that as long as she kept bucking off her riders she would be allowed to return to the hills and concentrate on producing more excellent foals!

6. Tanybwlch Berwyn
Registration number 1383 in the *Welsh Stud Book*,
Vol. XXVI
Grey, height: 13 hands, foaled 1924
Breeder: Mrs. Inge, Plas Tanybwlch,
Merionethshire

Tanybwlch Berwyn can rightly be described as the "Abraham" of the Section "B" Welsh Pony and consequently the Coed Coch Stud through Berwyn can be regarded as a "pioneer" stud.

Tanybwlch Berwyn twice competed at Royal Welsh Shows when in the ownership of his breeder Mrs. Inge; firstly at the 1930 Show when Section "B" and "C" competed together and Berwyn stood fourth to Royal Welsh Jack, Ceulan Comet (owned by my father) and Mab Y Brenin (*chapter 28.8*) owned by my grand-father. By 1939, the Section "B" ponies had been established in their own right and Berwyn stood second to Mr. Tom Jones Evans' Craven Cyrus (*chapter 14.13*). Amongst the ponies bred by Mrs. Inge before Berwyn went to Coed Coch were Tanybwlch Rhos (foaled in 1929 and a winning riding pony for Mrs. Hepburn), Tanybwlch Rhosdir (a first prize-winner at the 1936 Royal Welsh Show) and Tanybwlch Prancio, foaled in 1932 and a big winner in hand and under saddle for Miss Brodrick, she has had a big word

Tanybwlch Berwyn photographed in 1948 when 23 years old.

in deciding the future of the Welsh Mountain Pony through her descendants Coed Coch Planed, Coed Coch Pelydrog and Coed Coch
Pryd, all of which have been Royal Welsh Show Champions. Although
Tanybwlch Berwyn does not seem to have been officially transferred to
Miss Brodrick, it was sometime during the 1939–1945 war years that he
went to Coed Coch but his services had been used at Coed Coch for
many years prior to this e.g. Coed Coch Erlewyn (foaled in 1934) who
was second prize Section "A" stallion for Mr. Holden at the 1938 Royal
Welsh Show and who spent the latter years of his life in Cardiganshire
being g-g-sire of the 1970 Royal Welsh Champion mare Rowfant Prima
Ballerina through his son the Cardiganshire-bred Tanffynnon Twm
Shanco.

Mention has already been made of some of his noted Coed Coch
progeny: Coed Coch Siabod (foaled in 1945) Champion at the Royal
Welsh every year between 1950 and his export in 1953, Coed Coch
Silian Female Champion in 1952 and 1954 and Overall Champion in
1955 and the four full-sisters out of Tanybwlch Penwen viz Tanybwlch
Penllyn (foaled in 1937), Coed Coch Pilia (foaled in 1945), Coed Coch

Pendefiges (foaled in 1946) and Coed Coch Pluen (foaled in 1947). Tanybwlch Penllyn when owned by Mr. McNaught of the Clan Stud won the brood mare class at the 1951 Royal Welsh Show and is best known as the grand-dam of the famous Clan Pip. Pilia was a good winner under saddle where she won over thirty first prizes, Pendefiges won first prizes at the Royal Agricultural Society of England Shows of 1949 and 1950, Pluen won at the Royal Agricultural Society of England three times and produced some super riding ponies such as Coed Coch Prydyddes ridden to so many victories by Miss Deirdre Chambers.

215

The three Coed Coch sisters, Pilia, Pendefiges and Pluen were all sold on the 1959 Coed Coch Sale, Pilia to Lady Margaret Myddelton, Pendefiges to Mrs. Binnie of the Brockwell Stud and Pluen to Mrs. Crisp of the Kirby Cane Stud. Fortunately Coed Coch Penllwyd (foaled in 1953) daughter of Pendefiges was retained at the time of the sale; Penllwyd won at the Royal Welsh (twice), Shropshire and West Midland (twice) Bath and West, Royal Lancashire, Cheshire, National Pony Show etc and was dam of Coed Coch Priciau (Champion Royal Welsh Show 1966) and Coed Coch Dawn (Champion Royal Welsh 1974 and first prize mare in 1975). Indeed after the major Coed Coch Section "B" dispersal of 1959, all the eighty or so Section "B" ponies on the 1978 Sale traced back either to Penllwyd, her daughter Peioni by Coed Coch Blaen Lleuad or to another family originating from Downland Lavender.

The influence of Tanybwlch Berwyn on Welsh Ponies (Section "B") is only to be expected, what is surprising is his influence on the Section "A" ponies; to mention the following Royal Welsh Show Champions: Coed Coch Planed (1954), Clan Pip (1963 and 1964), Coed Coch Pelydrog (1964 and 1965), Clan Peggy (1966 and 1967), Treharne Tomboy (1967, 1968 and 1970), Ready Token Glen Bride (1968), Coed Coch Pryd (1969), Rowfant Prima Ballerina (1970), Coed Coch Norman (1971), Gredington Simwnt (1972), Dyfrdwy Midnight Moon (1972), Coed Coch Glenda (1973), Bengad Love in the Mist (1974), Rondeels Pengwyn (1975), Revel Cassino (1976 and 1977), Aston Super Star (1978) and Bengad Day Lily (1978). It will be seen from this extensive list that it is very few of the post-war Champions of Sections "A" and "B" who do not trace back one way or another to Tanybwlch Berwyn.

7. Dinarth Wonderlight
Registration number 9269 in the *Welsh Stud Book,*
Vol. XXXII
Bay, height: 12 hands 1 in, foaled 1936
Breeders: John Jones and Son, Dinarth Hall,
Colwyn Bay

Dinarth Wonderlight was sold (lot 29 at 8 guineas) at the Dinarth Hall Dispersal Sale on 27th October 1937 to Lord Howard de Walden who sold her on to Mr. Tudor Jones. On the same sale was her dam Irfon Marvel (lot 7 sold to Mr. John Berry for the same price of 8 guineas). This was an exceptionally successful family since Irfon

Marvel's other daughter Dinarth Henol was dam of the legendary Coed Coch Glyndwr (*chapter 6.1*); another daughter Meifod Beauty (foaled in 1934, by Bowdler Brightlight) became a very successful brood mare for Miss Ruth Hobbs of Llanelian.

After producing Berwyn Beauty in 1942, Wonderlight produced her full-sister Berwyn Marvel in 1947, both of which were soon sold to Miss Brodrick.

8. Coed Coch Glyndwr (*chapter 6.1*)

9. Criban Blonde
Registration number 8966 in the *Welsh Stud Book*,
Vol. XXXI
Cream, height: 12 hands, foaled 1932
Breeders: H. W. Richards and Sons, Criban,
Talybont-on-Usk, Brecon

Criban Blonde came from one of the oldest-established Criban families, her sire Criban Bumble Bee was by Criban Shot (*chapter 9.12*) out of Criban Busy Bee by Criban Kid; and the dam of Blonde was Criban Betsy by Criban Kid out of Criban Bess who was a daughter of the original Black Bess II (foaled in 1897).

When Coed Coch Glyndwr was exchanged from the Coed Coch Stud for the 1931 season for Mathrafal Tuppence, while there are very many Coed Coch (and neighbouring) ponies sired by Tuppence in 1932, Criban Winston seems to be the only Criban progeny of Coed Coch Glyndwr bred at Criban.

10. Mathrafal Broadcast
Registration number 1502 in the *Welsh Stud Book*,
Vol. XXX
Chesnut, off fore and both hinds white, height:
14 hands 3 in, foaled 1926
Breeder: E. Jones, Plasgwyn, Llansantffraid,
Montgomeryshire
Sire: Mathrafal Eiddwen (*chapter 25.8*)
Dam: Plasgwyn Polly by Llwyn Idloes Flyer

It was in 1935 that Mathrafal Broadcast went to Criban and there were eight yearling sons and daughters of his entered on the Criban Sale of 7th May 1937. Indeed, Mathrafal Broadcast himself was offered for sale (lot 8) but reached only 20 guineas and he was withdrawn at that figure.

Later that year, he was shown at the Royal Welsh Show at Monmouth where he stood second in the Welsh Cob stallion class to Cystanog Trotting Comet.

Mr. Llewellyn Richards used to ride Mathrafal Broadcast as whipper-in to the Talybont Hounds but does not think that he was as big as his registration suggests.

Mr. Richards then had Broadcast at his home at Oundle in Northamptonshire and Mrs. Alice McLean of Long Island, New York came over for one month every year to hunt with the Pytchley Hounds and every year she would hire a chauffeur-driven Daimler to drive her around the neighbouring countryside, and she had called every year to see Mr. Richards and his ponies. Late in 1937 she fancied Broadcast and bought him along with another stallion Criban Craven Comet (by Ceulan Comet) and eight mares: Criban Dunish, Criban Honey, Criban Magie, Criban Margaret, Criban Patch, Craven Sprightlight, Criban Roan Rose and Criban Sylvia and they all left for the U.S.A. along with one of Mr. Richards' prize-winning sheepdogs (who only understood Welsh!) on 1st December 1937.

Mrs. McLean used Mathrafal Broadcast to cross on her Polo ponies but she died a year or two afterwards and most of these ponies were dispersed throughout the U.S.A. without trace. For many years after the end of the war, Mr. Richards tried to assist American owners to trace these valuable blood-lines but very, very few of them were discovered.

11. Criban Mulberry

Registration number 8611 in the *Welsh Stud Book,*
Vol. XXVII
Bay, star, height: 12 hands 1 in, foaled 1924
Breeder: H. W. Richards, Criban, Talybont-on-Usk
Sire: Criban Cracker 1308
Dam: 7971 Criban Raspberry by Criban
Wild Wonder 1179
G-dam: 5452 Criban Duchess by
Invincible Taffy 593
G-g-dam: 1298 Roanie II
G-g-g-dam: 263 Vaynor Duchess (foaled 1897)

Criban Cracker was a successful sire at Criban after which he was sold to Mr. Jenkins, Lynwood, Pontyclun (whose grand-son breeds ponies today) and for whom, he won in the show ring.

Vaynor Duchess was one of the original Criban mares to be registered in the first volume of the *Welsh Stud Book*.

12. Sahara
Barb, white, height: 14 hands 3 in, foaled about 1908

Mrs. F. E. G. Betty bought Sahara when she was in Gibraltar in 1913. He came from a load of ponies from Morocco and was called Sahara since he was branded (Sahara Desert brand) with a necklace of spots in a double row.

When war broke out in 1914, Mrs. Betty shipped him to the United Kingdom and she hunted him in the Carmarthen and Brecon areas for two years, eventually selling him to Mr. Denis Aldridge at the 1919 Royal Welsh Show. It was while in the ownership of Mr. Aldridge that Mrs. Inge sent many mares to Sahara including Brynhir Black Star, dam of Tanybwlch Berwyn.

When Mr. Aldridge gave up breeding, he leased Sahara to Mrs. Bolam in the New Forest and that was where he died.

Sahara.

13. Brynhir Black Star
Registration number 6974 in the *Welsh Stud Book,*
Vol. XXI
Dark grey, height: 12 hands 1½ in, foaled 1916
Breeder: Walter Glynn, The Grange,
Bletchley, Bucks.
Sire: Bleddfa Shooting Star 73 (*chapter 4.1*)
Dam: 6884 Brynhir Flight by Grove Ballistite
(*chapter 5.6*)
Dam: 6660 Brynhir Georgina by Berkeley
George 127

Brynhir Black Star had a full-sister (a year younger) called Brynhir White Star. After producing Tanybwlch Berwyn in 1924, Black Star was mated to registered Welsh stallions producing Tanybwlch Bara in 1927 and Tanybwlch Bron in 1929. Her sister Brynhir White Star followed her to Tanybwlch, both visited Sahara in 1923, White Star producing a filly Tanybwlch Sierol.

14. Bowdler Brightlight (*chapter 7.8*)

15. Irfon Marvel (*chapter 6.7*)

16. Coed Coch Berwynfa
Registration number 2114 in the *Welsh Stud Book,*
Vol. XXXV
Grey, height: 13 hands 2 in, foaled 1951
Breeder: Miss M. Brodrick, Coed Coch, Abergele

One of the most successful breeders when it came to establishing the type of Hackney ponies over 100 years ago was Mr. Christopher Wilson of Kirkby Lonsdale, Westmorland owner of the stallion Sir George (winner of first prize at the 1872 Royal Agricultural Society of England Show). Mr. Wilson put Sir George to the best mares of his area, then put the female offspring in due time back to their sire and succeeded in producing an uniform type unknown at that time.

Coed Coch Berwynfa was the product of such breeding policy and he also was responsible for a remarkably consistent type. Berwynfa was not shown very much as a youngster but was third at the 1953 Royal Welsh Show and fourth in the adult class the following year. He was obviously going to grow well up to the 13 hands 2 in mark if not a little bit over

Coed Coch Berwynfa.

Coed Coch Pedestr (foaled in 1963). Sire Coed Coch Berwynfa. Dam Coed Coch Pannwl by Coed Coch Blaenlleuad followed by his son Wharley Caruso at Glanusk Show.

221

which would, of course, disqualify him from the show ring but add to his value as a stud stallion since he would then produce sizeable Section "B" ponies from both "A" and "B" mares. Berwynfa undoubtedly deserves his place amongst the greatest of Section "B" sires his progeny including the Champion mares Coed Coch Dawn, Coed Coch Priciau, Coed Coch Llawrig etc.

His progeny were in great demand at the 1978 Coed Coch Dispersal Sale a selection of which were: Coed Coch Llawrig (16 years old), Champion Bath and West, Great Yorkshire, National Pony show, Royal Agricultural Society of England etc, 2,000 guineas to Germany; Coed Coch Llywy (15 years old) Champion Three Counties, Anglesey, Denbigh and Flint etc 1,400 guineas to Germany; Coed Coch Penwn (15 years old) second Royal Agricultural Society of England, Champion Northern Counties, 1,400 guineas; Coed Coch Gala (14 years) 3,800 guineas, Coed Coch Dawn (12 years) Champion Ponies of Britain, Cheshire, Three Counties, Royal Welsh, Leicester etc 1,300 guineas; Coed Coch Alarch (6 years) 3,600 guineas; Coed Coch Olwen (4 years) 1,000 guineas to U.S.A.; Coed Coch Bridget (yearling) 1,000 guineas to Holland. Bridget was about the last to be sired by the magnificent Berwynfa and he passed away at Coed Coch in June 1978.

Finally a word must be mentioned about the great success of crossing Coed Coch Berwynfa with the Gredington family originating from the Foundation stock mare Silver (from which family also originated Chirk Caradoc and Chirk Crogan via Silver's daughter Gredington Bronwen).

The result of mating Silver to Criban Victor produced Gredington Milfyd (foaled in 1956) winner of the Section "B" mare class at the Royal Welsh Shows of 1962 and 1963. Milfyd mated to Berwynfa produced Gredington Tiwlip (big winner for Mrs. Mansfield) whose daughter Rotherwood Honeysuckle was Champion at the 1970 and 1978 Royal Welsh Shows.

Milfyd mated to Criban Victor produced Gredington Saffrwm who in turn mated to Berwynfa produced Miss Bale-Williams' Gredington Blodyn. What is interesting is that at the 1970 Royal Welsh Show Blodyn as winning mare stood Reserve Champion to Rotherwood Honeysuckle while to have her revenge at the 1971 show, Blodyn again stood first beating Gredington Tiwlip, her "aunt"!

14

Craven Cyrus foaled 1927
Downland Chevalier foaled 1962

1 Downland Chevalier 3951	**2** Downland Dauphin 3188	**4** Criban Pebble 1700
		8 Criban Grey Grit 1699
		9 9060 Criban Martha
	5 Downland Dragonfly	**10** Downland Serchog 2033
		11 Criban Heather Bell
3 10451 Downland Love in the Mist	**6** Star Supreme 2004	**12** Welsh Echo 1891
		13 9179 Lady Cyrus
	7 9331 Craven Sprightly Twilight	**14** Craven Greylight 1692
		15 9072 Gwyndy Sprite

1. Downland Chevalier

Registration number 3951 in the *Welsh Stud Book,*
Vol. XLV
Chesnut, star and stripe, off fore and near hind little
white, height: 13 hands 3 in, foaled 1962
Breeder: Mrs. Cuff, Plas Llangoedmor, Cardigan

Downland Chevalier certainly deserves his place amongst the influential Section "B" sires, he became top sire in the Welsh Pony & Cob Society sire ratings in 1973, a position which he has maintained every year since.

Chevalier was only shown as a yearling when he was Champion youngstock at the 1963 Ascot Stallion Show. By the time he was two-years-old he was obviously going over-height and consequently has not been shown since.

An idea of the prestige in which Chevalier is regarded by Section "B" breeders can be obtained from the fact that at the 1973 Fayre Oaks Sale, one service was offered by auction (proceeds donated to the Animal Health Trust) and this realised 740 guineas when the services of other sought-after sires realised 20 to 60 guineas (with the exception of

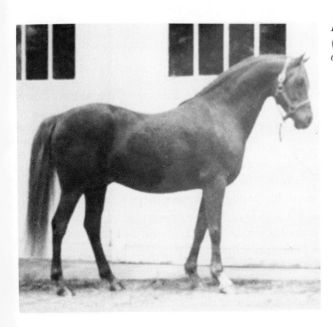

Downland Chevalier.
(Photograph courtesy
of Mrs. Cuff.)

225

Solway Master Bronze at 140 guineas and Downland Romance at 300 guineas).

This figure was not surprising when one considers the vast list of winners sired by Downland Chevalier which include: Abercrychan Cavalier (exported to Holland), Belvoir Zoroaster (championship winner in the United Kingdom and exported to Holland for a record figure), Baledon Squire (Male Champion Royal Welsh Show 1978), Downland Jamila (winner of Championships and first prize mare Royal Welsh 1976), Downland Mandarin (sire of all three winners at the 1979 West Midlands Stallion Show: Sunwillow Lindehorn, Varndell Right Royal and Keston Royal Occasion), Lydstep Ladies Slipper (many times Champion and Lloyds Bank Qualifier Royal Welsh 1977), Rotherwood Honeysuckle (many times Champion including Royal Welsh 1970 and 1978 and another Lloyds Bank Qualifier), Towy Valley Quail, Downland Dandini (successful sire), Penwood Mujib (successful sire), Downland Joyous and Downland Duet (both many times champion) and the super working pony Downland Smuggler. These are but a few of the progeny of Downland Chevalier which are making the sire a household name throughout the world.

2. Downland Dauphin
Registration number 3188 in the *Welsh Stud Book,*
Vol. XLIII
Brown, star, white on four legs, height: 13 hands,
foaled 1959
Breeder: Mrs. Cuff, Downland Stud, Llanddeusant,
Carmarthenshire

The year 1959 was a milestone in the history of the Welsh Pony Section "B" as signified by the births of four much-needed champion stallions Brockwell Cobweb, Chirk Crogan, Solway Master Bronze and Downland Dauphin, the first three gladly still (1979) alive and well, Downland Dauphin living for only six years but yet creating a blood-line which has greatly altered the course of the breed.

When Dauphin was in his youngstock days there were no classes for young Section "B" colts and Dauphin stood second to Criban Victor (*chapter 13.2*) fifteen years his senior, in the one-and-only male class. The following two years Dauphin gained third prizes in classes won by Solway Master Bronze at Royal Welsh Shows with two first prizes at the Ascot Shows in 1961 and 1964. In 1965 Dauphin stood second at Ascot, first (ridden) at Glanusk, second at the Royal Agricultural Society of

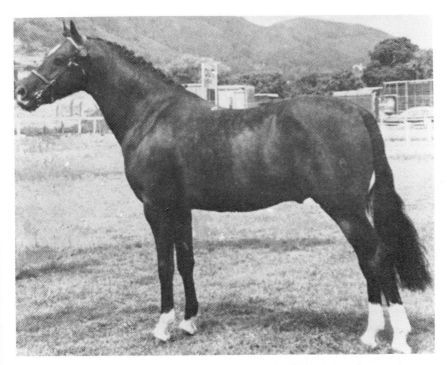

Downland Dauphin.

England, first at the National Pony Show and first at the Royal Welsh. Very soon after the Royal Welsh Show, Dauphin became very ill and despite constant hand feeding by Mrs. Cuff for seven weeks, Dauphin passed away without having reached his prime.

Despite his short life, Dauphin sired many influential stallions and mares. Of course pride of place must go to Downland Chevalier; others who have made a big mark are Bowdell Quiver (one of his last, foaled in 1966, Champion at the 1970 Royal Welsh and stud sire at Gredington), Lydstep Blondie (top-price at the Fayre Oaks Sale, dam amongst many other good ones of Lydstep Barn Dance, sire of Champion Tetworth Nijinsky, Downland Camelia (winner as Section "B" and 13 h and 2 in brood mare), Downland Misty Morning (Champion in hand and under saddle and twice Champion at the Royal Agricultural Society of England, 1968 and 1972), Downland Honeybee, Downland Demoiselle and Downland Sandalwood (all well-known winners), the Champion Welsh Part-bred Downland Sonata and the Champion Riding pony gelding Downland Red Gauntlet.

227

3. Downland Love-in-the-Mist

Registration number 10451 in the *Welsh Stud Book,
Vol. XXXVIII*
Grey, blaze near hind white, height: 13 hands 2 in,
foaled 1954
Breeder: Mrs. Cuff, Downland Stud, Presteigne,
Radnorshire

Love-in-the-Mist was a well-known winner in open 13 hands 2 in childrens riding classes followed by many wins in open brood mare classes at about the time when her most famous sons were foals. Amongst many brood mare wins were first prizes in 1961, 1962 and 1963 at the Three Counties Shows including the Championship at the last occasion. As a brood mare she produced a most formidable list:

1961 Downland Romance, colt, by Downland Roundelay
1962 Downland Chevalier, colt, by Downland Dauphin
1963 Downland Misty Morning, filly, by Downland Dauphin. A well-known winning mare including first prize at the 1972 Royal Welsh Show and Champion at the 1968 and 1972 Royal Agricultural Society of England Shows. Dam of the good sire Downland Manchino

Downland Misty Morning, daughter of Downland Love in the Mist.

1964 Downland Water Gypsy, filly, by Downland Dauphin, dam of the brilliant young sire and 1971 Royal Welsh Champion Downland Mohawk.

1965 Downland Madrigal, filly, by Downland Dauphin

1966 Downland Minerva, filly, by Downland Dominie

1967 Downland Maple Leaf, filly, by Ardgrange Llungwyn

1968 Downland Fleetfoot, colt, by Shawbury Bittermint (in Holland)

1970 Downland Mezzotint, filly, by Downland Dragoon

1973 Downland Melrose, filly, by Downland Toreador

1975 Downland Omega, colt, by Downland Toreador

Unfortunately Love-in-the-Mist died after producing Downland Omega in 1975. However, with this formidable list of famous progeny both male and female, she has gained her place amongst one of the great trend-setters of the Welsh Pony Section "B".

4. Criban Pebble (*chapter 8.4*)

5. Downland Dragonfly
Registration number 2185 F.S.2 in the appendix of
the *Welsh Stud Book, Vol. XL*
(Transferred to Section "A" in *Vol. XLI*)
Liver chesnut, broad blaze, white fetlocks in front,
white to hocks behind, foaled 1955
Breeder: Mrs. Cuff, Downland Stud, Llanddeusant,
Carmarthenshire

In order to show the value of Downland Dragonfly as a brood mare I start with a list of her progeny:

1958 Downland Dainty, filly, by Downland Serchog

1959 Downland Dauphin, colt, by Criban Pebble

1961 Downland Drummer Boy, colt, by Downland Roundelay. Drummer Boy was a successful sire with Mrs. Crisp of the Kirby Cane Stud and afterwards in the U.S.A. I had two daughters of his at Ceulan and both had exceptionally kind temperaments.

1962 Downland Destiny, filly, by Downland Dominie (dam of Downland Bouquet, Downland Periwinkle etc)

1963 Downland Demoiselle, filly, by Downland Dauphin (dam of Downland Dulcet, Downland Diadem, Downland Dancer etc)

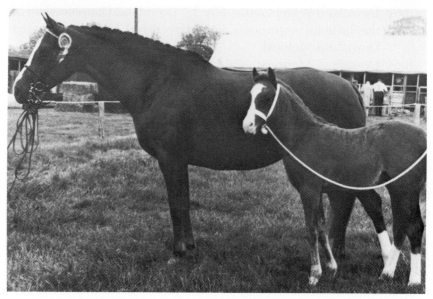

Downland Dryad daughter of Downland Dragonfly, with foal Downland Yeoman.
Photograph taken in 1972.

1964 Downland Deubtante, filly, by Downland Romance (dam of the well-known stallion Downland Tanglewood)

1965 Downland Dryad, filly, by Downland Romance. Dryad was a most beautiful mare, champion several times in youngstock and adult classes; she is dam of Downland Yeoman (Cennen Stud), Downland Decor, Downland Duet and Downland Dabchick, the latter being the top-priced animal at the 1978 Fayre Oaks Sale

1966 Downland Dandini, colt, by Downland Chevalier. Rather smaller than most of Chevalier stock; however a very successful sire at the Leighon Stud

1967 Downland Dragoon, colt, by Downland Chevalier. Exported to Germany but prior to this he sired Downland Kestrel, the top-priced animal at the 1977 Fayre Oaks Sale

1968 Downland Dalesman, colt, by Downland Romance (died as a yearling)

1969 Downland Delphine, filly, by Downland Romance (dam of Downland Damask, Downland Demelza etc)

1970 Downland Duellist, colt, by Downland Chevalier

1973 Downland Dubonnet, colt, by Downland Romance

I see in *Vol. XL* of the *Welsh Stud Book* that I had the considerable task of arranging the export of 28 Welsh Mountain Pony stallions and 161 mares to the U.S.A. I went to see Downland Dragonfly at Llanddeusant and was offered her for a very reasonable figure but was unable to send her to the U.S.A. since her transfer to Section "A" had not come through in time. Had Downland Dragonfly gone to the U.S.A. in 1958, the course of Section "B" breeding in the United Kingdom would be dramatically different and the Downland Dauphin/Downland Chevalier dynasty would not have occurred, a dynasty which has been responsible for the top-rated sire of the last six years plus many of the lower rated sires.

Downland Dragonfly was a little mare of exceptional quality as reflected in her list of influential progeny. She proved to be one of the most popular amongst the large band of "famous names" representing the Welsh Sections "A", "B", "C" and "D" which we assembled for a special Display at the 1972 Royal Welsh Show.

This was her last public appearance and she died in 1974.

6. Star Supreme
Registration number 2004 in the *Welsh Stud Book,*
Vol. XXXIV
Grey, star, white legs, height: 13 hands 1 in,
foaled 1949
Breeder: A. L. Williams, Blaentwrch, Farmers,
Llanwrda, Carmarthenshire

Star Supreme was shown by his breeder at the 1951 Royal Welsh Show (held at Llanelwedd which twelve years later was to become its permanent site) in the class for yearling or two-year-old colts, fillies or geldings. Unfortunately he met some stiff opposition from Mr. Emrys Griffiths' Revel Nance (bred at Vardra), Miss Brodrick's Coed Coch Pinc and Mrs. Hambleton's Llanerch Blue Girl who secured the prizes in that order.

Star Supreme was transferred to Mrs. Cuff in April 1953 and was used at the Downland Stud that year. Along with Downland Love-in-the-Mist foaled in 1954, also by Star Supreme was the colt Downland Gay Star out of Downland Grasshopper (foaled 1949 by Tregoyd Starlight out of Craven Good Friday) a grand old mare who spent her last days at Ceulan having previously produced the influential Kirby Cane Gopher for Mrs. Crisp. Gopher was originator of all the "G" strain at Kirby Cane: Kirby Cane Gauntlet, Golden Road, Guardsman etc.

After the 1953 stud season at Downland Star Supreme was gelded and went on to win many important awards under saddle.

7. Craven Sprightly Twilight

Registration number 9331 in the *Welsh Stud Book,*
Vol. XXXII
Bay, blaze, white hind fetlock, height: 11 hands 3 in,
foaled 1943
Breeder: W. Arthur Pughe, Gwyndy, Burbage,
Hinckley, Leicestershire
Owner: T. Jones Evans, Dinchope, Craven Arms,
Salop.

Mr. W. Arthur Pughe was almost an original member of the Welsh Pony & Cob Society having joined in 1906 when he lived at Gwyndy, Llanfyllin, Montgomeryshire and produced many fine "Gwyndy" ponies. In 1918 he moved house to Leicestershire but continued breeding very good Welsh Ponies and Cobs, Mr. Pughe was President of the Welsh Pony & Cob Society during 1944–1945 and died two years later.

On Mr. Pughe's death his ponies were dispersed all over the United Kingdom some of them making a big influence on the breed e.g. Gwyndy Limelight (Coed Coch); Craven Sprightly's Last, Craven Sprightly Twilight and Craven Sprite Light (Craven); Gwyndy Georgina (Miss Lumsden and later Mr. R. W. H. Jenkins for whom she won at Windsor); Gwyndy Light (Whitehall Stud), Gwyndy Penarth Delight and Gwyndy Penarth Relight (Mr. T. J. Powell), Gwyndy Royal Pearl (Major Careless) etc.

Craven Sprightly Twilight was sold by Mr. Tom Jones Evans to Mrs. Darby (President of the Welsh Pony & Cob Society in 1950–1951) who sold her along with her filly foal (later named Llanerch Blue Girl) to Mrs. Hambleton of the Llanerch Stud.

Mrs. Hambleton sold Sprightly Twilight to Mrs. Cuff in 1952 for whom she bred Downland Love-in-the-Mist in 1954 and Downland High Society (*Welsh Part-Bred Register*) in 1956 then on the Fayre Oaks Sale (6th October 1956) Mrs. Cuff sold her to Mr. Campbell Moodie for whom she continued as a valuable brood mare producing Ankerwycke Comet (1958), Man (1959), Twilight (1960), Sprightly Relight (1961) and Aurora (1962) and there are some of these families still producing under the Ankerwycke prefix.

8. Criban Grey Grit (*chapter 8.8*)

9. **Criban Martha** (*chapter 8.9*)

10. Downland Serchog
Registration number 2033 in the *Welsh Stud Book,*
Vol. XXXIV
Liver chesnut, blue eyes, near fore and both hinds
white, height: 11 hands 3 in, foaled 1951
Breeder: Mrs. K. Cuff, Downland Stud, Presteigne,
Radnorshire
Sire: Downland Dicon 1803
Dam: 8968 Criban Sweetly (*chapter 9.7*) by Criban
Marksman 1395

Downland Dicon (foaled in 1947) was sired by Revel Brightlight a very small but very correct stallion which we leased from Mr. Emrys Griffiths during the early 'fifties and he left us some very nice stock. Dicon was used extensively at the Downland Stud siring such as Downland Blythe Spirit (1951), Butterfly (1950), Image (1951), Leaf (1951), Limpet (1951), Moth (1950), etc; he was then gelded and won prizes under saddle at some major United Kingdom shows.

Serchog was used at stud from 1953 at Downland for four years then was sold to North Wales where he continued to sire some nice stock but of all his progeny, Downland Dragonfly is undoubtedly the most influential.

11. Criban Heather Bell
Registration number 197 F.S. 1 in the appendix of the
Welsh Stud Book, Vol. XXXII
Bay, star, height: 11 hands 2 in, foaled 1943
Sire: Criban Cockade 1627 (*chapter 12.6*)
Dam: Criban Bowbell No. 166 F.S. by
Silverdale Bowtint

Criban Bowbell must have been a very remarkable little mare, apart from producing Heather Bell (from whence came Downland Dauphin), she also produced Criban Belle (*chapter 16.7*) and from her, Criban Biddy Bronze and Solway Master Bronze (*chapter 16.1*).

Before Criban Heather Bell was sold to Mrs. Cuff, at Criban she produced the beautiful Criban Nylon (by Revel Springlight) in 1947 and Criban Red Heather (by Criban Loyalist *Welsh Part-Bred register*) in 1948.

Criban Red Heather was bred from two Welsh Mountain Pony strains and two Polo Pony strains, the intention being to combine the small native pony characteristics with the movement of the Thoroughbred and the balance and temperament of the Polo Pony. Criban Red Heather certainly fulfilled all this, her seventeen offspring being very successful winning as children's riding ponies, jumping and cross-country events both in the United Kingdom and abroad. Listed below are her offspring which were bred at Criban:

1952 Criban Dippy, filly, by Criban Loyalist; Dippy was dam of Criban Astra, Criban Venus, Criban Erica, Criban Galaxy etc.

1954 Criban Heather, filly, by Bwlch Valentino; Heather was sold to Mr. Eckley and she produced Champion Cusop Hostess who in turn was dam of the 1979 Reserve Champion at the Horse of the Year Show, Cusop Heiress.

1955 Criban Dart, colt, by Bwlch Valentino, exported to Mrs. Mackay-Smith (U.S.A.) where he sired some outstanding performance ponies. Dart was also a Champion Hunting Pony in the U.S.A.

Criban Dash, son of Criban Red Heather. Photograph taken at Glanusk Show 1963.

Criban Red Heather (foaled in 1948), daughter of Criban Heather Bell.

1956 Criban Viola, filly, by Bwlch Valentino, sold to the Bullen family she later was dam of Treharne Maxine (Royal Champion).

1957 Filly, by Bwlch Zingaree which died as a yearling.

1958 Criban Joy, filly, by Bwlch Valentino, sold to Mrs. Furness she produced the successful riding pony stallion Knowle Lightning.

1960 Criban Dash, colt, by Bwlch Valentino, he was sold to Mrs. Pennell and became Champion riding pony at the International Show.

1961 Criban Harebell, filly, by Bwlch Valentino was sold to Mrs. Taylor and she was a winning brood mare and dam of winners.

1962 Criban Tigerling, colt, by Criban Tiger Bay. He was a popular sire of riding ponies with Mrs. Joanna MacInnes.

Criban Red Heather was then sold to Mrs. Pennell where she produced Bwlch Red Wing (a Champion Section "B" mare in the ownership of Mrs. Carter), the world-famous Bwlch Hill Wind (now dead), Bwlch Hill Song, Bwlch Hill Mist, Bwlch Carrulla etc.

235

Criban Bowbell (*chapter 16.15*) followed her daughter Heather Bell to the Downland Stud where she produced Downland Wildflower (1955), Downland Smokey Eyes (1956) and Downland Coral (1959).

Heather Bell went to Downland in 1949 and was immediately produced under saddle in which category she won many prizes. Also that year she won a first prize in the Welsh (Section "B") mare class at the Royal Welsh Show and this was followed at this show with a fourth in 1951, second in 1952, third in 1953, fourth in 1954, and fifth in 1955; her daughter Downland Red Heather winning this class in 1958. In addition, Criban Heather Bell won several prizes at other shows such as the Royal Agricultural Society of England and the Bath and West. After her ridden showing days she produced Downland Red Heather (1953), Downland Dragonfly (1955), Downland White Heather (1956) and Downland Cameo (1958).

In 1959 she was sold in foal to Revel Challenge to Mrs. Crisp of the Kirby Cane Stud duly producing Kirby Cane Songbelle the following year followed by Kirby Cane Bustle in 1962 and Kirby Cane Hoodwink a well-known "performance" winner in 1963.

Criban Heather Bell deserves her place in any pony history, as a show mare, ridden child's pony, producer of some of the best Welsh Section "B" and riding pony strains and producer of top performers.

12. Welsh Echo

Registration number 1891 in the *Welsh Stud Book,*
Vol. XXXIII
Chesnut, white on forehead, both white hind socks,
height: 13 hands 2 in, foaled 1943
Owner: A. L. Williams, Blaentwrch Farm, Farmers,
Llanwrda, Carmarthenshire
Breeder: W. D. Williams, Post Office, Farmers,
Llanwrda, Carmarthenshire
Sire: Welsh Patriot 1651
Dam: Lady Valiant by Llethi Valiant 1238 (*chapter 26.12*)
G-dam: Goldflake by Myrtle Welsh Flyer (*chapter 29.8*)

Welsh Echo was one of only two Welsh Pony of Cob type stallions registered in *Vol. XXXIII* of the *Welsh Stud Book* (1949); such was the dearth of this type of pony in the immediate post-war years. Welsh Echo won a first prize in the Welsh Pony of Cob type stallion class at the

Welsh Patriot, sire of Welsh Echo photographed in the farmyard at Blaentwrch. (Photograph courtesy of University of Reading Museum of English Rural Life.)

Royal Welsh Show in 1949. His sire, Welsh Patriot (who was foaled in 1939 but died in 1948) had previously won the first prize of that class in 1947.

Welsh Patriot was a bay with star and two white hind fetlocks standing about 12 hands 3 in, he was sired by the big Cob stallion Cymro'r Wy (Mr. Tom Wood-Jones) and out of Mr. Alfred Williams' good mare Welsh Homage by Ceitho Welsh Comet (*chapter 24.2*) the grand-dam being Blaentwrch Firefly (foaled in 1914) by Bleddfa Shooting Star (*chapter 4.1*) produced at the time when Shooting Star was leased by Mr. Dafydd Evans, Llwyncadfor. Welsh Homage was Champion Cob type Pony at the 1937 Royal Welsh Show and third prize mare the following year.

237

13. Lady Cyrus

Registration number 9179 in the *Welsh Stud Book,*
Vol. XXXII
Light roan, wide blaze, four white legs, height:
13 hands 2 in, foaled 1941
Owner and Breeder: A. L. Williams, Blaentwrch,
Farmers, Carmarthenshire
Sire: Craven Cyrus 1441
Dam: 8328 Blaentwrch Firelight by Baedeker 500
G-dam: 8326 Blaentwrch Firefly (foaled 1914) by
Bleddfa Shooting Star 73
G-g-dam: 1847 Dolly Grey II (foaled 1902) by
Eiddwen Flyer II
G-g-g-dam: 271 Wild Duck (foaled in 1896)

Craven Cyrus was foaled in 1927, sired by King Cyrus (Arab bred by
Lady Wentworth sired by the World Champion Skowronek) and was
out of the delightful little Mountain Pony mare Irfon Lady Twilight by
Dyoll Starlight (*chapter 2.1*). He was described in the Craven Stud Sale
Catalogue (3rd October 1936) (lot 24) as "without doubt one of the best
sires of riding ponies alive today; he has the best of limbs and sweetest of
tempers". It was at this Sale that Craven Cyrus was purchased by Mr.
Williams and he stayed at Blaentwrch until he died.

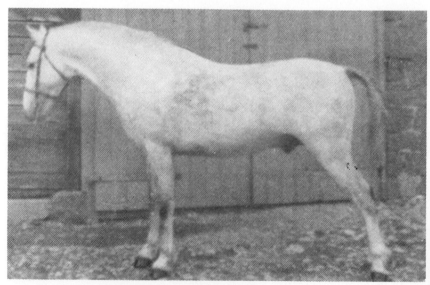

Craven Cyrus sire of Lady Cyrus and Craven Greylight.

It can safely be said that the Welsh Riding pony started with Tanybwlch Berwyn (foaled 1924) and Craven Cyrus (foaled in 1927); these were the only two strains until Reeves Golden Lustre came along in 1945, Criban Victor in 1944 and Solway Master Bronze in 1959.

What is not generally appreciated is the big effect which Craven Cyrus has had on the Welsh Mountain Ponies mainly through his daughter Wentworth Grey Dapples. Considering Royal Welsh Show Champions, the following are direct descendants of his: Clan Pip, Ankerwycke Clan Snowdon and Ready Token Glen Bride and of course, Clan Pip is responsible for the other Champions: Revel Cassino, Bengad Day Lily and Bengad Love-in-the-Mist. Craven Cyrus himself had been Champion at the 1939 Royal Welsh Show.

Lady Cyrus won a first prize in the Welsh mare class at the 1947 Royal Welsh Show beating Mrs. A. R. Hepburn's Primula and Craven Nell who had both done well under saddle.

14. Craven Greylight
Registration number 1692 in the *Welsh Stud Book,*
Vol. XXXII
Grey, height: 11 hands 3 in, foaled 1939
Breeder: Tom Jones Evans, Dinchope Farm,
Craven Arms, Shropshire
Sire: Craven Cyrus 1441 *(chapter 14.13)*
Dam: 8616 Gatesheath Dainty by Grove Sprightly
1036 *(chapter 5.1)*
G-dam: 7303 Dunchurch Venus by Bleddfa
Shooting Star 73 *(chapter 4.1)*

Gatesheath Dainty was a very well-known show mare during the years just before the Second World War e.g. she won the first prize and Championship at the 1938 National Pony Society Show and was second and Reserve Champion at the 1938 Royal Welsh Show. Dainty was one of the few ponies retained at Dinchope after the 1936 Sale and with Sprightly becoming an old man (he was 27 years old when his last foal, Craven Sprightly's Last was born) the stallions used mainly at Dinchope during the war years were Craven Greylight and Craven Tit Bit.

Apart from Craven Sprightly Twilight, Greylight sired Craven Iona (winner for Mrs. Cuff), Craven Blue Light and Craven Daylight at Dinchope. The breeding of Craven Daylight is interesting since he was by Craven Greylight and his dam Gatesheath Dainty is also, of course, dam of his sire; Craven Daylight was a big winner in South Wales for

239

Gatesheath Dainty, dam of Craven Greylight. (Photograph courtesy of G. H. Parsons.)

Mr. Edgar Herbert, later he was owned by Mr. Douglas Meredith and Mr. J. J. Borthwick (jointly), Mr. R. T. Evans and he ended his days as a tremendously successful sire at the Fayre Stud of Mr. Theron Wilding-Davies.

Craven Greylight was gelded in 1947 and sold to Miss Anne Lumsden as a riding pony.

The last time I saw Gatesheath Dainty was at the 1948 Shropshire and West Midland Show where, with Capt. Howson judging she stood second in the brood mare class (although she was 24 years old) to her beautiful daughter Craven Bright Sprite, winner of so many important awards for Mrs. Cuff both in hand and later under saddle. Third in this class was another of Dinchope's "old ladies" the bay Gwyndy Sprite (at 21 years) followed by Miss Brodrick's Coed Coch Seirian, Capt. Brierley's Brierwood Treacle and Criban White Wings and Mrs. Cyril Darby's Craven Blue Light (a daughter of Craven Greylight).

After the death of Mr. Tom Jones Evans, Gatesheath Dainty kept on breeding at Dinchope for Mr. Douglas Meredith producing 1948: Craven Dainty (dam of first Craven Dandy at Dinchope then several good mares at the Penmor Stud), 1950: Craven Dainty Lass then in 1951: her last foal (at 26 years) Craven Sprightly Light, an outstanding mare who won a Championship at the Royal Agricultural Society of England for Mr. Wilding-Davies before being exported to Australia (Fairway Stud) where she bred excellent stock.

15. Gwyndy Sprite
Registration number 9072 in the *Welsh Stud Book, Vol. XXXII*
Bay, blaze, white near hind leg, height: 11 hands 3 in, foaled 1927
Breeder: W. Arthur Pughe, Gwyndy, Grove Road, Hinckley, Leicestershire
Sire: Grove Sprightly 1036 (*chapter 5.1*)
Dam: 9069 Gwyndy Georgina II (foaled 1913) by Prince of Cardiff 84 (*chapter 6.8*)

On the death of Mr. Pughe, Gwyndy Sprite and her daughter Craven Sprightly Twilight were bought by Mr. Tom Jones Evans and as already mentioned when dealing with Gatesheath Dainty, Sprite was shown by Mr. Evans at the 1948 Shropshire Show when she was 21 years old. After the death of Mr. Tomes Jones Evans, Gwyndy Sprite was retained at Dinchope by Mr. Meredith producing Craven Debonair in 1949.

15
Reeves Golden Lustre

2 Ceulan Revoke 1720	**4** Ceulan Revolt 1719	**8** Coed Coch Glyndwr 1617
		9 8888 Coed Coch Serliw
	5 8849 Ceulan Silverleaf	**10** Llwyn Brilliant 1342
		11 5553 Seren Ceulan
3 Ceulan Silver Lustre	**6** Incoronax A.H.S.B.	**12** Raseem A.H.S.B.
		13 Incoronata A.H.S.B.
	5 8849 Ceulan Silverleaf	**10** Llwyn Brilliant 1342
		11 5553 Seren Ceulan

1

Reeves Golden
Lustre 3456

1. Reeves Golden Lustre

Registration number 3456 in the *Welsh Stud Book,*
Vol. XLIV
(originally registered in the Welsh Part-Bred
Register owing to having an F.S. dam but in 1960
allowed into the *Welsh Stud Book* to alleviate the
dearth of Section "B" stallions).
Chesnut roan, three white legs, height: 13 hands,
foaled 1945
Breeder: E. S. Davies, Ceulan Stud, Talybont,
Cardiganshire.

Golden Lustre's dam had always run wild on the Cardiganshire marshlands and in 1947 he was still out with the Ceulan mares, his dam, her filly foal and yearling sister (both by Ceulan Revelry, full-brother to Ceulan Revoke, sire of Golden Lustre). By now, he was probably feeling "the joys of spring" to which Ceulan Revelry would not take too kindly and Golden Lustre had to be rescued out of a ditch and revived with much beer! It was obvious now that it was time for him to be handled; it transpired that he had a very friendly temperament and he was soon sold to Mrs. D. Reeve Reeves of Penn, Buckinghamshire (along with his dam who still had never been touched and two sisters). And so it was that Golden Lustre led the group of loose ponies from Talybont to Llandre Railway station headed for Reeves Stud. The Ceulan ponies were well used to being driven along the roads since there were several miles between various grazing lands and there was very little traffic in those days.

In 1948 and for several years afterwards, Mrs. Reeve Reeves (who kept riding stables in Penn) visited Talybont with various groups of clients and ponies for riding holidays in the magnificent mid-Wales hills and Golden Lustre (and his dam) returned to their native heath several times, incorporating many prizes at mid-Wales shows amidst their three or four weeks of riding in the hills.

Until Golden Lustre was accepted into the *Welsh Stud Book,* he was used mainly on riding pony mares producing such well-known riding ponies as Cherry Pie, Golden Fantasy, Golden Link, Fluster and Silver Gilt. When the most famous riding pony mare of her time was put to stud and sent to Golden Lustre a pony magazine ran a competition for children to suggest the most suitable name for the foal. Indeed Reeves Golden Lustre was a household name in the riding pony world at that time. Also his photograph would have been seen by many thousands of

245

Reeves Golden Lustre, photographed as a two-year-old (1947).

Elphicks Harvest Gold, daughter of Reeves Golden Lustre. Photograph taken in 1974. (Photograph courtesy of Photonews.)

Pitkins, Clements Inn, London, WC2.) On page 53, he is striding out well with her but on page 120, he is lying down and looks quite happy to stay in this position as long as Imogen was prepared to feed him in this lazy pose!

Any Welsh ponies sired by him during this period obviously had to go back to the "Foundation stock" registry but many of his progeny of this period have made valuable contributions to the Welsh Pony Section "B" and by now have been up-graded through three generations into full-registration status.

Examples of his Foundation stock daughters are Elphicks Harvest Gold, Antonia and Reeves Golden Samphire. Elphicks Harvest Gold began a very successful family of winners for Miss Reader; Antonia was dam of the eminently successful riding pony Abercrychan Atonella and later Abercrychan Angelina and Abercrychan Cordelia (two of the highest-priced mares on the 1978 Fayre Oaks Sale); Reeves Golden Samphire was a big winner for the Downland Stud where she produced such well-known animals as Downland Sandpiper, Downland Sing Song, Downland Songbird and Downland Sandalwood, the latter being one of the foundation mares at the successful Tetworth Stud were she produced e.g. Tetworth Tropical Romance who, in turn, was one of the foundation mares for Mr. Hensby's Laithe Hill Stud, one of her daughters, Laithe Hill Tropical Sand being the second-highest priced Section "B" pony at the 1974 Fayre Oaks Sale (when she was only a yearling).

After 1960, when (along with Coed Coch Pawl etc.) he was accepted into the *Welsh Stud Book* his services were in the majority of cases required for registered Welsh mares; examples of his progeny being:

(i) the stallion Cusop Rockery foaled in 1964, a successful sire at the Shimpling Stud producing such as Shimpling Moon Frolic, dam of the successful Shrimpling Moon Tipsey.

(ii) In 1965, Golden Lustre stood at the Springbourne Stud, his produce in 1966 including the Royal Welsh Show Champion Springbourne Golden Flute (who fetched 1,200 guineas at the 1969 Fayre Oaks Sale and returned to Wales at 950 guineas at the 1976 Fayre Oaks Sale) and Clyphada Mystery, a successful brood mare at the Bengad Stud.

(iii) Golden Lustre spent 1966 at the Sinton Stud, his progeny including the well-known Sinton Court Perilustre and Sinton Lustre Bell (sold to Essex at the 1967 Fayre Oaks Sale).

2. Ceulan Revoke

Registration number 1720 in the *Welsh Stud Book, Vol. XXXII*

Grey, darker mane, tail and points, height 11 hands 2 in, foaled 1942

Breeder: E. S. Davies, Ceulan Stud, Talybont, Cardiganshire.

Ceulan Revoke was the oldest of three full-brothers, the other two being Ceulan Revelry (foaled 1943) and Ceulan Reveller (foaled 1944). Previous to these three colts there was a filly, again, a full-sister Ceulan Blue Vision, a well-known winner and producer of champions in the ownership of the Ty'r Sais Stud.

My father's intention was to drive these three colts with their sire Ceulan Revolt as a team of four but a family bereavement caused a change of plans and all four were sold one-by-one. Ceulan Reveller was sold to Mrs. Arkwright in Midlothian; he later returned to Wales where he stood as senior sire at some Welsh studs e.g. Cui, he gained a first premium for the Eppynt hill in 1955 and later we sent him to Mr. Simpson in the U.S.A.

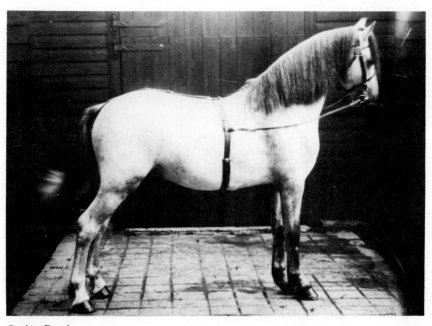

Ceulan Revoke.

Ceulan Revelry was sold to Mr. Tom Norman Lewis of the Bolgoed Stud where he won many prizes for many years both in hand and harness; he then spent his remaining days on Gower where he had almost the same effect on the Gower ponies as Dyoll Starlight or Coed Coch Glyndwr had on the ponies of Wales, from the day of his arrival on Gower, that area produced one champion after another e.g. both the winning Section "A" mare and the Champion Section "C" at the 1975 Royal Welsh Show were grand-daughters of his.

Ceulan Revoke was the first to be sold, he went to the Reeves Stud in 1945, was re-registered as Reeves Ceulan Revoke in the same year and gelded in 1947, after winning several prizes at Windsor and the National Pony Society Shows as a stallion. For some years after gelding, he worked as a riding school pony at Reeves Stables, then he was sold to the Duke and Duchess of Norfolk for whom he won several prizes ridden by their children. Another exhibitor who won many prizes with him was Mr. Bobby Black (brother to the world-famous whip Mrs. Cynthia Haydon). Revoke ended his days with Mrs. Parsons-Smith of the Roughets Stud.

3. Ceulan Silver Lustre
Registration number 191 F.S. in the *Welsh Stud Book,
Vol. XXXII*
Grey, near fore and off hind white, height: 13 hands,
foaled 1938
Breeder: E. S. Davies, Ceulan Stud, Talybont,
Cardiganshire.

As already related, when writing about her son, Reeves Golden Lustre, Silver Lustre ran wild on the Cardiganshire marshlands until 1947 when she was sold (along with Golden Lustre and her two daughters: the yearling Reeves Crystal and the foal Reeves Nantgarw) to Mrs. Reeve Reeves of Penn in Buckinghamshire. Silver Lustre was in foal again for 1948 so remained un-caught for her first winter in England. Unfortunately the foal died so it was decided that it was time that Silver Lustre was caught and within two months she won a third prize in the ridden Welsh class at the National Pony Society Show. This was the start of an extremely successful showing career which began at ten years old and carried on until she was twenty-two.

Amongst her winnings were eight successive first prizes in 13.2 hands open ridden classes in 1950 (ridden by Geoffrey Carter), the same year being Reserve for the Country Life Cup at the Royal Welsh Show. In

Ceulan Silver Lustre at the Beaconsfield and Penn Show 1950.

addition, she won a first prize at the Ponies of Britain Show four times. One achievement which is worthy of mention was the 1956 Henley Show where Golden Lustre stood first, his son Golden Emblem was second, Silver Lustre was third and a grand-daughter, Reeves Ruby was fourth. Her last show was at the 1960 Royal East Berks where she was Champion Mountain or Moorland Pony for the fourth time.

In 1954 the Ponies of Britain Club staged a show of native ponies at Olympia as part of the *Evening News* Town and Country Show; Silver Lustre was selected to represent the Welsh Pony and paraded twice a day, decorated with flowers and carrying a floral doll!

Silver Lustre will be remembered more for what she produced than what she won in the show ring despite the formidable total of the latter.

After Golden Lustre (foaled in 1945) were the two sisters Reeves Crystal and Reeves Nantgarw (both by Ceulan Revelry). Nantgarw was a big winner under saddle, Crystal was smaller and was sold to the Twyford Stud where she produced the three full-sisters Twyford Cuckoo, Chiante (Roman Stud, Holland) and Cobweb (Rondeels Stud, Holland). I was delighted to see the latter two in September 1979. Before Crystal left the Reeves Stud (in 1950) she produced Reeves Coral (by Ceulan Revolt); Coral was also for a time at the Twyford Stud where she produced Twyford Cossack (well-known sire in Ireland). I bought her in 1965 and had Ceulan Coral out of her, then she spent the rest of her life in the Mynd Stud producing some very good winners such as Mynd Cowrie (in 1966) by Downland Romance. Silver Lustre then produced another three full-sisters by Mrs. Yeomans' Kirby Cane Shuttlecock: Reeves Sapphire (won the Royal Agricultural Society of England for Mrs. Dorian Williams), Reeves Filigree (a big winner under saddle in Open classes and afterwards a brood mare in Cardiganshire) and Reeves Fairy Lustre winner of so many important Championships when owned by Miss Miriam Reader (including the 1973 Royal Welsh Show Championship). Two fillies sired by her grandson, Reeves Golden Emblem were Reeves Cameo and Reeves

Reeves Sapphire, daughter of Ceulan Silver Lustre. (Photograph courtesy of Blinkhorns.)

Reeves Fairy Lustre, daughter of Ceulan Silver Lustre. (Photograph courtesy of J. E. L. Mayes.)

Cinnamon, the latter better known as the dam of Master Cinnamon who was quoted in *Horse and Hound* in February 1968 as having been sold for a record price (1,000 guineas) for a leading-rein pony.

In 1964 the Reeves Stud moved to mid-Wales and Silver Lustre produced Reeves Silver Thread by Ceulan Vanadium. This is the family which now represents this strain at the Reeves Stud. In May 1968, when Silver Lustre was thirty years old, she was asked to take part in a National Stock Breeders Association display, mainly for overseas visitors and was given a terrific ovation for giving such a fine show despite her advanced years. This was her last public appearance and she died on 29th October 1970.

4. Ceulan Revolt

Registration number 1719 in the *Welsh Stud Book,*
Vol. XXXII
Red roan, little white on four legs, height: 11 hands
3½ in, foaled 1938
Breeder: E. S. Davies, Ceulan Stud, Talybont,
Cardiganshire.

Ceulan Revolt has the distinction of being the first-ever foal of the greatly influential Coed Coch Glyndwr. He won many prizes for Ceulan Stud in the immediate post-war years e.g. Champion in hand at the 1946 Lampeter Show and he also won in harness, often against Hackneys. Of all our ponies at that time, he was the favourite of my late brother's who would immediately harness him up and drive him for many miles on his arrival home on vacation from Veterinary College.

Ceulan Revolt was sold to Mr. Pickles of High Wycombe (who owned also two champion Arab stallions). Mr. Pickles showed Revolt a few times and did quite well with him at Shropshire and West Midland and Royal Agricultural Society of England Shows but came to the conclusion that there were not enough mares in that area to justify keeping a stallion and Revolt came back to Wales.

For Mr. Emrys Griffiths of the Revel Stud, Revolt secured three premiums for the Breconshire Black Mountains duing the early fifties. One of the most influential blood-lines to be created whilst at the Revel was Revolt's daughter Revel Fair Maid (foaled 1952, died 1972) who produced Weston Fair Lady, Weston Fair Charm, Weston Rawhide, Weston Mayfair, Weston Dorita, Weston Highwayman, Weston Pageant, Weston Fair Maid and her last foal, Weston Christmas Cracker foaled on Christmas Day 1971. This family has had a big influence on the Welsh Mountain Pony breed, just one of them, Weston Fair Lady producing such winners and champions as Weston May Day Lady, Weston Gay Lady, Weston May Queen, Weston Fairy Queen, Weston Pearly Queen, Weston Pearly Princess, Weston Mink Muff, Weston Sport, Weston Carnival, Weston Fair, Weston Brandy etc.

Ceulan Revolt's next owner was Mr. Willie Davies of the Eppynt Stud who won the premium with him for the Eppynt Mountains area. Mr. Davies then sold him to Mr. Llewellyn Richards where he sired some good stock such as the two roan stallions Criban Rocky and Criban Rockaway. A roan mare Criban Rock Dove (foaled during this period 1957/1958) came to Ceulan Stud in 1962 and produced eleven fillies for us during the period up to 1974 when she went to some good

253

friends of ours. Ceulan Revolt was then owned for a short time by Mr. W. M. Thomas of Talybont-on-Usk whose great-uncle had bred Moonlight, dam of Dyoll Starlight (*chapter 2.1*). From Mr. Thomas I bought a Revolt daughter, Strawberry Princess out of Strawberry Queen, daughter of Criban Biddy Bronze (*chapter 16.3*) whom Mr. Thomas had bred also. And I also bought Ceulan Revolt back and sent him to the Reeves Stud where he finished his days in great comfort. Ceulan Revolt was still siring good foals in Buckinghamshire in the early sixties, one of them a very nice grey filly, out of Ready Token Bo Peep, I bought whilst on our honeymoon from Lady Barclay and she was named Ceulan Honeymoon, later producing outstanding stock for the Egetofte Stud in Denmark.

5. Ceulan Silverleaf
Registration number 8849 in the *Welsh Stud Book*,
Vol. XXX
Grey, height 11 hands 3 in, foaled 1929

Silverleaf won a first prize at the Talybont Show in 1930 and was first and Reserve Female Champion at the 1932 Royal Welsh Show. Her first two foals, Ceulan Silver Belle and Ceulan Silver Gem (foaled in 1934 and 1935) were exported to Mr. Idelfonzo Stanga in Italy (along with Grove Will O'The Wisp, Craven Bywiog and Bowdler Barbara

Ceulan Silverleaf photograph taken in 1931. (Photograph courtesy of E. S. Davies.)

Ceulan Revelry as a two-year-old (1945). Son of Ceulan Revolt and Ceulan Silverleaf.

and Mr. Stanga published a book with individual photographs of his purchases and Welsh pony history), then followed a Foundation stock filly Ceulan Blue Moon (foaled 1936) by Saleve (T.B.) by Spion Kop; another Foundation stock filly Ceulan Silver Lustre (foaled 1938) by Incoronax (Arab) then a gap until the four by Ceulan Revolt: Blue Vision (1941), Revoke (1942), Revelry (1943), Reveller (1944), a filly Ceulan Cora (by Eryri Gwyndaf) foaled in 1948 won a second prize in an enormous class at the 1951 Royal Welsh Show before fetching the top-price of the 1952 Welsh Pony & Cob Society Sale, selling to Anne, Duchess of Rutland, who exported her to the U.S.A. a few years later.

Silverleaf's last two foals were Ceulan Valentine (born on St. Valentine's Day 1951) and Reeves New Leaf (exported to Dr. Crist, U.S.A.) foaled in 1953. This family is represented at the Ceulan Stud by Valentine's two daughters Ceulan Venus and Ceulan Vanity and various of Valentine's grand-daughters.

Silverleaf had quite a lot of successes in the mid-Wales show rings in the post-war years. At the 1946 Aberystwyth Show she won a first prize (in a class of twenty-two where her stable-mate Coed Coch Serliw was second) and then went on to be Supreme Champion Horse or Pony of the Show beating the Shires (very many of them in those days), Hunters, Riding ponies, Hackneys, the lot.

For her last years, Silverleaf lived in retirement, usually caring for other foals after they had been weaned. She died in 1960 aged thirty-one years.

6. Incoronax
Registered in the *Arab Stud Book, Vol. VIII*
Grey, off fore and two hind fetlocks white,
height: 14 hands 3 in
Breeder: Lady Wentworth, Crabbett Park,
Crawley, Sussex.
Owner: Moses Griffith, M.Sc., Capel Bangor,
Aberystwyth.

Incoronax ridden by Mr. Moses Griffith.

8. Coed Coch Glyndwr (*chapter 6.1*)

9. Coed Coch Serliw (*chapter 10.11*)

10. Llwyn Brilliant
Registration number 1342 in the *Welsh Stub Book, Vol.
XXV* (incorrectly registered in Section "B")
Also registered in *Vol. XXVII*, registration number
1420 (this registration cancelled in *Vol. XXV*)
Registration in Section "A", registration number
1342, *Vol. XXVIII*
Dark grey, star, height: 12 hands, foaled 1924
Breeder: Major W. M. Dugdale, D.S.O., Llwyn,
Llanfyllin, Montgomeryshire.
Owner: R. A. C. Pugh, Voelas, Glandyfi,
Cardiganshire.
Sire: Kilhendre Celtic Silverlight (*chapter 6.12*)
Dam: 2902 Lady Lightfoot

Llwyn Brilliant was bought by Mr. R. A. C. Pugh from his breeder as
a yearling. Mr. Pugh showed him at the 1927 Royal Welsh Agricultural
Society Show in the any-age stallion class where he stood seventh below
Lady Wentworth's Grove King Cole II (purchased one month pre-
viously at the Grove Sale, Llwyn Satan (*chapter 6.6*) and his full-brother,
Mrs. Sofer Whitburn's Llwyn Temptation, Caer Beris King Cole and
Grove Sprightly (also purchased one month previously). Llwyn
Brilliant was followed amongst this galaxy of stars by five others in this
good class. He was also shown by Mr. Pugh at the 1928 Royal Welsh
Agricultural Society Show (Wrexham) where he stood eighth, beaten
by Craven Master Shot, Llwyn Satan, Grove Will O'the Wisp, Caer
Beris King Cole, Trillo Columba, Wingerworth Eiddwen and Gates-
heath Magic, beating Coed Coch Pryfllwyd, Berwyn Ranger,
Tanybwlch Bryn and one or two more. It was in 1928 that he served
Seren Ceulan (who incidentally was Overall Champion Welsh Pony at
the 1928 Royal Welsh Show).
   Llwyn Brilliant was possibly the only Mountain Pony stallion in
North Cardiganshire during those years, most other breeders keeping
Welsh Cobs or ponies (Cob type). Llwyn Brilliant had served his time
(three years) with Mr. Pugh and was sold as a premium stallion to the
Cefn Bryn Society (Gower) where he was awarded the first premium in
1929. My father bought Kilhendre Celtic King Cup as a replacement

257

	£	s	d
cost of pony	3	13	6
rail fare: Llandre to Oswestry		9	0
Oswestry to Ellesmere		1	0
taxi to sale		5	0
taxi to station		5	0
Ellesmere to Borth		9	0
bus from Borth		1	0
paid man to walk pony to station		5	0
total cost of Kilhendre Celtic King Cup:	5	8	6

Very little is known of Llwyn Brilliant after 1929. Usually when a stallion becomes a premium stallion for one area, he is passed from one premium area to another every three years. Surprisingly, Llwyn Brilliant returned to private ownership being owned by Mr. Tom Jones Evans in 1935 who showed him at the National Pony Society Show at Islington to stand fifth to the same owner's Grove Sprightly, then Bowdler Brightlight, Caer Beris King Cole, and Craven Black and White.

11. Seren Ceulan (*chapter 24.3*)

12. Raseem
Chesnut Arab stallion, foaled 1922
Owner: Lady Wentworth, Crabbet Park, Poundhill,
Sussex

My father often had cards and booklets of the Crabbet Stud from Lady Wentworth, one such booklet dated 1924 lists 32 mares and 28 stallions mostly photographed. Raseem is No. 13 stallion and his photograph appears on page 32 of the booklet. (The photographs referred to are not reproduced here due to the emphasis on the Welsh breeds.) A later stud card quotes Raseem as "World Champion" standing at a stud fee of 500 guineas at a time when many champion Crabbet stallions stood at fees of 5 to 15 guineas. Raseem was by the magnificent No. 3 stallion Rasim (exported to Poland) out of No. 12 mare Rim.

Owner: Lady Wentworth, Crabbet Park, Poundhill,
Sussex.

Her sire was the world-famous Skowronek, a white Kehilan Ajuz of which Lady Wentworth wrote: "No more perfect specimen has ever been imported to England". Nisreen, dam of Incoronata, was a bay mare bred in 1919 and a daughter of Nasra, a foundation mare at Crabbet whose dam, Nefisa, was by Hadban purchased from Jakeen Ibn Aghil Sheykh by Lady Anne Blunt in 1883.

16

Solway Master Bronze foaled 1959

2	4	8
Coed Coch Glyndwr 1617	Revolt 493	Llwyn Tyrant 207
		9 145 Llwyn Flyaway
	5 8683 Dinarth Henol	**10** Llwyn Satan 1325
		11 6350 Irfon Marvel

1

Solway Master Bronze 3197

3	6	12
Criban Biddy Bronze	Criban Gay Snip 2163	Criban D-Day 1725
		13 9138 Criban Whalebone
	7 Criban Belle	**14** Bolgoed Squire 1681
		15 Criban Bowbell

1. Solway Master Bronze

Registration number 3197 in the *Welsh Stud Book,*
Vol. XLIII
Chesnut, blaze, four white legs, height: 12 hands 3 in,
foaled 1959
Breeder: Lady Reiss, Down Grange, Basingstoke,
Hants., England.

Solway Master Bronze was purchased by Miss Miriam Reader from his breeder in October 1959. Miss Reader had been promised first refusal on him before he was born if he turned out to be a colt since Miss Reader was very keen to own a colt of that breeding.

Master Bronze soon began to notch up some good wins for his new owner; at the 1960 Ponies of Britain Show, he ended up Reserve Supreme Champion. Later that year he was Champion Mountain and Moorland Pony at Essex County, a title which he won four times in all.

In 1961 he ventured into Wales and ended up as Royal Welsh Show Section "B" Champion for which he had to beat many well-known favourites; a rare feat for a two-year-old who had to compete in an any-age class. This particular championship he repeated again in 1962 and 1963, every time at the Royal Welsh shown by Mr. David Reynolds. Other noteable wins include the Champion Ridden Mountain and Moorland Pony (ridden by Miss Jane Bullen) at the 1962 National Pony Society Show, Champion Richmond Royal 1962, Champion Peterborough 1963, etc.

However successful he was in the show ring, Master Bronze is better known as an extremely successful sire. His first foal, Elphicks Honey B was unbeaten in first-ridden classes and was Champion riding pony at Windsor beating all the bigger ponies despite being only 11 hands 3 in. high. Honey B won many brood mare and Mountain and Moorland championships in later life. Elphicks Fidelio, out of Reeves Fairy Lustre was unbeaten as a foal and won two years running at the Ponies of Britain Show.

Elphicks Golden Gift won for three successive years at the Royal Agricultural Society of England Show in hand for the Hon. Mrs. Ponsonby and later won many prizes under saddle when owned by Mr. Daffurn. Elphicks Golden Grain won many times as a foal and was later (1970) Champion at the Newark and Notts Show. All these Elphicks winning ponies trace back on their dam's side to Ceulan Silver Lustre (*chapter 15.3*) through Elphicks Harvest Gold, Honey Moon and Reeves Fairy Lustre. One son, Lechlade Scarlet Pimpernel is siring many

263

Detail from the painting of Solway Master Bronze by Alison Guest (1973). Painting courtesy of Miss M. Reader.

Solway Master Bronze. (Photograph courtesy of J. E. L. Mayes.)

Elphicks Honey B, the first foal of Solway Master Bronze at the 1973 Ponies of Britain Show. (Photograph courtesy of Photonews.)

in-hand and under saddle winners and was sold to Dr. Mayze of New South Wales in April 1979.

Others of the progeny of Master Bronze are doing well in Performance classes such as Housemaster (half-thoroughbred), Deverell Paymaster, and Bronze Boy. At the 1978 National Pony Society Ridden Native Pony Championships held at Olympia in December three of the first four were his g-sons and g-daughters i.e. Criffell Caspar first, Burstye Kythnos second and Keston Royal Occasion fourth. Another Welsh Part-bred stallion Pendley Model was Supreme Champion at the Ponies of Britain Show.

Up to 1974 Master Bronze had sired 541 foals when he went to the Hon. Mrs. Ponsonby's stud where is is now standing to a very select number of approved mares.

Many of his progeny have proved their worth as kind-tempered mounts for young children. This characteristic they derive from their kind-tempered sire who, although he always shows off to best advantage if there is an appreciative audience present, is, when alone, kindness itself.

265

3. Criban Biddy Bronze
Registration number 1042 F.S. 2. in the Appendix of
the *Welsh Stud Book, Vol. XXXVI*
Liver chesnut, star, height: 12 hands, foaled 1950
Breeder: W. M. Thomas, Cui Farm,
Talybont-on-Usk, Brecon.

The family of Mr. Will Thomas had kept ponies on the Brecon
Beacons for many generations, especially at their previous farm, Pentre,
Abercanafon, Talybont-on-Usk; ponies such as Pentre Bucephalus
(foaled in 1908 and g-g-sire of Criban Shot, *chapter 9.12*), Pentre Taffy
foaled in 1899 and Dyoll Moonlight (foaled in 1896 and dam of the
immortal Dyoll Starlight (*chapter 2.1*). Mr. Thomas was well-known in
the Brecon area for the care he bestowed on his animals and Criban
Belle had been given to Mr. Thomas for retirement (Mr. Thomas had
Ceulan Revolt when he was a great age and in fact, it was from him that
I bought him back).

As soon as Mr. Llewellyn Richards (who had given Criban Belle to
Mr. Thomas) saw Biddy Bronze as a foal he suspected that here was

Criban Biddy Bronze.

something special and he bought the foal back at weaning time. The family and staff at Criban did not hold out any high hopes for Biddy Bronze, indeed Mr. Richards showed her in a small class at the 1953 Royal Welsh Show where she gained only a fourth prize. However, Mr. Richards having seen her as such a promising foal maintained that she would make a "good one" one day and he stated (which the staff did not believe!) that he would want a high figure for her.

Shortly afterwards Biddy Bronze was "spotted" by Miss Elspeth Ferguson who had gone to Criban to see a 14-hand pony which she had not bought. Miss Ferguson bought her immediately and within a very short time had sold her to Mrs. John Reiss (now Lady Reiss). It says a lot for the intuition of these two ladies who saw great things in this filly labelled by many as an "ugly duckling".

Under the ownership of Mrs. Reiss and ridden by her daughter Virginia Booth-Jones, Biddy Bronze swept all in front of her including championships against all heights at the major shows. Ailsa Smith-Maxwell writing of Biddy Bronze in the *Field* (18th July 1957) says: "Criban Biddy Bronze who has only just retired from the ring has more quality than is imaginable for a pure-bred native pony"; an excellent photograph accompanied the article.

And so Biddy Bronze retired to stud to make her mark on the Welsh and riding pony world mainly through her son and daughter (full-brother and sister) Solway Master Bronze and Solway Summertime, the latter dam of e.g. the riding pony stallion Treharne Raphael (Ty Gwyn Stud) by Bwlch Valentino.

4. Revolt (*chapter 6.2*)

5. Dinarth Henol (*chapter 6.3*)

6. Criban Gay Snip
Registration number 2163 in the *Welsh Stud Book,*
Vol. XXXVI
Bay, star, height: under 12 hands, foaled 1947
Breeder: Mr. H. Ll. Richards, The Allt,
Bwlch, Brecon

Criban Gay Snip had an accident as a two-year-old after serving only two mares and had to be put down. After the successes of his daughter Biddy Bronze and also his half-brother Criban Victor, Mr. Richards tried to trace the other foal but failed and she was never discovered.

7. Criban Belle
Registration number 527 F.S. 1. in the appendix of
the *Welsh Stud Book, Vol. XXXIII*
Bay, blaze, off hind fetlock white, height: 12 hands,
foaled 1945
Breeder: H. Ll. Richards, Allt, Bwlch, Brecon.

Criban Belle was far too young to be "pensioned off" with Mr. Thomas and when Biddy Bronze began "sweeping the board" many breeders became interested in her whereabouts and it was in fact Mr. Vivian Eckley of the Cusop Stud who succeeded in purchasing her and many famous Cusop ponies are descended from Criban Belle.

Mr. Eckley was doubly interested in Criban Belle since on the 1952 Criban Sale he had purchased lot 30, a brown three-year-old filly Criban Activity, the 1949 daughter of Criban Belle and she was proving to be a very hard nut to crack under saddle, especially in the ridden native pony classes e.g. she won outright the ridden Welsh Mountain pony trophy at the Royal Welsh Show.

Possibly the bargain of the 1952 Criban Sale was a yearling filly Criban Spice by Vardra Sunstar (*chapter 8.2*) out of Criban Belle that was purchased by Mr. Sid Davies for 18 guineas. Criban Bowbell, dam

Criban Activity winning the ridden Welsh pony class at the Royal Welsh Show.

of Criban Belle was also on this sale (lot 50) and this is where she was purchased by Mrs. Cuff to later become g-g-g-dam of Downland Chevalier (*chapter 14.1*).

8. Llwyn Tyrant (*chapter 6.4*)

9. Llwyn Flyaway (*chapter 6.5*)

10. Llwyn Satan (*chapter 6.6*)

11. Irfon Marvel (*chapter 6.7*)

12. Criban D-Day (*chapter 12.3*)
Registration number 1725 in the *Welsh Stud Book, Vol. XXXII*
Bay, star, height: 11 hands, foaled 1944
Breeders: H. W. Richards and Sons, Criban,
Talybont-on-Usk, Brecon.
Sire: Criban Grey Grit 1699
Dam: 9132 Criban Brenda

13. Criban Whalebone (*chapter 13.5*)

14. Bolgoed Squire (*chapter 12.2*)

15. Criban Bowbell
Registration number 166 F.S. in the appendix of the
Welsh Stud Book, Vol. XXXII
Chestnut, blaze, height: 13 hands, foaled 1939
Sire: Silverdale Bowtint
Dam: 8913 Criban Charity (foaled 1932) by Criban
Bumble Bee 1394 (*chapter 9.6*)
G-dam: 8611 Criban Mulberry (foaled 1924) by
Criban Cracker 1308 (*chapter 13.11*)
G-g-dam: 7971 Criban Raspberry (foaled 1920)
G-g-g-dam: 5452 Criban Duchess (foaled 1914)
G-g-g-g-dam: 1298 Roanie II (foaled 1900)
G-g-g-g-g-dam: 263 Vaynor Duchess (foaled in
pre-Stud Book times)

Silverdale Bowtint was a chestnut Polo Pony stallion standing 15 hands high foaled in 1926 and bred by Mr. Herbert Bright of the

269

Silverdale Stud. Mr. Llewellyn Richards had previously purchased Silverdale Loyalty (foaled in 1923), by Prince Friarstown out of Silvery II, from Mr. Bright and was offered Bowtint very cheaply after he got cast in his box at the Royal Show.

Silverdale Bowtint was sired by Cherry Tint *General Stud Book* (a very successful Polo Pony sire who had been exported to the Argentine and Bowtint's dam was Bowery *General Stud Book* a well-known mare who had won the Polo Pony progeny competition at the Polo Pony Show three times.

Bowtint himself had won a first prize at the Royal Agricultural Society of England Show and after a few years at Criban became perfectly sound again and was sold to Mr. Kiddie of South Africa.

Mr. Richards later had other Silverdale stallions at Criban, namely Silverdale Tarragon and Silverdale Aquilla and also Criban Loyalist a bay 13 hand stallion, son of Silverdale Loyalty out of Criban Harpist; Criban Loyalist being sire of Criban Red Heather (*chapter 14.11*).

Criban Charity was thought by Mr. Llewellyn Richards to be the best Welsh Mountain Pony mare ever to be bred at Criban. The reason why she was not shown in preference to e.g. Criban Socks (Mr. Richards claiming her to be a better mare than Socks) was that she spent all her life on the hills producing top-class foals.

Amongst the progeny of Criban Charity were: Criban Martha (foaled 1935) (*chapter 8.9*); Criban Faith (foaled 1943); Criban Gracie (foaled 1948), dam of Criban Pep; Criban Gracious (foaled 1949), sold to the Llanarth Stud at the 1952 Criban Sale (lot 29); and the stallion Criban Flag Day (foaled 1944).

Criban Bowbell started a whole dynasty of riding ponies mainly through her daughter Criban Heather Belle (*chapter 14.11*) (foaled in 1943) who spent most of her life in the ownership of Mrs. Cuff. Mrs. Cuff also bought Criban Bowbell (lot 60) at the 1952 Criban Sale and bred Downland Wildflower (1955), Downland Smokey Eyes (1956) and Downland Coral (1959) out of her.

17

True Briton foaled 1830

1	2	4	
True Briton	Ruler II	Ruler	
	3	6	12
	Douse	True Briton Trotter	Granby
			13
			Flower
		7	
		Old Douse	

1. True Briton

Registration number 839 in the *Hackney Stud Book,
Vol. I* (1884)
Corrected date of birth in the *Hackney Stud Book,
Vol. II* (1885), *pp. 334*
Black, foaled 1830
Breeder: John Walters, Llanfair Clydogau,
Cardiganshire.

True Briton was sold as a three-year-old to Mr. Thomas Jones, Stone Mason, New Court, Lampeter who travelled him for ten years and he died in 1843 when still in his prime. Mr. Charles Coltman Rogers writing in the early volumes of the *Welsh Stud Book* states: "True Briton must be described as the 'fons et origo' i.e. as far as we can go in all that was best of the far-famed trotting Cob of Wales".

Judging by the size of his hoof and height of the bones of his fore-leg (which were until recently at a blacksmith's shop at Llanwnen, near Llanybyther) True Briton was a horse standing 15 hands or more. True Briton was better known in his native area as "ceffyl du Twm Masiwn" i.e. the black horse of Tom the mason.

It is interesting that Bleddfa Shooting Star (foaled in 1901) (*chapter 4.1*) traces back to True Briton (foaled in 1830) in ten generations: Bleddfa Shooting Star out of Alveston Belle by Cymro by Beaconsfield (*chapter 22.1*) by Earl Beaconsfield by Caradog whose dam was by Cardigan Comet I (*chapter 19.4*) by Young Comet whose dam was by True Briton.

2. Ruler II

Registration number 2000 in the *Yorkshire Coach Horse
Stud Book*.

3. Douse

Breeder: John Walters, Llanfair Clydogau,
Cardiganshire.

Mr. Coltman Rogers, writing in the *Welsh Stud Book* is of the opinion that Douse was "an Arab mare bought from the gipsies". I prefer to think that she was a typical Welsh Cob mare since if she had been bought from the gipsies her breeding would be unknown and her dam would hardly have been Old Douse. I find other evidence in the fact that a Welsh Cob stallion Phenomenon III (foaled in 1875) was also

1892.

VALUABLE OPPORTUNITY TO BREEDERS OF HORSES:

BREED FROM FIRST-CLASS HORSES IF YOU BREED AT ALL.

Quality, Symmetry, Size, and Action, are the essential points in a good Roadster Stallion, and for all these you are most respectfully requested to inspect carefully that very celebrated Trotting Stallion,

PHENOMENON III.

The property of Mr. W. Jones, Pantyfen, Llanfihangel-ar-Arth,

Which will serve Mares this season at £3 3s. each Mare, and 5s. the groom.

A good Card is always made for every Stallion, but Phenomenon III.'s stock testifies to his merits to a much greater extent.

This celebrated Horse is jet black, with black points, 9 years old, stands 16¼ hands high, and in symmetry he is unequalled. He has a very powerful and arched neck, deep and slanting shoulders, wide breast, strong back and loins, superb arms and legs (measures 9½ inches below the knee), has elastic pasterns and sound feet. He is a perfect model of a well-bred horse, and is greatly admired for his trotting qualities, and he possesses one of the best constitutions in the world; and in the opinion of all competent judges, he has the full physical development and vigorous character of a progenitor, with precise and imposing carriage; has a high and sagacious temperament, delighting to obey, but scorning fear and rest.

PHENOMENON III. is by that very celebrated horse, Welsh Phenomenon, 859 in Stud Book, and was bred by that very eminent breeder of the best type of Cardiganshire Horses, D. Davies, Esq., of Pistill Einon, Cardiganshire. He was the winner of 10 prizes in the leading shows of South Wales. Grandsire, Broad's PHENOMENON, the winner of the Royal at Taunton, and there sold to the King of Italy for 1,000 guineas. G. grandsire, that very celebrated Norfolk Horse, Young Perfection, winner of the Royal in 1865. G.g. grandsire Young Catton, winner of the Royal at Lincoln. Catton by Bay Beckingham, by Grand Conqueror, by king George, which was sold to the Emperor of Russia for £370.

PHENOMENON III. combines the best Norfolk and the best Cardiganshire Trotting Blood, and cannot fail to get with suitable Mares, valuable Carriage Horses, Cavalry Horses, Bus, Van and Tramcar Horses, and good Roadsters, which are now in very great demand.

The Groom's fee to be paid the first time of serving, and the remainder on or before the 24th of June next, or 10s. extra will be charged for collecting same;

All mares agreed for and tried must be paid for.

David Jones, Printer, King-street, Carmarthen.

Stud card of Phenomenon III for 1892. (Stud card courtesy of Messrs. Rowlands Harris.)

274

registered in the *Hackney Stud Book*. Phenomenon III was bred by David Davies, Pistyll Einon, Cellan, Lampeter and David Davies' mother, Mrs. Jane Davies, Baylie, Cellan was a sister to John Walters of Llanfair Clydogau. The dam of Phenomenon III was Dido (foaled in 1869); g-dam: Old Dido, g-g-g-dam: Douse, g-g-g-g-dam: Old Douse.

4. Ruler
Registration number 1990 in the *Yorkshire Coach Horse Stud Book*.

British Ruler a descendant of Ruler with his owner Mr. John Jones, Aberduar, Llanybyther. This is one of the oldest known photographs of a Welsh Cob.

6. True Briton Trotter
Registration number 840 in the *Hackney Stud Book*,
Vol. II, pp. 97.
Foaled 1821
Breeder: John Walters, Llanfair Clydogau,
Cardiganshire.

Quoting from the *Hackney Stud Book*: "True Briton Trotter was sold by his breeder to his eldest sister Mrs. Jane Davies of Baylie, Cellan, Lampeter for £100. The horse was travelled by a farm servant of Mrs. Davies and the old man was still alive in October 1884 (when this registration was made) being then in his 88th year. The horse became blind when seven years old and was sold to a hotel keeper and ran as a wheeler in the mail from Llandovery to Trecastle every alternate day for fifteen years without a break".

It is interesting that a monument has been erected on the roadside between Llandovery and Trecastle commemorating an accident when a coach-load of passengers were killed at Christmas-time 1835 when a drunken driver drove the coach over the hedge and down a steep slope into the river below. True Briton Trotter was on this route at this time.

7. Old Douse
Owner: John Walters, Llanfair Clydogau, Cardiganshire.

John Walters was tenant and agent of the Carrington Estate in Cardiganshire. Looking at my painting of Old Douse as I write, her Welshness is striking and I'm sure she has nothing to do with "an Arab mare bought from the gipsies". The painting is signed SG RA and dated 1803 and SG has been recognised by a London professional to be Sawrey Gilpin (1733–1807). Sawrey Gilpin was a very popular animal painter in his day, Anthony Pasquin writes of him in 1794: "Mr. Gilpin is inferior to Mr. Stubbs in anatomical knowledge but is superior to him in grace and genius".

How was it then that this fashionable London painter came to mid-Wales to paint Old Douse? There are very few paintings of horses in Wales as distinct from many in England; the only ones in Wales being done for the titled families of which there again were very few. Most of the horse owners in Wales at this period and just later were very poor "peasant" farmers living with large families in two-roomed "crofts" with a stable being joined onto the "croft" and that is where the stallion lived, his every move being followed by the family in the next room.

These "croft" families have produced many notable men, typical of them being Dr. Thomas Jones, C.H., LL.D., Secretary to the Cabinet for many years and father of Baroness White and Mr. Tristan Jones (who purchased a Welsh Cob colt at Llanarth Sale 1966). Dr. Thomas Jones was President of the University College of Wales Aberystwyth until his death in 1955 and his grand-father Benjamin Jones, Gwynfil, Llangeitho was the groom who travelled Cardigan Comet I.

To return to Old Douse and Sawrey Gilpin; reference is seen that Sawrey Gilpin was commissioned by the "Board of Agriculture" to paint examples of "British livestock". The Board of Agriculture was set up in 1793 under the Presidency of Sir John Sinclair who was replaced

276

Old Douse and foal Flower. Detail from the painting by Sawrey Gilpin (1803).

as President by Lord Somerville from 1798–1800. There does not seem to be recorded a President from 1800 until 1806 (when Sir John Sinclair again became President, the Board being dissolved in 1819). However various publications were produced between 1800 and 1806 and the one by John Tuke for the North Riding of Yorkshire for 1801 quotes Lord Carrington as President. Also recorded in the British Museum Library Catalogue is a speech by Lord Carrington delivered to the Board of Agriculture on 15th March 1803, though whether he was still President is not indicated.

The only reason that I can see for Sawrey Gilpin to travel to Cardiganshire to paint a Welsh Cob mare is that it was part of the project commissioned by Lord Carrington, John Walters the owner of the mare being the agent for the Carrington estate in Cardiganshire.

Old Douse was painted by Sawrey Gilpin on a mahogany panel measuring 25 in × 32 in and my father remembered that his friend, Mr. Ernie Hutton (an expert on Hackney horses who exported several hundred of them to Spain) who lived in Suffolk had this painting and we bought the painting from Mr. Hutton. Mr. Hutton's father had bought the painting in 1898 (through Dafydd Evans, Llwyncadfor, father of Tom Jones Evans, Craven Stud). The history of the painting is written

277

on the back of the panel: "Painting given in 1858 to David Prosser, Brynderwen, Carmarthen (Secretary of the Carmarthen Show) who then gave it to the Reverend David Evans, Maesmawr, Llanybyther." Mr. Hutton (Senior) bought it in 1898 from the Reverend Evans. Reverend Evans kept several good Welsh Cob stallions in pre-Stud Book times, one such was Cardigan Driver, sire of Bold Buck the first stallion to be owned by Thomas Rees, father of David Rees and James Rees (*chapter 23*). The painting is titled "Old Douse and her foal, Flower by Flower of England".

12. Granby
Registered in the *General Stud Book, Vol. IV, pp. 226*
Foaled 1824

Granby is recorded as the sire of True Briton Trotter. It will be seen that from his date of birth this is not possible. Either the fact is incorrect or the date of birth is incorrect.

13. Flower
Chesnut, foaled 1803 (the foal in the painting)
Sire: Flower of England *Hackney Stud Book, Vol. 1*
Dam: Old Douse

Flower is recorded as having been a very famous trotting mare in the ownership of John Walters.

Song of Praise to Trotting Briton

Gymry anwyl! gwlad y bryniau
Megaist filoedd o gyffylau,
Ond y penaf o dy feibion
Ydyw'r enwog "Trotting Briton!"

CYDGAN – Os bydd parch byth i farch,
Os bydd parch byth i farch,
"Trotting Briton" gaiff y goron,
Gyda dynion hyd ei arch!

Ganwyd ef yn Ngheredigion,
O rieni oedd enwogion:
Bro y Ferwig gafodd fagu

Un a ddaeth yn "Flodyn Cymru."
    Os bydd parch, &c.

Mae'n barhaus yn cipio'r llawryf:
Am ei fod yn "drottiwr" heinyf:
Ar amrantiad rhed fel mellten,
A dilyna'r gwynt a'r glomen!
    Os bydd parch, &c.

Mae hiliogeth "Trotting Briton"
Yn mhob ardal lle mae dynion;
Mae yn fafrin gan blant Adda,
Bron bod fel yr Influenza!
    Os bydd parch, &c.

"Polly Briton," "Happy Lady,"
"Pretty Girl," a "Queen," a "Lilly,"
Dyna bump o'i ferched hawddgar,
Y cyflynaf ar y ddaear!
    Os bydd parch, &c.

Y mae merched "Trotting Briton,"
Yn cael ganddo waddol ddigon,
Nid cael can'punt neu ychwaneg,
Ond cael grym a nerth i redeg!
    Os bydd parch, &c.

Tri o fechgyn glan ein gwron
Ydyw "Bob," a "Jack," a "Briton,"
Hogiau chwim yn eu cerbydau,
'N curo'r awel ar eu teithiau!
    Os bydd parch, &c.

Rhedegfeydd y greadigaeth,
Anrhydeddir a'i hiliogaeth;
Ni aeth gwobr erioed i estron,
Lle'roedd teulu "Trotting Briton."
    Os bydd parch, &c.

Chwi amaethwyr sydd mewn poenau,
Gan wehilion o gyffelau,

Mynwch berlau o ebolion
Drwy groesawu "Trotting Briton."
        Os bydd parch, &c.

Mae y "Brython" yn foneddwr
Hawlia sylw pob amaethwr;
Nid·yw doctor mawr y Ferwig
Byth yn colli yn ei gynnyg!
        Os bydd parch, &c.

Ganddo cewch geffylau bywiog
O gyflymder yn goronog;
Gwell i ffermwr y'nt nag arian,
A gall dalu'r rhent dan chwiban.
        Os bydd parch, &c.

Fe fum i yn hir mewn trallod
Gyda meirch, rhai dioglyd hynod,
Ond pan gefais "Trotting Briton"
Gwnes fy ffortiwn o'i ebolion.
        Os bydd parch, &c.

                HEN FFERMWR O DDYFED.
                J. BRYNACH DAVIES.
Llanfyrnach.

Dear old Cambria! on thy highlands
Thou has reared thy horses thousands,
But thy celebrated paragon
Is the famous "Trotting Briton."

CHORUS – Of the horses that are brave,
            Of the horses that are brave,
            "Trotting Briton," gallant stallion,
            Will be champion till his grave!

Ceredigion was his birthplace,
And his parents were in highness;
The land of Verwig was the breeder,
And the home of the "Welsh Flower."
            Of the horses, &c.

Everywhere he is the winner,
For he is a lively trotter:
In an instant as the lightning,
Or the wind and dove he's running!
     Of the horses, &c.

Mr. Trotting Briton's family
Can be found in every country,
By Adam's children he is populous
As the Influenza famous!
     Of the horses, &c.

"Polly Briton," "Happy Lady,"
"Pretty Girl," and "Queen," and "Lilly,"
Are five of his brilliant daughters,
And the swiftest through the universe!
     Of the horses, &c.

"Trotting Briton," king of runners.
Gives good fortune to his daughters,
Not a hundred pounds of money,
But gives strength for running quickly.
     Of the horses, &c.

Who has sons as our champion,
Such as "Bob" and "Jack" and "Briton,"
Lively lads in their carriages
On their tours beyond the breezes!
     Of the horses, &c.

The creation's Trotting Matches,
Through his sons are made successes;
"Trotting Briton's" family never
Left a prize to any stranger!
     Of the horses, &c.

Farmers! you that are in torment,
With your horses without talent,
Seek for colts like pearls that glitter,
Welcome "Trotting Briton" clever!
     Of the horses, &c.

"Trotting Briton" is a 'squire,
Claims respect from every farmer;
Verwig's doctor with his doses
In his trial never loses!
　　Of the horses, &c.

He will give to your gladness,
Gallant horses crowned with swiftness,
Better than the money sterling,
And you'll pay the rent by whistling!
　　Of the horses, &c.

I have been in sad affliction,
Long with many a sluggish stallion,
But hurrah! through "Trotting Briton"
From his colts I made my fortune!
　　Of the horses, &c.

The above appreciation is reproduced to illustrate in some small measure the esteem which the Welsh Cob enjoyed in Cardiganshire some years ago. The stallion "Trotting Briton" being one of the greatest, moved an aspiring bard to express himself in this dedication. His stud card for 1890 brings this chapter to an appropriate close.

1890.   1890.

TO SERVE MARES THIS SEASON,

At £2 10s. each Mare, and 5s. the Groom,

(The Groom's Fee to be paid at the first time of covering, and the
remainder on or before the 10th of July next),

THAT CELEBRATED & WELL-KNOWN COB

TROTTING BRITON,

OF LLECHWEDDERI-UCHAF, LAMPETER.

The Property of Mr. JENKIN JENKINS.

TROTTING BRITON stands 15 hands 2 inches high, is of a
dark bay colour, with splendid actions, and was a very fast
Trotter, and has proved himself a sure foal-getter.

TROTTING BRITON has come out of very fast TROTTERS
on both sides (sire and dam) out of the well-known Stallions True
Briton (*Cefful du Tom Mason*) and Old Comet.

The Prizes taken by his Stock are far too numerous to mention
here, they being also well known to the Public as fast Trotters,
one of them is now with Mr. David Thomas, Trellwyn, Llanwñen,
he is the fastest Trotter in Wales, and has won 1st prizes in many
open Races this year and last year. Many of them have been sold
for the highest prices in the neighbourhood.

TROTTING BRITON won the first prize at Llanwnen Trotting Match in 1877, under 3 years old, and the first Prize as a
Cob at Newcastle Emlyn in 1879, (unfortunately he sprained the
sinews of his hind leg).

All mares tried by this horse and put to another will be charged Season Price.

The Groom will specify the time of attendance.

T. L. Davies & Co., Printers, Lampeter.

*Stud card of Trotting Briton for 1890. Trotting Briton is a descendant of True Briton.
(Stud card courtesy of Messrs. Rowlands Harris.)*

18

Trotting Comet foaled 1840
Cymro Llwyd foaled 1850 (about)
Old Welsh Flyer foaled 1861

1	2	4	8
Old Welsh Flyer	Trotting Comet	Flyer	Black Jack
			9 Black Bess
		5 Bess	10 Colt
	3 Trotting Nancy	6 Cymro Llwyd	12 Arab
			13 Brown

1. Old Welsh Flyer

Registration number 856 in the *Hackney Stud Book,*
Vol. I (1884), *pp. 340*
Brown stallion, standing 14 hands 3 in,
foaled in 1873
(The genealogies in the Welsh Stud Book quote his
date of birth as 1861, the same year that his sire
Trotting Comet died and this date is confirmed by
the fact that he won a first prize at Cardigan
Agricultural Show in 1868)
Breeder: David Davies, Bryngwyn, Llanilar.

When the breeder, David Davies died, Old Welsh Flyer was bought by Dafydd Evans who, at that time, was living with his uncle Richard Evans, Cefncae (now in ruin), Penuwch in Cardiganshire. The family later moved (taking Old Welsh Flyer with them) to Talryn near Llangeitho, then to Rhiwarthen Uchaf, Capel Bangor (near Aberystwyth where quite a few good Cobs are still bred) and then Dafydd Evans becane tenant of Rhoscellan Fawr at Clarach on the Wallog estate (adjoining the Gogerddan estate of Sir Pryse Pryse which is to have a large influence on the pedigree of Old Welsh Flyer). Dafydd Evans was responsible for bringing some of the most influential stallions into mid-Wales; his name reigned supreme in Cambrian cobland as the moulder of the destinies of Welsh Cobs in early Victorian days. Old Welsh Flyer was reputed to have had more "quality" than his sire, possibly through the effect of his grand-sire on the dam's side Cymro Llwyd and his Arab sire. It was a curious fact that Old Welsh Flyer and Jack Jones, his groom who travelled him far and wide for David Evans, had but one eye apiece!

One of the most influential sons of Old Welsh Flyer was Trotting Flyer 271 (*chapter 23.14*) (Alex Morton, Ayrshire) known in Wales as "Aberhenwen fach". It was recorded in the *Aberystwth Observer* of 24th January 1874 that a son of Old Welsh Flyer won a prize of £500 at a trotting match in London. This is equivalent to an enormous figure one hundred years later.

(In pre-Stud Book times much of the information regarding pedigrees, performance and progeny of stallions could only be obtained from stud cards. These were distributed during the Spring of each year, they were generally four page cards or leaflets and sometimes included advertisements for local businesses. Some are included here.)

1874.

TO
SERVE MARES THIS SEASON

At £1 each Mare, and 3s. the Groom,

(Or £2 each Foal, and 7s. the Groom,—Single leap, 10s. The Grooms Fee to be paid the first time of Serving—Single leap in the same manner. Season money to be paid last journey round, or 10s. extra will be charged. When the Groom agrees for a Foal, and the Mare sold before ascertaining that she is in Foal, the price will be charged.)

Season begins April, and ends the third Saturday in June.

RAILWAY COMET

*The Property of Mr. Evan James, Mynyddmawr,
Llanilar, Cardiganshire.*

RAILWAY COMET is 8 years old, and stands 15 and a half hands high. Is a splendid Bay Horse, of good action, and has proved himself a sure and good foal-getter. His stock are very fast trotters, and are sold at high prices. He was got by Young Trotting Comet; Young Trotting Comet won a prize at Machynlleth in 1863. Young Trotting Comet by Old Comet, whose dam was Mr. Poole's celebrated Trotting Mare; Old Comet by Flyer, which was the fastest trotter in Cardiganshire. RAILWAY COMET is out of a splendid Mare by Old Railway; Old Railway was allowed to be one of the best Horses and Trotters in England in his time; Old Railway by Hibernia; Hibernia by the Duke of Grafton's Symmetry, dam by Whalebone; Old Railway's dam by Fitzorvil.

Mares tried by this Horse and covered afterwards by another, or sold, or discontinued, will be charged for in full.

The Groom will specify the time & place of attendance.

William Williams, Printer, Aberystwyth.

Stud card of Railway Comet for 1874. Railway Comet was foaled in 1866 and was g-son of Trotting Comet. (Stud card by courtesy of "Ar gefn ei geffyl" Dr. Richard Phillips.)

288

18 76.

TO COVER THIS SEASON,

At £1 1s. each Mare, and 2s. 6d the Groom.
(The Groom's Fee to be paid at the first time of Covering and the remainder on or before the 30th of June next.)

That celebrated Fast Trotting,
Dun-coloured Horse,

'WELSH JACK,'

The Property of Mr. Thomas Daniel, Caecefnder, near Pennant, Cardiganshire.

WELSH JACK stands about 14½ hands high, of good symmetry and action, and has proved himself a sure foal-getter. He was got by Cymro Llwyd, out of an excellent fast-trotting Bay Mare, got by Old Comet, and grand dam was got by Comet Bach, and his great grand-dam was got by True Briton. WELSH JACK has been serving Mares after half-breeds, and his stock were sold for much more money ; and £600 each were offered for his two brothers to the late Lady Lundell, of Kington. One of his stock obtained a Prize of £10 at Llanwrtyd last year, and was highly commended.

Any Mare tried by this Horse, and put to another, or sold, will be charged the same.

Groom will specify the

J. DAVIS, MACHIN

Stud card of Welsh Jack (also known as Caecefnder) for 1876. Welsh Jack was foaled about 1860 and was a son of Cymro Llwyd. (Stud card courtesy of Messrs. Rowlands Harris.)

289

Stud card of Cardigan Flyer for 1881. Cardigan Flyer was foaled in 1873 and was a son of Welsh Flyer. (Stud card courtesy of Messrs. Rowlands Harris.)

Stud card of Young Welsh Flyer for 1885. Young Welsh Flyer was foaled in 1881 and was a son of Welsh Flyer. (Stud card courtesy of Messrs. Rowlands Harris.)

TO COVER THIS SEASON,

At £1 10s. each Mare and 2s. 6d. the Groom,

(The Groom's fee to be paid at the first time of trying the Mares, and the remainder on or before the 24th June next,)

THAT SPLENDID CHESTNUT COB

KING FLYER,

The property of Mr. Morgan Davies, Gors Inn, near Aberystwyth.

KING FLYER is rising 6 years old, stands about 14½ hands high, of a most excellent symmetry, possessing strong bone, great power, good action, free from any blemish. He was got by the celebrated horse Welsh Flyer, whose stock won the most prizes for trotting in England and Wales. Welsh Flyer by Old Comet, out of Trotting Nancy (the property of the late Hon. Capt. W. Vaughan, Crosswood), by Cymro Llwyd, which won the prizes at the Brecon Agricultural Show in 1851, 1852, and 1853; Trotting Nancy out of Brown, by Old Comet; Brown out of Darby, by Currycomb Welsh Flyer won the prize at the Cardigan Agricultural Show in .1868, and at the Llanwrtyd Entire Horse Show in 1875.

KING FLYER'S dam is by King Jack; King Jack by Wonderful Comet; Wonderful Comet by Young Comet; Young Comet by Old Comet. King Jack's dam was got by Old Express, who won a match of £100 at Cardiff, by trotting against one of the fastest horses in Wales, with 2 to 1 on. KING FLYER'S sister won the first prize of £50, for trotting in Alexandria Park, and was afterwards sold for £100. Another sister has been sold for £90. KING FLYER won the first prize at Llanbadarn Stallion Show in 1886.

☞ All Mares tried by this Horse, and afterwards put to another (without an understanding with the Groom), will be charged Season Price.

The Groom will specify the time and place of Attendance.

John Morgan, Printer, *Observer* Office, Aberystwyth.

Stud card of King Flyer for 1887 (about). King Flyer was a son of Welsh Flyer who was foaled in 1861. (Stud card courtesy of Messrs. Rowlands Harris.)

Season 1896.

A RARE OPPORTUNITY TO BREEDERS OF COBS,
AND CARRIAGE HORSES.

TO SERVE MARES THIS SEASON,

At £2. 2s. each Mare, and 5s. the Groom.

THAT CELEBRATED COB

WELSH JACK the SECOND,

The property of Mr W. Morgan, Tanfalier, Penuwch,
Llangeitho, Cardiganshire.

WELSH JACK the SECOND is by the world renowned horse
Welsh Jack, the property of Thos Daniel, Caecefnder, Penant; by
Cymro Llwyd winner of many First Prizes including the Brecon Agric-
ultural Shows in 1851-1852, and 1853.

WELSH JACK the SECOND's dam was got by Young Rainbow,
late the property of Mr. David Griffiths, Ffrwd, (655 Vol. 1 H.S.B.,)
a first prize winner in 25 Shows in different parts of England & Wales.
Young Rainbow was got by Old Rainbow, who was bred by Thos Davies,
Aberdihonw, Builth, and was considered the grandest trotter of his day,
obtained the First Prize in an open Trotting Match in France, and was
afterwards sold for 300 guineas, out of a splendid mare by Britton Comet,
by Old Comet.

WELSH JACK the SECOND though young has proved himself
a sure foal-getter, is rising 5 years old, stands 14 hands 2 inches high,
free from all natural blemish.

☞ All demands are to be paid at the end of the season. For further particulars
apply to the Groom.

*Stud card of Welsh Jack the Second (Tanfalier) for 1896. Welsh Jack the Second was a son
of Welsh Jack (Caecefnder). (Stud card courtesy of Messrs. Rowlands Harris.)*

2. Trotting Comet (also known as Old Comet)

Registration number 834 in the *Hackney Stud Book*
Dark brown, height: 15 hands 1½ in, foaled in 1836
(the Welsh genealogies say foaled 1840, died 1861)
Breeder: Mr. Poole, Peithyll, agent of the
Gogerddan estate.

Trotting Comet was much fancied at Gogerddan by Dr. Evans of Aberystwyth who persuaded his brother Richard Evans, Cefncae, Penuwch (uncle of Dafydd Evans) to buy him. He became such a household name in Wales that there was a great rush for his services and "Comet" bloodlines spread like wildfire (even one Comet Comet 108 *Welsh Stud Book*). To quote Mr. Charles Coltman Rogers: "Comets in Cardiganshire are as thick as the blackberries of a hedgerow in October". Breeders three or four generations later proudly boasted descent from "Old Comet" e.g. the stud card of Eiddwen Flyer. Some present-day Welsh Cobs can claim ten or more separate lines of descent to Trotting Comet. Trotting Comet was buried in the gooseberry

Comet Bach (foaled in 1891) and a Welsh Cob Premium stallion in 1912; owned by Sir Edward Webley Parry Pryse, Bart. Sire Cardigan Briton. Dam by Young Comet.

garden at Cefncae. This house is now in ruins, though Richard Evans' other abode, Plasnewydd, also in Penuwch, is still thriving.

There was another Comet (known as Comet Bach) registered in the *Hackney Stud Book* number 931 (foaled in 1845) and recorded as the sire of Old Welsh Flyer. He was, in fact sired by Trotting Comet (and therefore half-brother to Old Welsh Flyer). He was owned and bred by Jack Jones of Pontardulais (the same Jack Jones with one eye). The *Welsh Stud Book* genealogies quote him as being foaled in 1861 but later quote him as having travelled Radnorshire in the late fifties so possibly neither *Welsh Stud Book* nor *Hackney Stud Book* dates of birth are correct. This Comet Bach sired some useful stock including Wonderful Comet, the sire in turn of King Jack (g-sire of High Stepping Gambler, *chapter 23.8*). With so many "Comets" it is not surprising that the early genealogists faced a difficult task. Trotting Comet was usually known as "Old Comet"; his son, Comet Bach in his younger days was known as "Young Comet" then gradually, as he became older he too became "Old Comet"!

Quoting from the stud card of Young King Jack (1897) (*chapter 23.9*) (son of King Jack *chapter 21.10*) three generations from Old Comet: "It will be seen by the white mark on Young King Jack that he is bred from the first Comet which was marked similar" wherever that mark was. With so many Comets (as indeed with the Flyers, Expresses etc.) it was an advantage to the Welsh breeders of that era (and to anyone researching into these families at a later date) that they would have been 100 per cent Welsh speaking and could easily distinguish between the various colloquial names such as Comet Cefncae, Caebidwl, Tyreithin etc.

3. Trotting Nancy

Was owned by the Hon. Capt. W. Vaughan, of Crosswood, Aberystwyth.

4. Flyer

Flyer was bred at Glanymor, Clarach around the time when William IV came to the throne of England and was later owned by Mr. Pryse Loveden of Buscot Park, Berkshire and Gogerddan (the latter is now the home of the Welsh Plant Breeding station). Mr. Pryse Loveden was later Sir Pryse Pryse, father of Sir Lewes Loveden Pryse who was President of the Welsh Pony and Cob Society in 1921–1922. Flyer was a strong black horse, a good trotter but blind.

5. Bess

Little is known about Bess apart from the fact that she was a chesnut Cardiganshire trotting mare of some renown.

6. Cymro Llwyd
Dun, foaled around 1850

A stallion who had an enormous influence on the Welsh Cob breed e.g. the present-day Llanarth Braint has 13 crosses of Cymro Llwyd in his pedigree. He was bred by Mr. Jones of Growen, near Merthyr Tydfil, sired by an Arab (imported by Mr. Crawshay, an iron-master of Cyfarthfa Castle, Merthyr Tydfil) from a mare called Brown owned by Mr. Jones of Growen.

Cymro Llwyd won prizes at the Brecon Agricultural Shows in 1851, 1852 and 1853 amongst many other prizes. He was owned by Dafydd Evans for many years and travelled extensively (e.g. travelled in Montgomeryshire in 1862) and was later owned by Mr. Thomas Daniel, Tanyrallt, Cockshead, Tregaron.

Stud cards for Cymro Llwyd, already referred to, record the sire of Cymro Llwyd as Welsh Jack which is now regarded as being incorrect in favour of Mr. Crawshay's Arab. One of his most famous sons was Welsh Jack (Caecefnder) and my father was once told by Miss Margaret Daniel of Banc-y-cwrt, Llidiart Maengwyn, Llangeitho (daughter of Thomas Daniel, Cockshead) that he was a bright cream (palomino) with long flaxen mane and tail, though his stud card for 1876 says "dun".

8. Black Jack

Black Jack and his sire, Cauliflower were both owned and bred by Mr. Pryse Loveden at Buscot Park in Berkshire and brought to Gogerddan in mid-Wales (his other estate). Black Jack and Cauliflower were both of the "lighter cart type", the sort of animal referred to as "Equus Operarius" in the *Laws of Hywel Dda*.

9. Black Bess

There is no further information about Black Bess than imagination can supply. Rumour assigned to her a rather unauthenticated and more picturesque origin. It was asserted by the lover of legends without any further reason than a similarity of name that she was a true lineal descendant of the famous Black Bess which carried Dick Turpin from London to York!

10. Colt

Owned by Mr. James, Llwyniorwerth Isaf, near Aberystwyth.

12. Arab stallion

Imported by Mr. Crawshay, Cyfarthfa Castle, Merthyr Tydfil.

13. Brown

Mare owned by Mr. Jones of Growen, Merthyr Tydfil. Brown was sired by Old Comet Brown out of a mare called Derby by Curry Comb (Thoroughbred).

19

Cardigan Comet I foaled 1860
Cardigan Comet II foaled 1872
Cardigan Comet III foaled 1880

1	2	4	8
Cardigan Comet III	Cardigan Comet II	Cardigan Comet I	Comet
			9 mare
		5 Nora Creina	10 King William IV
	3 Lady Poll	6 Confidence	
		7 Lock	14 Harkaway
			15 Magnet

1. Cardigan Comet III

Registration number 2885 *Hackney Stud Book,*
Vol. 8, p. 17
Chesnut stallion, height: 15 hands 3 in,
foaled 1880
Breeder: James Jones, Clydey Rectory, Newcastle
Emlyn, Carmarthenshire.
Owner: David Lewis, Gilfachgoch, Blaenpennal,
Tregaron, Cardiganshire.

Cardigan Comet III won several prizes in the show ring including first Aberaeron 1883, first Carmarthen 1884, first Llanelly 1885, first Llandysul 1886, first Llanybyther 1886, second Llanon 1886, second Llanbadarn 1886, second Newcastle Emlyn 1886 and first Alltrodyn Arms 1886.

He was an influential sire e.g. Cardigan Comet IV, another big stallion standing 16 hands, foaled in 1884, and Cardigan Comet V (also known as Young Cardigan Comet and foaled in 1898) standing 15 hands 1½ in.

2. Cardigan Comet II

Registration number 2396 *Hackney Stud Book,*
Vol. 7, p. 14
Bay stallion, height: 15 hands 2 in,
foaled 1877
Breeder: W. Davies, Goyallt, Llangeitho.
Owner: Enoch Morgan, Fedw Farm, Llangeitho,
Cardiganshire.

Cardigan Comet II again was a well-known prizewinner including: first Tregaron 1878, first Carmarthen 1880, first Llanelly 1880, first Llanelly 1881, second Carmarthen 1881.

When William Davies, who lived at Blaenwern, Llangybi got married in 1876 and went to live at Goyallt, Llangeitho, his mother gave him a mare called Nora Creina as a wedding gift, and she was in foal to Cardigan Comet I. In 1877, Nora Creina duly produced a colt foal and Enoch Morgan (who had Comet I at Fedw at that time) bought Comet II from William Davies in 1878 for £45. Incidentally Goyallt and Fedw are neighbouring farms.

Comet II was used extensively as a sire, he travelled Radnorshire for two seasons. He was described as full of quality and a splendid all-

Cardigan Comet II
(foaled in 1877).

round "goer" with extravagant action. It was stated that he could travel from Llangeitho to Llandovery in a trap (a distance of over 30 miles) without breaking from a trot.

One of his sons, Merry Stanton, bred by Mr. J. Thomas of Stanton-on-Arrow (*Hackney Stud Book 2591*) was sold for £600 to go to America.

In old age, Comet II was put down and buried in a field at Glanmarch, Llangeitho. Much is written on the effect of Hackneys on Welsh Cobs therefore it is interesting to note that the Supreme Female Champion at the 1909 National Hackney Show was Mel Valley Best of All, sire: Tregaron Horace; dam: black mare by Alonzo the Brave (*chapter 20.6*); g-dam: black mare by Cardigan Comet II.

4. Cardigan Comet I
Registration number 1254 *Hackney Stud Book*
Bay stallion, foaled 1860
Breeder: T. Talbot
Owners: W. and J. Morgan, Birch Hill, Llangeitho,
Cardiganshire.

It was recorded that at Carmarthen in 1868, Cardigan Comet I had to beat 17 others. Prizes: first Aberaeron 1861, first Aberystwyth 1861, first prizes Cardigan 1864,5,6,70, first prizes Aberaeron 1865,6,8,70, first prizes Carmarthen, 1868,70,1,2,3. Here was a stallion with a phenomenal show record.

SEASON   1890.

TO COVER MARES THIS SEASON,

At £2 2s. each Mare, and 5s. the Groom,

The Groom's fee to be paid at the first time of trying the Mares, and the remainder
on or before the 12th day of July next,

THAT PROMISING YOUNG CARRIAGE STALLION,

CARDIGAN COMET THE IV.

The Property of DAVID THOMAS, Farm, Talgarreg, Llandyssul.

CARDIGAN COMET THE IV. is rising 5 years old, stands 16 hands high, of a most quiet and docile temper, and has those virtues which are seldom combined in the same horse, viz., bone, with clean fetlocks, and the grandest action. He was got by Cardigan Comet III., which was bred by the same owner.

Cardigan Comet the III. by Cardigan Comet II., by old Cardigan Comet, by Young Comet, by old Comet.

Cardigan Comet the III. has won the following First Prizes, viz.,—Aberayron in 1883, Carmarthen in 1884, Llanelly in 1885, Llandyssul Entire Horse Show held at Alltyrodin Arms, and Llanybyther in 1886. Cardigan Comet the II. was the Prize winner at Tregaron when a yearling, also at Carmarthen and Llanelly in 1880 and 1881, and Carmarthen in 1886.

Cardigan Comet the III.'s dam was got by Confidence, by Cleveland.

Cardigan Comet the IV.'s dam, Star, is a very fine mare by that well-known horse Cardigan Driver. Star's dam was by Thomas Jones' (New Court) old black horse.

So Cardigan Comet the IV. comes out of a good Pedigree, and when put to suitable mares is likely to develop all his good points in his stock.

Mares tried by him and afterwards covered by another will be charged for, unless otherwise arranged by the Groom.

Cardigan Comet the IV. will attend Lampeter, Llandyssul, Newcastle Emlyn, &c., every alternate week.

For other places of attendance apply to the Groom.

Printed by David Jones (late C. & D. Jones), 60, King-street, Carmarthen.

Stud card of Cardigan Comet IV (foaled in 1885), son of Cardigan Comet III. (Stud card courtesy of Messrs. Rowlands Harris.)

Season 1891.

TO SERVE MARES THIS SEASON,
At £2 5s. each Mare, and 5s. the Groom.
(The Groom's Fee to be paid at the first time of serving, and the remainder on or before the 30th of JUNE).

THAT CELEBRATED YOUNG HORSE
ODWYN COMET
The Property of Mrs. SARAH EVANS, Deryodwyn, Llangeitho, Cardiganshire.

ODWYN COMET stands 15–3 hands high, rising 4 years old, is of perfect symmetry and proportions, has capital action, and docile temper. He was got by Cardigan Comet II., Cardigan Comet II. by Cardigan Comet, Cardigan Comet by Young Comet, Young Comet by Old Comet.

CARDIGAN COMET II. won the First Prize at the Tregaron Agricultural Show when entered as a Yearling; also First Prizes at Carmarthen and Llanelly in 1880; First Prize at Llanelly in 1881; Second Prize at Carmarthen in 1881; and First Prize at Carmarthen in 1886.

ODWYN COMET'S dam was got by "Gomer," which is considered to be the best Brood Mare in the District, and her Offsprings were all sold at high prices. ODWYN COMET'S great grand dam was got by Old Comet.

From the above Pedigree, it may be seen that **ODWYN COMET** possesses first-class blood.

Stations and time of attendance will be specified by the Groom.

Mares tried by him and afterwards covered by another will be charged for.

Jenkin Thomas, Machine Printer, Market Square, Tregaron,

Stud card of Odwyn Comet (foaled in 1887) son of Cardigan Comet II. (Stud card courtesy of Messrs. Rowlands Harris.)

*Stud card of Gwynfil Comet (foaled in 1889) son of Cardigan Comet IV. (Stud card
courtesy of Messrs. Rowlands Harris.)*

305

Wonderful Comet

Will serve a limited number of Mares at

£2 10s. each Mare, 5s. the Groom

which is to be paid first time of service, remainder first week in June, 1902, afterwards five per cent. will be charged for collecting.

WONDERFUL COMET, 7 years old, stands nearly 16 hands high, is a beautiful dark chestnut, has plenty of nice flat bone and substance, clean legs, best of feet, extraordinary action, and a sure foal getter. Pedigree as follows:

Sire Cardigan Comet II. H.S.B.
g sire Cardigan Comet
g g sire Young Comet
g g g sire Old Comet

Dam Annie by Young Tom Steel

Bred by that famous horse breeder T. Edwards, Esq., Rhydyfrwig, Cardiganshire and was got by that noted prizetaker Tom Steel out of a most superior and valuable mare by Sailor Tregaron, g dam by Old Comet.

Wonderful Comet's dam was own sister to Fly, Mr. D. Griffith's Ffrwd celebrated chestnut trotting mare, the world-renowned winner of so many trotting matches and show ring, speed and action, through England and Wales in both saddle and harness. All interested in horse breeding will find that this young sire descends thoroughly from the best strain of horses Wales ever produced.

His produce generally fetch from £50 to 120 guineas. A match pair were sold for 250 guineas in 1889. A cob mare was bought for His Majesty in Lampeter 1901 for 120 guineas. All these can be referred to.

Certificates of Soundness.

" We hereby Certify that we have on Feb. 19th, 1902 and March 4th, 1902, examined at the request of Mr. T. Edwards, Pottre Farm, now Mr. D. J. Davies', Tynygarn Pony Stud, the chestnut stallion Wonderful Comet. We find the stallion to be sound and perfectly free from hereditary disease."

(Signed),   W. G. PATRICK, M.R.C.V.S., Lon.
              D. J. JONES, M.R.C.V.S.
              JAMES STEEL, M.R.C.V.S.

☞ Prizes will be given at local shows for best suckers by this horse where he is travelling this season

Any Mare tried by this horse and afterwards put to another will be charged for.

All Mares at owner's risk. Good accommodation for Mares at grass moderation charge.

Time and place of attendance may be specified by the Groom.

Stud Card of Cardigan Comet V (foaled in 1898) son of Cardigan Comet III. (Stud card courtesy of Messrs. Rowlands Harris.)

It is believed that Mr. Enoch Morgan, Fedw Farm, bought Comet I from Mr. David Walters or from his son-in-law James Davies, of Pentrebrain, Llanddewi Brefi (the late J. O. Davies, was still breeding excellent Welsh Cobs at Pentrebrain when he passed away at over 90 years of age in 1978).

Comet I perished in a fire that destroyed the stable at Fedw Farm and it is still believed in the district that this was an act of sabotage in order to get rid of a stallion of whom other stallion owners were so jealous. Dr. Thomas Jones, C.H., LL.D., writing in *Rhymney Memories* states that his grandfather, Benjamin Jones, Gwynfil, Llangeitho was the groom who travelled Cardigan Comet I and that a black leather collar adorned with 14 brass shields recording the prizes listed here still survives with members of the owner's family in Cardiganshire.

307

6. Confidence (*chapter 20.10*)

8. Comet
Registration number 931 in the *Hackney Stud Book*

This Comet has already been described along with his sire Trotting
Comet (*chapter 18.2*) and also (*chapter 21.10*) as g-sire of King Jack.

9. Mare by True Briton (*chapter 17.1*)

20

Alonzo the Brave foaled 1866
Welsh Flyer III foaled 1877
Welsh Flyer IV foaled 1893

2 Welsh Flyer III	4 Old Welsh Flyer	
	5 Blaze	10 Confidence

1

Welsh
Flyer IV

3 Polly	6 Alonzo the Brave	12 Trotaway
	7 Polly Brown	14 Trotting Comet

1. Welsh Flyer IV

Registration number 6613 in the *Hackney Stud Book, Vol. 15* (1898)
Dark chestnut, height: 14 hands 3 in, foaled 1893
Owner and breeder: Aaron Davies, Greenfields,
Four Crosses, Montgomeryshire.

2. Welsh Flyer III

Registration number 4074 in the *Hackney Stud Book, Vol. 9* (1892)
Chestnut, height: 15 hands, foaled 1877
Breeder: Miss Griffiths, Caebidwl, Rhydlewis,
Newcastle Emlyn, Carmarthenshire.
Owner: David Ellis, Commins, Llangwryfon,
Aberystwyth (uncle of the well-known Dr. Ellis).

This stallion was known locally as "Ceffyl Dafydd Cwmins" or "Ceffyl Caebidwl".

Stud card of Welsh Flyer III foaled in 1877.

SEASON 1899.

TO COVER THIS SEASON at £2 each Mare and 5s. the Groom. The Groom's Fee to be paid at the first time of serving, and the remainder on or before the 1st July next, or 10s. extra will be charged for collecting,

THAT SPLENDID CHESTNUT COB, THE ORIGINAL

WELSH FLYER III.

(4074 Hackney Stud Book, Vol. IX.)

Was bred by Miss Griffiths, Cae-Bidwl, Newcastle Emlyn, and is the property of Mr. D. Ellis, Commins, Llangwyr-yfon, near Aberystwyth.

WELSH FLYER III. is a very fast trotter, stands 15½ hands high, is of perfect symmetry and proportions, beautiful action, most docile temper, and has proved a sure foal-getter. He was got by Welsh Flyer, which won the prize at the Cardigan Agricultural Show in 1868, and at Llanwrtyd Entire Horse Show in 1875. Welsh Flyer was got by Old Comet, whose dam was Mr. Poole's celebrated trotting mare, which was never beaten: Old Comet by Flyer, which was the fastest trotter in Cardiganshire. Welsh Flyer III.'s dam was got by Old Confidence, one of the best horses of his time, his grand dam by the famous trotting Gambler, one of the fastest horses in Wales.

WELSH FLYER III. has won the following Prizes:—At Newcastle Emlyn, April, 1884; at New Inn, April 27th, and Llanybyther May 2nd, 1887; and at New Inn, April 25th, 1888.

All Mares tried by this Horse and served by another without the Groom's consent, or sold after being tried, will be charged Season Price. The Owner will not be responsible for any accident that may occur to any Mare, but every care will be taken to prevent accidents.

EVANS BROS., Printers, &c., 17, Pier Street, Aberystwyth.

---

3. Polly
Dark chesnut, foaled 1875
Breeder: The late Edward Andrew, Revel, Berriew,
Montgomeryshire
Owner: Aaron Davies, Greenfields, Four Crosses,
Montgomery

Registration number 10420 in the *Hackney Stud Book, Vol. 14* (1897) where it is also recorded that Polly produced a colt foal by Welsh Flyer III in 1893.

4. Old Welsh Flyer 856 *(chapter 18.1)*

There were other Welsh Flyers descended from the Old Welsh Flyer *856 Hackney Stud Book.*

(i) Glanne Welsh Flyer, foaled 1871, died 1902, son of the Old Welsh Flyer he was owned by W. T. Jones, Glanne, Builth Wells and travelled Breconshire and Radnorshire for 25 years. His stock were much sought after and fetched good prices. He was the sire of Pencaerhelem 23 *Welsh Stud Book, Vol. I* (foaled 1886) g-g-g-sire of Brenin Gwalia *(chapter 23.1)*.

Pencaerhelem was registered as "sire: Welsh Flyer". With so many Welsh Flyers in existence, luckily the breeder of Pencaerhelem later was more specific and in *Welsh Stud Book, Vol. II* quoted which Welsh Flyer, in fact, was the sire of Pencaerhelem.

(ii) Welsh Flyer, owner, L. P. Jones, Dolwner, Llandrindod Wells.

(ii) Young Welsh Flyer (stud card 1885 included here).

(iv) Young Flyer (Tregaron).

6. Alonzo the Brave
Registration number 22 in the *Hackney Stud Book,
Vol. I* (1884)
Bay, black legs, height: 15 hands 3 in, foaled 1866
Breeder: Henry Redhead, Leverington, Norfolk.
Owner: 1871–1873 Mr. Powell, Butington Hall,
Welshpool, Montgomeryshire.
After 1874 Richard Evans, Cefncae, Llangeitho and
later his nephew Dafydd Evans, Rhiwarthenuchaf,
Aberystwyth.

Along with Trotting Comet, foaled 1836 *(chapter 18.2)*, Cymro Llwyd foaled 1850 *(chapter 18.6)* and True Briton, foaled 1830 *(chapter 17.1)*,

Alonzo the Brave has the distinction of being amongst the four stallions which had the greatest influence on the Welsh Cob breed during the fifty years 1830–1880.

Alonzo the Brave blood appears in the pedigrees of 16 of the 70 stallions registered in the first two volumes of the *Welsh Stud Book* (compared with 38 who trace descent from True Briton).

Alonzo the Brave's ancestry traces back to the Darley Arabian (imported to the United Kingdom in 1714) through the blood of many Shales, Original, Scot Marshland, the redoubtable Sampson, Blaze (foaled in 1733) and Flying Childers, who was by the Darley Arabian.

The great-grandsire on the dam's side, Premier was a Thoroughbred; sired by Priam who was in turn sired by the Derby winner Emilius. The prizes won by Alonzo the Brave include a first prize of £10 at Newnham in 1871, 1st prizes at Montgomeryshire Show in 1873/4; 1st prize at the North Cardigan Society's Show at Aberystwyth in 1875; prizes at Builth Wells, Talgarth, Penybont, Carmarthen and Brecon (£30) in 1876; 1st prizes Builth Wells and Penybont 1877; 1st prizes at Talgarth, Montgomery and Penybont 1878; 1st prizes at Llanelly, Penybont and Builth Wells 1879 etc.

Alonzo the Brave was travelled for many seasons by Richard Evans (and later by Dafydd Evans). It was while travelling a son of Alonzo the Brave in Anglesey that Richard Evans died and he was buried where he died. An influential strain arising from Alonzo the Brave was that of Evolve (W. H. Jones, Black Lion, Llangurig) whose dam, Daisy, was a daughter of Alonzo the Brave.

Alonze the Brave died in 1896 at 30 years of age still in the ownership of Richard Evans.

10. Confidence
Registration number 158 in the *Hackney Stud Book*,
Vol. I (1884)
Black-brown, height: 15 hands 2 in, foaled 1867
Owner: Henry D'Oyly, Hempnall, Long Stratton.

This is a very influential stallion in the history of the Hackney; his breeding is recorded in the *Hackney Stud Book* for six generations well back into the eighteenth century.

At the time of his registration, he had 22 registered sons also in the *Hackney Stud Book* including Reality 665 (foaled 1875) a noted prize-winner and sire of winners including (later in 1886) Evolution 2058, sire of the previously mentioned Evolve and owned by R. T. Hawkins,

Coedmawr, Builth Wells for whom he won many prizes (including 1st prize at the 1890 Royal Agricultural Society of England Show in Plymouth) and travelled Radnorshire and Breconshire in 1897–98. (See also *chapter 23.13*).

12. Trotaway

Registration number 833 in the *Hackney Stud Book, Vol. I* (1884)

Dark chesnut, height: 15 hands 2½ in, foaled 1859

Breeder: Robert Case, Hilgay, Norfolk.

Owner: T. L. Read, Downham Market, Norfolk.

Sire: Fireaway (Betts') (foaled 1852) by Fireaway (Burgess') (foaled 1844)

Dam: Case's bay mare by Fireaway (Flanders')

g-dam: Miller's brown mare by Shales by Marshland Shales (foaled 1802)

14. Trotting Comet (*chapter 18.2*)

21

Eiddwen Flyer I foaled 1877
Eiddwen Flyer II foaled 1888
Eiddwen Flyer III foaled 1895

	2 Eiddwen Flyer II 2	4 Eiddwen Flyer I 421	8 Old Welsh Flyer
1 Eiddwen Flyer III 5			9 Mare
		5 Black Bess	10 King Jack
	Mountain Pony mare	6 Cymro Llwyd	

1. Eiddwen Flyer III
Registration number 5 in the *Welsh Stud Book, Vol. I.*
Blue roan, height 12 hands 2 in, foaled 1895
Breeder: J. Thomas, Pencarreg, Llanybyther,
Carmarthenshire.
Owner: Professor Tom Parry, Neuadd Llansilio,
Cross Inn, Llandysul, Cardiganshire.

Eiddwen Flyer III has the distinction of being registered in the *Welsh Stud Book* next to Dyoll Starlight (*chapter 2.1*), a stallion to which he stood second at the Royal Agricultural Society of England Show in Cardiff in 1901.

The Livestock Journal of 28th June 1901 reports: "Messrs Parry and Jones coming second with the blue roan Eiddwen Flyer III by Eiddwen Flyer II, a very sweet-headed five-year-old with lots of substance and big quarters, rather of the harness type".

The Journal of the Royal Agricultural Society of England reports: "This was a good class. The second prize pony (Eiddwen Flyer III) was of great merit but of rather a stronger character than the winner (Dyoll Starlight)".

Eiddwen Flyer III stood at stud with Professor Tom Parry at a Stud fee of one guinea (tenant farmers) with grass accommodation for mares at 2/6 per month.

Neuadd Llansilio was about the next farm to Werville Brook (birthplace of the legendary Greylight in 1900) where there lived a Mr. Blackwell one of the first Inspection judges of the Welsh Pony & Cob Society.

One of the most influential lines originating from Eiddwen Flyer III was via his daughter Wedros Gem (bred by Mr. Evan Jones the blacksmith of Caerwedros, near New Quay in Cardiganshire), she in turn was dam (by Bleddfa Shooting Star) of the lovely grey mare Ness Thistle (winner of Championships at the Shropshire and West Midland, Conway, Lampeter, Pontardulais, Church Stretton etc for Mr. Lyell of Neston, Cheshire). Wedros Gem was also dam (by Eiddwen Flyer V, 324) of Wedros Betty Wyn who was dam of the spectacular chestnut harness mare Ness Sunflower (*chapter 7.10*).

Another of the progeny of Wedros Gem which had a great influence on Welsh Mountain ponies was Grove Arclight who was generally considered to be the best of Greylight's sons. After a very successful show ring career (first and Champion at the Royal Agricultural Society of England in 1914, first Royal Welsh in 1914 etc.) he produced some

1902

WELSH MOUNTAIN PONY STALLION

(Winner of Second Prize Royal Show. Cardiff, 1901).

Eiddwen Flyer III.

(W.P.C S. No.............)

Colour: Blue Roan.   Height 12·2.   Foaled 1896.

SIRE: EIDDWEN FLYER II. by EIDDWEN FLYER by WELSH FLYER (856), the celebrated one-eyed Cardi Trotting Cob.

DAM: WELSH MOUNTAIN PONY by CYMRO LLWYD (out of the famous TROTTING NANCY), the "Denmark" (177) of Welsh Ponies.

PRESS NOTICES.

LIVE STOCK JOURNAL, 28th June, 1901.

WELSH MOUNTAIN PONIES, CARDIFF ROYAL SHOW.

"Messrs. Parry and Jones coming second with the blue-roan Eiddwen "Flyer III. by Eiddwen Flyer II., a very sweet-headed five-year-old, with lots "of substance and big quarters, rather of the harness type."

FARMER & STOCKBREEDER YEAR BOOK, 1902.

PONIES IN 1901. (Royal Show, Cardiff.)

"The real Welsh Classes were very good as respects the few leading "specimens. Messrs Parry and Jones's Eiddwen Flyer III., a blue-roan of "quite remarkable build, substance and action, and a hard one to beat, was "placed second."

JOURNAL OF THE ROYAL AGRICULTURAL SOCIETY.
Vol. 62.   1901.

WELSH MOUNTAIN PONIES.

"This was a good class. The Second Prize Pony (Eiddwen Flyer III.) was "of great merit, but of rather a stronger character" (than Starlight).

SERVICE FEE (Tenant Farmers) - ONE GUINEA.

Grass Accommodation for Mares, 2/6 per month.

TELEGRAPHIC ADDRESS—PARRY,

NEUADD, CROSS-INN,

LLANDYSSUL.

Stud card of Eiddwen Flyer III for 1902.

318

exceptional stock at the Grove Stud after which he was sold for a high figure for export to Argentina (the first Welsh Mountain Pony to be exported to that country).

2. Eiddwen Flyer II
Registration number 10 in the *Welsh Stud Book,*
Vol. I
Chesnut, height 13 hands, foaled 1888
Breeder: William Evans, Hafod, Lledrod,
Cardiganshire
Owner: Thomas Evans, Tynyreithin, Bronant,
Cardiganshire.

There were two stallions registered in *Vol. I of the Welsh Stud Book* under the name of Eiddwen Flyer II (both sired by Eiddwen Flyer I). The one above was very popular in Cardiganshire where he was known as "Tyreithin"; the other one (*no. 32 Welsh Stud Book*) was foaled in 1894 and stood 15 hands, his dam and grand-dam also both 15 hands were rather ignominiously given the male names: Punch and Comet. Since the smaller one was foaled before the larger one, the latter was usually known as Eiddwen Flyer IV.

Eiddwen Flyer II was one of many famous animals that ended their days at Dinarth Hall. My father often went to Dinarth and knew where he had been buried "just outside the garden wall", a spot which was built over in the late nineteen forties.

The breeding of Klondyke (*chapter 24.12*), g-sire of my father's first pony Seren Ceulan, is interesting since his sire, Young Messenger was by Eiddwen Flyer II and his dam Lady Eiddwen was by Eiddwen Flyer I.

Young Messenger was known as "Cardi Mawr" (the big Cardiganshire man) after his owner Dafydd Evans (who was a man of very tall stature) rather than after the height of the stallion, although Young Messenger stood at 15 hands or more. Dafydd Evans was the son of the Hafod Farm Bronnant, later of Cwmgwenyn Farm, Llangeitho, a financially prosperous family. Dafydd Evans married the daughter of the Hafodlas Farm, Llangeitho and so was neighbour to William Jones, Hafodlas Uchaf, owner and breeder of Eiddwen Flyer I. According to Dr. Richard Phillips' "Ar gefn ei geffyl", Dafydd Evans squandered his money through keeping his stallions, having to sell Hafodlas to buy the smaller Pengelli, eventually selling Pengelli to buy Pantcoch and receiving financial assistance from the parish.

319

Eiddwen Flyer II (foaled in 1888) photographed at Dinarth Hall, Colwyn Bay.

4. Eiddwen Flyer
Registration number 421 in the *Welsh Stud Book*
(recorded in 1911)
Registration number 2053 in the *Hackney Stud Book*
(recorded in 1889)
Chesnut, height: 14 hands 2 in.
Owner: William Jones, Hafodlasuchaf,
Llangwyryfon, Cardiganshire.(The *Hackney Stud
Book* quotes William Jones also as the breeder, the
Welsh Stud Book quotes "breeder: unknown").

Both *Hackney Stud Book* and *Welsh Stud Book* quote the date of birth as 1880 but his stud card (printed in 1880) offers him at stud in 1880 and gives his date of birth as 1877.

There are only two photographs of individual animals featured in *Vol. I* of the *Welsh Stud Book*. One is of the Welsh Mountain Pony stallion Dyoll Starlight (who completely changed the fate of the breed; *chapter 2.1*) and the other was the Welsh Cob stallion Eiddwen Flyer. Such was the respect which early members of the Welsh Pony & Cob Society had for these two stallions that their photographs also illustrated the Society's Certificates (which accompanied medals for championship awards) up until the year 1930.

Mr. Thomas John Jones of Dinarth Hall, owner of Eiddwen Flyer II also several other famous ponies e.g. Bowdler Brightlight, Criban Socks, Ceulan Comet etc.

Eiddwen Flyer certainly deserves to be amongst the "great Cob sires". Early breeders always referred to Eiddwen Flyer with great reverence, proudly claiming descent of their animals from "Eiddwen Bach" ("Little Eiddwen" as he was affectionately known in Cardiganshire). He left hundreds of good Cobs in Cardiganshire and Montgomeryshire (where he travelled in 1892–1896).

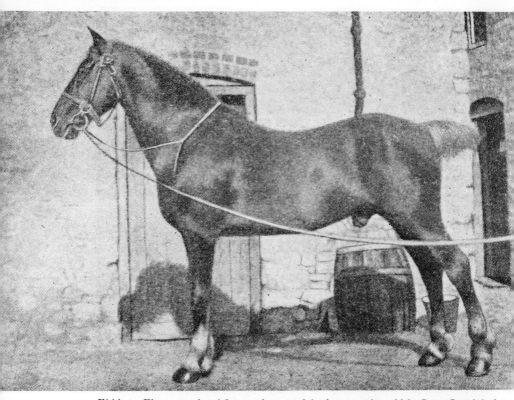

Eiddwen Flyer reproduced from a photograph in the possession of Mr. Percy Dugdale from Welsh Stud Book, Vol. I.

Eiddwen Flyer was a big winner in the show ring in such far-off places as Stourbridge, Crewe, Ruthin, Swansea, Oswestry and Kington and with travelling so difficult in those days, one wonders how he managed to get to these far-off shows. His wins include prizes in harness and under saddle. The name "Eiddwen" was derived from a lake "Llyn Eiddwen" which lies high on a Cardigan summit.

Eiddwen Flyer died in 1902 but his blood had made an enormous impact on the Welsh Cob breed. Surprisingly he also had a big influence on the Mountain Pony breed e.g. Coed Coch Glyndwr (*chapter 6.1*) has six strains of Eiddwen Flyer; four on his dam's side through Klondyke (foaled 1894 and owned by my mother's great uncle John Thomas, the Mill, Tre'rddol) and two on the sire's side.

One daughter of Eiddwen Flyer to excel in harness was Lady Go Bang a chesnut mare, foaled in 1896 she measured 13 hands 1 in. Bred by W. Williams in Ciliau Aeron, Cardiganshire she won most of her prizes in the ownership of George Griffiths, Cape Hill, Smethwick.

Lady Go Bang (foaled in 1896), daughter of Eiddwen Flyer.

Eiddwen Flyer ridden by his owner Mr. William Jones. (Photograph courtesy of Mr. John Roderick-Rees, B.A.)

These prizes included Dublin, Belfast, York, Oxford, Gloucester, Shrewsbury, Bath, Cardiff, Swansea, Aberdare, Kington, Hay, Brecon, Maidenhead, Devon etc. etc; what a well-travelled little mare!

One photograph shows Eiddwen Flyer ridden by his owner, William Jones, Morfa Bychan, Llanfarian, Aberystwyth (later of Brynchwith, Llangwyryfon where his grand-son Dan E. Jones still breeds good Welsh Cobs). David Rees (who had this photograph) thinks it was a good likeness of him and not at all like the *Welsh Stud Book* photograph.

John Jones, Coed Coch relating on how high Eiddwen Flyer used to step said that he once saw him step over a wheel-barrow!

5. Black Bess

6. Cymro Llwyd (*chapter 18.6*)

8. Old Welsh Flyer (*chapter 18.1*)

9. mare by Welsh Jack (Caecefnder) (*chapter 18.6*) by Cymro Llwyd (*chapter 18.6*)

10. King Jack
Registration number 1022 in the *Hackney Stud Book, Vol. II* (1885)
Chesnut, foaled 1860
Breeder: M. Davies, Cross Inn, Aberystwyth
Sire: Wonderful Comet 1225 *Hackney Stud Book* by
Comet 931 *Hackney Stud Book* (Comet Bach) by Old
Comet 834 (*chapter 18.2*)
Dam: by Express 964 *Hackney Stud Book*.

Wonderful Comet 1225 *Hackney Stud Book* was bay, foaled in 1854 and owned by Mr. Rowlands, Ystrad Caron, Tregaron, Cardiganshire.

Comet 931 *Hackney Stud Book* (Comet Bach) was bay, foaled in 1845 and owned by Mr. David Williams, Llwyncolfa (where some excellent Welsh Cobs are still bred today), Tregaron.

Express 964 *Hackney Stud Book* was brown and foaled in 1853. Breeder: William Edwards, Pwll, Aberystwyth. Owner in 1860: David E. Jones, Old Abbey, Cardiganshire. Owner in 1870: D. Havard, Cwmtaf, Merthyr Tydfil, Glamorganshire.

Not only did King Jack have a big influence on the breeds of Welsh ponies and Cobs himself through Eiddwen Flyer but also through his son Young King Jack, g-sire of High Stepping Gambler II (*chapter 23.4*).

22

Beaconsfield foaled 1887

2 Earl Beaconsfield	4 Caradog	8 Welsh Jack
		9 Mare
		10 Young Rainbow

1

Beaconsfield
27

3 Black Bess	6 Glanne Welsh Flyer	12 Old Welsh Flyer
	7 Bess	14 Young Rainbow
		15 Mare

1. Beaconsfield
Registration number 27 in the *Welsh Stud Book,*
Vol. I
Chesnut, height: 14 hand 2 in, foaled 1887
Breeder: John Webb, Aberbutran, Garth R.S.O.
Owner: George Webb, Cilmery Farm, Builth Wells

This is the stallion referred to as "Southin" in the letter of O. G. Owen, describing the g-sire of Alveston Belle (*chapter 4.3*). In his younger days, Beaconsfield won many prizes around the Builth Wells area; from six years onwards, he spent considerable time travelling in North Wales and won many prizes at Pwllheli, Portmadog and Ffestiniog.

2. Earl Beaconsfield
Liver chesnut, height: 14 hands 2 in, foaled 1877

3. Black Bess
Black, 14 hands

4. Caradog
Height: 14 hands 3 in, foaled 1872
Owned by Mr. S. Jones, Talfedw, Llangeitho,
Cardiganshire

Caradog's stud card for 1877 claims him to be "of perfect symmetry and proportion, of beautiful action and of most docile temper". He was got by Welsh Jack, Welsh Jack by Cymro Llwyd (*chapter 18.6*) out of an excellent fast-trotting mare got by Old Comet (*chapter 18.2*) and grand-dam by Comet Bach; his great-grand-dam was got by True Briton (*chapter 17.1*) Caradog's dam was got by that celebrated fast-trotting horse Cardigan Comet (*chapter 19.4*) which at different times and places won 16 prizes; great-grand-dam by Young Nelson.

Caradog won the first prize at Aberaeron in March 1875 and also first prize at Llanwrtyd in April 1876. Caradog was g-g-sire of High Stepping Gambler (*chapter 23.8*), and also g-g-sire of Ceitho Welsh Comet (*chapter 24.2*).

6. Glanne Welsh Flyer (*chapter 20.4*)

8. Welsh Jack (*chapter 18.6*)

1877.

TO COVER THIS SEASON,

AT £1 10S. EACH MARE, AND 2S. 6D. THE GROOM,

The Groom's Fee to be paid at the first time of serving, the remainder on or before the 26th of June next,

THE FAMOUS HORSE

CARADOG,

The property of Mr. S. Jones, Talvedw, Llangeitho, Cardiganshire.

CARADOG is five years old, and stands 14 hands 3 inches high, is of perfect symmetry and proportion, of beautiful action, and of most docile temper. He was got by Welsh Jack, Welsh Jack by Cymro out of an excellent fast-trotting Mare, got by Old Comet, and grand dam by Comet Bach; his great grand dam was got by True Briton. Cymro won the prizes at the Brecon Agricultural Show in 1851—52—53. Caradog's dam was got by that celebrated fast-trotting horse Cardigan Comet, which at different times and places won 16 prizes; great grand dam Young Nelson.

Caradog won the 1st prize at Aberayron in March, 1875, also the 1st prize at Llanwrtyd in April, 1876. The first of his offspring won the 1st prize at the Tregaron Agricultural Show in 1876.

When the Groom agrees for a Colt, and the Mare is sold before he ascertains whether she is in foal, the Season price will be charged. Mares tried and given to another will be charged for.

The Groom will specify the time and places of attendance.

J. Morgan (late Cox), Printer, Pier St., Aberystwyth.

9. mare by Cardigan Comet (*chapter 19.4*)

10. Young Rainbow
registration number 655 in the *Hackney Stud Book, Vol. I*
Black, height: 14 hands 3 in, foaled 1874
Breeder: Mr. Curtis, Farnham, Berkshire
Sire: Rainbow (Thomas') by King George
Dam: by True Briton (*chapter 17.1*)

Young Rainbow was known in Wales as "Cel du bach" and was

328

Stud card of Cardigan Rainbow for 1882. Cardigan Rainbow was a son of Rainbow. (Stud card courtesy of Messrs. Rowlands Harris.)

owned by Mr. D. Griffiths, Ffrwd, in 1881. He was a good sire, two of his sons Cardigan Rainbow (Messrs. Rowlands, Mabwshen) and King Jack The Second (foaled in 1881 and bred by William Davies, Penbryn, Bronant, Llanilar) being popular stallions in mid-Wales.

Another popular stallion in mid-Wales was Rainbow Comet (foaled in 1899) whose dam, Rose was sired by Young Rainbow. Rainbow Comet's stud card claims that Young Rainbow travelled the same round for 15 years and was a winner of 23 first prizes, his stock for years fetching the highest prices in Cardiganshire.

(Old) Rainbow was bred by Mr. Thomas, Aberduhonw, Builth

TO SERVE THIS SEASON

A limited number of Mares at £2 2s. each Mare, and 2s. 6d. the Groom.

The Groom's Fee to be paid at the first time of serving, and the remainder on or before the 1st day of July next.

THAT GRAND YOUNG STALLION

'RAINBOW COMET,'

The property of Mr. David Jones, Bwlchwernen, Llangybi, Derry Ormond, R.S.O.

RAINBOW COMET is a beautiful bay, stands 15 hands high, and 3 years old. He is without doubt one of the most promising young stallions of the present day. He is a brilliant all-round mover, combined with high and level action, and is probably going to make the fastest Cob Stallion that has travelled the district for years. His breeding will carry him a long way, as he was got by Beauty Boy, which was without a doubt the most fashionable stallion that ever travelled Wales, and was very highly commended at the Royal Agricultural Show held at Cambridge in 1894.

BEAUTY BOY'S sire Silver King, 1559, was 15-2 hands high, by Golden Star, 989, winner of fifty prizes, he was by Star of the East, 798, which won the championship at Paris Exhibition, and first at the Agricultural Hall, Islington (three times), and at the Royal Show, Great Yorkshire, and all the principal shows in England, he was by Star of the West.

Silver King, the sire of Beauty Boy, won the following prizes :—six firsts, and six seconds, at such places as Keighley, Airdale, Wharfedale, Otley, Doncaster, Bradford, Middleton, Royal Manchester, Liverpool, North Lancashire and Worsley.

Dam of Silver King, 1015, Triffil's Fireway, 249, obtained first at the Great Royal Show at Manchester in 1869, also at Budwith, Ross, Cottingham, Sutton, and Care, also the first prize of £20 at the Great Yorkshire, 1868.

Silver King, the sire of Beauty Boy, was admitted to be one of the fastest trotters in the county of Norfolk, and was also well-known in trotting matches.

BEAUTY BOY'S dam was a pure Welsh mare, bred by Miss Davies, Pantyfedwen, Cardiganshire, a dark bay, and was got by the renowned horse Welsh Flyer, 856. She was a very fast trotter, and strains back to the blue blood of the old Cardiganshire breed. She was bought since at a long price for breeding purposes, and has proved herself a most valuable mare to breed from. The following are some of her offsprings :—one winning first prize at a trotting match at Pomona Gardens ; another won first at Glossop ; another won second for the best show, speed, and action at Bakewell Show ; one won a mile trotting match in England in 2 minutes 46 seconds, reaching the winning post 14 seconds before the rest ; one was sold to the Sudbury Stud Company, Blackpool, at a fabulous price ; one was sold to Chas. S. Mynors, Esq., for 300 guineas. The above will show clear to anyone that this mare was the right sort to breed from.

RAINBOW COMET'S dam Rose was got by that renowned sire Rainbow (Curtis), known in Wales as (Ceffyl du bach), 655 Vol. 1., H.S.B., who travelled 15 years the same round. He was a winner of 23 first prizes, and his stock for years fetched the highest prices in Cardiganshire. Rainbow's pedigree can be seen in full in the Hackney Stud Book. Rainbow Comet's grand dam was got by Cardigan Comet the First (Cel bach Pentrebrain). Rainbow Comet's dam is half-sister to Stala, winner of nine first prizes at Lampeter and other places. Now it will be seen by the pedigree (both sides) of this young horse, that he is not an inferior one. His speed producing power is guaranteed by a good pedigree, and he must make a very valuable and impressive sire, and as like begets like, we shall have fine results from this young stallion.

1906.   1906.

Number **20** in Stud Book Welsh Pony and Cob Society.

A Rare Opportunity to Breeders of Cobs and Carriage Horses.

TO SERVE MARES THIS SEASON,

At £1 10s. each Mare, and 2s. 6d. the Groom.

THAT CELEBRATED HORSE,

"KING JACK THE SECOND,"

The property of Mr. William Davies, Penbryn, Bronant, Near Aberystwyth.

KING JACK the 2nd is of Chestnut colour, and stands 14-2 hands high. King Jack the 2nd, by Young Rainbow (Cel-du-bach), late property of Mr. D. Griffiths, Ffrwd, whose stock is well known throughout Wales. Young Rainbow was got by Old Rainbow (bred by Mr. Thomas, Aberdihonw, Builth), was got by King George, who was sold for £400

KING JACK the 2nd's dam is the noted Trotting Polly, the property of William Rees, Esq., Waunfawr, Tregaron. Trotting Polly has taken 1st prizes in numerous places in Cardiganshire and elsewhere. This Trotting Polly is also the dam of Young Caradog, the property of John A. Jones, Esq., Dowlais, which has taken 1st prizes at Bedwellty, Rhymney, Neath, Blackwood, &c. Trotting Polly was got by King Jack, by Wonderful Comet, by Comet bach, by Old Comet, and has taken 1st prize for action and speed, in 1884, at Cribin, Aberaeron, Llanon, Pontrhydfendigaid, Ysbytty Ystwyth, Rhayadr, Radnorshire; two 1st prizes at Ty'nllidiart, and two 1st prizes at Pontllanio in 1887; second prizes too numerous to mention.

This is a proof that King Jack the 2nd, is related to the best trotters ever known.

KING JACK the 2nd is of splendid action, quite worthy of his predecessors as a trotter, and has proved himself a sure foal getter. Some of his stock have won 1st prizes every year at the Horse Shows all over the country for show in harness and trotting, and others sold for very high figures, from £40 to £50.

☞ All demands to be paid at the end of the Season. For further particulars, apply to the Groom.

Printed by Jonathan Thomas, The Square, Tregaron.

Stud card of King Jack the Second (foaled in 1881) for 1906. King Jack the Second was a son of Rainbow. (Stud card courtesy of Messrs. Rowlands Harris.)

Wells and was claimed to be "The fastest trotter in South Wales". Old Rainbow was sold in 1874 to Mr. Castle of Thame, Oxfordshire for 150 guineas, he took the first prize in France the same year and was afterwards sold for 300 guineas. King George was sold for £400.

12. Old Welsh Flyer (*chapter 18.1*)

15. mare by Trotting Lion by Dandelion

23

High Stepping Gambler II foaled in 1902
Mathrafal Brenin foaled in 1911
Gwalia Victor foaled in 1924
Brenin Gwalia foaled in 1934

1 Brenin Gwalia 1656	2 Gwalia Victor 1431	4 High Stepping Gambler II 143	8 High Stepping Gambler I 33
			9 Fanny
		5 Hendraws Doll	10 Briton Flyer
			11 Polly
	3 Cymraes	6 Mathrafal Brenin 873	12 Trotting Railway II 529
			13 Dolly 5648
		7 Doll	14 Flying Express 624
			15 Polly

1. Brenin Gwalia

Registration number 1656 in the *Welsh Stud Book,*
Vol. XXXII
Chesnut, blaze, four white legs, height: 14 hands 2 in,
foaled 1934
Breeder: Lloyd Rees, Tynewydd, Llandefalle,
Breconshire.
Owners: David Rees and Son (John Roderick Rees,
B.A.), Bear's Hill, Penuwch, Tregaron,
Cardiganshire.
(Bear's Hill 1920–1939; Berthlwyd 1939–1954 and
back to Bear's Hill 1954–)

John Roderick Rees and his father David Rees were minutely and intimately concerned with Brenin Gwalia, his feeding, his working and his showing for 30 years and 6 months.

He was 6 months old when he arrived at Bear's Hill, in the early darkness of the evening of 1st December 1934, John Rees' birthday. And what a birthday present! His breeder, Lloyd Rees (no relation), Tynewydd, Llandyfalle, Talgarth, Breconshire had brought him to meet Mr. David Rees at the cattle pens at Brecon market. There he was loaded on to John's uncle's lorry from a ramp (as the lorry had sides but no stock tail-board) the lorry being used for purposes other than the carriage of animals. Disembarkation at Bear's Hill was over a hedge and on to a carefully arranged landing pad in the field! He was in the Cardi-land of his forefathers, there to remain for evermore.

That he was to be a stallion, if a male, was a secular predestination from the moment of conception. Mathrafal Brenin had died in 1928, High Stepping Gambler II in 1933. Gwalia Victor, alone, was left to keep the flag of the little stud flying. The colt from Llandyfalle had the blood of all three in his veins. On the sire's side, Brenin Gwalia was a son of Gwalia Victor and the sixth generation of Cob stallions, father-to-son, in the Rees family. The seventh generation was Trotting Comet (*chapter 18.2*) (again of Penuwch) about the furthest step you can reach in the recorded history of the Welsh Cob.

The name "Brenin Gwalia" was an obvious combination. His arrival at Bear's Hill aroused a good deal of curiosity. John Rees remembers Tom Jones Evans, Craven Arms, on a premium tour of inspection, casting his eyes over the colt in 1936 and prophesying great things for him. As yet he was but a colt and John a boy. John had to lead him out to the field and he already showed promise of the extraordinary action

335

which was to be one of his hallmarks. Most often, he broke loose and made a bee-line for the yard and his stable! As a yearling he was out at grass with Gwen, their trusty old chesnut pony by Trotting Jack. That was the last time the stars looked down on him. From year 1 to year 31, he always had a roof over him, only spending the occasional half-day in a paddock by the house.

In 1936, David Rees was travelling Gwalia Victor in parts of Carmarthenshire and the Gower. An affliction disabled him for a fortnight and his two-year-old son, Brenin Gwalia had to step into the breach. John well remembers his going out of the yard and his return after a fortnight, having held his own well and served 16 mares. From then on, he was for a time, the reserve at home. At week-ends, home from school John took him to mares within walking distance. He showed his characteristic docility and was easy to handle. Eventually, he shared duties with his sire and ultimately took over the premier spot. He gained a premium at his first attempt and was twelve times in succession premium stallion for Cardiganshire, more often North Cards but sometimes the South, always taking in the mid-County where he was based.

Regarding premiums, matters were different then in two respects: the judges visited the applicants' homes and saw the stallions individually on their own ground. Secondly, a premium stallion had to travel, which meant walking a distance of 15 to 20 miles a day, every week-day for 3

336

summer months, calling at customers' farms en route. It was hard, unrelenting pressure for the conscientious, which tested the mettle of man and beast, not least the little pony which carried the groom alongside the stallion. Bryn Arth Titch, barely 13 hands high, carried David Rees for 20 seasons. She lived to be 27 years and was a high-actioned and most sure-footed of animals, exploding the myth that riding horses have to be "daisy-cutters".

It speaks volumes for the acceptability of man and stallion that Brenin Gwalia, always led by David Rees, served over 100 mares per season and that over the same ground with occasional slight variation, throughout his long career. Twelve different judges in successive years awarded him a Cardiganshire premium; one other wanted him to move to Breconshire for a season. It was both inconvenient and unnecessary for David Rees to do so: he travelled the same Cardiganshire patch competing against the "fresh" stallion. Brenin served 128 mares, the new stallion 14 mares. There was no suggestion of a switch thereafter!

Mr. David Rees photographed in 1948. Mr. Rees was owner of Brenin Gwalia, Gwalia Victor, Mathrafal Brenin and High Stepping Gambler II.

If QUALITY, STYLE, STRENGTH and ACTION, combined with the very best Welsh Trotting Blood that has ever travelled England and Wales are the essentials of a successful Stock-getter, they are to be found in marked degree in that Typical, Superior and Well-Bred Young Welsh Cob Stallion.

Brenin Gwalia

Foaled 1934.

sire—Gwalia Victor 1431 W.S.B.
g sire—High Stepping Gambler II. 143 W.S.B.
g g sire—High Stepping Gambler I. 33 W.S.B.
g g g sire—Welsh Briton.
g g g g sire—Briton Comet.
g g g g g sire—Old Comet.

dam—Cymraes by Mathyrafal Brenin 873 W.S.B.
g dam—Doll by Flying Express 624 W.S.B.
g g dam—by Pencaerhelem 23 W.S.B.
g g g dam—by Old Trotting Railway (better known as Bedlinog Horse).

BRENIN GWALIA, a blaze-faced chestnut, with four white limbs, a flaxen mane and tail, stands 14.8 h.h., and goes great guns all round. He holds the Ministry's Certificate for soundness, and is descended from absolutely sound cobs, on both sides. The majority of Welsh Cob Stallions travelling to-day, have unsound ancestors. This is a remarkable fact which must appeal to every judicious Stock-breeder, for unsound horses are worthless.

Little need be said by way of recommend-ation of Brenin Gwalia's pedigree. He is be-lieved to be the only Welsh Cob Stallion liv-ing, who is descended from Supreme Cham-pions on both sides High Stepping Gambler II. 143 W.S.B., winner of 65 first prizes, in-cluding silver cups and medals, at all the leading shows in England and Wales, includ-ing the Royal Welsh 1908, 1909, and the Royal A.S. of England, 1919, at 17 years old, needs no words of praise. His showyard career, and the eulogistic terms in which competent judges of the breed still speak of him, provide a glittering tribute to this celebrated Welsh Cob.

Mathyrafal Brenin 873 W.S.B., a great winner in the Show Ring, including the Prince of Wales' 50 guineas Challenge Cup at the Royal Welsh Show 1924-25, and 3rd in the 15 hands class at the Royal Show, Cardiff, 1919, is too highly esteemed by Stock-breeders, and admiring showyard crowds, to need commendation. Indeed this sterling trotter was one of the most perfect specimens of his kind.

Both of Brenin Gwalia's grandsires were exported as equine pioneers of Welsh Cob breeding in two Continents; Trotting Railway II. 529 W.S.B., to Australia, where he triumphed at leading shows, including 1st Sydney; High Stepping Gambler I. 33 W.S.B., to South Africa where he was serving mares at £10 10s. each at the stud of Mr. J. R. Hill, at Bloemfontein, Orange River Colony.

Brenin Gwalia's g g g sire, holds a re-cord, which is, probably, unequalled in the annals of Welsh Cob breeding. Two of his progeny,—Cardigan Lass and Welsh Prince, won the Trotting Competition at Alexandra Park, beating all the leading trotters of the day. And no fewer than 20 stallions were sired by this equine celebrity.

That Brenin Gwalia is directly descended, on both sides, from Welsh Cobs of incompar-able merit, and the leading prize-winners for half a century, is clearly shown by the above pedigree. Two of his forefathers have blazed the trail for Welsh Cob breeding in two Con-tinents, and although they clung to their native heath, the transcendent sires, Mathy-rafal Brenin and High Stepping Gambler II. have written their names, indelibly, on the page of equine history. They represent long service at the helm of life; Brenin Gwalia re-presents youth at the prow.

TERMS.

Will serve a limited number of Mares at £2/2/0 each Mare (bona-fide Tenant Farmers £1/1/0) and 2/6 Groom's fee. No alteration in the service fee in any way. Groom's fee to be paid first time of serving; Service Fee due first time of serving and to be paid on or before the 24th day of June next.

Neither the Owner nor the Groom will be responsible for any accident that may occur through trying or serving Mares, either to the Mare or the man in charge, nor for any ill effects that may occur to the Mare after serving, but the utmost care will be taken.

All Mares tried by this horse and not brought forward, or disposed of in any way will be charged for, card price.

If anything happens to BRENIN GWALIA a substitute will be provided and must be accepted.

FOR FURTHER PARTICULARS, APPLY TO THE OWNER:—

D. REES,
Bear's Hill Stud, Penuwch,
Tregaron, Cards.

D. R. Evans & Co., The Bridge Press, Lampeter.

Stud card (1938) for Brenin Gwalia.

A successful stallion greatly depends on the man in charge, he has to be both hardworking and a man of the people; that David Rees was. He also has to keep his horses in peak condition; that norm was invariably attained. Brenin Gwalia was a born showman. David Rees usually took him at the walk around the ring: then John took over. He needed no prompting nor spurring to do his best. With his proud crest, his perfect symmetry, his almost transparent bone, the silkiest of feathers, his walk-on-air movement and tremendous action, high and traditional be it noted, he gravitated automatically towards the head of the line. Being eight times in succession Champion Welsh Cob stallion at Lampeter is about as high as you can go in competition. Before entering the ring, he often trembled a little; "nerves" affect the best performers. Something that seems to have deserted shown stallions nowadays is the fiery spirit which he radiated on parade. Very much the lamb in domestic surroundings, he pretended to be a lion in combat.

A highlight of his showing career was at the 1947 Royal Welsh Show at Carmarthen where he put up a great show handled alternatively by John Rees and my father E. S. Davies and won the Male Championship. In 1948 he was selected by the Welsh Pony & Cob Society to represent the breed at the International Horse Show at the White City, London; here he proved to be the favourite with the spectators and was always held back when the others had gone out to give a second "show".

Brenin Gwalia's last appearance in a show ring was at Llandovery in 1954. He was 20 years old but had lost none of his freshness nor his agility. It turned out to be a rather remarkable re-union and it was poetic justice that the old maestro should win. Placings were first: Brenin Gwalia; second: Llwynog-y-Garth; third: Pentre Eiddwen Comet.

Wyre Star, daughter of Brenin Gwalia driven by Mr. Gwil Evans.

One facet of Brenin Gwalia's life story which the world at large may be ignorant of, was his capacity for work. So intelligent was he that when you donned stallion gear on him he was the spirited Pegasus; when you put his head through a collar he was the docile servant of the soil. He was trained to plough and harrow alongside Bryn Arth Titch, our good but fiery old pony, when he was only two-years-old. Pulling the mower, the cart, the gambo, the trap, he was homely and unhurried as to the manner born. He was a beautiful harness horse: no wonder that he sired such harness performers as Meiarth Royal Eiddwen and Wyre Star and was grand-sire of both the Champion Harness Cob and the Champion Harness Pony at the 1978 Royal Welsh Show.

The first field that John Rees ploughed was Cae Glanrafon (the field by the river) on Berthlwyd Farm, Cross Inn, Llanon, Cardiganshire, behind Brenin Gwalia and Blaenwaun Flora Temple (the 1929 Royal Welsh Show Champion Mare and daughter of High Stepping Gambler

Rhosfarch Frenin, son of Brenin Gwalia the present-day stallion of the Rees family with Mr. John Roderick Rees. Photographed when Champion at Aberystwyth Show.

340

II) in the spring of 1941. Being a novice, John ploughed one way, trailing back. Brenin Gwalia wore a big collar. It is still in John's possession and it was his pleasure quite recently when asked to lend it to adorn a rustic looking set for a B.B.C. Television programme. Miss Beryl Evans took a cine-film of Brenen Gwalia ploughing alongside his daughter, Bryn Arth Madonna. This film was once shown at the A.G.M. of the Welsh Pony & Cob Society but was later, unfortunately, lost in transit.

David Rees cared for him superbly but also worked him hard. However, he had a long and mellow retirement from 20 to 31, dying at 31 years in 1965. John was one of those that dug his grave, the same grave in which he had seen the body of High Stepping Gambler II being put 32 years earlier (at 32 years of age), in Y Cae Bach (the small field) at Bear's Hill. He was fertile to the last, producing one filly in his last week of life. He spent 16 years at Bear's Hill and 15 years at the Rees' other home at Berthlwyd.

Now John has Rhosfarch Frenin, one of his few remaining sons, the seventh generation in the Rees family. Moreover Brenin Gwalia has over twenty stallion grandsons from Aberdeen to Melbourne, from Lleyn to East Anglia. John Rees' one-stallion Welsh Cob Stud is the oldest in existence having devolved father-to-son without a break from the 1870's to 1979.

2. Gwalia Victor
Registration number 1431 in the *Welsh Stud Book*,
Vol. XXVII
Bay, blaze, white off hind fetlock,
height: 14 hands 2 in, foaled 1924
Breeder: J. Lloyd Davies, Hendraws Farm,
Rhydlewis, Henllan, Cardiganshire.

It has been a policy of the Rees family to breed a young stallion from the best of their current ones ever since John Rees' grandfather developed the family's connections with Welsh Cobs. Thus there is a genealogical chain binding their stallions from John Rees' present Rhosfarch Frenin to his grandfather's Welsh Briton and Gwalia Victor is a link in this unbroken chain.

Gwalia Victor was foaled in 1924 when his sire was 22 years old (incidentally Brenin Gwalia was 26 years old when he begot Rhosfarch Frenin), and Mr. David Rees bought him as a foal from his breeder. High Stepping Gambler II, Mathrafal Brenin and Gwalia Victor were

341

Gwalia Victor with Mr. David Rees photographed while travelling Brecon and Radnor. Note the feed on the girth etc.

stud stallion with the Rees family at the same time; Mathrafal Brenin died in 1928, Gambler II lived on to 1934, the year that his grand-son Brenin Gwalia was born.

Gwalia Victor was a compact, blocky cob, very symmetrical, short-backed, short-legged, strong-boned, with a neat head and small ears, elegantly curved at the tips; full of a controlled power, strength without coarseness, of a rich, polished bay with black points, a white right hind sock and a narrow blaze. He had a wiry toughness that was truly Welsh and took very hard travelling on foot from farm to farm in his stride. In a farmyard he would invariably stand "at attention", without prompting. His walk was very nimble and light-footed.

He may not be as well-known as some of the Rees' stallions, but point for point, in aggregate, he was not inferior. His "hour" was the late 20's and 30's, the years of the locust, when economic survival was the predominant theme in agriculture. Trade in colts and fillies was de-pressed; the heartless slaughter-trade (as now) swept good and bad together into oblivion. It was not a time for the emergence of heroes, equine or human.

Although not shown extensively, Gwalia Victor had considerable success; at the Lampeter Stallion Show, he was Champion Cob in 1929, 1930 and 1931. Above all, he was the breeder's stallion who invariably had good seasons e.g. he served 128 mares in 1931.

Gwalia Victor often travelled Breconshire, Radnorshire or the Gower with part of Carmarthen. Travelling Brecon in 1933 he produced Brenin Gwalia; travelling the same area in 1931 he produced Pistyll Sunset, dam of Llanarth Goldcrest, sire of Llanarth Braint (*chapter 27.1*).

342

Stud card (1937) for Gwalia Victor.

343

Gwalia Victor is the grand-sire on both sides of Favourite who was dam of Chancerie King Flyer, Champion Chancerie Polly etc. When Brenin Gwalia became the main stud horse for the Rees family, it was decided to find a good home for Gwalia Victor. This was found with Douglas Neale (Neale and West, Shipowners, Cardiff) who had a farm at Nant Fawr, Lisvane and Gwalia Victor lived there happily in semi-retirement until his death at 24 years in 1948.

3. Cymraes
Registration number 137 F.S. 2. in the appendix of
the *Welsh Stud Book, Vol. XXXII*
Chesnut, blaze, height 14 hands 3 in, foaled 1929
Breeder: Lloyd Rees, Tynewydd, Llandyfalle,
Breconshire.

John Rees remembers visiting Tynewydd to see Cymraes with his father and Mr. D. Ivor Lewis of the Glancrychan Stud and describes Cymraes as a "well-made, blocky chesnut with substance upstairs and downstairs with quality to boot". Cymraes was at the apex of a long line of Breconshire Cob mares; that shrewd judge, Mr. Gwilym Morris of the Pistyll Stud knew all the Cobs in Breconshire and considered this family to be among the very best.

4. High Stepping Gambler II
Registration number 143 in the *Welsh Stud Book,
Vol. IV*
Bay, star, white near hind fetlock, height: 14 hands
1 in, foaled 1902
Breeders: Evan and David Davies, Penrhiw, Silian,
Lampeter, Cardiganshire

High Stepping Gambler II, a rich dark bay with a star and near hind white sock, was a tightly-coupled, full-bodied cob, with a near head, a wonderful rangy outlook, strong bone of steely quality and hard-wearing feet; in short, a rare combination of quantity and quality. Add to this a proud, fiery nature – it needed a true horseman to handle him in his prime – and the superb action of the original variety. No wonder that he dominated the show ring for many years. In his day there were red-blooded specimens of the old lineage, as yet undiluted, striving for honours; it was also the heyday of the Hackney and the current fashion was weighted in their favour. A Welsh Cob had to have distinctive

High Stepping Gambler II with Mr. David Rees. Photographed in 1909.

qualities, in mixed classes, to beat them in their own metier. Gambler was capable of this on account of his supremely spirited displays. He was shown only in hand; in those days Welsh Cob stallions were not driven and ridden in shows; at fairs they showed their trotting paces alongside a ridden pony. There was not the profusion of stallion classes in general shows either; stallion shows were often occasions apart at eve-of-travelling season exhibitions. Gambler won 65 first prizes and was never unplaced. The two peaks of his show career were winning the championship at the 1909 Welsh National (as it was then called) and similar honours at the Royal Show of England at Cardiff in 1919. In 1908 he had been reserve champion at the Welsh National.

Afterwards, Evan Davies sold Gambler to his nephew, Harry Rees who shortly afterwards sold him to his brother, David Rees, father of

If quality, style, strength, and action, combined with the very best Welsh Trotting blood that has ever travelled England and Wales, are the essentials of a successful Stock getter, they will be found in a marked degree in that Superior and Well Bred Pure Welsh Cob,

HIGH STEPPING GAMBLER II.
143 W.S.B.

The Property of E. H. Rees, Cwmgwceni Stud Farm, Llangeitho, Cardiganshire.

Will Serve a limited number of Mares this Season at £3 3s. Bona-fide Tenant Farmers, £2 2s., each mare, and 5s. the Groom.

The Groom's Fee to be paid the first time of Serving and the remainder on or before the 24th of June next, or 5s. extra will be charged for collecting without further notice. This Rule will be strictly adhered to.

HIGH STEPPING GAMBLER stands 15 hands high, is of a beautiful bay colour, strong bone, grand all round action, and one of the fastest trotters in Wales. He is full of quality and perfect in symmetry. Has a splendid constitution, combined with good temper, and has proved himself a most sure and impressive sire, and his young stock are most promising, they possess strong bone and beautiful high step, and he has already sired some tip-top Cobs which are prize winners in open competitions. Several of these have been sold for satisfactory prices. All his stock even from ordinary mares are most promising. His pedigree is unequalled in point of purity of the Welsh Trotting Breed, embracing some of the best sires and dams, including a number of prize takers. He was got by Stepping Gambler I., 36 W.S.B., a horse which won numerous prizes, by Welsh Briton, by Briton Comet, by Old Comet, by Flyer, whose dam was Pool's celebrated trotting mare, which was never beaten.

HIGH STEPPING GAMBLER II. 143, dam Fanny, by Young King Jack, by King Jack 1002 W.S.B., by Wonderful Comet 1225 H.S.B., by Comet Bach 931, by Old Trotting Comet 834, dam by Express 964 H.S.B. His sire, Stepping Gambler I., was one of the best and fastest all-round Cobs of his day, sired most valuable Cobs and sold at satisfactory prices.

High Stepping Gambler I. was exported to South Africa, end of season 1903, and kept by J. R. Hill, Esq., at his valuable stud at Schultz House, Monument Road, Orange River Colony, South Africa, and serving mares at £10 10s. each mare.

High Stepping Gambler II.'s, Half-Brothers and Half-Sisters, by the renowned High Stepping Gambler I. have won hundreds of prizes at the leading Shows of Great Britain, in fact, his stock both in the Show Ring and Sale Yard are at the top of the tree.

High Stepping Gambler II. has had a most successful Show yard career, amongst his winnings being:—The H.R.H. the Prince of Wales' 50 guineas Challenge Cup for the best Welsh Cob of the Old Welsh Type, open to Wales and Monmouthshire. He has won several First and Special Prizes on different occasions at Lampeter, Aberayron, Welsh National, Aberystwyth, two years in succession, Taunton, Marshbrook, Carmarthen, Newcastle Emlyn, and Llandyssul.

From the above it will be seen that High Stepping Gambler II. is undoubtedly one of the best horses of Welsh breeding standing for service at the present day. Breeders, therefore, cannot do wrong in giving this horse a trial.

Mares tried by this horse and afterwards put to another horse or not brought forward will be charged for. Any dispute that may arise between Groom and Hirer, the Conditions of this Card shall be final. If anything should happen to High Stepping Gambler II. a substitute will be provided, and must be accepted. The Owner, nor the Groom, if necessary to be employed, will not hold himself responsible for any accident that may occur through trying or serving mares, but the utmost care will be taken.

D. R. Evans & Co., Stud Card Printers, Lampeter.

Stud card (1911) for High Stepping Gambler II.

346

John Rees. Then began a period of unparalleled success. The 1909 entries at Aberystwyth were an illustrious crowd. The Champion mare was H. P. Edwards' Pride of the Hills, sold shortly afterwards to go overseas for the then princely sum of 500 guineas.

John Rees still has the special girth made for High Stepping Gambler II which is all covered with medals, commemorating some of his prizes: forty-eight in all. The medals were made too big for all his successes to be incorporated on the one piece of leather; here is the list:

Board's Premium, 1912, 1913, 1914, 1915, 1916, 1917, 1918, 1919.

1907: First Lampeter. 1908: First Lampeter: Reserve Champion Welsh National.

1909: First, Silver Medal and Prince of Wales Cup, Welsh National; first Taunton; first Marshbrook.

1910: First Aberaeron; first Aberystwyth; first Cardigan; first Lampeter; first Llandyssul; first Newcastle Emlyn.

1911: First Llanelly; first Carmarthen; first Newcastle Emlyn; first Llandyssul; first Lampeter; first Cardigan.

1912: First Lampeter; first Newcastle Emlyn; first Llandyssul; first Tragaron; first Cardigan.

1913: First Tregaron; first Llandyssul; first Cardigan; first Newcastle Emlyn.

1914: First Crymych; first Llandyssul; first Lampeter; first Cardigan; first Newcastle Emlyn.

1916: First Carmarthen.

1917: First Carmarthen.

1919: First and Silver Medal, Royal of England, Cardiff; first Carmarthen; first Narberth.

In 1917, Gambler was awarded a double premium of £100, probably unique in the history of premiums.

High Stepping Gambler II was very much a hard-working stud horse, whose services provided his master with his bread and butter. His old service books have been preserved and no horse could have had better seasons. He regularly served over 100 mares per season and on one occasion attained 187. In Carmarthenshire he once covered 100 mares in the first month of the season, that county being then an early breeding area.

The lively demand and inflated prices of the First World War swept away many of his best progeny. Here are some of the most noted of those that remained: Blaenwaun Flora Temple: Champion Mare Royal Welsh Agricultural Society, Cardiff 1929; second Caenarvon 1930, dam of Thomas Rees' last two stallions, also Bryn Arth Madonna and Bryn

Arth Stepping Gambler, grandsire of Llanarth Brummel (he was second at the Royal Welsh Agricultural Society Show, Machynlleth).

Gwalia Victor 1431, sire of Brenin Gwalia, and a chip off the old block. High Stepping Gambler III, a dashing grey, whose stud card carried a challenge to any Welsh horse to trot a mile, which was never taken up. Flower: the dam of the noted stallion Llethi Valiant (*chapter 26.12*). Llwyn Gambler: of Major Marshall Dugdale's noted stud at Llwyn, Llanfyllin. Pantclynhir Welsh Gambler, bought by the Radnorshire Welsh Cob Breeding Society. Gambler Again (foaled in 1916) owned and bred by my mother's great-uncle, John Thomas, who previously owned Klondyke, Total etc.

Included here is the report taken from the *Livestock Journal* written by Capt. T. A. Howson (Lancastrian) about the Welsh Cob stallion class at the 1919 Royal Agricultural Society of England Show at Cardiff:

The class for Stallions foaled in or before 1913, over 14 hands, was an altogether better one, and at its head was placed the dark bay seventeen-year-old High Stepping Gambler II 143 by High Stepping Gambler 33, dam by Young King Jack. This horse is full of old Welsh blood and, though age may be telling slightly on his back, he is the type required. He has a beautiful cob head and eye with a great, long, reachy neck and outlook, shows the characteristic silky tufts on his heels, and goes with both hinds up and a display of action. He is a grand cob type and as such deservedly won. Rumour saith he works to earn his daily bread. Second was Llwynog-y-Dyffryn 882, a chestnut seven years of age by Briton Flyer 622, dam a Gomer mare. This horse has nothing like the type nor quality shown of the winner. He has a plain head and is altogether more of the Suffolky order in appearance. In action he is prone to trail his hocks.

Third stood Mathrafal Brenin 873, a blaze-faced chestnut with three white limbs. A courageous, tight-made "stuffy" cob, he has good limbs and character and feather, and he goes great guns all round – indeed, in point of action he could teach some Hackneys at the show a thing or two. He lacks the winner's beauty somewhat, but he is a "mighty cob" of the Borrovian order, and in the writer's view should have gone second. Reserve went to Abernant Express 826, a chestnut by Seven End . . . and, h.c. was Young Briton Comet 2nd 780.

Within two years, after Mr Butler's death (he would never have parted with Brenin), David Rees bought Mathrafal Brenin so that he and Gambler became stable-mates at Penuwch. As Lancastrian again put it: "Since Mr Butler's death he has been sold by Mr T. J. Evans, now of Craven Arms, but late of Henllan to Mr David Rees the owner of the charming, brown High Stepping Gambler II 143."

It is interesting to note that the champion Welsh Pony (Cob type) at Cardiff 1919, was Penuwch Cymro Bach, owned by David Thomas, a neighbour of David Rees, and a son of Trotting Jack 528, a Cob deserving of much greater recognition. And barely a mile away lay the bones of Old Trotting Comet, beneath the gooseberry bushes on old Richard Evans' smallholding.

Gambler died in the autumn of 1934, with the falling of the leaves and young John Rees was there when he was buried in the home paddock at 32 years of age. John was also there, 31 years later, when Gambler was joined by his grandson Brenin Gwalia.

5. Hendraws Doll
Dark bay, height: 14 hands 3 in
Owner: Joseph Lloyd Davies, Hendraws Farm,
Rhydlewis, Cardiganshire

6. Mathrafal Brenin
Registration number 873 in the *Welsh Stud Book*,
Vol. XVI
Chesnut, blaze, four white legs, height: 14 hands 1½ in, foaled 1911
Breeder: William Watkins, Garnlydan, Beaufort,
South Wales

In the world of people there are certain pivot figures around whom events seem to revolve; this is equally true of animals and Welsh Cobs are no exception. Any student of Welsh Cob pedigree must agree that one of the dominant influences among cob sires, as reflected in the blood lines of those horses that have been exhibited during the last 25 years, is that of Mathrafal Brenin 873 *Welsh Stud Book*. If David Rees, had not bought him in 1921 and travelled him until his death in 1928, about 75 per cent of recent, and comparatively recent, prize-winning Cobs would never have emerged in their present form (Incidentally, it would be hard to name one of the remaining 25 per cent that has no dash of the blood of one of David Rees' earlier stallions in him or her). The following is a selection of well-known Welsh Cobs, who are all derived from Mathrafal Brenin through one channel or another:

Brenin Gwalia, Mathrafal, Llwynog y Garth, Cahn Dafydd, Meiarth Royal Eiddwen, Hendy Brenin, Heather Royal Eiddwen, Rhystyd Prince, Honyton Michael ap Braint, Llanarth Brummel, Verwig Mathrafal, Lyn Cwmcoed, Fron Arth What Ho, Gwynau Boy, Rhosfarch Frenin and Rhystyd Welsh King. Among the mares, Parc Lady, Meiarth Pride, Meiarth Welsh Maid, Parc Pride, Geler Queen, Tyhen Mattie, Rhosfarch Morwenna, Princess, Piercefield Lady Lilian, Lili Cwmcoed, Llanarth Flying Saucer, Llanarth Nest, Geler Daisy and Gwynau Puss. Not to mention thousands of equal, or possibly greater potential, who have passed unsung through farmyard and sale ring.

Brenin's dam in 1911 had borne her foal on the mountain, sometime in March, and Mr. Watkins discovered one morning that the colt was suffering badly from "strangles". A gambo had to be taken up the mountainside to bring him home. He recovered and developed into a promising youngster, winning first prizes at all local shows except one.

Stud card (1923) for Mathrafal Brenin.

SEASON 1923.

——o——

If QUALITY, STYLE, STRENGTH and ACTION

combined with the Very Best Welsh Trotting Blood that has ever travelled England and Wales, are the essentials of a

SUCCESSFUL STOCK GETTER,

they will be found in a marked degree in that

SUPERIOR AND WELL-BRED WELSH COB

MATHYRAFAL BRENIN

873 W.S.B.

M.B. stands 14.2 h.h., is of a beautiful chestnut colour, has strong bone, and always moves like a piece of perfectly-geared machinery, going free and fast, with well-balanced action. His conformation leaves nothing to be desired, and his quality is of a superior type. It is many years since such a Welsh Cob Stallion stood for service in this country, for he imparts in all his stock bone, courage, speed and action.

350

At the end of the day, the judge sought to buy Mr. Watkins' colt, but the owner's pride in his horse was not to be bought in this manner; he insisted that the judge should buy the one he had considered to be the better horse!

At first, Mathrafal Brenin was called Young Railway (after his father). Rising four, Young Railway was sold to Mr. Price, The Antelope Inn, Dowlais (owner of Trotting Railway II, who had in the meantime been exported to Australia). Mr. Price died and on his death, his children sold the stallion to a Merthyr butcher, who very soon transferred him to Mr. Meyrick Jones, Mathrafal, Mont. There he remained but a year or so, sufficient time for him to be re-baptised "Mathrafal Brenin." His next owner was Mr. F. Butler, a butcher and horse-lover of St. Albans, Hertfordshire. After two years, Mr. Butler died. This was in 1921. It was from Mr. Butler's widow that David Rees bought Mathrafal Brenin and he owned him until the stallion's death, a

M.B.'s Sire, Trotting Railway, 529 W.S.B., is a Horse which won numerous Prizes in this country and Australia, including 1st Sydney. Trotting Railway by Wild Buck, by Cardigan Briton. M.B.'s Dam, Doll, 5648 W.S.B., by Evolve.

From the above it will be seen that M.B. is undoubtedly one of the best Horses of Welsh Breeding. Full advantage should be taken by Breeders of this wonderfully bred Cob.

M.B. is a Winner of several Prizes, including 3rd Royal Show, Cardiff, in the 15 hands class, giving away 2 inches in height. He won 3 First and 2 Seconds in 1921, and First and Silver Medal, Cilkenin, 2nd Llanelly, 1st United Counties, Carmarthen; 2nd Welsh National, Wrexham; also 2nd for The Prince of Wales Challenge Cup for the old Welsh type; reserve for the Welsh Cob Silver Medal at Wrexham in 1922. He is undoubtedly the Fastest of his height in Wales.

TERMS.—Will serve a limited number at £3 3s. each Mare; Tenant Farmers and Tradesmen, £2 2s. each Mare; and 5s. the Groom's Fee.

Groom's Fee due first time of serving, and the remainder on or before the 24th of June next, or 10s. extra will be charged for collecting after last journey round.

Mares tried by this Horse and not brought forward will be charged for.

And if anything happens to Mathrafal Brenin a substitute will be provided, and must be accepted.

The Owner and the Groom will not hold themselves responsible for any accident that may occur through trying or serving Mares, but the utmost care will be taken.

M.B. holds the Ministry of Agriculture's Licence for 1922.

M.B. was the Board's Premium Cob in Brynaman district, and stood the Four seasons previously at stud in Hertfordshire, and travelled three seasons in Carmarthenshire. He gave the greatest satisfaction in both places.

For further particulars, apply to the owner, D. REES, Bear's Hill Stud, Penuwch, Llanio Road, Cards.

* * * * *

FROM THE REPORT OF THE "LIVE STOCK JOURNAL," JUNE, 1919, OF THE ROYAL SHOW, CARDIFF.

Third, stood Mathyrafal Brenin, 873, a blazed faced chestnut, with three white limbs. A courageous, tight made, "stuffy" cob, he has good limbs and character and feather, and he goes great guns all round; indeed in point of action he could teach some Hackneys at the show a thing or two. He lacks the winner's beauty somewhat, but he is a mighty cob, of the Borrovian order, and in the writer's view should have gone second.

Cambrian News (Aberystwyth), Ltd.

Mathrafal Brenin with Mr. David Rees. Photograph 1924.

week before the end of the travelling season in 1928, aged 17 years. This
was the fruitful period of his life, in the progeny sense, when the various
strands of pedigree which have persisted so clearly to this day, were
woven into the fabric of the Cobs of Wales.

It has already been reported on how Mathrafal Brenin stood third to
David Rees' High Stepping Gambler II at the 1919 Royal Agricultural
Society of England Show at Cardiff. David Rees was greatly impressed
with Mathrafal Brenin and he asked Mr. Butler whether he would be
prepared to sell him. The answer was: "I will never part with Brenin."
Sadly, fate intervened; early in 1921 Mr. Tom Jones Evans told David
Rees of Mr. Butler's death and that his horses were for sale. A representative of the Royal Veterinary College was interested in Mathrafal
Brenin for export. David Rees immediately contacted St. Albans and
was invited to come and inspect the stallion. A long train journey from
Tregaron in Cardiganshire and a midnight horse-and-cab itinerary
across London, brought him to his sister's house, a London dairy. The
following day, he and his brother Harry, went up to St. Albans. A man
in a blue butcher's smock took Brenin on a lead out into a big park,
riding a tall Hackney, who dwarfed the little cob, alongside. He made a
wonderful show and confirmed David Rees' intention of bringing him
back to his ancestral homeland. It was not an easy matter. The sum of
£400 was asked for him, a nine-year-old stallion. This was a big sum to

ask of a Cardiganshire smallholder in the hungry twenties. The deal was not immediately clinched but on the following day, from the house of the parents of Dr. Martyn Lloyd-Jones (the now famous minister of Westminster Chapel), both Cardiganshire Welshmen, the stallion was bought on the telephone for £290 and eventually duly entrained for Cardiganshire.

During that first season, he was travelled alternate weeks in Cardiganshire and Carmarthenshire, walking alongside a pony as was always David Rees' practice, but travelling by train from Lampeter to Carmarthen when moving ground.

Six times in all, David Rees exhibited him for a travelling premium at Lampeter. Each time he was passed by, despite his record and continuing successes. In one notable year, the Cardiganshire selectors turned down Mathrafal Brenin, Ceitho Welsh Comet and Trotting Jack, names that are enshrined for posterity in Cob lore. At the same time and place, Breconshire representatives chose the three as Premium stallions for their county. Breconshire awarded Mathrafal Brenin a premium during the three remaining seasons of his life. It was two days before he died suddenly of anthrax at the Camden Arms, Brecon, that he produced Cymraes, who was to become the dam of Brenin Gwalia.

Mathrafal Brenin put up a very good "show" at the 1922 Royal Welsh Show (Wrexham) but had to be content with second place. However at the 1924 Show (Bridgend) (judge: Mr. W. Arthur Pughe) and 1925 (Carmarthen) (judge: Mr. T. H. Vaughan) he took the Cob Supreme Championship, Prince of Wales Cup. At Bridgend the cup was presented to David Rees by Lord Noel Buxton the first Labour Minister of Agriculture whose comments were reported in the *Royal Welsh Journal* as: "I congratulate you most heartily on winning such a magnificent cup with such a magnificent animal".

That, then is the story of Mathrafal Brenin, a Welsh Cob great in everything except inches, combining a docile nature with pride and great beauty, a rare mover and a progenitor of much that is enduring in the history of the breed.

7. Doll

Registration number 136 F.S.1 in the appendix of the
Welsh Stud Book, Vol. XXXII
Chesnut, height: 14 hands 2 in, foaled 1916
Breeder: Lloyd Rees, Tynewydd, Llandyfalle,
Brecon.

353

1901.

To Cover this Season

At £3 3s. each Mare, and 5s. the Groom.

The Groom's Fee must be paid the first time of serving, and the remainder on or before the 24th June next, or 5s. extra will be charged for collecting.

THAT PURE-BRED WELSH COB STALLION

High-stepping Gambler

(The property of Mr Evan Davies, Penrhiw, Silian, Lampeter.)

HIGH-STEPPING GAMBLER stands 15 hands high, is rising 6 years old, and was got by Welsh Briton; Welsh Briton by Briton Comet; Briton Comet by Old Comet; Old Comet by Flyer, whose dam was Mr. Pool's celebrated mare which was never beaten.

HIGH STEPPING GAMBLER'S dam was got by Caradog. She is a beautiful mare, with good all round action, and very fast; won several prizes in farmers' races; also won 1st Prize in an open race at Synod Inn Trotting Matches. Caradog is a winner of great many prizes, and a wonderful stock-getter. He was the sire of the world-renowned trotter—the Earl of Beaconsfield. Caradog was by Welsh Jack, Welsh Jack by Cymro Llwyd. Caradog's dam by Cardigan Comet I, sister to Cardigan Comet II. (Stud 2396).

Please note his blood and trace his pedigree, and it will be seen that High-Stepping Gambler has descended from the pure old Welsh blood.

HIGH-STEPPING GAMBLER won 1st prize at Carmarthen Entire Horse Show, 1897. 7 entries; 2nd in a large class at Llanelly, 1897; also, 1st prize at Llanybyther, 1899 and 2nd prize, Newcastle Emlyn, 1900. He was bred by Mr. Denis Davies, Ty'r-Esgob.

HIGH-STEPPING GAMBLER is a beautiful bay in colour, possesses the best of legs, and is free from any hereditary unsoundness, and, if put to suitable mares, he cannot fail to get first-class high-stepping cobs, which are at present time in great demand, and realize a very good price.

HIGH-STEPPING GAMBLER has proved an excellent foal-getter, and his stock are very promising. They possess strong bone, and very likely to become extraordinary trotters.

All Mares tried by this horse and served by another, without the Groom's consent, or sold after being tried, will be charged season price.

The Groom will specify the times and places of attendance.

M. Davies, Printer Stationers' Hall, Lampeter.

Stud card (1901) for High Stepping Gambler. (Stud card courtesy of Messrs. Rowlands Harris.)

8. High Stepping Gambler I

Registration number 33 in the *Welsh Stud Book, Vol. I*

Bay, star and stripe, off fore coronet and both hind
fetlocks white, height: 15 hands, foaled 1894

Breeder: D. Davies, Tyresgob, Llanon,
Cardiganshire

Owner: Evan Davies, Penrhiw, Silian, Lampeter,
Cardiganshire

Sire: Welsh Briton by Old Briton Comet *Hackney Stud
Book 1374* (foaled in 1859)

by Old Trotting Comet *Hackney Stud Book* 834
(*chapter 18.2*)

out of mare by True Briton 839 (*chapter 17.1*)

Dam: Darby (chesnut, 15 hands) by Caradog (*chapter 22.4*)

by Welsh Jack (*chapter 18.6*) by Cymro Llwyd
(*chapter 18.6*)

Welsh Briton was the first stallion to be owned by Thomas Rees
father of David Rees. Evan Davies, owner of High Stepping Gambler
was David Rees' uncle.

In *Vol. I, Welsh Stud Book* there are three great stallions sired by Welsh
Briton viz Briton Comet 30 (also owned by Thomas Rees), High
Stepping Gambler 33 and King Briton 34; all three standing at 15 hands
or over.

Evan Davies exported High Stepping Gambler to the stud of J. R.
Hill, Schultz House, Bloemfontein, Orange River Colony, so his
imprint in his native land was thus cut short.

9. Fanny

Sire: Young King Jack (chesnut, 15 hands 2 in) (Moses
Williams)

by King Jack *Hackney Stud Book* 1022, chesnut,
foaled 1860

by Wonderful Comet 1225 *Hackney Stud Book*
by Comet Bach 931 *Hackney Stud Book*
by Old Trotting Comet 834 *Hackney Stud Book*
(*chapter 18.2*)

Fanny was a bay mare whose dam Darby was bought as a sucker
from somewhere in South Cardiganshire, pedigree unknown.

1897.   **1897.**

To cover this Season at £2 2s. each Mare, and 5s. the Groom.
(The Groom's Fee to be paid at the first time of Covering, and the remainder on or about the 1st day of July next).

THAT SPLENDID CHESTNUT COB

"YOUNG KING JACK"

The Property of Mr. Moses Williams, Glandwr, Lledrod, Aberystwyth.

Young King Jack stands 15 hands 2 in. high, possessing strong bone, great power, splendid action. most excellent symmetry, free from any natural blemish, he has proved a sure toal getter, and his stock are very promising. He was got by King Jack, King Jack by Young Comet, by Old Comet. Young King Jack's dam was got by Briton Comet, Briton Comet by Trotting Comet, Trotting Comet by Young Comet by Old Comet. Young King Jack's grand-dam was also got by Old Gomer. It will be seen by the white mark on Young King Jack that he is bred from the first Comet, which was marked similar. Young King Jack's stock has been sold for long prices, making as much as 80 guineas.

Young King Jack has won t e following Prizes. viz. : The Premiums at the Aberystwyth Agricultural Show, at Llanon Entire Horse Show (First Prize), also at Aberaeron (First Prize).

Young King Jack's brother, from the same sire and dam, won First Prizes at Aberystwyth Agricultural Shows in 1882, 1883 and was sold on the latter date for £50, when 3 years old, and a few months later, again sold for 100 guineas.

"This is to certify that I have this day examined an Entire Horse, the property Mr. Moses Williams, Aberystwyth. I find him sound."
April 27th, 1897.   E. THOMAS, M.R.C.V.I.S., Carno.

ROUTE—

MONDAY.—Lion, Welshpool, for the market ; Lion, Berriew, for the night.
TUESDAY.—Nag's Head, 9 ; Abermule, 10 ; Black Boy, Newtown, for the Market ; Unicorn, Caersws for the night.
WEDNESDAY.—Kerry, 11 ; Sarn for the night. No mares taken in the morning.
THURSDAY.—Anchor by 10 ; The Mill, Newcastle, for the night.
FRIDAY.—Six Bells, Clun, by 9 ; Bishop's Castle for the market ; Churchstoke for the night.
SATURDAY.—Chirbury by 9 ; Marton by 11 ; Worthen by 2 ; Westbury by 4 ; Half-way House Buttington, by 5 ; Middletown ; to Mr. Pryce, Llwynmelin, Buttington, until Monday Morning.

☞ **All Mares tried by this Horse are at Owner's risk.**

Phillips and Son, Printers and Bookbinders, Newtown.

Stud card (1897) for Young King Jack, sire of Fanny. (Stud card courtesy of Messrs. Rowlands Harris.)

356

To quote from the 1897 Stud card for Young King Jack:

Young King Jack is coming,
You can tell him by his walk,
He is the horse that trots so fast,
And makes the people talk,
Look at his feet and legs,
His breeding and his strength.

10. Briton Flyer (Cefnlleithtre)
Sire: Cardigan Briton (Ceffyl Pregethwr)
Dam: by Welsh Flyer III *(chapter 20.2)* (known as
both Caebidwl Horse and Dafydd Ellis
by Old Welsh Flyer *(chapter 18.1)*

Not registered in the *Welsh Stud Book* and a different Briton Flyer from Briton Flyer 60 (D. Moses, Cwmnewynydd, Brecon who won first prizes at the Bedwellty Shows of 1896 and 1897).

Briton Flyer was a dark brown stallion, standing about 15 hands and is said to have been a "true type of the Old Welsh breed".

11. Polly
Bay mare, 14 hands 2 in, by Heart of Welsh Flyer, bay, 15 hands

12. Trotting Railway II
Registration number 529 in the *Welsh Stud Book, Vol. XI*
Dark brown, star, near front white foot, height: 14
hands 2 in, foaled 1905
Breeder: Goronwy Price, Gelliargwellt Uchaf, Gelligaer who
sold him to John Price, Antelope Hotel, Dowlais, Glamorganshire.
Sire: Wild Buck by Cardigan Briton (ceffyl Taihirion
or ceffyl Pregethwr)
Cardigan Briton was g-son of Welsh Briton
Wild Buck was travelled in Glamorgan by Mr. Tom
Davies, Derlwyn Fach, Llangeitho
Dam: Dolly bay, 13 hands 3 in, by
Trotting Railway I

Trotting Railway II won a second prize in hand at the 1910 Entire Horse Parade at Caerphilly and another second prize in harness. By 1911 he had been exported to Mr. D. F. Davies, Grahamstown, New

Pencaerhelem sire of Polly 15. Pencaerhelem was foaled in 1886.

Trotting Railway II photographed after export to New South Wales in 1911.

Evolve foaled in 1898, sire of Dolly with the late Mr. Harry Llewellyn. (Photograph courtesy of Mr. Mostyn Isaac.)

South Wales for whom he won a third prize at the Royal Easter Show, Sydney, in harness, competing against Hackneys.

13. Dolly

Registration number 5648 in the *Welsh Stud Book, Vol. XVI*

Chestnut, white hind socks, height: 14 hands 1 in, foaled 1906

Breeder: Henry Davies, Pontygwarth Farm, Newport, Monmouthshire

Owner: William Watkins, Garnlydan, Beaufort, Breconshire

Sire: Evolve, black stallion with white points, height: 14 hands 2 in, by Evolution 64 *Welsh Stud Book* and 2058 *Hackney Stud Book*

Dam: A Welsh Cob mare, winner of numerous prizes

Evolution, foaled in 1886 was bred by Arthur Gittus of Worlington in Suffolk for whom he won three first prizes at the London Hackney Shows 1890–1892 amongst many other prizes throughout the United Kingdom. Then in 1897 he came to Wales, to Mr. R. T. Hawkins of Coedmawr, Builth Wells and won first prizes at the Builth Wells,

Penybont and Llanidloes during 1897–1898. A son of Evolution named Evolution II sired some good ponies in the Brecon area e.g. Criban Cochybondy (foaled in 1914).

14. Flying Express

Registration number 624 in the *Welsh Stud Book, Vol. XII*
Brown, star, height: 14 hands 3 in, foaled 1910
Breeder: J. F. Ricketts, Trebarried, Talgarth, Breconshire
Owner: Jack Davies, Danyrallt, Upper Chapel, Breconshire
Sire: Dorando 371
Dam: 1178 Fan (chestnut, blaze, height: 15 hands
1 in, foaled in 1894)

Dorando was a chestnut stallion, measuring 13 hands 1 in and foaled in 1906; his sire was Pencaerhelem 23 and his dam Puss by Trotting Flyer 271. Trotting Flyer 271, a chestnut stallion foaled in about 1880, was a well-known sire in South Wales where he was known as "Aberhenwenfach". Bred by Mr. E. Davies of Hafod, Llanwrda he spent most of his life with Alex Morton, Gowanbank, Darvel, Ayrshire, one of the most famous persons in the history of the Hackney pony. Trotting Flyer is said to have had an enormous influence on the ponies in Scotland at the beginning of this century. In Wales he was influential as well mainly through his son Llew Llwyd 162 (Tom Matthias) who was also registered as Gwesyn Flyer 90 *Welsh Stud Book*.

15. Polly

Registration number 135 F.S. in the appendix of the
Welsh Stud Book, Vol. XXXII
Chestnut, height: 14 hands 2 in, foaled 1912
Breeder: J. Rees, The Mill, Felinfach, Breconshire
Sire: Pencaerhelem 23
Dam: A mare by Old Trotting Railway I

Pencaerhelem (foaled in 1886) was a chestnut stallion, standing 14 hands 2 in and bred by T. Davies, New House, Garth, Brecon. He was owned for most of his life by Edward Owen of Pencaerhelem, near Builth Wells. His sire was Welsh Flyer (*chapter 18.1*) and his dam was Black Bess by Eiddwen Flyer (*chapter 21.4*) and g-dam Bess a 15-hand bay mare by Cardigan Comet (*chapter 19.4*).

Pencaerhelem won several prizes in the Builth Wells area during 1890 to the time of his registration in the *Welsh Stud Book, Vol. I*.

24
Ceitho Welsh Comet (foaled in 1913)
Ceulan Comet (foaled in 1926)

1 Ceulan Comet 1490	2 Ceitho Welsh Comet 774	4 Caradog Flyer 379	8 Young Caradog
			9 Star
		5 5069 Rhystyd Black Bess	10 Cardigan Flyer 699
			11 Bess
	3 5553 Seren Ceulan	6 Total 320	12 Klondyke 12
			13 Chesnut
		7 5806 Aeronwen Ceulan	14 Satisfaction
			15 971 Ffynon Queen

1. Ceulan Comet

Registration number 1490 in the *Welsh Stud Book,*
Vol. XXIX
Photograph *Welsh Stud Book, Vol. XXX, page 36,* Welsh
Pony & Cob Society Journal, 1964, *page 28*
Black, white on both hind pasterns, height: 13 hands,
foaled 1926
Breeder: E. S. Davies, Ceulan Stud, Talybont,
Cardiganshire

Ceulan Comet was well accustomed to the show ring having been the foal at foot of Seren Ceulan when she won the brood mare class at the 1926 Royal Welsh Show (Bangor). He won a few local prizes in young-stock classes but his first competition at the Royal Welsh Show was in 1930, when at only four-years-old he stood second to the twelve-year-old Royal Welsh Jack (whose Royal Welsh Show career was indeed chequered: second in 1925, third in 1926, sixth in 1927, first in 1928, 1929 and 1930 and finally second in 1933). Third in this class was Mab Y Brenin (*chapter 28.8*) (sire of Mathrafal) owned by my grandfather, L. O. Williams and Tanybwlch Berwyn (*chapter 13.6*) was fourth. Although these four stallions were registered in Section "B" of the *Welsh Stud Book*, it must be understood that all that had to be in common was a question of height (i.e. over 12 hands 2 in and under 13 hands 2 in). The first three were Welsh Ponies (Cob type) i.e. the present-day Section "C" whilst Tanybwlch Berwyn (foaled 1924) was one of the originators of the present-day Welsh Ponies Section "B".

Ceulan Comet put up a tremendous show to win the stallion class at the 1931 Royal Welsh Show (Llanelly) and the judge, Mr. T. J. Jones of

Ceulan Comet photographed when Champion at the 1934 Royal Welsh Show. (Photograph courtesy of G. H. Parsons.)

Ceulan Comet Daily Mail *newspaper cutting, 26th July 1934.*

the Dinarth Hall Stud bought him from my father after he had been awarded the Section Championship. Under the ownership of the Dinarth Stud, he repeated his Championship at the 1932 Royal Welsh Show (Llandrindod) where Mr. Meyrick Jones, Mathrafal judged. Incidentally at this show, his maternal half-sister Ceulan Silverleaf (see *chapter 15.5*) was reserve Champion female.

At the 1933 Royal Welsh Show (Aberystwyth) Mr. Matthew Williams judged and he was reserve Champion to his son Dinarth Comet (who had won the two or three-year-old colt class). These positions were reversed the following year at the Llandudno Royal Welsh Show where Ceulan Comet was Champion with Dinarth Comet second in the adult stallion class. Writing about him in the Royal Welsh Agricultural Society Journal, Capt. Howson says: "Here was an outstanding Champion in Ceulan Comet who has a tip-top pony head, a lengthy outlook, great power and substance and quite captivating movement. He was subsequently sold at a good figure and exported to Australia to join Mr. Hordern's Stud."

This is what the judge Mr. Tom Mathias had to say about him: "The stallion Ceulan Comet, in type and manner of movement, revealed ability to enthuse the ringsiders to rounds of applause – he was an easy winner of the Championship of this Section."

Whilst at Ceulan, Comet had sired some good ponies in the North Cardiganshire area e.g. Dinarth Comet foaled in 1931 out of Caran Black Bess. He was used extensively during his stay at Dinarth Hall, one daughter Dinarth Lady Love bought by my grandfather at the Dinarth Dispersal Sale (a black mare, foaled 1934, Section "A") won first prizes at Shrewsbury, the Three Counties, Chester, Royal Welsh and Craven Arms. One son, Dinarth Greylight (again Section "A" out of the same dam as Dinarth What Ho) was used at the Twyford Stud siring e.g. Twyford Gay Lad who has produced several different Section "A" strains in the United Kingdom at the present time. Other breeders, e.g. Mr. Tom Jones Evans of the Craven Stud used Ceulan Comet, thus spreading the blood in other directions e.g. Craven Comet purchased by the Criban Stud at the 1936 Craven Sale and shortly afterwards exported to the U.S.A.

Mr. Ken Armstrong writing in the 1970 Welsh Pony & Cob Society Journal, outlines the influence which Ceulan Comet had on Mr. Hordern's Milton Stud in Australia (where previously Cream of Eppynt and the famous Greylight had been imported) and later on the Nattai Stud of Mr. Hordern's daughter Lady Creswick. Mr. Armstrong writes: "The daughters of Ceulan Comet have proved wonderful brood mares, he giving them lovely 'rein' with substance and possessing excellent legs and bone with strength in their gaskins. Lady Creswick has consistently shown her ponies with success in led, ridden and driven classes."

Dinarth Greylight (foaled in 1934) son of Ceulan Comet. Dinarth Greylight was used extensively for siring Mountain ponies e.g. at Twyford Stud.

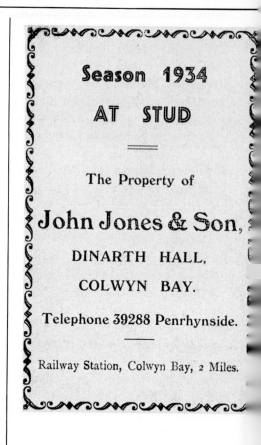

Stud card (1934) for Ceulan Comet.

Whenever one sees reports of sales in Australia, descendants of Ceulan Comet demand high prices. One of the most successful studs in Australia (Owendale) lays great importance on Ceulan Comet bloodlines (Darrell Owen's grandfather, Stan Shepherd was head groom at Nattai in the 1930's and 1940's and was Comet's handler) and Mrs. Owen purchased a Twyford Gay Lad descendant (for more Ceulan Comet blood) whilst in the United Kingdom in 1978.

2. Ceitho Welsh Comet

Registration number 774 in the *Welsh Stud Book,*
Vol. XIV
Black, white inside off hind fetlock, height: 14 hands
2 in, foaled 1913
Breeder: David Lloyd, Talwrncoch, Llanrhystyd,
Aberystwyth
Owner in 1915: Richard Morgan, Lluest-y-broga,
Llangeitho, Cardiganshire

That great authority on Welsh Cobs, Mr. D. O. Morgan writes in the 1964 Welsh Pony & Cob Society Journal of Ceitho Welsh Comet as the one which he remembers best. "Bred over fifty years ago in the heyday of Welsh Cob breeding, this little black horse known as Cel du bach Lluest-y-broga, was very much talked of. I remember him best, not as being the last word in Welsh Cob conformation (in fact he was not frequently seen in the show ring) but for his tremendous influence on the breed throughout his stud career. Probably he has gone down in history as one of the most impressive sires known to the breed. Himself being a good and game little Cob, he certainly produced his superiors galore, not only from the best mares mated to him (and there were many in those days) but equally as good from what some breeders would term now as nondescript mares."

Ceitho Welsh Comet's stud card shows him to have had a little success in the show ring himself: first prize Brynamman 1915, second Lampeter 1918, first Lampeter and second Tregaron 1919, second Llandovery 1924 and finally a first prize at Tregaron in 1925. However his stud card continues: "No sire in the history of Welsh Cobs has been so impressive as Ceitho Welsh Comet and his progeny have invariably been at the top at all mid-Cardigan Shows for many years. Three of his sons are today War Office Premium stallions in Wales. Three others have been exported to Spain at prices which constitute a record for Welsh Cobs, others have been sold to go to Ireland for Stud purposes. His greatest triumph however was at the Royal Welsh Show at Bridgend in 1924 where Cardiganshire won the £200 prize given by the President for the best group of Welsh stock. In the Cob classes they secured two first prizes and two seconds in the four classes provided and in the Pony Section they again won two firsts and two seconds in a similar number of classes: No stallion of any breed has ever equalled this performance at a National Show."

At the 1924 Royal Welsh Show, his daughter Wyre Lady was reserve

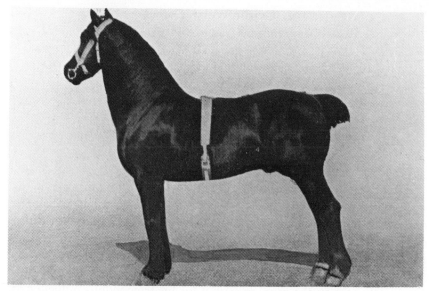

Ceitho Welsh Comet. (Photograph courtesy of Welsh Stud Book.)

for the George, Prince of Wales Cup (won by Mathrafal Brenin, *chapter 23.6*). Also in the stallion class, his son, Llethi Valiant (*chapter 26.12*) stood second, being fourth in 1925, second again in 1926, first and Reserve Champion to the mare Pant Grey Star (*chapter 29.5*) in 1928, fifth in 1929, and winner of the George, Prince of Wales Cup in 1931 (Craven Cymro, winner of the stallion class not being resident in Wales).

One daughter of his, Pantlleinau Blodwen (*chapter 28.11*) (grand-dam of Cahn Dafydd) was a consistent competitor at Royal Welsh shows winning fourth prizes in 1924 and 1925, second in 1926, and 1928, seventh in 1929, third in 1930, first in 1931 and second (her last appearance) in 1932. The best known of Ceitho Welsh Comet's daughters were Dewi Black Bess (*chapter 25.5*) (winner of the Prince of Wales Cup in 1935 and Teify of Hercws (winner of the Prince of Wales Cup in both 1936 and 1937). When these two great rivals (both twelve years old) met at the 1938 Royal Welsh Show, the judge, Capt. Howson wrote that: "they took a little sorting out", adding: "Black Bess has a lovely neck and lookout and quality all through and was the first to be pulled in; but, though she stood inspection well enough so far as make and shape went, she seemed to lack a little freshness and to be a little listless in her action on the day and so she had to yield top place to Tiefy of Hercws who, though perhaps a wee bit heavy in the neck, is a rare substantial short-legged sort."

These are typical descriptions of the lovely animals sired by Ceitho Welsh Comet.

In those days of stallions travelling it was a very sad day indeed when Ceitho Welsh Comet was put off the road, failing his veterinary inspection (the defect was said to be cataract, though none of his progeny was reported as suffering from this). The Premium stallions were not always recorded in the *Welsh Stud Book*, however for 1928, Ceitho Welsh Comet is recorded as travelling Breconshire in the ownership of Mr. S. P. Owen of Tygwyn, Brecon. Eventually he returned to his native area to the Meiarth Stud at Bwlchyllan where he continued to sire exceptional

---

PEDIGREE :

Ceitho Welsh Comet

(Ceffyl du Lluestybroga).

774 Vol. 14, W.P. & C.S., Section C.

Colour, Black.   Aged 12.   Height 14-2 h.h.

SIRE—Caradog Flyer 379 W.P. & C.S., by Young Caradog, by Caradog, by Welsh Jack, y Cymro Llwyd.

DAM—Black Bess 5069, Vol. 14 W.P. & C.S., y Cardigan Flyer, by Welsh Flyer III. (Ceffyl afydd Ellis), by Welsh Flyer.

Caradog Flyer was known throughout Wales s one of the best Sires and Show Horses of his ay.

——:o:——

SHOWN AND RECORD.

Ceitho Welsh Comet was never extensively shown, as the owner's great aim at all nes was to keep him in best form for Stud.

He won—First Prize Brynamman, 1915.
Second Prize Lampeter, 1918.
First Prize Lampeter, 1919.
Second Prize Tregaron, 1919.
Second Prize Llandovery, 1924.

SEASON 1925.

Important to all who wish to breed Welsh Cobs and Ponies from the best strain of Welsh Blood.

THAT REMARKABLE HIGH-STEPPING COB,

CEITHO WELSH COMET

774 Vol. 14, W.P. & C.S., Section C.

The War Office Premium Stallion in Cardiganshire, 1925.

Will serve a limited number of approved mares this season at £2 2s. per mare and 5s. Groom's Fee.

OWNER :
Mr. O. R. OWEN, Gamrhew, Babel, Llandovery

BREEDER :
Mr. D. LLOYD, Talwrncoch, Llanrhystyd, Cards

CEITHO WELSH COMET is a Black Cob, 12 years old, and stands 14-2 h.h.

The most impressive and successful Sire in the history of Welsh Cobs.

IMPORTANT—He holds the Ministry of Agriculture Licence for 1925.

L. Thomas, Printer, Llandovery.

card (1925) for Ceitho Welsh Comet.

369

Teify of Hercws, daughter of Ceitho Welsh Comet. Teify of Hercws was Champion at the 1936 and 1937 Royal Welsh Shows. (Photograph courtesy of G. H. Parsons.)

stock e.g. Welsh Rebound (foaled 1934) third prize Welsh Cob stallion at the 1937 Royal Welsh Show. It was at Meiarth that he died in 1936 at twenty-three years of age.

In the same way as Dyoll Starlight and Coed Coch Glyndwr altered the fate of the Welsh Mountain Pony; undoubtedly Ceitho Welsh Comet had as great an effect as any other stallion this century on the Welsh Cob and Welsh Pony (Cob type) breeds.

3. Seren Ceulan
Registration number 5553 in the *Welsh Stud Book, Vol. XVI*
Photograph *Welsh Stud Book, Vol. XXVIII, page 28*
Grey, height: 12 hands 2 in, foaled 1910
Breeder: Lewis Lewis, Tynygraig, Talybont, Cardiganshire
Owner: E. S. Davies, Ceulan Stud, Talybont, Cardiganshire

Seren Ceulan won a few prizes for Lewis Lewis, such as a second prize at the Talybont Show in 1912, three firsts at Borth, Machynlleth and Talybont in 1913, and two seconds (with a grey filly foal at foot by Klondyke) at Talybont in 1914. With my father she won two first prizes at Talybont Show in 1916 along with a magnificent Welsh Pony & Cob

Society silver medal (the original ones designed by Charles Coltman Rogers). During her lifetime she won another seven medals.

Sir Lewes T. Loveden Pryse, Bart. of Gogerddan (whose family was responsible for the Trotting Comet family, *chapter 18*) was elected President of the Welsh Pony & Cob Society in 1921 and to commemorate the fact presented a splendid Challenge Cup to the Talybont Show to be awarded to the best registered Pony or Cob, male or female at the show. Seren Ceulan was the only animal ever to win this award (1922, 1923 and 1924) and consequently won it outright.

At Royal Welsh Shows Seren Ceulan won her fair share of prizes: 1925 (Carmarthen) second prize mare to Kerry Queen and first prize group (along with Kerry Queen and the two winners of the youngstock classes owned by Mr. S. O. Davies and sired by Parc Satisfaction, a son of Ceitho Welsh Comet); first and reserve Champion 1926 (Bangor)

Seren Ceulan with Mr. E. S. Davies at the 1928 Royal Welsh Show. (Photograph courtesy of G. H. Parsons.)

Penllas
Llangeitho
Llanio Rd
Cards
22. 6. 25.

Dear Sir

In answer to your
letter of the 6th inst I beg to inform
the terms for Ceitho Welsh Com
for this season is 30/- per mar
but your case is a little differ
for our service so I will adv
you to bring your mare to
Tregaron on Tuesday for he wi
attend Brynawel Temperan
Hotel Tregaron every Tuesda
throughout the season if will
send her down when she is in
season & the owner himself
will be there with him. So I send
you his route card where he
will attend throught the week

Yours Faithfull
O. R. Owens
For Ceitho Welsh Com

Letter from Mr. O. R. Owens, dated 22nd June 1925 arranging the service of Seren Ceulan to Ceitho Welsh Comet.

and first and Champion 1928 (Wrexham) where she beat four former winners (Flemish Cymraes, Flemish Eiddwen, Cilwen Lady Lilian (*chapter 26*) and Kerry Queen in that order) to win the brood mare class.

Seren Ceulan died in 1931 and Capt. Howson wrote an obituary notice for her in the Royal Welsh Agricultural Show Journal, part of which read: "Seren Ceulan who died recently at the age of 21, was a pony of that grand old-fashioned order for which her native county has so long been famous. Full of substance, yet full of quality withal – and abounding in free, swinging action – this great little mare (for she was only 12.2 hands in height) won many honours in Welsh showyards . . . it is interesting to know that her dam is still alive and going strong with five-and-twenty summers on her head."

When one considers that Seren Ceulan had only seven progeny three of which were lost without trace, another viz Aven Bun was sold to Mr. Frank Minorpio for a harness pair with Aven Glitter (purchased from Miss Lort) and was not bred from and of the remaining three, two were exported i.e. Brenin Cymru (foaled in 1925 and was exported to the Argentine in 1929) and Ceulan Comet (foaled in 1926 and exported to Australia in 1934) it is surprising that Seren Ceulan blood was so influential on the Welsh breeds mainly through her last foal, her daughter Ceulan Silverleaf (foaled in 1929) (*chapter 15.5*).

4. Caradog Flyer
Registration number 379 in the *Welsh Stud Book, Vol. IX*
Bay, height: 15 hands,
foaled 1896
Breeder: David Benjamin, Trafleuchaf, Llangeitho,
Cardiganshire
Owner: Richard Morgan, Lluestybroga,
Llangeitho,
Cardiganshire

Very little is known about Caradog Flyer. The stud card of Ceitho Welsh Comet quotes that: "Caradog Flyer is well-known throughout the Counties of Cardigan, Carmarthen and West Glamorgan as one of the best old typical Welsh Cob stallions at present in Wales and his stock are the best on the minds of the multitude."

The stud card of Caradog Flyer for 1913 shows that he was still travelling in Cardiganshire at 17 years of age and still in the ownership of Richard Morgan.

Caradog Flyer

(379 W.P. & C.S. Section D.)

CARADOG FLYER is a beautiful Dark Brown Horse, stands 15 hands high, on good sound wearing legs. He is an excellent worker, and has proved himself a wonderful stock getter. He was got by that well known horse Young Caradog (Caerllugest Horse) ; Young Caradog by Caradog which won 1st prizes at Aberayron and Llanwrtyd in 1876 ; 1st at Newcastle-Emlyn in 1877 and 1880. He was the sire of the wonderful trotter Earl Beaconsfield. Caradog by Welsh Jack, Welsh Jack by Cymro Llwyd, winner of several 1st prizes. Caradog's dam by Cardigan Comet the 1st, winner of 21 prizes.

CARADOG FLYER's dam by Welsh Flyer by Old Comet by Flyer, she won the 1st at Lampeter 1877, and his g-dam won prizes at Lampeter 1877—79—81 and 1884 ; at Aberayron in 1878—80 and 1882 ; at Aberystwyth in 1877—79—82 and 1884. She was bred at Nantymedd, Llanfair-Clydogau.

It will be seen by the pedigree of this Stallion Caradog Flyer, that he is bred on pure Welsh Lines, and descended, on both sides, from a pure strain of trotters.

The Owner (nor the Groom) will not be responsible for any accident that may occur to Mares in any shape or form, nor as to time of attendance, but the utmost care will be taken.

All Mares tried by this Horse and afterwards covered by another, sold, exchanged, dead, or otherwise disposed of, or not brought forward, will be charged card price. If anything happens to this Horse another must be accepted.

For Route and other particulars apply to the Owner or the Groom.

374

5. Rhystyd Black Bess
Registration number 5069 in the *Welsh Stud Book,*
Vol. XIV
Black, height: 14 hands 2 in, foaled 1896
Owner and Breeder: David Lloyd,
Talwrncoch,
Llanrhystyd, Cardiganshire

Although foaled in 1896, Rhystyd Black Bess was not registered until 1915 i.e. after her influential son Ceitho Welsh Comet was produced. Of Rhystyd Black Bess, the stud card of Ceitho Welsh Comet states: "Black Bess is a typical Welsh Cob mare, coming out on both sides of the best old Welsh type. She was certified last season (1915 at nineteen years old) to be absolutely sound by the Board of Agriculture's Veterinary Inspector and secured Free Service by the Board's Premium Cob."

6. Total
Registration number 320 in the *Welsh Stud Book,*
Vol. VIII
Chesnut, star, white off hind, height: 13 hands 1 in,
foaled 1904
Owner and Breeder: John Thomas, London House,
Trerddol
(The Breeder in *Welsh Stud Book* is not correct, Total
was bred by John Davies of Cefngwairog but spent
most of his life with John Thomas whose sister Jane
Williams, Clettwr Hall, was my
great-grandmother).

Total won reserve prizes at the Aberystwyth Cob Society's Shows in 1908 and 1909. His stud card describes him as "a dark chesnut, free mover, fine action, a model in figure and proves a good stock-getter on account of the blood and quality he possesses."

Total certainly was a good stock-getter; in addition to Seren Ceulan who won a Royal Welsh Show Championship, there was Temptation (also bred by John Thomas) who in 1914 won Championships at both the Royal Welsh and Royal Agricultural Society of England (Shrewsbury) and was afterwards exported to W. H. Millspaugh, Ohio, U.S.A. (in 1915).

Total was exported to Mr. Laurie Wilson of New Zealand and soon after arrival, won a first prize in a class of 14.

SEASON   1910.

TOTAL

(By Klondyke),

The property of Mr John Thomas, The Mill, Tre'rddol, Glandyfi, R.S O.

Will Serve Mares this Season,

At £1 1s. each Mare, and 2s. 6d the Groom The Groom's Fee to be paid at the first time of Serving.

TOTAL, No. 320 Vol. VIII. W.S B., Reserve at the Aberystwyth Cob Society's Shows 1908-1909, also Highly Commended at the Welsh National Show at Aberystwyth Foaled in 1904, stands 13-1 h.h., a dark chestnut, free mover, fine action, a model in figure, and proves a good stock getter, on account of the blood and quality he possesses.

Sire—the celebrated and well-known KLONDYKE, No. 12 Vol. 1, W.S.B., the winner of numerous first prizes, including the first in his class at the National Show at Aberystwyth 1905. Afterwards sold to W. S. Miller, Esq., of Forest Lodge, Brecon, for £100.

Dam—A fine Chestnut Pony, winner of several prizes; last heard of was sold for £55 when only 3 years old. Her sire, Lord Ventry, 4386 H.S B., a good cob, winner of many first prizes; also the Aberystwyth Cob Society's prize.

G. Dam—A very good action pony by Eiddwen Flyer I., No. 2053 H.S.B.

Lord Ventry, by Ganymede, 2076 H.S.B , which was sold to T. Mitchell, Esq., for 2 000 guineas. Ganymede, by Danegelt 176, was sold to Sir Walter Gilbey for 5,000 guineas. Danegelt, by Old Denmark 177, Old Denmark by Sir Charles 768.

Lord Ventry's Dam Water Rose 4874 H.S.B., by Callis World 1483.

All Mares at owner's risk. All Mares tried by this Horse and afterwards put to another will be charged for.

WILL ATTEND ABERYSTWYTH AND MACHYNLLETH.

Stud card (1910) for Total.

Temptation, son of Total. Temptation, foaled in 1909 won a first prize at the Royal Agricultural Society of England Show. (Photograph courtesy of Sport and General.)

7. Aeronwen Ceulan

Registration number 5806 in the *Welsh Stud Book,*
Vol. XVII
Grey, height: 12 hands 2 in, foaled 1905
Owner: Lewis Lewis, Tyngraig, Talybont,
Cardiganshire
Breeder: J. Lewis, Ffynonddu, Talybont,
Cardiganshire

Aeronwen Ceulan was a well-known show mare in North Cardiganshire. Seren Ceulan (foaled 1910) was her first produce; thereafter she produced a grey filly by King Jack 20 in 1912; another grey in 1914 by Trotting Jack 528. The only other of her progeny that I know of was Cream Bun a dark cream stallion, foaled 1920 by Llanio Trotting Comet 872 which was second in the Welsh Pony stallion class at the 1923 Royal Welsh Show (Welshpool) when owned by my grandfather, L. O. Williams and was later (1925) Champion Welsh Pony at the

Cream Bun, Champion at the 1925 Royal Welsh Show. Cream Bun driven by Mrs. E. S. Davies was a son of Aeronwen Ceulan.

Royal Welsh Show (Carmarthen) when owned by John Jones and Son of Dinarth Hall. Aeronwen Ceulan won a first prize at Talybont Show when 26 years old and newspaper reports in 1934 (when her grand-son Ceulan Comet was exported to Australia) quote her as "still alive and well and running out at Tyngraig".

8. Young Caradog

This stallion belonged to pre-Stud Book times and was known locally as Caerllugest Horse. Young Caradog was by Caradog (*chapter 22.4*) (S. Jones, Talfedw, Llangeitho) by Welsh Jack by Cymro Llwyd (*chapter 18.6*). Caradog was g-g-sire of High Stepping Gambler (*chapter 23.8*); g-g-sire of Ceitho Welsh Comet (*chapter 24.2*) and g-sire of Beaconsfield (*chapter 22.1*) who was g-g-sire of Bleddfa Shooting Star (*chapter 4.1*).

9. Star

Star was by Welsh Flyer by Old Comet by Flyer (*chapter 18.4*). She won prizes at Lampeter 1877, 1879, 1881 and 1884, at Aberystwyth 1877, 1879, 1882 and 1884, and Aberayron 1878, 1880 and 1882. She was bred at Nantymedd, Llanfair Clydogau.

10. Cardigan Flyer
Registration number 699 in the *Welsh Stud Book*,
Vol. XIII
Chesnut, star, height: 14 hands 2 in, foaled 1886
Owner and Breeder: Jenkin Davies, Lluestygarn,
Llanrhystyd, Cardiganshire

There was another more well-known Cardigan Flyer, foaled 1873 and owned by David Evans, Trewern-Fawr, Tregaron, but the Cardigan Flyer, g-sire of Ceitho Welsh Comet was sired by Welsh Flyer III (*chapter 20.2*) (Dafydd Ellis) from a black mare by King Jack (*chapter 21.10*).

11. Bess

Bess was of pre-Stud Book era, a bay with height of 14 hands 2 in she was sired by Welsh Jack by Cymro Llwyd (*chapter 18.6*). She was described on the stud card of Ceitho Welsh Comet as "famous as one of the best Welsh type mares in the district."

12. Klondyke

Registration number 12 in the *Welsh Stud Book, Vol. I*
Re-registered as Forest Klondyke in *Welsh Stud Book, Vol. VIII, page 13*
Chesnut, star, off hind white fetlock, height: 12 hands 3 in, foaled 1894
Breeder: John Thomas, The Carrier, Trerddol, Cardiganshire
Owner: John Thomas (no relation to breeder), The Mill, Trerddol

Klondyke was sired by Young Messenger (Cardi Mawr) by Eiddwen

Welsh Cob group photograph taken in 1911. Mr. and Mrs. L. O. Williams (grandfather and grandmother of the author) between the carriages. Mr. L. O. Williams owned Cream Bun and was a nephew of the late John Thomas who owned Total, Klondyke, etc.

379

Flyer II (*chapter 21.2*) by Eiddwen Flyer 2053 *Hackney Stud Book*. The dam of Klondyke was 128 Lady Eiddwen winner of trotting races at Talybont, Towyn, Dolgellau and Machynlleth between the years 1895 and 1904 (my father remembered her and said she was a little black mare about 12 hands 1 in, foaled in 1888). Lady Eiddwen was by Eiddwen Flyer 2053 *Hackney Stud Book* (*chapter 21.4*) by Old Welsh Flyer 856 *Hackney Stud Book* by Old Trotting Comet 834 *Hackney Stud Book* (*chapter 18.2*).

Klondyke won first prizes in 1896 and 1897, a first at Machynlleth in 1897, seconds at Machynlleth in 1898, 1899, 1900 and 1901. In 1905 he was Champion at the Aberystwyth Welsh National Show where he was sold to Mr. W. S. Miller, Forest Lodge, Brecon for £100.

Klondyke won a first prize for Mr. Miller at the 1906 Brecon Show. Mr. Miller had the largest Mountain Pony stud in the United Kingdom and there are dozens of "Forest" progeny of Klondyke registered between the years 1906–1910.

Mr. Miller, when once judging at Talybont Show told my father that some of the best "Forest" ponies which he ever bred were sired by Klondyke. However with many of his daughters becoming of breeding age, Klondyke was sold to Mr. David Lloyd, Pwllpridd, Lledrod (later of the noted Meiarth Stud, Bwlchyllan) who travelled him for some years in Cardiganshire and he died with Mr. Lloyd.

13. Chesnut

Chesnut was not registered, she was described on the stud card of Total as "winner of several prizes; last heard of was sold for £55 when only three-years-old. Her sire Lord Ventry 4386 *Hackney Stud Book* was a good Cob, winner of many prizes, also the Aberystwyth Cob Society's prize. Lord Ventry by Ganymede 2076 *Hackney Stud Book* which was sold to T. Mitchell for 2,000 guineas. Ganymede by Danegelt 176 which was sold to Sir Walter Gilbey for 5,000 guineas."

14. Satisfaction

Satisfaction was not registered but was known as "ceffyl gwyn bach Blaengorphen". His stud card (for 1906) states that his owner was John Jones, Mountain, Llanrhystyd; previously John Edwards, Blaengorphen, Tregaron.

My father was once told by a Mrs. Margaret Morgan, Castell, Bethania that Satisfaction was bred at Pant, Bethania and sold at the

Stud card (1906) for Satisfaction. (Stud card courtesy of Messrs. Rowlands Harris.)

Pant Sale for £1.15.0 as a foal. She said that he jumped out of the ring before the bidding stopped but that the auctioneer said that he need not be caught and brought back in since everyone there had seen him! He was bought there by the Rev. Evan Evans, Piggin Isaf, Penrhiw, Trawsnant (cousin of Mrs. Margaret Morgan). Rev. Evans rode Satisfaction on his preaching journeys, often serving mares on these journeys! Rev. Evans sold Satisfaction to Mr. John Edwards where he became a well-known sire; John Edwards then sold him to John Jones

381

who, father was told, sold him to some gipsies but when he was an old pony, Messrs. Rowlands Brothers of Mabwshen recognised him, bought him back and he died at Mabwshen when very old.

15. Ffynon Queen
Registration number 971 in the *Welsh Stud Book*, *Vol. III*
Owner and Breeder: L. R. Lewis, Ffynonddu, Clarach, Aberystwyth
Chesnut, star, height: 12 hands 1 in, foaled 1900

Ffynon Queen was sired by Eiddwen Flyer II (*chapter 21.2*) out of a chesnut mare called Bess by King Jack (ceffyl Morgan Y Gors). Ffynon Queen won a second prize at Talybont Show in 1902 and of the twenty-two medals awarded by the Welsh Pony & Cob Society in 1903, the Stud Book records that the medal at the Talybont Show was won by Ffynon Queen so, in this respect, she is included along with some of the greatest names: Prince of Cardiff, Greylight, Llwyn Prince of Wales and Wild Duck (Blaentwrch).

25

Mathrafal Eiddwen (foaled 1914)
Dewi Black Bess (foaled 1926)
Dewi Rosina (foaled 1934)
Pentre Eiddwen Comet (foaled 1946)
Llanarth Flying Comet (foaled 1968)

1 Llanarth Flying Comet 6835	2 Pentre Eiddwen Comet 1796	4 Eiddwen's Image 1703	8 Mathrafal Eiddwen 965
			9 8937 Dewi Rosina
		5 Dewi Black Bess	10 Ceitho Welsh Comet 774
			11 Bess
	3 Llanarth Flying Saucer	6 Llanarth Braint 1854	12 Llanarth Goldcrest 1793
			13 9643 Llanarth Kilda
		7 Llanarth Rocket	14 Llanarth Prince Roland 1712
			15 Llanarth Fortress

1. Llanarth Flying Comet

Registration number 6835 in the *Welsh Stud Book, Vol. L*
Black, both hind white fetlocks, height: 14 hands
2 in, foaled 1968
Owner and Breeder: Miss Pauline Taylor, Llanarth
Stud, Llanarth, Cardiganshire

Llanarth Flying Comet is the most successful of all the young Cob stallions exhibited in the 'seventies; he came out as a yearling at the 1969 Royal Welsh show, went straight to the top and has stayed there ever since! Never has a Cob stallion enjoyed such fantastic success: first prize as a yearling in 1969, ditto again in 1970 and 1971 with Reserve Male Championships on both occasions, then he entered the adult fray where as a fresh four-year-old he held off all opposition, gained the Male Championship and stood Reserve for the George, Prince of Wales cup. Flying Comet had a rest from the 1973 Royal Welsh Show since Miss Taylor was the judge; however he came back in great form to be recipient of the Supreme award in 1974, 1976, 1977 and 1978. These are

Llanarth Flying Comet photographed in 1978.

only a few of the major awards which have fallen to Llanarth Flying Comet, amongst the numerous championships which have gone his way, apart from the Royal Welsh Show successes, possibly his next most noteable are four times qualifying for the Lloyds Bank award at the Horse of the Year Show and in 1975 being "Pony of the Year and Reserve overall Champion and Supreme Champion in 1979. The visitors from Wales attending this major event have been justifiably very proud of their representantive.

Standing reserve to him at the 1978 Royal Welsh Show was Parc Rachel and the first prize foal was the produce of Parc Rachel and Llanarth Flying Comet so the influence of this successful stallion will be with us for many more years to come.

2. Pentre Eiddwen Comet

Registration number 1796 in the *Welsh Stud Book*,
Vol. XXXII
Bay, white off hind fetlock, height: 14 hands 2 in,
foaled 1946
Breeder: J. O. Davies, Pentrebrain, Llanddewi Brefi,
Tregaron, Cardiganshire
Owner (after 1950): John Hughes, Rhydlas Uchaf,
Llanrhystyd, Cardiganshire

The first time I saw Pentre Eiddwen Comet was at the 1949 Royal Welsh Show (Swansea) where he won the two- or three-year-old Welsh Cob class having previously that year stood third in the any-age stallion class at the Royal Agricultural Society of England Show. The Royal Welsh Agricultural Society judge, Capt. T. A. Howson wrote of him: "A bold and free-moving bay three-year-old colt with a neat head, a reachy forehand, a good strong back and loins and a well-set tail, he promises to develop into a typical Cob stallion of the old Welsh school."

How true that prophecy turned out to be! In 1951 Pentre Eiddwen Comet secured the George, Prince of Wales Cup, the supreme acclaim in Welsh Cobland, an award which he was to win again five years later (as well as an additional thrice Male Champion at the Royal Welsh Agricultural Shows) and he is followed by three of his sons who have, between them, won this award six times to date (1978).

It was at this same 1951 Royal Welsh Show at Llanelwedd (which in 1963 became the permanent site for the Royal Welsh Agricultural Society Shows) that Pentre Eiddwen Comet brought the house down and the grandstand to its feet when he won the Tom and Sprightly Cup

(judged by the popular applause of the spectators) an award which he won a total of five times. Apart from his Royal Welsh Agricultural Society Championships his career there was somewhat chequered. He stood third to Mathrafal and Llwynog y Garth in 1952, he won in 1953, was third to Meiarth King Flyer and Brynarth Stepping Gambler in 1954, second to Caradog Llwyd in 1955 then won for four successive years only to be fourth in 1960, seventh in 1962, fifth in 1963 and 1964, second in 1965, seventh in 1967 and sixth on his last Royal Welsh Agricultural Society appearance in 1968 at twenty-two years of age.

Pentre Eiddwen Comet made his presence felt as a sire throughout the Principality by his participation in the Premium scheme where he was an exceptionally popular stallion, always kept in great form by his devoted owner, he appeared just as fiery and active travelling the various counties as he was when waiting to go into battle in the show ring. He travelled North Cardiganshire for four years (1951–1954) followed by a year in Brecon and another year in Carmarthen before returning for a further two year stint in North Cardiganshire, a year in South Cardiganshire and two years in Carmarthen before the con-ditions of award of a Premium were altered and stallions could stand at home and Pentre Eiddwen Comet was awarded a further three

Premiums. In his later years, it was found that his services were in very great demand and mares travelled from all over the United Kingdom to his court until he died in the early 'seventies.

Usually when in-breeding is practised, it is the mating of "cousins" or the "Rigmaden system" as demonstrated so successfully by Mr. Christopher Wilson of Westmorland with his Hackney ponies. In the case of Pentre Eiddwen Comet it was more of "scissors" mating: Dewi Rosina is his half-sister and also his grand-dam on his sire's side. However, this breeding, although unorthodox, produced results since naming first his sons who have achieved Royal Welsh Show Championships it is a formidable list: Tyhen Comet (1966 and 1969), Nebo Black Magic (1971 and 1973) and Llanarth Flying Comet (1972, 1974, 1976, 1977 and 1978). Other sons who have achieved lesser (though nevertheless noteworthy) fame include Parc Welsh Flyer, Felin Prince, Oak Hatch Flight (exported to South Africa), Llanarth Valiant's Image and Redwood Cardi Comet.

3. Llanarth Flying Saucer
Registration number 1134 F.S.2 in the appendix of
the *Welsh Stud Book, Vol. XXXVII*
Chesnut roan, blaze, near hind sock white, height:
13 hands 2 in, foaled 1951
Owners and Breeders: The Misses Taylor and
Saunders Davies, Llanarth Stud, Cardiganshire

Llanarth Flying Saucer was shown extensively in the Section "C" brood mare class at Royal Welsh Shows winning a second prize to Dyffryn Rosina in 1956, another second prize in a mixed-sex class to Teifi Brightlight in 1958, and again second to the same stallion in 1960, fourth in the mare class to Pride of the Prairie, Gerynant Rosina and Lili Cwmcoed in 1962, fourth to Pride of the Prairie, Menai Ceridwen and, Gerynant Rosina in 1964; whilst in 1965 she was awarded the Section "C" Championship and consequently retired from the show ring.

During all these years she had also been a prolific producer of foals and it is for the successes in this category that her outstanding accomplishments are best remembered:

1954 Llanarth Speedwell, filly, by Llanarth Hywel ap Braint
1956 Llanarth Flying Kite, filly, by Llanarth Hywel ap Braint. A very good producer at Llanarth Stud e.g. Llanarth Kate in 1972

388

Llanarth Flying Saucer photographed when Champion at the 1965 Royal Welsh Show. (Photograph courtesy of Les Mayall.)

1957 Llanarth Sentinel, colt, by Llanarth Hywel ap Braint. A well-known sire for Sir Nigel Colman, Mr. Jeffrey Davies and Trewysgoed Stud.

1958 Llanarth Dancing Satellite, filly, by Fronarth What Ho (exported to U.S.A. Mrs. Ingersoll).

1959 Llanarth Meteor, colt, by Menai Ceredig. One of the senior stallions at Llanarth Stud; a great performer in harness having won the Harness Championship at the Royal Welsh Agricultural Society Show (1972).

1960 Llanarth Sparkling Satellite, filly, by Llanarth Sparkle. A good producer at the Bolgoed (S) Stud e.g. Bolgoed (S) Fusilier.

1961 Llanarth Hedydd, filly, by Menai Ceredig.

1962 Llanarth Simnel, colt, by Llanarth Cerdin (sold to Dwyfor Stud).

Llanarth Meteor, son of Llanarth Flying Saucer.

1963 Llanarth Sissel by Llanarth Cerdin (sold to Dwyfor Stud).

1965 Llanarth Sensyllt, colt, by Llanarth Carel (sold to Dwyfor Stud).

1966 Llanarth Saethyd, colt, by Llanarth Cerdin (sold to Dwyfor Stud).

1967 Llanarth Siriel, colt, by Cymro Lan (sold to Dwyfor Stud).

1968 Llanarth Flying Comet, colt, by Pentre Eiddwen Comet.

1969 Llanarth Flying Rocket, filly, by Pentre Eiddwen Comet. Dam of Llanarth Touch and Go (Scole Stud), Llanarth Flyer (Austria), Llanarth Rainbow etc.

1971 Llanarth Jack Flyer, colt, by Tyhen Comet. Exceptional colt, winner of many awards.

1972 Llanarth Sian, filly, by Tyhen Comet (dam of Champion Llanarth Sally).

1973 Llanarth Brenin Siarl, colt, by Tyhen Comet. A young stallion of great promise, based in North Wales.

1975 Llanarth Lloyd, colt, by Nebo Black Magic (sold to Wansdyke Stud).

1976 Llanarth Jack Flash, colt, by Nebo Black Magic (exported to Marc Bullen, Australia).

What a remarkable record; 19 foals and all alive (1979).

4. Eiddwen's Image
Registration number 1703 in the *Welsh Stud Book,*
Vol. XXXII
Bay, star, white near hind fetlock, height: 14 hands,
foaled 1940
Owner and Breeder: J. O. Davies, Pentrebrain,
Llanddewi Brefi, Cardiganshire

Very little is known about Eiddwen's Image apart from the fact that many breeders who saw him claim that he was no "show specimen" although the progeny of two National Champions. He illustrates the fact that breeding is more of an art that an exact science and perhaps more of a gamble than either. However he makes a good link between his famous sire, Mathrafal Eiddwen and his more famous son Pentre Eiddwen Comet.

One daughter of Eiddwen's Image was Pentre Black Bess (foaled in 1945) her dam being Eiddwen's Pride who was three-quarters sister to Eiddwen's Image, both being sired by Mathrafal Eiddwen and Eiddwen's Pride being a daughter of Dewi Black Bess (g-dam of Eiddwen's Image). Pentre Black Bess spent most of her life in North

Pentre Rainbow photographed when Champion at the 1962 Royal Welsh Show. Dam: Pentre Eiddwen's Model, g-dam: Eiddwen's Model, g-g-dam: Dewi Black Bess.

Wales with Mr. Hugh Owen, Ty Helen, Caernarfon where she produced e.g. the black stallion Tywysog Menai (by Mathrafal, *chapter
28.4*) in 1950.

Eiddwen's Pride (foaled 1940) had a full-sister Eiddwen's Model
(foaled in 1939) and both were sold to the Hon. Mrs. Oscar Guest of
Hay-on-Wye, producing such as Vanguard in 1947. Both these mares
were then bought back by Mr. J. O. Davies, Eiddwen's Model winning
a third prize for him at the 1951 Royal Welsh Show. It was a very wise
move to buy back these two mares, Eiddwen's Model becoming g-dam
of the 1962 Royal Welsh Champion Pentre Rainbow and the 1963 and
1965 Royal Welsh Champion Pentre Eiddwen's Doll (daughter of
Pentre Rainbow); also Eiddwen's Pride produced Pentre Eiddwen
Flyer, sire of Brenin-y-Bryniau.

*Brenin y Bryniau at Lampeter Show 1963. Sire Pentre Eiddwen Flyer. G-dam: Eiddwen's
Pride, g-g-dam: Dewi Black Bess.*

5. Dewi Black Bess
Registration number 19 F.S.2 in the appendix of the
Welsh Stud Book, Vol. XXX
Black, white off hind fetlock, height: 14 hands 2½ in,
foaled 1926
Owner: J. O. Davies, Pentrebrain, Llanddewi Brefi,
Cardiganshire
Breeder: William Williams, Penbwlch Mawr,
Llangeitho, Cardiganshire

One day in 1926 Mr. J. O. Davies was riding home to his farm
(Pentrebrain, where four generations of his family had been breeding
Welsh Cobs) from Tregaron alongside Mr. Williams who was riding
Bess No. 18 F.S.1. Mr. Davies was so impressed with the paces of Bess
that he enquired of Mr. Williams if there was more of this family around
and it so transpired that Mr. Williams had her daughter at home, a filly
foal by the noted Ceitho Welsh Comet. It is sad to relate that Bess died
that same night. Shortly afterwards, Mr. Williams had a dispersal sale
and Mr. Davies bought the foal for £4.10.0. and duly registered her as
Dewi Black Bess No. 19 F.S.2.

Dewi Black Bess soon started to win prizes at Cardiganshire Shows
one of her most successful days being at the 1932 Lampeter Show where
she won three first prizes, the Williams Challenge Cup and the Welsh
Pony & Cob Society silver medal. At the Pontrhydyfendigaid Show one
year after winning the Welsh Cob brood mare class in the morning, she
had her heavy shoes removed and later in the afternoon won the trotting
race!

Her first taste of the Royal Welsh show ring was in 1933 (Aberystwyth) where she stood fifth in a strong class won by Cwmcau Lady Jet
(owned by Dinarth Hall) who had won previously in 1930 and 1932 and
later also won in 1934. At the 1934 Show (Llandudno) Black Bess was
third to Cwmcau Lady Jet and Sian Gwalia owned by my grandfather.
It was in 1935 that Dewi Black Bess was to have her day when, not only
did she beat Cwmcau Lady Jet, Sian Gwalia and Teifi of Hercws
(another daughter of Ceitho Welsh Comet) in the brood mare class but
she also beat the winning stallion Myrtle Welsh Flyer (*chapter 29.8*)
(another by Ceitho Welsh Comet) for the George, Prince of Wales
Championship award. For the next three years, the mare class was won
by Teifi of Hercws and in 1938 Black Bess was second.

Reference has already been made to Dewi Black Bess' enormous contribution as a brood mare producing Eiddwen's Model (1939),

Dewi Black Bess photographed when Champion at the 1935 Royal Welsh Show. (Photograph courtesy of G. H. Parsons.)

Eiddwen's Pride (1940), Pentre Eiddwen Comet (1946) etc between them all, responsible for thirty of the Royal Welsh male and female Championships between 1951 and 1979.

The only time that I can recall seeing Dewi Black Bess was at the Aberystwyth Show on 20th August 1947 where she stood sixth in the barren mare class. At twenty-one years old she was only a shadow of her former self and I prefer to visualise her as depicted in the photograph taken in 1935 which shows a very magnificent mare indeed.

6. Llanarth Braint *(chapter 27.1)*

7. Llanarth Rocket
Registration number 645 F.S.1 in the appendix of the
Welsh Stud Book, Vol. XXXIV
Chesnut, broad blaze, height: 13 hands 2 in,
foaled 1947
Breeders: The Misses Taylor and Saunders-Davies,
Llanarth Stud, Cardiganshire

When Rocket was three-years-old she was mated to Llanarth Braint, she produced Llanarth Flying Saucer in 1951 (incidentally also Llanarth Braint's first foal) and then she was sold as a riding pony to the Isle of Man where she was last heard of at thirty years old and still thriving. It is a matter of great regret to all at the stud that Rocket was not kept to produce another "Flying Saucer" and all the success which that would entail.

8. Mathrafal Eiddwen

Registration number 965 in the *Welsh Stud Book,*
Vol. XVIII
Bay, near hind white fetlock, height 14 hands 2 in,
foaled 1914
Breeder: Evan Lloyd, Caedtalog, Llanerfyl,
Welshpool, Montgomeryshire
Owner: H. Meyrick Jones, Mathrafal, Meifod,
Montgomeryshire
Sire: King Flyer 35
Dam: 4295 Polly of Maesglynog by Cymro Du
G-dam: 4318 Vyrnwy Lass by Eiddwen Flyer 421

Mathrafal Eiddwen was bought from his breeder as a four-year-old by Mr. Meyrick Jones who registered him under the Mathrafal prefix. Mr. Meyrick Jones had previously owned his sire, King Flyer (foaled in 1894) who had spent the first fifteen years of his life at stud in Cardiganshire until Mr. Jones bought him, took him to Montgomeryshire and won the George, Prince of Wales Cup at the Royal Welsh Show with him twice (1913 and 1914) at ages when most stallions would have long-since retired.

King Flyer (foaled in 1894), sire of Mathrafal Eiddwen.

1910.   1910.

TO SERVE THIS SEASON

At £2 10s. each Mare, and 5s. the Groom.

The Groom's Fee to be paid at the first time of covering, and the
remainder on or before the 24th day of June next.

THAT SPLENDID WELSH COB

KING FLYER

No. 35 IN WELSH PONY AND COB STUD BOOK.

(Late CEL BACH GLANDULAS).

*The property of Mr. John Jones, Green Hill, Llanfair Clydogau,
near Lampeter, Cardiganshire.*

KING FLYER stands 15-2 hands high. and is of a beautiful
Brown Colour. He was got by Young Welsh Flyer, by Welsh
Flyer, by Old Comet, by Flyer, the fastest horse that ever
travelled Wales.

KING FLYER was awarded 3rd prize at Carmarthen in 1899 ;
3rd in 1901 ; 2nd at Llandovery in 1902 ; 2nd at Llandovery in
1903 ; 3rd at Carmarthen and 3rd at Llanelly in 1908.

KING FLYER'S stock find a ready sale, some of his progeny
have realized high prices.

KING FLYER'S dam was got by Young Trotting Comet by
Old Comet, by Flyer, out of Brown Bess, by Black Jack, Black
Jack out of Black Bess, which was never beaten at any Match.
Therefore it is clearly understood that King Flyer descends from
pure trotting blood, and has proved himself a sure foal getter.
Foals got by him last year have been sold for £10 and £11 each.

The Groom will specify the time and places of attendance.

All mares tried by this horse and afterwards put to another will
be charged full price.

*The Owner of the horse nor the Groom will not be responsible for any accident
which may occur to any mare during time of covering.*

D. R. Evans & Co., Stud Card Printers, Lampeter.

Stud card for King Flyer for 1910. (Stud and courtesy of Messrs. Rowlands Harris.)

King Flyer was a stallion of magnificent proportions, possessing such
excellent bone and limbs; his fault, if one wanted to be very critical, was
that he was possibly long in his head, a characteristic which he did not
pass on to his progeny.

Mathrafal Eiddwen soon notched up a few prizes in the Royal Welsh
show rings with a second prize in 1923 (Welshpool) to Mr. Tom Jones
Evans' Llwynog Flyer. The next two years saw the other Mathrafal

396

stallion, Mathrafal Brenin (*chapter 23.6*) owned by Mr. David Rees in his supremacy. It was then in 1926 with Mr. Tom Jones Evans judging at the Bangor Royal Welsh Show that Mathrafal Eiddwen first won the coveted Prince of Wales Cup with the eminently successful sire, Llethi Valiant standing second.

Mathrafal Eiddwen repeated this award at the 1927 Royal Welsh Show (Swansea) under Major Dugdale of the Llwyn Stud. The 1928 Show (Wrexham) saw Mr. Edgar Herbert officiating; Mr. Herbert's favourite mare was Pant Grey Star (*chapter 29.5*) (whom he had placed Supreme Champion at Tregaron the previous year) and in the stallion class, he thought Llethi Valiant a better match for this mare so Mathrafal Eiddwen had to be content with second place.

Mathrafal Eiddwen had his revenge over Llethi Valiant at the 1929 show, where, with Mr. J. R. Bache judging, Eiddwen won and Llethi Valiant was relegated into fifth place. This was also Eiddwen's third notch on the Prince of Wales Cup, a feat which he repeated for the fourth (and last) time in 1930 under Mr. T. E. Jenkins.

Mr. Jenkins writing of Mathrafal Eiddwen in the Royal Welsh Journal describes him as "although he is getting to the end of his showyard career, he is a grand old horse and full of Welsh character".

Among his progeny during his period at Mathrafal was Mathrafal Broadcast (foaled in 1926) whose blood flows in the veins of so many of the Section "B" ponies through his grand-son Criban Victor (*chapter 13.2*). In the early 'thirties Mathrafal Eiddwen sired some good Cobs at Dinarth Hall including Edgware Sunrise (foaled 1932, out of Cilwen Lady Lilian, *chapter 26*) one of four in Mr. Bertram Mills' famous coach team which were exported to Mr. van Sinderen of Wall Street, New York in 1937. He then passed through various hands until he became the property of Mr. J. O. Davies of Pentrebrain in 1937 (at the age of 25 years). It was during these last three years (he died in 1940) that he had his greatest influence on the Welsh Cob breed. Mated to Mr. Davies' Dewi Black Bess (No. 5) he produced (in 1939) Eiddwen's Model and (in 1940) Eiddwen's Pride. Eiddwen's Model was dam of Gwalchmai Welsh Model, and grand-dam of Pentre Rainbow (Champion Cob stallion Royal Welsh 1962) and Pentre Eiddwen's Doll (Champion at the Royal Welsh in 1963 and 1965). Eiddwen's Pride was dam of Pentre Eiddwen Flyer who, in turn, sired the well-known Brenin-y-Bryniau.

The most important mating of Mathrafal Eiddwen was in 1939 to Dewi Black Bess' daughter Dewi Rosina (No. 9) producing Eiddwen's Image (No. 4) who in turn, sired the immortal Pentre Eiddwen Comet. Thus the blood of Mathrafal Eiddwen, four times Royal Welsh Show Champion himself, is responsible for such a long list of later champions.

9. Dewi Rosina
Registration number 8937 in the *Welsh Stud Book, Vol. XXXI*
Black, height: 14 hands 1 in, foaled 1934
Breeder: J. O. Davies, Pentrebrain, Llanddewi Brefi,
Tregaron, Cardiganshire
Sire: Blaenwaun True Briton 1351
Dam: Dewi Black Bess No. 19 F.S.2

Dewi Rosina was the foal at foot of Dewi Black Bess when the mare won a third prize at the Llandudno Royal Welsh Show; in her own right, Dewi Rosina won the foal class at the Llanilar Show. After producing some foals at Pentrebrain (such as Eiddwen's Image, No. 4, foaled in 1940) Dewi Rosina was sold in 1944 to Mr. Roscoe Lloyd who at that time was living at Drefach, Llanybyther (later at Derwenfawr, Crugybar, Llanwrda) for whom she produced Derwen Welsh Flyer (1945), Derwen Welsh Comet (1946), Derwen Derwena (1949) etc. It was also at this time that she began being shown in earnest winning seven first prizes (including championships at Cardigan, Llangwyryfon and Crugybar) in 1946, five first prizes in 1947 including the Championship at Lampeter and Llangwyryfon and a second prize (to Meiarth Welsh Maid *chapter 29.3*) at the Royal Welsh Show. In 1949 at this show she stood second to Meiarth Welsh Maid. Then, in 1951 at seventeen years old, she won for the first time at the Royal Welsh under the expert judge Mr. D. O. Morgan of the Parc Stud. Her final

Dewi Rosina with Mr. Roscoe Lloyd.

appearance at the Royal Welsh was in 1953 where Mr. A. L. Williams placed her supreme Champion and therefore her name became engraved (at the age of nineteen years) on the George, Prince of Wales Cup.

The blood of Dewi Rosina is to be found all over the world, recently through Pentre Eiddwen Comet, Nebo Black Magic and Llanarth Flying Comet blood to Australia, Canada etc but an interesting original export was Derwen Welsh Comet who was exported to Pakistan to cross with the native mares to produce Polo ponies.

10. Ceitho Welsh Comet (*chapter 24.2*)

11. Bess
Registration number 18 F.S.1. in the appendix of the
Welsh Stud Book, Vol. XXX
Black, height: 14 hands 1 in, foaled 1919
Breeder: William Williams, Penbwlch Mawr,
Llangeitho, Cardiganshire
Sire: Dewi Welsh King 775
Dam: Poll No. 17 F.S. by King Flyer 415
G-dam: Mag by Welsh Flyer (856 *Hackney Stud Book*)
(*chapter 18.1*)

As already written in connection with her daughter, Dewi Black

399

Bess, Bess was a very good trotting mare. Unfortunately she died in 1926 when only seven-years-old.

12. Llanarth Goldcrest (*chapter 27.2*)

13. Llanarth Kilda (*chapter 27.3*)

14. Llanarth Prince Roland
Registration number 1712 in the *Welsh Stud Book, Vol. XXXII*
Liver chesnut, blaze, white off hind pastern, height:
14 hands 2 in, foaled 1944
Owners and Breeders: Misses Taylor and Saunders
Davies, Llanarth Stud, Cardiganshire
Sire: Brenin Gwalia 1656 (*chapter 23.1*)
Dam: 9114 Llanarth Firefly by Blaenwaun True
Briton 1351

Llanarth Firefly (foaled 1933) was the first registered Welsh Cob mare to be purchased (in 1936) by Miss Taylor. Bred by Mr. E. A. Lloyd at nearby Aberayron, she was sired by the 1936–1938 Premium stallion Blaenwaun True Briton out of Bess of Llwynbrain a daughter of Plynlimmon Champion (who was registered in the Pembrokeshire Pack Horse Section of the *Welsh Stud Book*.)

The first breeding programme attempted at Llanarth Stud was the mating of Firefly to the reigning Champion Welsh Cob stallion Brenin Gwalia and this produced Llanarth Prince Roland, the second Welsh Cob to be foaled at the Llanarth Stud, the first being Llanarth Vega (foaled in 1942) also by Brenin Gwalia.

Llanarth Prince Roland was sold as a stallion to South Wales where he continued as a popular stallion for some years.

15. Llanarth Fortress
Registration number 297 F.S. in the appendix of the
Welsh Stud Book, Vol. XXXII
Red-roan, star, white off hind sock, height: 13 hands
2 in, foaled 1943
Owners: Misses Taylor and Saunders Davies,
Llanarth, Cardiganshire
Breeder: R. Jones, Court Farm, Gwenddwr, Builth Wells

Driving along a lovely stretch of road by the River Wye near Builth

Wells in 1945, the Misses Taylor and Saunders Davies saw a roan two-year-old filly being ridden by some small children; they immediately took a fancy to her and bought her. Having no recorded parentage, she was duly registered as F.S. in the appendix of the *Welsh Stud Book*. From an investigation of the high calibre of her descendants, then here obviously was a typical Welsh Pony of Cob type of old, germane bloodlines (though not recorded) and although there are many other mares which have had a great influence on Cob breeding at the Llanarth Stud (and on the breed throughout the world) pride of place amongst the Llanarth females must go to little Llanarth Fortress.

Strangely enough Fortress bred only one filly i.e. Llanarth Rocket (and Rocket's one and only foal was the famous Flying Saucer) though she bred several colts notably her last two (by Llanarth Braint) being Fortel (well-known for his placid temperament with disabled riders) and Beaufort, a very well-known harness winner. For many years Fortress was owned by Miss Taylor's sister who kept her only for riding and when she eventually returned to Llanarth, she was too old to breed any more.

Llanarth Fortress ridden by Miss Gillian Cuff.

Llanarth Fortel, son of Llanarth Fortress ridden by Miss Pauline Taylor.

I well remember doing the commentary on the display of famous Welsh Ponies and Cobs at the Royal Welsh Show. Fortress appeared ridden by Miss Taylor and they received an enormous ovation when I announced that their combined ages exceeded a century. Fortress died in her thirtieth year quietly as she would have wished while grazing with the other mares – no fuss, no nursing and no trouble.

26

Cilwen Lady Lilian foaled 1917
Llethi Valiant foaled 1921
Myrtle Rosina foaled 1924
Lyn Cwmcoed foaled 1960
Menai Fury foaled 1963
Synod William foaled 1969

1 Synod William 8244	2 Menai Fury 4382	4 Gredington Oswallt 2858	8 Coed Coch Planed 2154
			9 Gredington Llinos
		5 11517 Menai Ceridwen	10 Caradog Llwyd 2069
			11 11462 Menai Queen Bee
	3 11585 Gerynant Rosina	6 Valiant Flyer 1765	12 Llethi Valiant 1238
			13 8002 Deinol Bloss
		7 9094 Dyffryn Rosina	12 Llethi Valiant 1238
			15 8584 Myrtle Rosina

1. Synod William

Registration number 8244 in the *Welsh Stud Book,*
Vol. LII
Bay, star, near fore and both hind fetlocks white,
height: 13 hands 1 in, foaled 1969
Owners and Breeders: Mr. and Mrs. Cerdin Jones,
Gellihen, Talgarreg, Llandyssul, Cardiganshire

It was not long before Synod William found himself in the show ring. At the 1970 Royal Welsh Show, he was places second in a large class open to yearling colts and fillies and also to two and three-year-old fillies. His full-brother (a year older) Synod Cerdin, later to achieve international fame when driven by Mrs. Deirdre Colville, won the older colt class at that show and was proclaimed Reserve for the Section Championship.

At the 1971 Royal Welsh Show, Synod William was Champion Welsh Pony (Cob type); at two-years-old he is the youngest to achieve this feat. He did not then compete at Royal Welsh Shows until 1977 when he repeated this Championship win; however in the meantime his stock had been well to the fore, all three winning foals at the 1974 Show were his and he won the progeny group class in 1977 and 1978.

Synod William.
(Photograph courtesy
of Idris Aeron.)

405

Synod Roger, Champion Welsh Pony (Cob type) at the 1979 Royal Welsh Show. Son of Synod William. (Photograph courtesy of Idris Aeron.)

Outside Wales, he has also made his mark in the show ring, such as being twice Champion at Royal Agricultural Society of England Shows in 1976 and 1977. The 1977 Royal Agricultural Society of England was quite an event, Synod William was Champion Welsh Pony Section "C" shown in hand, his full-brother Synod Cerdin was Champion in the Private Driving Competition!

Synod William was also Champion at the 1975 Ponies of Britain Show, whilst within Wales he won a first prize and stood reserve to his son Synod Ranger at the 1976 Lampeter Stallion Show. Synod William is still in his prime (1979) and has many other great heights to which to climb yet.

2. Menai Fury

Registration number 4382 in the *Welsh Stud Book*,
Vol. XLVII
Bay, star, off fore white fetlock, height: 12 hands 2 in,
foaled 1963
Owner and Breeder: Willie Jones, Pantydefaid,
Llandyssul, Cardiganshire

Menai Fury arrived on the Welsh Pony (Cob type) scene at a time when the total numbers within the United Kingdom did not reach 50; there were insufficient numbers to warrant youngstock classes at the Royal Welsh Show; indeed, until 1961 there was only one class offered where stallions competed against mares. When two classes were staged in 1961, the two contenders in the stallion class (as also in 1962) were the aged Teify Brightlight (foaled in 1936) and Menai Fury's brother Llanarth Cerdin.

Thus Menai Fury was able to exert a big influence on this valuable breed, 80 or more representatives nowadays often competing at the Royal Welsh Show, a far cry from the days when there were not this number in the United Kingdom. In the show ring, Menai Fury found it hard to make it to the top, possibly on account of his lack of inches, winning five second prizes at Royal Welsh Shows in 1966, 1967, 1968, 1970 and 1974, eventually winning in 1976. However a stallion is best

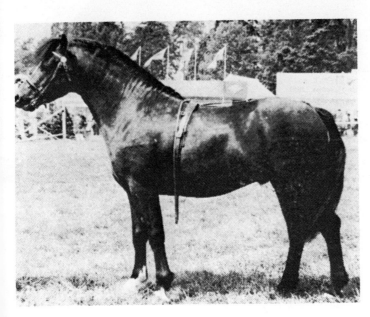

Menai Fury.

judged by the stock which he produces and in this, Menai Fury leaves nothing more to be desired; his stock producing a lasting effect to the second and third generation.

3. Gerynant Rosina
Registration number 11585 in the *Welsh Stud Book*,
Vol. XLI
Black, star, near fore and both hind white fetlocks,
height: 13 hands 1 in, foaled 1955
Breeder: W. J. Jones, Gerynant, Cellan, Lampeter,
Cardiganshire

Mr. W. J. Jones did not feel very pleased with himself at the 1959 Royal Welsh Show at Margam. He had bred Gerynant Rosina in

Gerynant Rosina.

*Tydi Rosina, daughter of
Gerynant Rosina.
(Photograph courtesy of
Les Mayall.)*

Tydi Red Rose, daughter of Tydi Rosina.

409

1955; the previous year he had bred Pride of the Prairie (out of Piercefield Lady Lilian; half-sister, same dam Dyffryn Rosina to Gerynant Rosina) which he had sold back to Mr. Freddie Lewis of the Piercefield/Dyffryn Stud, and Mr. John Berry at Margam placed Pride of the Prarie first with Gerynant Rosina second!

One person who took a fancy to Gerynant Rosina at Margam was Cerdin Jones (who had been brought up very near to Rhyderwen where the reigning Champion mare Queenie lived) but on enquiring of W. J. Jones was told that she was not for sale. Shortly afterwards, Mr. Jones died and Cerdin bought Gerynant Rosina and her colt foal at Llanybyther Market for £72. For Cerdin Jones she won second prizes at the Royal Welsh Shows in 1962 and 1963 with a third prize in 1964. In 1960 Cerdin Jones mated Gerynant Rosina to the very correct (if small) Cob stallion Meiarth Royal Eiddwen (*chapter 29.7*); this mating producing the lovely Tydi Rosina whose photograph illustrated the Welsh Pony & Cob Society brochures for many years. Tydi Rosina is still hale and hearty at the Synod Stud producing one champion after another; two of her better-known having died very prematurely, a great loss to the breed; Tydi Cerdin Reserve Champion at the 1969 Royal Welsh Show died just as he was launching on being a great sire and his sister the lovely Tydi Red Rose, Champion at the 1972 Royal Welsh Show, died as she was producing her second foal.

Later progeny of Gerynant Rosina are as follows:

1963 Tydi Rosita, filly, by Meiarth Royal Eiddwen
1964 Tydi Rosette, filly, by Lyn Cwmcoed
1965 Tydi Rosie, filly, by Llanarth Cerdin
1967 Tydi Rosemary, filly, by Hendy Brenin (dam of Champions: Synod Roger and Synod Ranger)
1968 Synod Cerdin, colt, by Menai Fury
1969 Synod William, colt, by Menai Fury

4. Gredington Oswallt
Registration number 2858 in the *Welsh Stud Book*,
Vol. XLI
Grey, faint blaze, near hind white coronet; height: 11
hands 2 in, foaled 1958
Breeder: Lord Kenyon, Gredington, Whitchurch,
Salop.

Gredington Oswallt was sold as a foal on the Fayre Oaks Sale in

October (lot 106) for 30 guineas to Mr. Jack Lloyd of the Meiarth Stud. In his new ownership, Gredington Oswallt won some prizes at mid-Wales Shows and became a much-sought-after sire.

After siring some very useful stock in Wales, Gredington Oswallt was sold to Belgium and when I judged there on 19th November 1978, he was in great form carrying his twenty years very lightly.

5. Menai Ceridwen
Registration number 11517 in the *Welsh Stud Book*,
Vol. XLI
Dun, near fore fetlock white,
height: 13 hands 2 in,
foaled 1953
Owner and Breeder: Willie Jones,
Pantydefaid,
Llandysul, Cardiganshire

Menai Cerdiwen is regarded as one of the saviours of the Welsh Pony (Cob type) having produced two major sires, Menai Fury and Llanarth Cerdin, the latter sired by Llanarth Marvel and foaled in 1959. Menai Ceridwen was a well-known winner at mid-Wales Shows including fourth at the 1963 Royal Welsh Show, second in 1964 and a first prize at the 1964 Aberystwyth Show.

Menai Ceridwen.

6. Valiant Flyer
Registration number 1765 in the *Welsh Stud Book,*
Vol. XXXII
Black, white on four legs, height: 14 hands 2 in,
foaled 1940
Breeder: T. J. Jones, Deinol, Glynarthen, Llandysul,
Cardiganshire
Owner: E. J. Thomas, Trebleiddied Farm,
Whitland, Dyfed

Valiant Flyer pulled a butcher's van for Mr. David George in Pembrokeshire in his early days and spent his latter years with Mr. Griff Jones, Rhydyrwen, Synod Inn (owner of the famous Queenie). It is thought that he never competed in the show ring; however he was also sire of Mr. J. H. Davies' well-known winning mare Teify Welsh Maid, Champion of the 1955 Royal Welsh Show amongst many other noteable winnings. Two sons of his which were to have a big effect on Cob breeding were Prince Valiant (foaled in 1955) and Nebo Valiant (foaled in 1956) both out of the exquisite Champion mare Queenie. Prince Valiant sired Brondesbury Welsh Maid and Nebo Valiant sired the good winning mare Valiant Queenie.

Valiant Queenie, sire Nebo Valiant, son of Valiant Flyer.

412

Royal Welsh Show 1955, Welsh Cob brood mare class. From the left: Teify Welsh Maid (champion) daughter of Valiant Flyer, Polly of Hercws, (almost hidden) Teify Morina, Wyre Star and Gwlith y Mynydd.

7. Dyffryn Rosina

Registration number 9094 in the *Welsh Stud Book, Vol. XXXII*
Chesnut, narrow blaze, two white hind fetlocks, height: 13 hands 2 in, foaled 1938
Breeder: Joseph Lewis, Peithyll, Bow Street, Cardiganshire

Dyffryn Rosina was foaled in 1938 when her breeder, Mr. Joseph Lewis lived at Blaendyffryn, Llandysul and this was the year when her dam, Myrtle Rosina (in the ownership of Mr. Lewis) won the Championship at the Cardiff Royal Agricultural Show of England (no Royal Welsh Show that year, but a combined event).

Re-emerging after the war years, Dyffryn Rosina stood second to Mr. Griff Jones' noted Queenie at the 1947 Royal Welsh Show. Mr. Lewis had in the meantime moved to Peithyll Farm and his son, Mr. Freddie Lewis farmed at Piercefield just outside Aberystwyth. A photograph which I took at the 1947 Lampeter Show shows Dyffryn Rosina standing first (class 34) with Queenie second, Mr. D. T. Davies' Dulas Dol third and Messrs. Peter Davies and Son's Teify Pride II fourth.

Lampeter Show 1947. From the right: Mr. Freddie Lewis with Dyffryn Rosina, Mr. Griff Jones with Queenie, Mr. D. T. Davies with Dulas Doll and Mr. Peter Davies with Teify Pride II.

At the 1949 Royal Welsh Show, Dyffryn Rosina was again second to Queenie with Rosina's daughter Piercefield Lady Lilian, owned by Mr. Freddie Lewis standing third.

Piercefield Lady Lilian certainly later made her mark on the Welsh Pony (Cob type) breed during the ownership of the Dowager Viscountess Chetwynd when she bred such as Lyn Cwmcoed and Lili Cwmcoed. Lyn Cwmcoed, foaled in 1960, was a Premium stallion for fourteen years, top-rated sire for 1974, 1975, 1976, 1977 and 1978; winner of 32 Championships including a Fredericks Horse of the Year qualifier at the Royal Welsh Show; what a record!

Dyffryn Rosina and Piercefield Lady Lilian stood second and fourth again at the 1950 Royal Welsh Show (class won by Queenie) and for the next three or four years, numbers of this versatile breed throughout the United Kingdom had reduced to such critical totals that classification for them at the Royal Welsh Shows were abandoned.

During this period, Dyffryn Rosina and her daugher Piercefield Lady Lilian were both sold to Mr. W. J. Jones, Cellan, Lampeter and when numbers had recovered sufficiently by 1956 to allow classes for them at the Royal Welsh Show, Dyffryn Rosina emerged in the ownership of Mr. Jones to win the brood mare class from Llanarth Flying Saucer (*chapter 25.3*). As already written, Mr. Jones bred Gerynant Rosina from Dyffryn Rosina in 1955 and Pride of the Prairie from Piercefield Lady Lilian in 1954. Pride of the Prairie was later bought by Mr. Freddie Lewis for whom she won a second prize at the 1957 Royal Welsh Show, third in 1958, first in 1959, third in 1960, second in 1961 and first in 1962 and 1964.

Piercefield Lady Lilian meanwhile (late fifties) had been sold to the Dowager Viscountess Chetwynd in whose ownership she stood fifth at the 1963 Royal Welsh Show with her daughter Lili Cwmcoed (foaled in 1958) being third; Lili going on to win this class in 1966, 1968 and 1969 and beating her full-brother Lyn Cwmcoed for the Section Championship in 1968.

Champion Lili Cwmcoed. (Photograph courtesy of Les Myall.)

Champion Lyn Cwmcoed. (Photograph courtesy of Idris Aeron.)

8. Coed Coch Planed
Registration number 2154 in the *Welsh Stud Book,*
Vol. XXXVI
Light grey, height: 11 hands 1 in, foaled 1952
Breeder: Miss M. Brodrick, Coed Coch, Abergele
Sire: Coed Coch Madog 1981 (*chapter 10.1*)
Dam: 9507 Coed Coch Pelen by Tregoyd Starlight
1577 (*chapter 3.1*)

Coed Coch Planed at a very early age was obviously something quite special. He came out at the major shows in 1953 in the ownership of his breeder and caused quite a stir by his exceptional action and personality, winning first prizes at Shrewsbury, Three Counties, Bath and West and at the Royal Welsh Show. In 1954 he was just as spectacular and won just as many prizes, in fact, at the Royal Welsh Show with Mr. A. R. McNaught judging, after winning the two or three-year-old colt class he was proclaimed Male Champion for which he beat his illustrious sire Coed Coch Madog. By 1955, Planed had become the property of Lord Kenyon and this showing season was just as successful with my

Coed Coch Planed.

father judging at the Royal Welsh he again won a first prize in the colt class and was reserve to Madog for the Male Championship. After entering the adult stallion class, Planed did not quite make it to the top but he will always be remembered as one of the "characters" of the show ring, a truly magnificent animal with spectacular movement he was just lacking those inches when it came to top-class competition.

However what he lacked in stature, he made up for as a sire, particularly as a sire of beautiful mares.

A photograph taken in March 1979 and published in *Horse and Hound* showed that he had lost none of his sparkle despite his 27 years as a sire, he is still a great force with which to be reckoned.

9. Gredington Llinos
Registration number 1517 F.S.2 in the appendix to
Welsh Stud Book, Vol. XXXIX
Red roan, hind fetlocks white, height: 11 hands 3 in,
foaled 1955
Breeder: Lord Kenyon, Gredington, Whitchurch,
Salop.
Sire: Gaerstone Beacon 1856
Dam: Cui Pancake No. 1165 F.S.1 by Criban
Snowball 1746

Gredington Llinos was a very good sort of mare, typical and hardy with a typical "Gaerstone Beacon" head, short with great width between the eyes; she came to Ceulan for stud purposes in 1971, duly producing a colt foal by Revel Light. After producing Oswallt, Gredington Llinos was sold to Mrs. Greasley producing four "Rawthey" fillies during 1962–1965; from here she went to the Wharley Stud where she produced Wharley Caruso in 1968 (top stallion in Denmark for some years), Wharley Lancelot (colt) (1970), Wharley Twilight (colt) by Revel Light (1972), Wharley Cascade (filly) by Shawbury Cockade (1973), Wharley Eclipse (colt) by Revel Light (1974), Wharley Ladybird (filly) (1975) (first prize leading-rein pony British Show Pony Society Championships 1979) etc. Her dam, Cui Pancake remained at Gredington for some years producing some good daughters, Gredington Manod (1956), Gredington Ophelia (1958) and Gredington Rhuddos (later good producer for Polaris Stud) (1960). Cui Pancake was exported to Denmark in 1961 and I saw her in 1965 with the Brothers Michaelsen at Hedensted; a great moving mare despite then being twenty years old.

Gredington Llinos. (Photograph courtesy of Mrs. B. M. Howe.)

10. Caradog Llwyd
Registration number 2069 in the *Welsh Stud Book, Vol. XXXV*
Dun, star, white hind fetlocks, height: 14 hands 3 in,
foaled 1949
Breeder: J. T. Williams, Penfeidr, Verwig,
Cardiganshire
Sire: Cardi Llwyd 1665 (*chapter 27.6*)
Dam: 9750 Verwig Fly by Llethi Valiant 1238
(*chapter 26.12*)

Caradog Llwyd was bought by Mr. John Evans, Dolgwyddau, Bethania, Llanon, Cardiganshire (who had owned his sire, Cardi Llwyd) and remained with John Evans for the rest of his life. Caradog Llwyd soon started earning his keep also as Premium stallion for Carmarthenshire in 1953, South Cardiganshire in 1954, North Cardiganshire in 1955 and every following year in various areas up until 1967. Caradog Llwyd also had many encounters in the show ring; his

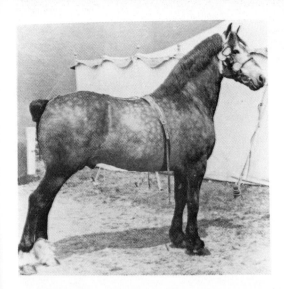

Caradog Llwyd.

owner possessing rather an explosive temperament, sometimes these encounters became somewhat heated! His best performances at Royal Welsh Shows were in 1953 where he stood third to Pentre Eiddwen Comet (*chapter 25.2*) and Llwynog-y-Garth and in 1955 when he won the stallion class only to be beaten for the Male Championship by the colt winner, Cefn Parc Boy (foaled in 1952, died December 1979). Caradog Llwyd was a typical Welsh Cob, tightly coupled and possessing an impressive head; he left behind some very good breeding daughters.

11. Menai Queen Bee
Registration number 11462 in the *Welsh Stud Book, Vol. XLI*
Grey, height: 13 hands 2 in, foaled 1937
Owner and Breeder: William Jones, Pantydefaid,
Llandysul, Cardiganshire
Sire: Welsh Rebound 1609 by Ceitho Welsh Comet
774 (*chapter 24.2*)
Dam: 11461 Menai Queen Bess by Bleddfa Shooting
Star 73 (*chapter 4.1*)
G-dam: 4546 Clettwr Polly (foaled in 1907) by Llew
Llwyd 162

As already written in the chapter on Bleddfa Shooting Star, he was not patronised as much as he should have been when hired by Dafydd Evans, Llwyncadfor. One exception was Mr. Timothy Evans of Pantmoel, Llandysul who bred Menai Queen Bess in 1914.

419

Menai Queen Bee (foaled in 1936).

Menai Ceredig, son of Menai Queen Bee.

Menai Queen Bee was the shepherding pony at Pantydefaid and carried Mr. William Jones' father (who weighed 18 stones) for many years. When Queen Bee was sixteen years old it was decided to breed out of her before it became too late and she was mated to Caradog Llwyd, producing Menai Ceridwen in 1953; then followed the influential Menai Ceredig in 1955, Llanarth Carel in 1959 and the Section "B" Menai Shooting Star in 1961, the last foal out of Queen Bee at the grand age of twenty-five years; she died the following year.

12. Llethi Valiant

Registration number 1238 in the *Welsh Stud Book, Vol. XXIII*
Black, height: 14 hands, foaled 1921
Breeder: John Richards, Cnwcapedward, Llanarth, Cardiganshire
Sire: Ceitho Welsh Comet 774 (*chapter 24.2*)
Dam: 7861 Llethi Flower by High Stepping Gambler II (*chapter 23.4*)
G-dam: Fan by Pregethwr (Cardigan Briton)
G-g-dam: Polly by Welsh Flyer (*chapter 20.4*)

Llethi Valiant paid many visits to the Royal Welsh Shows in his younger days: winning a second prize in 1924, fourth in 1925, second in 1926, first in 1928, fifth in 1929, and a second on his last visit in 1931. The winner usually in that era was Mr. Meyrick Jones' Mathrafal Eiddwen and we have already seen (*chapter 25.8*) why Mr. Edgar Herbert was thought to prefer Llethi Valiant in 1928. In 1931 however, it was Mr. Tom Jones Evans' Craven Cymro who beat him in the stallion class but not being a resident within the Principality, was not allowed to compete for the George, Prince of Wales Cup and therefore the name of Llethi Valiant joins the other great names, engraved on this magnificent trophy; unfortunately by default rather than when Llethi Valiant himself shook off his opposition.

In 1929 when Llethi Valiant stood only fifth under Mr. J. R. Bache, his dam, Llethi Flower was also present competing in the brood mare class; however, she did not find favour either, standing fifth in a class won by Mr. Thomas Rees' Flora Temple. Llethi Valiant certainly left his mark at stud, perpetuating the valuable blood of Ceitho Welsh Comet.

The working Cob mare which we had at Talybont through the war was 8917 Ceulan Chessie, a daughter of Llethi Valiant she was bred by

Stud card of Llethi Valiant for 1926. (Stud card courtesy of Messrs. Rowlands Harris.)

Evan Jones, Llawrcwrt, Talgarreg out of a daughter of Trotting Jack 528; a very honest mare with kind temperament.

13. Deinol Bloss
Registration number 8002 in the *Welsh Stud Book, Vol. XXIV*
Bay, star, near fore and both hinds white, height: 12 hands 2½ in, foaled 1923
Breeder: David Morris, Deinol, Glynarthen, Henllan, Cardiganshire
Sire: Myrtle Welsh Flyer 1020 (*chapter 29.8*)
Dam: 8302 Bloss By Garabaldi Comet II 711
G-dam: 877 Blossom by Odwyn Comet
G-g-dam: Spot by Old Garabaldi Comet
G-g-g-dam: Hornet by Old Comet (*chapter 18.2*)

Deinol Bloss was surprisingly small when one considers her breeding.

422

The dam was a bay mare with black points standing 14 hands 2 in by the very big Garabaldi Comet II (standing over 16 hands); the grand-dam Blossom was by Odwyn Comet (another stallion noted for his height of over 16 hands); the grand-dam Spot was a dark bay mare of 15 hands 2 in by the Old Garabaldi Comet, a brown stallion of 15 hands 3 in.

This old Garabaldi strain was best known for its height; a strain which has percolated through to present-day Cobs through the Madeni families, some of which still grow to around the 16 hands mark.

15. Myrtle Rosina
Registration number 8584 in the *Welsh Stud Book,*
Vol. XXVI
Red roan, height: 12 hands 3 in, foaled 1925
Breeder: Thomas Davies, Cilwen Farm,
Newcastle Emlyn
Owner at time of registration: Mr. Tom James,
Myrtle Hill, Llechryd, Cardiganshire
Sire: Baedeker 500
Dam: 6664 Cilwen Lady Lilian by Trotting Jack 528
(*chapter 27.14*)
G-dam: 2316 Myrtle Lady Trustful by Trustful *138*
Welsh Stud Book, 2741 Hackney Stud Book

Cilwen Lady Lilian (foaled in 1917) can be regarded as the foundation stone of this wonderful family of Welsh Ponies of Cob type. Her dam Myrtle Lady Trustful (foaled in 1902) was sold by Mr. Tom James, Myrtle Hill to Thomas Davies of Cilwen; the sire of Lady Trustful being one of Tom James' first stallions, the noted roan Hackney stallion Trustful, bred by J. Reeve of Wisbech, a stallion who was the originator of many generations of roans in South Cardiganshire.

Cilwen Lady Lilian made her debut at the 1923 Royal Welsh Show, where with Tom James judging, she duly won her class from Maj. Dugdale's Llwyn Coralie and Mr. Lyell's Ness Sunflower (*chapter 7.10*) (what this famous little Mountain Pony mare was doing amongst the Cob type-ponies, one cannot imagine). Lady Lilian met stronger opposition at mid-Wales local Shows that year than she did at the "Royal Welsh", however her flag was not to be lowered and she won in all a first and Welsh Pony & Cob Society medal Tivyside, first Cardigan, two firsts at Crymmych, Llandysul, Pencader, Lampeter

Cilwen Lady Lilian, dam of Myrtle Rosina.

and Llanllwni and a silver cup at Talgarreg, quite an impressive collection!

At the 1926 Royal Welsh Show, Tom James won the stallion class with Baedeker, sire of Myrtle Rosina. Baedeker was a 12 hands 2 in bay Hackney pony stallion bred by Miss Eurgain Lort of the Castellmai Stud, his sire being the well-known Traveller's Joy (foaled in 1906) by the famous Hackney pony Sir Horace 5402 *Hackney Stud Book* out of Biddy Brown by Sir George 778 *Hackney Stud Book*; the dam of Baedeker being Cassy Brown II out of Cassy Brown I by the great Casius 2397 *Hackney Stud Book* (John Jones, Whitegate Stud, Wrexham).

Second to Baedeker at the 1926 Royal Welsh Show was Cream Bun, the dun stallion which my mother used to drive before she was married and he was a brother to Seren Ceulan (*chapter 24.3*) with which my father won the brood mare class that year.

Cilwen Lady Lilian did not appear at the Royal Welsh Show after 1923 until 1927 when she had become the property of John Jones and Son of Dinarth Hall and won a third prize in 1927 and fourth in 1928 (class won by Seren Ceulan).

At the 1929 Royal Welsh Show, Lady Lilian was absent, Seren Ceulan had died and Tom James won the class with Lilian's daughter Myrtle Rosina who had previously won the filly class at the 1927 Show, and was second in the filly class at the 1928 Show.

Myrtle Rosina. (Photograph courtesy of G. H. Parsons.)

Lady Lilian re-appeared for John Jones and Son at the 1930 Show and wrested the winning rosette from her daughter; Lilian also being awarded the Section Championship.

Mr. Thomas John Jones of Dinarth was the judge at the 1931 Show so Lady Lilian had a rest; my father won the Section Championship with Ceulan Comet (*chapter 24.1*), Mr. Jones having the courage of his convictions buying him on the spot!

The formidable Dinarth Hall string had a field day at the 1932 Royal Welsh Show winning the Championship with Ceulan Comet and the Reserve Championship with Lady Lilian.

Myrtle Rosina (second to her dam) had been bought by my father's great friend Mr. Tom Wood-Jones (who later owned the world-famous Hackney ponies Bossy and Broompark Sir John). Dr. Richards Phillips writing in *Ar Gefn Ei Geffyl* gives some very interesting facts about the well-known stallion owners of the nineteenth and twentieth centuries. Of Tom James (1857–1942) he writes that: "He was brought up as one of two brothers on a fairly prosperous farm but being the second son, left to work as a coal miner at Ferndale but soon returned to travel the stallion Ceffyl Y Pregethwr (Cardigan Briton) (*chapter 1*). When he settled at Myrtle Hill he had many well-known stallions which provided him with a comfortable living until he spent too much money on drink!"

Cilwen Lady Lilian was again first and Champion for Dinarth Hall at

Dinarth Hall Show string 1933. From the left: Ceulan Comet, Dinarth Comet and Cilwen Lady Lilian.

the 1933 Royal Welsh Show with her daughter Myrtle Rosina (still in the ownership of Mr. Wood Jones though she was quoted as "for sale") standing second. Indeed this class was a family affair throughout since, of the five mares present, first and second were mother and daughter, third was Dewi Pride whose dam Teifi Pride was fourth and another daughter of Teifi Pride named Meurig Pride was fifth! Lady Lilian was again first (Reserve Champion to Ceulan Comet) at the 1934 Royal Welsh Show and, at the age of seventeen took to retirement. Myrtle Rosina was third for Mr. Wood Jones at the 1935 Royal Welsh Show then re-appeared in the ownership of Mr. Joseph Lewis at the 1938 Show where she was Champion, her daughter Dyffryn Moonlight (bred by Mr. Wood Jones in 1934 by Bowdler Brightlight) being third. At the last pre-war Show with Mr. Matthew Williams judging Myrtle Rosina was Champion female with Dyffryn Moonlight second.

By the time the war was over, Myrtle Rosina's showing days were over, Mr. Joseph Lewis and son Freddie Lewis then having her other daughter Dyffryn Rosina (No. 7) to show.

426

27
Cardi Llwyd foaled 1931
Llanarth Braint foaled 1948

1	2	4	8
Llanarth Braint 1854	Llanarth Goldcrest 1793	Pistyll Gold Flake 1723	Paith Flyer II 1538
			9 8656 Pistyll Nance
		5 9184 Pistill Sunset	**10** Gwalia Victor 1431
			9 9656 Pistyll Nance
	3 9643 Llanarth Kilda	**6** Cardi Llwyd 1665	**12** Ceitho Welsh Flyer 1080
			13 8935 Gwyryfon Nancy
		7 Poll	**14** Camddwr Trotter 1185
			15 Gipsy

428

1. Llanarth Braint

Registration number 1854 in the *Welsh Stud Book,*
Vol. XXXIII
Palomino (later turned chesnut), height: 14 hands
2 in, foaled 1948
Owners and Breeders: The Misses Taylor and
Saunders Davies, Llanarth Stud, Cardiganshire

When Llanarth Braint arrived on the Welsh Cob scene in 1948 (as the result of an un-planned mating with a two-year-old colt) he was not immediately accepted with any enthusiasm amongst the Cardiganshire breeders of that period. The reigning stallions in mid-Wales at that time were such as Brenin Gwalia, Meiarth Royal Eiddwen, Cardi Llwyd, Churchill and Brenin Cardi, all of the tightly moulded ilk with high, harness-type action. Llanarth Braint, although bred from similar stock on his dam's side, was descended from the more rangy "Breconshire"-type Cob on his sire's side and he inherited the forceful long-striding movement associated with these families. Also his palomino colour did not help as far as being accepted with the die-hard breeders was concerned, the majority of the Cobs were bays, browns or blacks with an occasional chesnut or roan; there had been very few palomino Welsh

Llanarth Braint.

Llanarth Braint in harness (driven by Miss Saunders-Davies) showing his enormous extension.

Cobs since the time of Cymro Llwyd (*chapter 18.6*) one hundred years previously.

It was in fact eight years later before Llanarth Braint entered the Royal Welsh Show fray; there was a desperate shortage of Cob stallions in those days, only two competing at the 1956 Royal Welsh Agricultural Society Show where Braint stood second to Pentre Eiddwen Comet (*chapter 25.2*), and for the next three years, Braint was placed third behind Pentre Eiddwen Comet and Llwynog Y Garth.

However, whilst the Welsh Cobs very rarely competed outside Wales, the Llanarth ladies sportingly travelled Braint much further afield, thus advertising the breed to far and wide and at the 1958 Ponies of Britain Show at Harrogate, Braint not only won the Championship for Welsh Cobs but won a first prize under saddle, another first in harness and ended up by being proclaimed Supreme Champion of the whole show! Perhaps what was equally important was the fact that, in the Welsh Cob class, the next five to him were all his progeny!

After four successive third prizes at the Royal Welsh Shows (1957, 1958, 1959, 1960), Llanarth Braint stood at the top of the ten-strong stallion class judged by Mr. Dafydd Edwardes in 1961 and he also stood reserve to Parc Lady (*chapter 28.7*) for the George, Prince of Wales Cup.

By this time, the situation on the Welsh Cob scene had improved considerably and competition was fierce as in pre-war shows.

From 1961 onwards, Llanarth Braint's luck at Wales' premier show varied considerably, his best two later achievements being in 1964 and 1967 when, on both occasions, he stood second to his sons: in 1964 to Llanarth Brummel and in 1967 to the Frederick's Champion, Honyton Michael ap Braint.

Llanarth Braint's "moment of glory" was without doubt at the 1969 Royal Agricultural Society of England Show where, at nineteen years of age, he put up the show of his life with Len Bigley (who had just joined the stud) to stand Champion Welsh Cob followed by various of his descendants of all ages and sexes.

So much for Llanarth Braint's show ring career. Future generations of Welsh Cob fanciers will probably remember him more for his influence on the Welsh Cob breed; indeed were it not for the presence of Llanarth Braint at the Llanarth Stud in 1961 when Miss Saunders Davies decided to return to the Academy of Music, Miss Taylor would have almost certainly given up her Welsh Cob interests and the University of Wales and indeed, all Wales, would have been so much the poorer.

In the days when Welsh Cob Premium stallions travelled various areas Llanarth Braint was awarded premiums for Pembrokeshire in 1955, for Carmarthen in 1957, 1958 and 1959 and South Cardiganshire in 1960 and 1961. After this date, the stallions were awarded premiums to stand at home and Llanarth Braint was awarded premiums in 1962, 1963, 1964, 1965 and 1966. Thus Llanarth Braint has left an indelible mark on the Welsh Cob breed over a very large area and over very many years. What says much for the kind temperament of Llanarth Braint is the fact that during these years of travelling, he was always led by a groom riding a mare, Llanarth Firelight, daughter of the original mare, Llanarth Firefly.

Equally as important, perhaps more so, was the influence which Llanarth Braint had on the Llanarth Stud. One daughter, Llanarth Flying Saucer (*chapter 25.3*) produced one champion after another. Without doubt, his most successful mating was with Rhosfarch Morwena who had already produced Rhosfarch Frenin and Rhosfarch Gwalia before she was purchased by the Llanarth Stud. After going to Llanarth this lovely matron produced eleven foals by Braint (as well as others e.g. Llanarth Morgan by Cymro Lan).

The produce of the mating of Rhosfarch Merwena to Llanarth Braint are:

1964 Llanarth Morwena, filly, a well-known winner in the North and exceptionally successful producer for the Scole Stud.

1966 Llanarth Medwyn ap Braint, colt, producing nice stock for Mr. Hughes at Hay-on-Wye.

1967 Llanarth Marc ap Braint, colt, originally exported to Holland, he was later sold on to France and I placed him first in a very strong stallion class at Poitiers in September 1978.

1968 Llanarth Morfydd, filly, one of the most valuable of the young mares at Llanarth producing Mabon (1972), Mydrian (1973), Myfanwy (1975) etc.

1969 Llanarth Meredith ap Braint, colt, this outstanding stallion needs no introduction, youngstock Champion at the Royal Welsh Show he has been Champion at the Royal Agricultural Society of England, Ponies of Britain, Lloyds Bank qualifier etc but more important he is siring exceptional stock throughout the United Kingdom e.g. Rhystyd Fashion Reserve Female Champion at the 1978 Royal Welsh Show and Rhystyd Meredith Male Champion at the 1979 Royal Welsh Show. Llanarth Meredith ap Braint qualified for the 1979 Lloyds Bank Championship of the Horse of the Year Show at the Bath and West Show; he also topped the 1979 Welsh Pony & Cob Society Welsh Cob sire ratings.

1970 Llanarth Math ap Braint, colt, a striking dun stallion owned

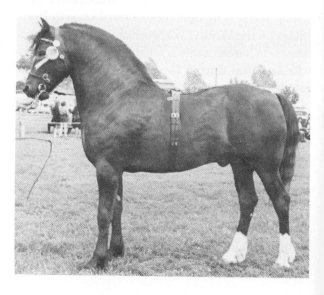

Llanarth Meredith ap Braint, Lloyds Bank qualifier 1979, son of Llanarth Braint. (Photograph courtesy of Monty.)

Rhystyd Meredith, Champion Welsh Cob Stallion, Royal Welsh Show 1979. Sire: Llanarth Meredith ap Braint.

originally by Mr. and Mrs. Haak of the Uplands Stud, he is now a very well-known dressage animal in Ottawa.

1971 Llanarth Martyn ap Braint, colt, a chesnut stallion doing good work for the Welsh Cob breed in Sweden.

1972 Llanarth Mari, filly, chesnut, the first Welsh Cob foal to be sold at auction for 1,000 guineas, she was purchased by Mr. D. W. Betts of Nottingham.

1973 Llanarth Miranda, filly, still at Llanarth.

1974 Llanarth Maldwyn ap Braint, colt, he was flown to Mr. Thomas Davies' Brynarian Stud in British Columbia on 8th January 1975 (photograph in 1976 Welsh Pony & Cob Society Journal, *page 143*). He is the most like Meredith of all of them and stands at 16 hands. There are so few Welsh Cobs in Canada, and Maldwyn is a magnificent ambassador for the breed.

1975 Llanarth Mair, filly, still at Llanarth.

The extended movement of Llanarth Braint was something not often experienced amongst Welsh Cobs and Llanarth Stud developed this attribute to great advantage both under saddle and in harness. It seems

433

Llanarth Braint. The bronze by Lorne McKean.

Llanarth Goldcrest.

that some strains of Welsh Cobs naturally possess the extension of movement that has to be instilled into other breeds for dressage purposes and Llanarth Braint progeny have proved eminently suited for this purpose, both in the United Kingdom and overseas.

Thus it was that on 20th May 1978 a very large number of well-wishers attended the thirtieth birthday party of Llanarth Braint and he died on 6th January 1979.

In the words of the Welsh hymn-writer, John Roberts of Caergybi: "Braint, Braint yw cael cymdeithas gyda'r saint". "Braint" is Welsh for "honour" or "privilege" and Miss Taylor considers it a great privilege to have spent 30 years of her life in the company of this wonderful progenitor.

2. Llanarth Goldcrest

Registration number 1793 in the *Welsh Stud Book,*
Vol. XXXII
Bright chestnut, off hind white coronet,
height: 15 hands,
foaled 1945
Breeder: Gwilym Morris, Pistill,
Llanfihangel
Talyllyn, Brecon.
Owners: The Misses Taylor and Saunders Davies,
Llanarth.

The Misses Taylor and Saunders Davies had already bought from Mr. Gwilym Morris Llanarth Dragon Fly (foaled 1941), three-quarter sister to Llanarth Goldcrest, having the same dam (Pistyll Sunset) and sired by Paith Flyer II (g-sire of Llanarth Goldcrest). The mating of Llanarth Goldcrest to Llanarth Kilda in 1947 was un-planned since he was only two-years-old at the time. However the result looked so promising (Llanarth Braint) that Goldcrest was retained at the stud producing Llanarth Firelight in 1950 and the well-known harness mare (in the ownership of Mrs. Gulbenkian) Llanarth Mirabel in 1953.

It was at a Royal Welsh Show where the Misses Taylor and Saunders Davies had both Goldcrest and Braint (and could keep only one stallion) that the advice of that eminent judge Mr. E. G. E. Griffith was sought as to which one of the two should be retained. Mr. Griffith pointed to Braint saying: "Goldcrest has served his purpose". Soon afterwards Goldcrest was gelded and being a superb riding animal was soon sold.

435

3. Llanarth Kilda
Registration number 9643 in the *Welsh Stud Book,*
Vol. XXXIII
Bay, near hind fetlock white, height: 13 hands 2 in,
foaled 1944
Breeder: John Evans, Dolgwyddau, Bethania,
Llanon, Cardiganshire
Owners: The Misses Taylor and Saunders Davies,
Llanarth, Cardiganshire

The purchase of Llanarth Kilda was a wise political move on the part of the Misses Taylor and Saunders Davies since the stallion owners of that time were always at war with one another and having used the services of one stallion, a breeder had to support the progeny of other stallions if one wanted to keep the peace!

It was not known that Kilda had been served by Llanarth Goldcrest in 1947 (it still is not known whether he jumped a fence to her or vice-versa) and she was offered for sale at Llanybyther Market with a reserve price of 30 guineas. In the sale ring, the top bid for her was 26 guineas, but outside the ring Miss Taylor was finally offered 29 guineas, but she was adamant that it had to be 30 guineas or Kilda would return home. Well, return home she did as if by some mysterious instinct Miss Taylor knew she should. Next year Kilda duly produced Llanarth Braint who was her only offspring at Llanarth since she was sold in 1949.

4. Pistyll Goldflake
Registration number 1723 in the *Welsh Stud Book,*
Vol. XXXII
Chesnut, blaze, height: 15 hands, foaled 1941
Owner and Breeder: Gwilym M. Morris, Pistyll,
Llanfihangel Talyllyn, Brecon

Pistyll Goldflake was one of a very well-known family of big, "coach-horse"-type Breconshire Welsh Cobs tracing back all the way in the same stud to Manest Express, standing 15 hands 1½ ins high registered in *Vol. I Welsh Stud Book.*

Pistyll Goldflake was a very influential stallion in the Breconshire area having been awarded premiums to travel the area every year from 1947 to 1954 (inclusive) with the exception of 1949 when the Breconshire premium was awarded to Brenin Cardi. I remember calling in at

Pistyll Goldflake.

Pistyll and, coming from Cardiganshire, being amazed to see such a "rangy" Welsh Cob.

The last time I saw him was at the 1953 Royal Welsh Show (Cardiff) where, with Mr. A. L. Williams judging, he stood fifth behind Pentre Eiddwen Comet (*chapter 25.2*), Llwynog-Y-Garth (*chapter 28*), Caradog Llwyd (*chapter 26.10*) and Mathrafal (*chapter 28.4*) and was followed by Pannau Prince, Llanarth Braint, Meiarth Royal Eiddwen (*chapter 29*) and Talley Black Prince.

In January 1955 Pistyll Goldflake was sold to Bernardo Duggan of Beunos Aires; the Argentinian Government often importing a large Welsh Cob stallion to produce "gaucho" ponies.

5. Pistyll Sunset
Registration number 9184 in the *Welsh Stud Book,*
Vol. XXXII
Bay, height: 14 hands, foaled 1932
Owner & Breeder: Gwilym Morris, Pistill,
Llanfihangel Talyllyn, Brecon

In addition to Llanarth Goldcrest (foaled in 1945), this mare produced Llanarth Dragonfly in 1941 and two other full-sisters to Goldcrest: Pistyll Gold Lass in 1950 and Pistyll Sunshine in 1948. Pistyll Gold Lass was fourth at the 1951 Royal Welsh Show in the yearling class and Sunshine third in the two or three-year-old class.

437

6. Cardi Llwyd

Registration number 1665 in the *Welsh Stud Book,*
Vol. XXXII
Dark dun, height: 14 hands 3¾ in, foaled 1931
Breeders: Parry Bros, Llwynfynwent, Llangwyryfon,
Cardiganshire
Owner: John Evans, Dolgwyddau, Bethania,
Llanon, Cardiganshire

Cardi Llwyd and his owner, John Evans lived together crofter fashion on the edge of a rough moorland, listening to one another's movements all day long and thinking of nothing else. One can well imagine, therefore, the fierce battles which raged in some immediate post-war show rings in mid-Wales when this stallion faced stallions owned by similarly devoted stallion men, each one idolising his own stallion as if it were part and parcel of the owner himself. The 1941 Stud card for Cardi Llwyd quoting him as Premium stallion for Brecon and Radnor for that year (a statement not upheld by the annual records in the Stud Books!) is reproduced here.

Cardi Llwyd was the Premium stallion for South Cardiganshire in 1948 and 1950. His best known son was the compact Caradog Llwyd

Cardi Llwyd.

438

Stud card of Cardi Llwyd for 1941. (Stud card courtesy of Messrs. Rowlands Harris.)

(foaled in 1949) winner of premiums from 1954 to 1966, he was placed third at the 1953 Royal Welsh Show to Pentre Eiddwen Comet and Llwynog Y Garth and won the class in 1955 only to be beaten for the Male Championship by the colt winner Cefn Parc Boy.

7. Poll

Registration number 429 F.S.2 in the Appendix to
the *Welsh Stud Book, Vol. XXXIII*
Liver chesnut, near hind white sock, height: 13
hands 1 in, foaled 1928
Owner: John Ll. Jones, Rhosymaen, Bethania,
Cardiganshire
Breeder: Rhys Benjamin, Tanquarrel, Pont
Newydd, Llanilar, Cardiganshire

8. Paith Flyer II

Registration number 1538 in the *Welsh Stud Book,*
Vol. XXX
Dark Chesnut, near fore and near hind white, height:
15 hands, foaled 1927
Owner and Breeder: James Scott, Penglanowen,
Rhydyfelin, Aberystwyth
Sire: Vyrnwy Flyer 923 by King Flyer 35 (*chapter 25*)
Dam: 7264 Paith Trilby by Danish Applause
(*Hackney Stud Book*)

Paith Flyer II was of a bigger, more "rangy" type than that favoured in his native Cardiganshire, therefore it is not surprising that he found most favour in Breconshire or in Radnorshire where he was awarded premiums in 1938 and 1939. Possibly this attribute came from his dam's side, Paith Trilby (foaled in 1913) she being by the stylish Hackney, Danish Applause. My father knew Paith Trilby well; he often remarked how lively and active she looked after a hard day's work pulling a milk cart (Mr. Scott had a milk round in Aberystwyth); he wrote about her: "A great old mare, a treat to see her even after working all day and even when she was getting on in years."

Paith Flyer's sire, Vyrnwy Flyer was bred by David Jones, near Welshpool in 1914; he was a bay horse, standing 15 hands, by King Flyer out of Bess of Neuadd by Welsh Flyer III and g-dam Comet by Eiddwen Flyer. David Jones sold Vyrnwy Flyer to Davies, Hen Shop, Llanegryn, Towyn for whom my mother's Uncle Dick, Bryngryffty rode

.:: Season 1926. ::.

THE NOTED WELSH COB STALLION

"Vyrnwy Flyer"

Foaled 1914.   Height, 14-3 hands.

No. 923 Welsh Stud Book, Vol. XVII.

Sire.—King Flyer No. 35, Vol. 1, by Young Welsh Flyer, and Young Welsh Flyer's dam was the noted bay mare, Bess, by Young Trotting Comet (Comet Bach) by Old Comet, the original of Cardiganshire.

The dam of Vyrnwy Flyer, Bess of Neuadd, by Welsh Flyer III., No. 4324 Welsh Stud Book, Vol. XII., and his g.-dam by Eiddwen Flyer, No. 421, Welsh Stud Book.

Every possible care and attention will be given to mares, but no responsibility can be accepted in any way whatever. All mares served once will be charged for. Every attention being given to the mares to ensure as far as possible their being in foal. **All Committee selected Mares charged according to rules.** Other mares as follows :—

Landlords, £2 2s.; **Tenant Farmers,** 30/-.
Groom's Fee, 5/-, to be paid first time of serving.
All accounts to be paid in full on or before last visit.

Owners of mares are respectfully asked to endeavour to send same at the appointed time, so as to keep all appointments punctually.

No Business done on Sundays.

Route :
Farmers' Arms, Aberystwyth, **Every Monday** ; Llanilar, 5-30 p.m.; at Lledrod for the night. **Tuesday.**—Tregaron, Dolfawr for the night. **Wednesday.**—Swyddffynon, 10 a.m.;   Pont Llanafan, 12 noon ;   Lodge Farm, 2 p.m. ; Llanfihangel, 4 p.m. **Thursday.**—Capel Seion 10 a.m.; Maesbangor, 2 p.m.; Peithyll for the night. **Friday.**—Talybont, 10 a.m.;   Borth, 1 p.m., through Clarach to Bow Street, 5 p.m.; Llanbadarn, 7 p.m., home for the night. **Saturday.**—Glanrhos, 10 a.m.; Llanrhystyd, 12 till 1 ; Llangwyryfon, 3·p.m.;   home for week-end .

Headquarters.—Farmers' Arms.

Any further particulars apply to Owner—
E. HUGHES, Cefncoch Stud Farm,
Rhydyfelin, near Aberystwyth.

441

him to win many trotting races. Vyrnwy Flyer was then sold at a Welsh Pony & Cob Society Sale at Lampeter in 1924 to Mr. Jim Hughes, Cefncoch, Rhydyfelin (father to John Hughes who owned Pentre Eiddwen Comet and brother-in-law to James Scott) who later had him gelded and sold to the United Dairies, where he spent many years working on the streets of London. Vyrnwy Flyer's best known daughter was Lady Wyre, dam of that very good mare, Wyre Star. Two of the families from Paith Flyer II for which my father had great admiration were his son Penarth Warrior (bred by our good friend Mr. Tom Powell in Radnorshire, who had so many good Mountain ponies too) and his daughter Ithon Polly bred by Mr. D. Powell of Newbridge on Wye. Penarth Warrior (foaled in 1940) mated to Ithon Polly (foaled in 1937) produced (in 1946) Ithon Kitty who was bought back by Mr. J. J. Hughes of Cefncoch (after producing some lovely mares for Mr. Suckley of Oswestry). A daughter of Ithon Kitty bred at Cefncoch is Cefncoch Lady Lynne, six of whose sons and daughters have been sold at Llanarth Sales (up to 1978) for quite considerable prices.

9. Pistyll Nance
Registration number 8656 in the *Welsh Stud Book*,
Vol. XXVII
Chesnut, height: 14 hands, foaled 1925
Owner and Breeder: Gwilym Morris, Pistill,
Llanfihangel Talyllyn, Brecon
Sire: Trotting Jack 528
Dam: Pistill Chess by Berwyn Fly 515
G-dam: Pistill Bess by Manest Express 36

The sire Trotting Jack (foaled in 1908) was a very popular stallion in mid-Wales. The dam and grand-dam were from a strain which had been kept by the Morris family of Pistill and their cousins, the Morrises of Manest Court since pre-Stud Book times.

Pistyll Nance won a first prize at Brecon Show in 1926; she repeated this feat also in 1927 and the same year stood fifth in the Cob youngstock class at the Royal Welsh Agricultural Society Show (Swansea) beaten by Brenin Cymru owned by my grand-father and bred by my father, by Mathrafal Brenin (*chapter 23.6*) out of Seren Ceulan (*chapter 24.3*).

The next time Pistyll Nance appeared at the Royal Welsh Show was in 1929 (Cardiff) where she stood fourth in the mare class to Blaenwaun Flora Temple, Pant Grey Star and Lan Carnation. The next time the Royal Welsh Show was staged in Cardiff (1938), Pistyll Nance re-

442

appeared to stand third to Teify of Hercws and Dewi Black Bess. Pistyll Nance produced both Pistyll Gold Flake and Pistyll Sunset, sire and dam respectively of Llanarth Goldcrest.

In her later years, Pistyll Nance was owned by Mr. Llewellyn Richards who competed with her in a ridden class at Islington. When a display of Cobs was held at Llanarth in the 'sixties, Mr. Richards gave a spanking display riding her g-g-son, Llanarth Braint!

10. Gwalia Victor (chapter 23.2)

12. Ceitho Welsh Flyer
Registration number 1080 in the Welsh Stud Book,
Vol. XX
Bay, white off hind pastern, height: 15 hands 1 in,
foaled 1917
Breeder: John Price, Boidie Farm, Lampeter, Cards.
Owner in 1921: Richard Morgan, Lleust-y-broga,
Llangeitho, Cardiganshire
Owner in 1933: William Howells, Bryntairllyn,
Penuwch, Tregaron

It can be seen from his stud card that Ceitho Welsh Flyer was a stallion of the top class; prize-winner from 1921 to 1932, winner of eleven premiums from 1921 to 1931 and whose pedigree contains the famous names of Cardigan Flyer, Briton Comet (Trefwtial) and Old Briton Comet (Tynfron).

13. Gwyryfon Nancy
Registration number 8935 in the Welsh Stud Book, Vol. XXXI
Bay, star, height: 14 hands 1 in, foaled 1922
Owner and Breeder: Evan Parry, Llwynfynwent,
Llangwyryfon, Cardiganshire
Sire: Welsh Model 620
Dam: 7141 Gwyryfon Betty

Welsh Model (foaled in 1910) was a very influential sire and was owned by Richard Morgan, Lleuest-y-broga who also owned Ceitho Welsh Comet (chapter 24.2) and Ceitho Welsh Flyer (chapter 24.14).

Gwyryfon Betty (foaled in 1915) was sired by an unregistered stallion with the strange name of King Betty out of Polly, a 13 hand 2 in cream mare by Satisfaction (chapter 24.14).

Stud card of Welsh Model for 1919. (Stud card courtesy of Messrs. Rowlands Harris.)

444

SEASON 1933.

Important to all who wish to breed Welsh Cobs and Ponies from the best strain of Welsh blood.

THAT REMARKABLE HIGH STEPPING COB

Ceitho Welsh Flyer

Reg. in Vol. 20 W.P. & C.S. No. 1080, Section D.

Mares will be served at a fee of £1, and a Groom's fee of 2/6 each mare.

The Groom's fee to be paid at the first time of service, and the remainder on or before the 20th day of June next.

Owner—Mr. William Howells, Bryntairllyn, Penuwch, near Tregaron.

Breeder—Mr. John Price, Boidie Farm, Lampeter.

Ceitho Welsh Flyer is a rich Dark Bay Cob, coming 16 years old, stands 15-1 h.h. Strength of bone and constitution are here combined with the elasticity and fascination of speed and action.

Ceitho Welsh Flyer's dam, Peggy, is a typical Welsh Cob Mare, won first prize as sucker, first as yearling, second as two-year-old, two firsts as brood mare, secured free service by the Board's Premium Cob every time applied and her stock have secured several first prizes and have commanded high prizes.

g dam Teify won 11 first prizes.

g g dam Jolly won 12 first prizes.

Lovely Boy's dam, by Young Comet, the Treprior Horse. Lovely Boy won first prizes at Newcastle-Emlyn, Llanon, Aberayron, Llwyn-rhydowen, Cardigan and Aberystwyth.

From the above pedigree one will at a glance see that Ceitho Welsh Flyer is descended from a well-known strain of excellent cobs.

He who is wise will excercise his wisdom profitable by securing the services of this splendid cob.

Premium Horse—Carmarthen, 1921; Gower, 1922: Pembroke, 1923-24; Mid-Carmarthen, 1925; Pembroke, 1926; Mid-Glamorgan, 1927; Pembroke, 1928-29; Carmarthen 1930-31.

445

Welsh Model.

Trotting Jack, foaled in 1908, sire of Camddwr Trotter.

NORTH CARDIGANSHIRE PREMIUM HORSE.

THE TYPICAL WELSH COB STALLION.

To Serve this Season a limited number of Mares at £2 2s. each Mare and 2s. 6d. the Groom.

TROTTING JACK,

528 W.S.B.,

THE PROPERTY OF

Mr. W. DAVIES, Pistyllgwyn, Llanddewi Brefi.

TROTTING JACK. 528, is of Chestnut colour, stands 14-2 hands high, rising 10 years old. He is without doubt one of the most promising young Stallions of the present day. He is a brilliant all round mover, and combines high and level action, and is probably going to make the fastest Cob Stallion that has travelled the district for years.

TROTTING JACK, 528, is winner of First Prizes in Tregaron and Llandyssul and 2nd in Lampeter in 1913. 1st in Tregaron, 1914, 1st prize at Llandyssul, 1914, 2nd prize and Reserve Silver Medal at the Royal Show, Shrewsbury, 1914, and 1st prize and Silver Medal at the Welsh National, Newport, 1914, 1st prize at Llandyssul, 1916.

A Cob by Trotting Jack won the 20 Guinea Cup for the best typical Welsh Cob at Tregaron Horse Show in 1916, so by this it can be seen that his stock are very promising.

Sire, King Jack II , 20 W.S.B., by Young Rainbow, a winner of 23 First Prizes.

Dam, Welsh Flower, 3680, W.S.B, by Cardigan Flyer, 699, W.S.B. Great Dam by Welsh Jack by Cymro Llwyd.

447

14. Camddwr Trotter

Registration number 1185 in the *Welsh Stud Book,*
Vol. XXII

Dark chesnut, height: 13 hands 2 in, foaled 1917
Owner and Breeder: John Williams, Tanquarrel,
Bronant, Aberystwyth
Sire: Trotting Jack 528
Dam: Madam Llwyd (dun) by Cymro Bach (dun)
by Cymro Llwyd (*chapter 18.6*)

15. Gipsy

Registration number 428 F.S.1 in the Appendix of
the *Welsh Stud Book, Vol. XXXIII*
Bay, off hind sock white, height: 14 hands,
foaled 1924
Owner: J. Scott, Aberbrwynen, Llanfarian,
Aberystwyth
Breeder: Rhys Benjamin, Tanquarrel, Pont
Newydd, Llanilar, Cardiganshire
Sire: Eiddwen Gleam 1070
Dam: Black No. 427 F.S. by Cardigan Briton II 611

Eiddwen Gleam, foaled in 1916, was a chesnut with a blaze and white hind legs of height about 14 hands. He was bred by Mrs. Jones Brynmiherin, Ystrad Meurig and owned by Mr. H. S. Williams, Garnuchaf, Bethania, Llanon. He derived his name from his grand-dam Lady Eiddwen who was by Eiddwen Flyer II (*chapter 21.2*).

28

Mathrafal (foaled in 1936)
Cahn Dafydd (foaled in 1942)
Parc Lady (foaled in 1948)
Parc Rachel (foaled in 1966)

2 Cahn Dafydd 1758	**4** Mathrafal 1629	**8** Mab Y Brenin 1555
		9 9040 Poll of Golfa
	5 9150 Gwenogwen	**10** Ceitho Welsh Flyer 1080
		11 7811 Pantlleinan Blodwen
3 13533 Parc Pride	**6** Pentre Eiddwen Comet 1796	**12** Eiddwen's Image 1703
		13 Dewi Black Bess
	7 9977 Parc Lady	**14** Mathrafal 1629
		15 9536 Parc Welsh Maid

1

19935 Parc
Rachel

1. Parc Rachel

Registration number 19935 in the *Welsh Stud Book,*
Vol. XLIX
Bay, star, near hind fetlock white, height: 14 hands
2 in, foaled 1966
Breeder: S. D. Morgan, Pen Parc, Lampeter,
Cardiganshire

Parc Rachel was introduced to the show ring very early in life; she was the foal at foot of Parc Pride at the 1966 Royal Welsh Show when Pride stood second to Derwen Rosina in a ten-strong class containing many of the most famous names of the day and Rachel went on to win an equally strong foal class; she could have had no better introduction to the show ring. Rachel's full-brother Parc Dafydd (foaled in 1964) (later stud stallion at Twyford) also met with success that day standing second in a very strong class of two and three-year-old colts to Brenin Dafydd who was later to become Champion of the 1970 Royal Welsh Show.

The year 1966 was only the start to Parc Rachel's brilliant Royal Welsh Show career; in 1967 she won a very large yearling filly class and

Parc Rachel. (Photograph courtesy of Idris Aeron.)

451

stood Reserve Female Champion, an achievement which she repeated in 1968, then in 1969 she went one stage better, after winning the two or three-year-old class she beat the winning mare Tyhen Mattie to be proclaimed Female Welsh Cob Champion and Reserve Supreme Champion to the winning stallion Tyhen Comet. I know of no other case where the same Welsh Cob, male or female has won four successive youngstock classes at the premier show within the Principality of Wales; no wonder that she had greater achievements in store!

In 1970 to give the Parc Cobs a rest, Mr. Sam Morgan judged at the Royal Welsh Show; however in 1971 and 1972 Parc Rachel re-appeared to win the George, Prince of Wales Cup. In 1973, Rachel stood second to Tyhen Mattie, but this was no disgrace since the class included another three champions and Mattie had previously won the class in 1969 and 1962 and had stood second in 1960, 1961 (both to Parc Lady), 1965, 1967, 1968 and 1970 and also been third or fourth for the other years.

Rachel was Champion again in 1975 and Reserve Champion to Llanarth Flying Comet (*chapter 25.1*) in 1976 and 1978.

2. Cahn Dafydd
Registration number 1758 in the *Welsh Stud Book,*
Vol. XXXII
Bay, height: 14 hands 3 in, foaled 1942
Breeder: Llewellyn Phillips, Cahn Hill Improvement
Scheme, Pwllpeiran, Devil's Bridge, Cardiganshire

Cahn Dafydd was fancied as a three-year-old when he was looking in very poor shape by Mr. Iorwerth Osborne Jones (who had a very good eye for a pony or Cob despite its condition) and purchased for £28. With some care and attention, Cahn Dafydd improved his condition considerably, he spent the rest of 1945 working on the farm often working alongside the farm mares, such a kind disposition did he possess. Cardiganshire at that time was full of famous Cob stallions such as Brenin Gwalia (*chapter 23.1*), nevertheless Cahn Dafydd attracted some attention including Mr. Roscoe Lloyd's celebrated mare Dewi Rosina (*chapter 25.9*) who visited him in 1946 producing a good colt Derwen Welsh Comet who was later exported to Pakistan. Another visitor in 1947 was Eiddwen's Pride (*chapter 25.4*) who also had a colt, Pentre Eiddwen Flyer the sire of Brenin-y-Bryniau.

Mr. Osborne Jones tried his luck in the show ring at the 1947 Royal Welsh Show (Carmarthen) where the judge was Mr. Morgan Evans, brother of Mr. Tom Jones Evans of the Craven Stud. It was a very strong class, I spent most of the time watching Brenin Gwalia (*chapter 23.1*) who was shown jointly by my father and by John Roderick Rees (son of the owner David Rees, cousin to Mrs. Osborne Jones) and he could be quite fiery at the best of times! It was Brenin Gwalia's day; he put up a great show, followed by Mathrafal (sire of Cahn Dafydd), Meiarth Royal Eiddwen (*chapter 29.7*) (a son of Brenin Gwalia and another who put up a terrific "show"), Churchill, Brenin Cardi (son of the third, Meiarth Royal Eiddwen), Pistyll Gold Flake (*chapter 27.4*), Cahn Dafydd and Tywysog Gwalia in that order.

I'm sure that Cahn Dafydd's connection would agree that he was no great "show" horse; some of the show rings' greatest have produced nothing of note; others like Cahn Dafydd who may be no "oil painting" often produce one champion after another. I always think that if an animal is regally bred, he or she is more likely to produce the "tops" than a "flash in the pan" who may be a dazzling beauty but whose ancestors were nothing to write home about.

Mr. Osborne Jones sold Cahn Dafydd on 27th March 1948 to Mr. Greenwood of Moss Farm, Davyhulme, Manchester for whom he won some prizes before being sold to Ireland where all tracks of him were lost for about ten years until suddenly, Mr. Moses Griffith (who had been in charge of Cahn Hill until 1939) discovered him in Ireland and bought him and returned him to North Wales where Mr. Griffith used him on some of his own mares.

Luckily for Cardiganshire breeders, Jones Brothers, Frongoy Stud bought him in 1960 and brought him back to Llanon where he stayed

Brenin Dafydd, Champion at the 1970 Royal Welsh Show, son of Cahn Dafydd.

until his death in 1966. It was during this period that he had the greatest influence on the Welsh Cob breed and he ranks as the leading sire of Royal Welsh Show Champions during the post-war years 1947–1978, a feat all the more remarkable since all these champions were foaled during the last six years of his life and for four of these years, he was over twenty years old! These champions are Brenin Dafydd (foaled 1964 and Champion in 1970), Derwen Rosina (foaled in 1962 and Champion in 1966, 1967 and 1968), Cathedine Welsh Maid (foaled in 1961 and Champion in 1970 and 1974) and Parc Rachel (foaled in 1966 and Champion in 1971, 1972, 1975, 1976 and 1978).

In addition to the named champions, there are others who have made their mark on the breed such as: Farian Prince (foaled in 1961), Parc Dafydd (foaled in 1964), Hewid Dafydd (foaled in 1965), Gwron Brenig (foaled in 1963) and Fronarth Welsh Jack (foaled in 1965) and the mares Geler Ann and Geler Eirlys (full-sisters foaled in 1964 and 1966) and Rhandir Rosina and Rhandir Margarita (full sisters, also full sisters to Derwen Rosina, foaled in 1963 and 1965), Cefncoch Lady Lynne (foaled in 1964) etc.

To this formidable list can be added very many more second-generation Cahn Dafydd stock proving to be of great influence also.

3. Parc Pride
Registration number 13533 in the *Welsh Stud Book, Vol. XLIV*
Bay, star, near fore and off hind white, height: 14 hands 2 in, foaled 1960
Breeders: D. O. Morgan and Sons, Coedparc, Lampeter, Cards.

The cross of Pentre Eiddwen Comet with Parc Lady (representing a total of eleven Royal Welsh Show Championships between them) proved exceptionally successful producing Parc Comet, Parc Prince, Parc Pride, Parc Delight, and Parc Welsh Flyer all noteworthy but probably Parc Pride is the most noteworthy of all of them.

Parc Pride herself had a successful run in the show ring, her Royal Welsh record being a second in 1966, third in 1968 and fourth in 1969 all in very strong company before she gave way in the show ring to her illustrious daughter.

Apart from producing Parc Rachel, there were many others of note from this good mare: Parc Dafydd (super tempered stallion and exceptional sire at Twyford Stud), Parc Violet (exported to Holland), Parc

454

Parc Pride. (Photograph courtesy of Les Mayall.)

Nest (a big winner at mid-Wales Shows before being sold in 1976 to Mrs. Colville of the Persie Stud where she has continued her winning ways and maintaining the high standard of this family as a brood mare), Parc Doreen and Parc Lucky Strike (full sister and brother to Parc Nest, the latter is also making a name for himself at Stud, I have had two foals by him and was well pleased with them), Parc Boneddwr (foaled in 1975, by Ceredigion Tywysog) standing at stud at Parc and Parc Enchanter who is standing at Mr. Haynes' Crickhowell Stud.

4. Mathrafal
Registration number 1629 in the *Welsh Stud Book*, *Vol. XXXI*
Chesnut, blaze, near fore pastern white, height: 14 hands 3 in, foaled 1936
Breeder: David Griffiths, Golfa, Welshpool.
Montgomeryshire

Very soon after birth, this colt was bought by Mr. Meyrick Jones of Mathrafal Stud, where so many famous Cob stallions had dwelt

455

"MATHRAFAL"

No. 1629   W.S.B.

CHESTNUT   15 h.h.   LICENSED

Sire : "Mab-y-Brenin"   { "Mathrafal Brenin" 873
8902 "Hafan Polly" (Vol. xxx)
by "Temptation"

Dam : 9040 "Poll-o'r-Golfa"   { "Manavon Flyer" 883
1676 "Poll" (Vol. v)
by "Welsh Flyer II"

1st Super Senior Champion at Royal Welsh, Caernarvon, 1952. Several times winner of the "George, Prince of Wales" Challenge Cup, and Royal Champion.

Winner of Kilvrough Cup; Society Medal and 1st Prize best type Welsh Cob.

Sire of many Show winners including :—

2nd Senior Champion
1st Junior Champion
1st two-year-old, and of others at Caernarvon Royal Welsh 1952.

FEE — £3. 0s. 0d.   **GROOM — 2s. 6d.**

For further particulars, apply—

**E. DILLWYN RICHARDS,
CWM RISCA FARM,**
Telephone : Aberkenfig 204.   **TONDU, Bridgend.**

Stud card of Mathrafal for 1953.

previously and Mr. Jones abandoned his usual practice of using Mathrafal as prefix, baptising the colt as simply "Mathrafal".

Mathrafal duly won a first prize at the 1937 Montgomeryshire Show. At the 1938 combined Royal Agricultural Society of England and Royal Welsh Show (Cardiff) with Capt. Howson judging he won the young-

Mathrafal in action.

Mathrafal when Champion at the 1952 Royal Welsh Show.

stock class from Oakford Welsh Flyer, Garibaldi Welsh Flyer and Cahn Scott and went on to win the Male Championship from the winning stallion Mr. D. O. Morgan's Parc Express, g-sire of Parc Lady.

Mathrafal's career was then interrupted by the war years; Mr. Meyrick Jones had sold his farm at Mathrafal and had gone to live with

457

Llwynog-y-Garth, Champion at the 1949, 1950 and 1960 Royal Welsh Shows. Son of Mathrafal.

his daughter at Bicester near Oxford but kept up regular correspondence with my father. In May 1946 he wrote: "Do you know of someone who would be interested in having Mathrafal; I would sell or hire him on very reasonable terms to someone who would look after him well. He is looking very well but wasted in Oxfordshire." In January 1947 he wrote again: "I have sold Mathrafal to an old friend at Llangollen".

Thus Mathrafal became the property of Mr. R. T. Evans of Llandyn Hall (later home of the Weston Stud) for whom he won a second prize at the 1947 Royal Welsh Show, third in 1949 and a second in 1950. Capt.

458

Howson writing of Mathrafal in the 1947 Royal Welsh Journal states that he is "a big stallion, a different type from the winner" (Brenin Gwalia). Mathrafal then changed hands again coming to South Wales, the property of Mr. Dillwyn Richards of Cwm Risca Farm, Tondu, Bridgend, a farm noted in South Wales agricultural circles for its progressive agricultural methods; for Mr. Richards, Mathrafal was third in 1951, Champion in 1952, and fourth in 1953. Then after having his name amongst the "greats" on the George, Prince of Wales Cup, he was to change hands for the fourth and last time when he became the property of Jones Brothers of Frongoy Stud, at eighteen years old in just the same way as the Jones Brothers six years later brought his son Cahn Dafydd, he also at eighteen years of age. Mathrafal's last Royal Welsh Show appearance was in 1954 in the ownership of the Jones Brothers when he stood fourth to Meiarth King Flyer, Brynarth Stepping Gambler and Pentre Eiddwen Comet. Mathrafal's influence on the breed is best assessed by the number of champions he produced and what, in turn, they are still producing.

Amongst his sons and daughters who have won Royal Welsh Show Championships are: Llwynog-y-Garth (foaled in 1944, champion in 1949, 1950 and 1960), Cefn Parc Boy (foaled in 1952 and Champion in 1955), Pentre Rainbow (foaled in 1955 and Champion in 1962) and Tyngwndwn Cream Boy (foaled in 1957 and Champion in 1963) along with the mares Parc Lady (foaled in 1948 and Champion in 1956, 1958, 1959, 1960 and 1961) and Tyhen Mattie (foaled in 1956 and Champion in 1962 and 1973). What a remarkable total, six animals representing a total of thirteen Royal Welsh Show male and female Championships; when this is considered along with the eleven Champions produced by his son Cahn Dafydd (also Champions from his daughters such as Tyhen Comet out of Tyhen Mattie) it constitutes a very formidable list.

5. Gwenogwen
Registration number 9150 in the *Welsh Stud Book*,
Vol. XXXII
Dun, height: 14 hands 2 in, foaled 1937
Breeders: Cahn Hill Improvement Scheme,
Pwllpeiran, Aberystwyth

Gwenogwen was sold by Cahn Hill to Mr. Iorwerth Osborne Jones (who later had Cahn Dafydd) who sold her to Mr. Roscoe Lloyd who was residing at that time at Garth Villa, Drefach, Llanwenog and who registered the mare as 9150 Gwenogwen. Later (in 1946) Cahn Hill (unaware that Mr. Lloyd had registered the mare) registered her as 9337 Cahn Blodwen (also in *Vol. XXXII*) at the same time as they registered her full sister 9336 Cahn Bess (foaled in 1935).

6. Pentre Eiddwen Comet (*chapter 25.2*)

7. Parc Lady
Registration number 9977 in the *Welsh Stud Book, Vol. XXXV*
Bay, near fore and both hind legs white, height:
14 hands 2 in, foaled 1948
Breeder: D. O. Morgan, Coedparc, Lampeter,
Cardiganshire

Without doubt, here is one of the most beautiful of Welsh Cobs ever. After winning locally in mid-Wales she made her visit to the Royal Welsh Show in 1956 where, with Mr. J. O. Davies judging she won the female Championship and stood reserve to Pentre Eiddwen Comet who was winning the George, Prince of Wales Cup for the second time. In 1957 she was defeated in her class by Mr. T. Evans' Princess by Brenin Gwalia but then went on to win the Prince of Wales Cup four years in succession under the judges: Mr. Tom Thomas, Mr. John Berry, Mrs. I. M. Yeomans and Mr. Dafydd Edwardes. This then represented her retirement from the show ring, in the meantime she had continued to

Parc Lady.

Parc Comet (foaled in 1955), the first of the progeny of Parc Lady, ridden by Mrs. Elizabeth Carson. (Photograph courtesy of Les Mayall.)

win countless Championships at lesser Shows such as Lampeter, Newcastle Emlyn, Cardigan, Llanilar, Talybont, Pontardulais etc. During all these years of showing and for the following six years she was well occupied in producing offspring many of which have made their mark on the breed:

1955 Parc Comet, colt, by Pentre Eiddwen Comet; unfortunately for the breed he was gelded when young and in the ownership of Mr. Jackson (after winning the Royal Welsh in 1956). However he proved to be a good advertisement for the breed under saddle when owned by the Lady Honor Llewellyn and won at the Royal Welsh ridden by Mrs. Elizabeth Carson.

1956 Parc Princess II, filly, dun by Caradog Llwyd. Won numerous prizes as a foal at mid-Wales Shows, also second prize at the 1957 Royal Welsh Show. Sold in 1958 and now with Mrs. Mary Edwards of the Cascob Stud and producing exceptional stock.

1957 Parc Duchess, filly, dun, by Caradog Llwyd. Bred Parc Flyer, Parc Comet II, Parc Eleri and Parc Jolly for Mr. T. R. Morgan and was then sold to Belgium but bought back in 1976 by Mrs. Mountain and her 1977 colt by Parc Dafydd has returned to the Parc Stud.

1958 Parc Prince, colt, black, by Pentre Eiddwen Comet. Sold to Argentine in 1960

461

Parc Delight (foaled in 1961), daughter of Parc Lady. (Photograph courtesy of T. M. Gibson.)

1959 Parc Express II, colt, chesnut by Mathrafal. Sold as a colt foal to Mr. Dunn (breeder in London). I had two very good foals by him, one, Ceulan Mandarin later being a consistent winner of Private driving classes.

1960 No. 3 Parc Pride.

1961 Parc Delight, filly, bay, by Pentre Eiddwen Comet, full-sister to Parc Pride, she won the foal class at the Royal Welsh Show and then sold in 1963 to the Twyford Stud.

1963 Parc King Flyer, colt, black by Dewi King Flyer. Sold as a yearling to Mr. Mark Ongley

1966 Parc Welsh Flyer, colt, bay by Pentre Eiddwen Comet. He was a winner at the Lampeter Stallion Shows in 1967 and 1969. In 1969 we were offered him at a very reasonable figure to export to the U.S.A. but it is fortunate for the breed that he stayed in Wales! Since then he has won many Premiums for mid-Wales including three times being Champion Premium stallion at Lampeter, Champion of the breed at the 1974 Royal Agricultural Society of England Show etc.

1967 Parc Commando, colt, chesnut by Parc Dafydd. He was sold in 1968 to Mr. S. O. James of the Trefaes Stud where he sired some very good stock including the winning mare Trefaes Sylvia. Now owned by Mr. and Mrs. Haak of the Uplands Stud in Hampshire.

I last saw Parc Lady in April 1977, and apart from her docked tail, one would never have guessed that she was well into her late 'twenties. Parc Lady passed away peacefully in June 1978.

8. Mab y Brenin

Registration number 1555 in the *Welsh Stud Book*,
Vol. XXX
Black, height: 13 hands 2 in, foaled 1924
Breeder: Isaac Edwards, Lletyllwyd, Llandre,
Cardiganshire
Sire: Mathrafal Brenin 873 (*chapter 23.6*)
Dam: 8902 Hafan Polly by Temptation 527
(*chapter 24.6*)

It was in *Vol. XXX Welsh Stud Book* that Section "B" first became labelled with its present-day significance i.e. "Ponies of Riding type" however it is difficult to see how the majority of these entries could be categorised as such: Hafan Polly (above) (by Temptation and g-dam of the fifteen-hand Cob stallion Mathrafal) was one of these! Mab y Brenin certainly belonged to what is currently classified as Section "C" and as such, was shown by his breeder to stand fifth at the 1927 Royal Welsh Show (Swansea) under Maj. Marshall Dugdale of the Llwyn Stud. The placings were first: Mrs. Hughes' Cefncoch Country Swell (who had competed in the Cob section the previous year and stood fourth to Mathrafal Eiddwen) second: Ormond Welsh Comet (S. O. Davies brother-in-law of Mr. D. O. Morgan), third: Mr. James Scott's Paith Flyer (*Vol. XXI* quotes him as being 14 hands 1 in Paith Flyer II, g-g-sire of Llanarth Braint was 15 hands), fourth: Mr. Tom James' Baedeker (*chapter 26.15*), fifth: Mab-y-Brenin and sixth: Mr. D. J. Jenkins' Royal Welsh Jack (who won the class for the next three years and was second to Ceulan Comet for another two years).

By 1930, Mab-y-Brenin had been bought by my grandfather, Mr. L. O. Williams and he stood third at the Royal Welsh Show to Royal Welsh Jack and Ceulan Comet (only four-years-old). Tanybwlch Berwyn (*chapter 13.6*) was fourth in this mixed "B"/"C" stallion class.

By 1932 grandfather had sold Mab-y-Brenin to Mr. Herbert

Threadgold of Welshpool who considered him to be a Welsh Cob and won fourth prize at the Royal Welsh Show that year in the Cob stallion class to Caerseddfan Stepping Flyer, Craven Cymro and Paith Flyer II. On 23rd April 1936 a Mr. H. Lee of Minsterley, Salop wrote to my father stating he had just bought him and asking for particulars of what he had bought! There seems to be no later record of him.

9. Poll of Golfa
Registration number 9040 in the *Welsh Stud Book, Vol. XXXI*
Dark chesnut, narrow blaze, white off hind coronet, height: 14 hands 2 in, foaled 1927
Breeder: David Evans, Cwmllwynog, Llanfair Careinion, Welshpool, Montgomeryshire
Sire: Manavon Flyer 883
Dam: 1676 Poll (foaled in 1898) by Welsh Flyer II

10. Ceitho Welsh Flyer (*chapter 27.12*)

11. Pantlleinau Blodwen
Registration number 7811 in the *Welsh Stud Book, Vol. XXIII*
Dun, white near hind, height: 14 hands, foaled 1920
Breeder: Rowland H. Jones, Pantlleinau, Moriah, Tregaron, Cardiganshire
Sire: Ceitho Welsh Comet (*chapter 24.2*)
Dam: Blodwen by Trotting Jack 528 (*chapter 27.14*)

Pantlleinau Blodwen came from a very well-established strain of Welsh Cobs in the Tregaron area; Myrtle Welsh Flyer (*chapter 29.8*) twice winner of the George, Prince of Wales Cup, was a son of Polly of Pantlleinau from the same strain.

In the ownership of Mr. Rowland Jones of Pantlleinau she won twenty-three first prizes and three silver cups during 1922 and 1923, a much-travelled filly and at the Royal Welsh Show at Bridgend (1924) stood third for Mr. Jones in the brood mare class won by Wyre Lady (another daughter of the prosperous Ceitho Welsh Comet). If Pantlleinau Blodwen was well-travelled in the ownership of her breeder, it was nothing compared with what lay in store for in 1925 she was sold to the Dinam Estates (David Davies M.P., later Lord Davies) and her Royal Welsh record reads: 1925 (Carmarthen) fourth, 1926

(Bangor) second, 1927 (Swansea) fifth, 1928 (Wrexham) second, 1929 (Cardiff) seventh, 1930 (Carnarfon) third, 1931 (Llanelly) first, 1932 (Llandrindod) second, 1933 (Aberystwyth) sixth. What an achievement, ten consecutive Royal Welsh Shows! Pantlleinau Blodwen was then sold to the Cahn Hill Improvement Society where she bred Cahn Bess (in 1935), Gwenogwen (in 1937) etc.

A good strain of Cobs are still being bred at Pantlleinau fifty years later, such as Pantlleinau Blodwen II (foaled in 1977).

12. **Eiddwen's Image** *(chapter 25.4)*

13. **Dewi Black Bess** *(chapter 25.5)*

15. **Parc Welsh Maid**
Registration number 9536 in the *Welsh Stud Book, Vol. XXXIII*
Bay, star, two white hind fetlocks, height: 14 hands
3 in, foaled 1942
Breeder: D. O. Morgan, Coedparc, Lampeter, Cardiganshire
Sire: Parc Express 1623 *(chapter 29.4)*
Dam: 9535 Parc Delight (foaled in 1936) by
Cardigan Jack 1580
G-dam, 9025 Ormond Jolly (foaled in 1927) by
Welsh Model 620 *(chapter 27.13)*
G-g-dam: 9024 Ormond Delight (foaled in 1923) by
Tyssul Bangorian 970
G-g-g-dam: 525 Jolly II (foaled in 1894) by Grand Express

Parc Welsh Maid won a first prize and was Reserve Champion at the North Breconshire Show, Builth Wells in 1947. At the 1948 Lampeter

Parc Welsh Maid photographed at Lampeter Show, 1948.

465

Show she stood fourth (with Mr. Matthew Williams judging) to Meiarth Welsh Maid (*chapter 29.3*), Polly of Hercws and Hercws Bright Star. She was again fourth in 1949 at Lampeter; what celebrated company there was at Lampeter Show in those days, it seems as if all the rivals came together to Lampeter for their final fight of the year, such names as Eirlys Gwenog, Oakford Charming Bess, Dewi Rosina, Meiarth Welsh Maid, Towy Black Bess, Groten Ddu, Polly of Hercws, Hercws Bright Star, Eiddwen's Model, Sheila, Daisy Gwenog, all were present at the 1949 Lampeter Show.

It was Mr. D. O. Morgan also who bred Ormond Jolly and Ormond Delight under his former prefix; Ormond Jolly was fourth to Pant-lleinau Blodwen at the 1931 Royal Welsh Show; she also won at the Bath and West, Carmarthen and Gower Shows. Ormond Jolly was dam also of Parc Express.

The g-g-g-dam Jolly II goes back to pre-Stud Book times and was reputed to be a winner of many trotting races.

29

Myrtle Welsh Flyer (foaled 1917)
Meiarth Welsh Maid (foaled 1940)
Meiarth King Flyer (foaled 1949)

1 Meiarth King Flyer 2025	2 Pant Grey Prince 1741	4 Parc Express 1623	8 Myrtle Welsh Flyer 1020
			9 9205 Ormond Jolly
		5 8651 Pant Grey Star	10 Penal Satisfaction 1074
			11 Bess
	3 9109 Meiarth Welsh Maid	6 Llethi Valiant 1238	12 Ceitho Welsh Comet 774
			13 Llethi Flower
		7 Meiarth Pride	14 Mathrafal Brenin 873
			15 Coedmawr Pride

1. Meiarth King Flyer

Registration number 2025 in the *Welsh Stud Book, Vol. XXXIV*

Dark bay, star, off hind fetlock white, height: 15 hands, foaled 1949

Breeders: David Lloyd and Son, Meiarth, Bwlchyllan, Lampeter, Cardiganshire

Meiarth King Flyer took the show ring by storm at the very wet 1954 Royal Welsh Show (Machynlleth) where, with Mr. Douglas Meredith judging he went straight to the top beating the seasoned campaigners Brynarth Stepping Gambler, Pentre Eiddwen Comet (*chapter 25.2*), Mathrafal (*chapter 28.4*), Brenin-y-Gogledd, Gwarffynon Artful Briton, Llanarth Braint (*chapter 27.1*) and Emlyn Gwalia in that order. (King Flyer had previously won the colt class at the 1951 Royal Welsh Show). The 1954 show was a very successful one for Messrs. David Lloyd and Sons since not only did Meiarth King Flyer win this good class but his dam Meiarth Welsh Maid also won her class and the coveted George Prince of Wales cup; also a yearling filly by King Flyer out of his dam was second in the yearling class and the two-year-old full-brother was third in the colt class.

The following year at the Haverfordwest Show, King Flyer was relegated to third place (his dam went down to seventh) behind Caradog Llwyd and Pentre Eiddwen Comet. However, Meiarth King Flyer made amends by winning the Welsh Cob harness class from Llwynog-y-Garth, Llanarth Braint (who had beaten him in harness the previous year), Wyre Star and Emlyn Gwalia. In his capacity as

Meiarth King Flyer.

Stud card of Meiarth King Flyer for 1956. (Stud card courtesy of Messrs. Rowlands Harris.)

harness winner, Meiarth King Flyer competed against twelve other contestants for the Tom and Sprightly Applause cup, gaining reserve place behind Mr. Havard's Hackney Wonder Boy but beating the Welsh Cob breed class winners, also some famous names amongst the other Welsh breeds such as Coed Coch Madog, Coed Coch Planed etc.

470

Meiarth King Flyer in action.

Meiarth King Flyer had not been used extensively at stud but had been mated back to his mother every year from 1951 to 1956. Then in 1956 he was awarded the Premium to travel in North Cardiganshire; however this arrangement was cut short and on 19th July 1956 he was exported to the Ministrie de Guerra in Spain.

2. Pant Grey Prince
Registration number 1741 in the *Welsh Stud Book,*
Vol. XXXII
Grey, blaze, height: 14 hands 3 in, foaled 1943
Breeders: J. and E. J. Davies, Pant Farm, Llanddewi
Brefi, Tregaron, Cardiganshire

3. Meiarth Welsh Maid
Registration number 9109 in the *Welsh Stud Book,*
Vol. XXXII
Dark bay, star, height: 15 hands, foaled 1940
Owner and Breeder: David Lloyd, Meiarth,
Bwlchyllan, Lampeter, Cardiganshire

Meiarth Welsh Maid stood out as the tallest competing show ring

Meiarth Welsh Maid (Photograph courtesy of University of Reading.)

Meiarth Pure Line, son of Meiarth Welsh Maid, with his owner Mr. John Berry. Mr. Tom Thomas is the driver.

Meiarth Modern Maid, daughter of Meiarth Welsh Maid with Mr. E. S. Davies, Aberystwyth Show 1964.

mare during the years 1947 to 1960 and as such met with varying fortunes either doing very well such as winning the Royal Welsh Show Championships awards in 1947, 1949, 1950 and 1954 or if the judge went for the smaller more compact type of Welsh Cob she would end up down the line such as fifth in 1951 and seventh in 1955. She would meet with similar fates at all her shows e.g. fifth at the 1949 Lampeter Show, Champion in 1955!

Probably the best way to describe Meiarth Welsh Maid is to quote from the writings of Capt. T. A. Howson who judged her at the 1949 Royal Welsh Show where she was awarded the Championship: "Brought out in very good form, she is a stylish mare with a neat and intelligent head, a reachy front and a good top line combined with depth through the shoulders, deep and well-sprung ribs and ample bone and substance while she moves with power and freedom. Probably most equines, like most humans, have their critics and some critics of

473

Ceulan Mandarin, Champion of the 1969 British Driving Society Show, son of Meiarth Modern Maid, driven by Mrs. M. A. Thrower.

Welsh Maid contend that she is on the big side for a Cob – and that appears to be about the worst that they can find to say about her."

For breeding, surprisingly Welsh Maid was usually mated to her relatives such as to her half-brother Meiarth Royal Eiddwen or to her son Meiarth King Flyer. To Royal Eiddwen in 1944 she produced Meiarth Pure Line who was premium stallion for Anglesey for 1951, 1952 and 1953 when owned by John Berry and also won for him at Royal Welsh Shows a third in 1950 and sixth in 1952.

In 1948 and 1949, Welsh Maid produced the grey Meiarth Grey King and Meiarth King Flyer, both by Pant Grey Prince. Then between 1951 and 1956 she was mated only to her son, Meiarth King Flyer producing in 1952: Meiarth Welsh Flyer (never registered, third prize Royal Welsh 1954) 1953: Meiarth Coronation Maid (never registered, second prize Royal Welsh 1954) 1954: Meiarth Welsh Gem, first prize at the 1955 Royal Welsh Show and in 1959 bred Meiarth Royal Maid by Brenin Gwalia (*chapter 23.1*) 1955: Meiarth Welsh Flyer; when I saw him in October 1956 he was owned by Mr. O. M. Evans, Cwmcae, Talybont, breeders of the 1930, 1932, 1933 and 1934 Royal

474

Welsh Show winner Cwmcau Lady Jet by Trotting Jack (*chapter 27.14*). 1956: Meiarth Welsh King (gelded).

In 1957, Meiarth Welsh Maid was mated to Brenin Gwalia producing the good mare Meiarth Modern Maid which we bought in 1962. Unfortunately for us she produced only colts, Ceulan Mandarin in 1963, Matador in 1964 and Meteor (by Madeni Welsh Comet) in 1965. We sold Modern Maid to Mr. and Mrs. Sowerby of the Arth Stud, Yorkshire and she is still (1979) producing top-class foals such as Arth Merryman (a successful sire in North Wales) and Arth Maid of Honour (winner at Royal Welsh for Dr. June Alexander) as well as the stock retained at the Arth Stud.

4. Parc Express
Registration number 1623 in the *Welsh Stud Book,*
Vol. XXXI
Black, star, off hind white fetlock, height: 14 hands
2½ in, foaled 1935
Owner and Breeder: D. O. Morgan, Coedparc,
Lampeter, Cardiganshire

The stud card for Parc Express states that he stood at over 15 hands and that he was "very typical, and is a powerful mover with plenty of

Parc Express.

SEASON 1940.

Pedigree and Particulars of
that Typical

WELSH COB STALLION

"Parc Express"

(1623) Vol. XXXI W.S.B.

"PARC EXPRESS" (1623), bred by D. O. Morgan, is exceptionally well bred, jet black in colour, stands over 15 h.h., very typical, and is a powerful mover, with plenty of bone and brimming over with quality. He is a prolific winner, including 1st at the Royal, and out of a strain of horses that has won Prizes all over the country.

His sire, "Myrtle Welsh Flyer" (1020), is recognised as one of the most perfect Welsh Cobs yet seen out, and his performance in the Show Yard goes to prove his outstanding qualities. "Myrtle Welsh Flyer" has won at the Royal Show of England, the Royal Welsh and the Bath and West Shows, as well as innumerable other prizes at Shows all over the country, and he has won the Prince of Wales Challenge Cup several times. "Myrtle Welsh Flyer" has left some of the finest Cobs in Wales, and "Parc Express" is recognised by keen judges as one of his best sons.

His dam (9025) "Ormond Jolly," by "Ceitho Welsh Model" (620) was one of the most classy Cobs Wales ever produced, and out of the finest strain of Cobs in the country. "Ceitho Welsh Model" was a Premium Horse in Breconshire, Carmarthenshire, Glanmorganshire and Cardiganshire, and left some celebrated winners. "Ormond Jolly" herself was a big winner and won at the Bath and West, Royal Welsh, Carmarthen, Gower and other big Welsh Shows.

His g dam (9024) "Ormond Delight" was also a prolific winner at all the best Welsh Shows. She had great action and was most typical.

His g g dam (535) "Jolly II," Vol. I, by "Grand Express" was also a very big winner and a first-rate trotter, and on many occasions won in the keenest company.

It can be clearly seen that the breeding of "Parc Express" contains the Bluest of Blood, and advantage should be taken of such a wonderfully bred Cob.

TERMS—Will serve Mares at £1 each, and 2/6 Groom's Fee.

Service Fee becomes due at time of first service and must be paid before the end of July, 1940 ; after that date extra will be charged for collecting. Mares tried by this Horse and not brought forward will be charged for.

The Owner and the Groom will not be responsible for any accident that may occur through trying or serving mares, but the utmost care will be taken. For further particulars, apply to to the Owner :

D. O. MORGAN, Coedparc, Lampeter, Cards.

bone and brimming over with quality". Parc Express was introduced into the show ring very early in life winning second Lampeter, second Cothi Bridge, third Pontardulais, second Llanedy, second Gower, first Newcastle Emlyn, first Talsarn and a second at Llangeitho, all as a foal.

Parc Express later won the first prize in the Welsh Cob stallion class at the 1938 Royal Agricultural Society of England (combined) Royal Welsh Show at Cardiff and was the Cardiganshire Premium stallion for 1940.

5. Pant Grey Star
Registration number 8651 in the *Welsh Stud Book*,
Vol. XXVII
Grey, four white legs, height: 14 hands 1 in,
foaled 1922
Breeders: J. Davies and Sons, Pant Farm, Llanddewi
Brefi, Cardiganshire

J. Davies and his two sons (the last, Edward passed away in December 1979) had kept a good strain of Welsh Cobs at Pant for many years. Their good bay mare Polly of Pant (g-dam of Pant Grey Star) had been bred by them in 1906 and was a good winner at Cardiganshire Shows in the years before the first war e.g. she won the Welsh Pony & Cob Society medal and certificate at the 1912 Lampeter Show. At 19

Polly of Pant, g-dam of Pant Grey Star. (Photograph courtesy of Bustin.)

477

Pant Grey Star Champion at the 1928 Royal Welsh Show with Mr. E. Davies. (Photograph courtesy of Mr. Elwyn Benjamin.)

and 21 years Polly of Pant was the oldest mare to have won first prizes at Royal Welsh Shows (1925 under Mr. T. H. Vaughan of Sychtyn and 1927 under Maj. Dugdale of the Llwyn Stud). Also at the 1925 Royal Welsh Show, Polly had won the Cardiganshire Cob group prize (her photograph appears in the Royal Wesh Journal) along with her grey grand-daughter, named Betty, foaled 1923 who had the same dam, (the un-registered daughter of Polly of Pant named just "Bess") as Pant Grey Star.

Excitement was growing over the forthcoming 1928 Royal Welsh Show to be held at Wrexham, Mr. Edgar Herbert had been nominated to judge the Cobs and ponies. Judging at the 1926 Lampeter Show, Mr. Herbert had placed (class 19) Messrs. W. T. and O. M. Evans' Cwmcau Lady Jet first (she was later to win at Royal Welsh Shows in 1930, 1932, 1933 and 1934) beating the Messrs. Davies' Polly of Pant and Pant Grey Star. The following year at the Tregaron Show (class 9), Mr. Herbert had reversed this decision putting Pant Grey Star first in a class of ten beating Cwmcau Lady Jet (writing to my father he said the decision was made on movement). What well-known names in Welsh Cob history exhibited at Tregaron that day the other exhibitors being Daniel Benjamin, Penylan, Swyddffynnon; Morgans Bros., Berthdomled, Lledrod; John Owens, Taihirion, Blaenpennal; M. L. Williams, Pengelly, Ystrad Meurig; James Jones, Bronhelem, Llanddewi Brefi; J. Edwards, Llwyncolfa Coed, Blaenpennal; D. Edwardes, Tannfynnon, Penuwch and H. T. Evans, Cefnmabws, Llanrhystyd.

As it turned out the anticipation of great things at the 1928 Royal Welsh Show was ill-founded in the Welsh Cob Section (as distinct from the Mountain Pony and Pony, Cob type classes which had very large entries of the best ponies in the United Kingdom). Only four Cob brood mares turned up and the only one of note for Pant Grey Star to beat was Pantlleinau Blodwen (*chapter 28.11*). Pant Grey Star then beat the winning stallion Llethi Valiant (*chapter 26.12*) to win the George, Prince of Wales cup, a feat which her grand-dam (despite being reserve twice) had failed to do. Mr. Herbert writing in the Royal Welsh Journal states "the grey which stood on top of her class won with something in hand". Pant Grey Star also has the distinction of being the only grey ever to have been Champion Welsh Cob at the Royal Welsh Shows. The old Polly of Pant was in no way finished either and at 22 years beat Pant Grey Star into second place at the Lampeter Show of 1928 (class 18) with Mr. Meyrick Jones of Mathrafal judging.

Pant Grey Star had several more visits to Royal Welsh Shows but just failed to make her mark again, her later record being second in 1929, fourth in 1930 and second in 1933.

6. Llethi Valiant (*chapter 26.12*)

7. Meiarth Pride
Registration number 133 F.S.2 in the appendix of the
Welsh Stud Book, Vol. XXXII
Bay, white hind socks, height: 14 hands 3 in
Owner: David Lloyd, Meiarth, Bwlchllan,
Lampeter, Cardiganshire
Breeders: Misses Jenkins, Coedmawr, Llangeitho,
Tregaron, Cardiganshire

It is not recorded when Meiarth Pride (foaled 1927) was transferred

Meiarth Royal Eiddwen, son of Meiarth Pride.

from her breeders to Mr. Lloyd of the Meiarth Stud who registered her. However along with her registration in the *Welsh Stud Book* it states that Meiarth Pride was a "winner of over two hundred and fifty first prizes and many cups and championships". With this wonderful showing record it is surprising that Meiarth Pride did not put in an appearance at any Royal Welsh Show before 1939. It is surprising also that not one of the usual "bevy of beauties" appeared to challenge once more at the 1939 Show, the stalwarts of that decade were missing, such as Teify of Hercws, Dewi Black Bess, Sian Gwalia, Cwmcau Lady Jet, Hwylog Peggy, Pant Grey Star. As it was, only three mares appeared in 1939 at Caernarfon and Meiarth Pride won the class and the female Championship. This is not to say that she might not have won if the others had been there since judges who remember her say that she was a very beautiful mare and to quote Matthew Williams the judge at Caernarfon "a nice sort of bay with dashing action".

What is even more surprising with this mare with such an outstanding showing record is that only two progeny were ever registered out of her, Meiarth Welsh Maid as already described and the previous year: Meiarth Royal Eiddwen by Brenin Gwalia (*chapter 23.1*) (the foal was only three days old with Pride at the Royal Welsh Show). Meiarth Royal Eiddwen was Premium stallion for South Cardigan while in the ownership of his breeders in 1943, he was then sold to Mr. D. J.

480

Richards of Llanelly for whom he stood third to his sire and Mathrafal (*chapter 28.4*) at the 1947 Royal Welsh Show. Capt Howson writing in the *Royal Welsh Journal* said that he had some friends at the ringside who would have placed him second or even first!

SEASON 1943.

IMPORTANT TO BREEDERS OF WELSH COBS AND PONIES.—Bred from the Winning Blood you know for Quality, Style, Courage and Action This Cob Stallion has only Champion Winning blood in his veins

Meiarth Royal Eiddwen

No. 1680 W.S.B.

A Smart Chestnut, on the best of feet and a dashing goer. Stands 15 h.h. Foaled 1939.

He is the PREMIUM WELSH COB for South Cardigan, Season 1943. He holds the Ministry's Licence and has proved to be a sure foal-getter.

sire—Brenin Gwalia, Vol. XXXII, No 1656.
g. sire—Gwalia Victor, Vol. 1431. W.S.B.
dam—Meiarth Pride, Vol XXXII, No. 133.
sire—Mathrafal Brenin, No. 873 W.S.B.

Meiarth Pride is well known all over Wales. She has won over 250 Firsts and Champion Prizes, including Champion Medal at the Royal Welsh, Carnarvon, 1939

Meiarth Royal Eiddwen will serve a limited number of Mares at

£1/10/- each; Tenant Farmers, £1/1/- each.

Neither the Owners nor the Groom will be responsible for any accidents in trying and serving Mares, but the best care will be taken. All Mares tried by this Horse will be charged for.

For route and particulars apply to the Owners—

DAVID LLOYD & SON,
Meiarth, Bwlchyllan, Lampeter.

D. R. Evans and Co., The Bridge Press, Lampeter.

Stud card of Meiarth Royal Eiddwen. (Stud card courtesy of Messrs. Rowlands Harris.)

Golden Gem. Sire Llanarth Braint. Dam Eiddwen Chess by Meiarth Royal Eiddwen.

Meiarth Royal Eiddwen then spent several years in the ownership of Mr. Taylor of Arborfield, Berkshire for whom he won many important prizes in harness before he returned again to his native Cardiganshire in the ownership of Mr. Jim Rees (brother to Mr. David Rees, Brenin Gwalia) for whom he won some more premiums such as Pembrokeshire in 1959; he died in 1963. Meiarth Royal Eiddwen was a flashy chesnut, closely resembling his sire, his best-known successful line today being through his daughter Eiddwen Chess dam of Golden Gem, Dilys Rhosyn, Dilys Stardust, Dilys Rain-drop etc. Golden Gem has certainly left her mark on Welsh Cob breeding in the South of England producing altogether 12 foals including Dilys Golden Rain, Dilys Golden Harp etc.

Another very popular and successful Meiarth Royal Eiddwen line is through his son Hendy Brenin (1944, died 1975). Hendy Brenin was Champion cob foal when he was sold to Mr. Jones of Llwynhendy at the Llanybyther autumn sale of 1944 and he stayed with Mr. Jones for 18 years before becoming the property of Mr. Idris Davies of Usk in whose ownership he died. Hendy Brenin's dam was Lady Welsh Flyer by Myrtle Welsh Flyer (*chapter 29.8*) out of Pontfaen Lady Model, Champion Welsh Cob of the 1922 and 1923 Royal Welsh Shows.

482

8. Myrtle Welsh Flyer

Registration number 1020 in the *Welsh Stud Book,*
Vol. XIX
Dark chesnut, blaze, off fore and both hind legs
white, height: 14 hands 2½ in, foaled 1917
Breeder: Humphrey Ellis, Pantlleinau, Moriah,
Tregaron, Cardiganshire
Owner: Tom James, Myrtle Hill, Llechryd,
Cardiganshire
Sire: Ceitho Welsh Comet (*chapter 24.2*)
Dam: 4766 Polly of Pantlleinau by Messenger
G-dam: Socks by Cardigan Flyer

Myrtle Welsh Flyer was bred at Pantlleinau from the same strain of
noted Welsh Cobs as Pantlleinau Blodwen (*chapter 28.11*). When he was
two-years-old he became the property of Tom James who often kept
(and travelled) as many as thirteen stallions at Myrtle Hill (the story of
Tom James is told in *chapter 26.15*)

Myrtle Welsh Flyer had a distinguished show ring career over a very
long period of time starting at the Royal Welsh Show in 1926 with a
third prize beyind Mathrafal Eiddwen (*chapter 25.8*) and Llethi Valiant
(*chapter 26.12*). Myrtle Welsh Flyer then was second to Mathrafal
Eiddwen in 1927, 1929 and 1930. He then did not appear until 1933
when he was awarded the Championship by Mr. Matthew Williams, he
was absent again in 1934 but re-appeared in 1935 to win his class and be
Reserve Champion to Dewi Black Bess (*chapter 25.5*). He won his class
again in 1936 under Mr. Llewellyn Richards but did not find favour in

*Myrtle Welsh Flyer with
Mr. Tom James in 1939.
(Photograph courtesy of
P. B. Abery.)*

MYRTLE WELSH FLYER

Chestnut Blaze, Flaxy Mane and Tail, 3 White Markings. Foaled in 1917. 14.3 h.h.

Sire—Ceitho Welsh Comet (774, Vol. 14 W.P. & C.S.)
    g. sire—Caradog Flyer (379, W.P. & C.S.)
    g.g. sire—Young Caradog, by Welsh Jack, by Cymro Llwyd.
Dam—Polly of Pantlleinau (4766, Vol. 13 W.C. & S.B.)
    Sire—Messenger.
    g. dam—Socks by Cardigan Flyer (Trewern Horse).
    The Messenger was got by Eiddwen Flyer, Eiddwen Flyer by Welsh Flyer, Welsh Flyer by Old Comet, Old Comet by Flyer, Flyer out of Brown Bess, Brown Bess by Black Jack—all celebrated trotters.

MYRTLE WELSH FLYER is licensed for the 1934 season. Premium Horse, Carmarthen County, 1921; Premium South Cardigan 1922; Premium North Cardigan 1923; Premium Gower (Glam.) 1924; Premium West Brecon 1925; Premium South Cardigan 1926; Premium North Cardigan 1928; Premium Carmarthen 1929-30-31.

PRIZES WON BY MYRTLE WELSH FLYER.

First at Stallion Show, Carmarthen. First Lampeter. First Newcastle-Emlyn. First Cardigan. Royal Welsh Shows—2nd Reserve Champion, Bangor; Second Reserve Champion Carnarfon; 2nd Reserve Champion, Cardiff; 1st Champion Medal and Prince of Wales Cup at Aberystwyth.

CONDITIONS.

(1) All mares are absolutely at owner's risk. (2) All mares tried by this horse will be charged for. (3) Fees due June 23rd, 1934, and must be paid to the Groom on his last round, or 5/- extra for collecting. (4) The Groom's fee at time of service. (5) A limited number of mares only accepted. (6) T. James reserves to himself the right to vary the route or substitute another horse should occasion arise. (7) No allowance for barren mares, and no barrens will be served by this Horse at reduced price.

Fee: £3.   Tenant Farmers: £1 10s.

Grooms Fee up to Five Mares, 2/6.

Alteration in Fee will on no account be made.

The property of

Mr. Tom James, Myrtle Hill, Llechryd, Cards.

the championship which went to the two mares Mr. J. D. Evans' Teify of Hercws and Sian Gwalia owned by my grandfather, L. O. Williams, as reserve.

Myrtle Welsh Flyer then did not appear until the 1939 show when Matthew Williams for the second time awarded him the George, Prince of Wales Cup. At this show, aged twenty-one, Myrtle Welsh Flyer looked in great form considering that he was a stallion who had

*Stud card of Peris
Satisfaction, son of
Penal Satisfaction.*

THE TYPICAL WELSH COB STALLION

" Peris Satisfaction "

Property of Mr. J. Ll. JONES, Garnwialen, Bethania

Fee: £1 0s. 0d. each mare; 2/6 Groom Fee.

"PERIS SATISFACTION" is of a Grey colour,
stands 14 hands 1 in. high, of the much-desired Old
Welsh Type, seldom seen nowadays; with great
strength and substance and a brilliant all-round
mover, with purest old Welsh blood in his veins.

Sire, "Pennal Satisfaction," 1074, Vol. 20, W.S.B.
Grandsire, "Trotting Jack," W.S.B., 528.
Great grandsire, "King Jack II.," W.S.B., 20.
Great Great Grand Sire, "Young Rainbow."

Dam, "Peris Polly," by "Cardigan Briton II.," No. 611.
Grand Dam, "Bess," by "Welsh Jack II."
Great Grand Dam, "Polly," by "Express Lion."

Gymru! Cedwch i fyny yr Hen Ach Gymreig drwy
ddefnyddio y Cobyn prydferth hwn; yr hwn sydd o
waed pur, ac o achau yr hen Gobs y dyddiau gynt,
pa rai sydd wedi gwneyd y Cobyn Cymreig mor
enwog.

Y mae "Peris Satisfaction" yn un o'r rhai mwyaf
mwynaidd ei natur, yn weithiwr di-ail, ac yn stocwr
diguro.

For terms and Route apply Owner.

All mares tried at Owner's risk, but every care
will be taken.

All demands to be paid at the end of the Season.

All Mares tried by this will be charged Card Fee.

---

earned his keep the hard way travelling Wales e.g. Premium stallion
for Carmarthenshire 1921, South Cardiganshire 1922, North Cardiganshire 1923, Glamorganshire 1924, West Breconshire 1925, South
Cardiganshire 1926, North Cardiganshire 1928, Carmarthenshire
1929, 1930 and 1931 etc. Considering the enormous number of progeny
sired by Myrtle Welsh Flyer during this period it is surprising that so
few of his blood-lines exist in the present-day Welsh Cobs.

485

9. Ormond Jolly (*chapter 28.15*)

10. Penal Satisfaction
Registration number 1074 in the *Welsh Stud Book, Vol. XX*
Grey, star, height: 14 hands, foaled 1916
Owner: John Evans, Penlan, Blaenpenal, Tregaron,
Cardiganshire
Breeder: Rees Evans, Caemawr, Blaenpenal,
Tregaron
Sire: Trotting Jack 528 (*chapter 27.14*)
Dam: Bess (grey) by Satisfaction (*chapter 24.14*)

Penal Satisfaction was quite a popular stallion in the mid-Cardigan-
shire area; one son of his named Peris Satisfaction (never registered in
the *Welsh Stud Book* although eligible) was owned by Mr. J. Ll. Jones,
Garnwialen, Bethania and he also was used quite a lot at stud.

11. Bess (not registered)
Brown mare, 14 hands 2 in
Owners: J. Davies and Sons, Pant Farm, Llanddewi
Brefi, Cardiganshire
Sire: not recorded
Dam: 4302 Polly of Pant, (winner at Royal Welsh
Shows in 1925 and 1927).

12. Ceitho Welsh Comet (*chapter 24.2*)

13. Llethi Flower (*chapter 26.12*)

14. Mathrafal Brenin (*chapter 23.6*)

15. Coedmawr Pride
Registration number 132 F.S.1 in the appendix *Welsh
Stud Book, Vol. XXXII*
Bay, black points, 14 hands 2 in, foaled 1922
Owners and Breeders: Misses Jenkins, Coedmawr,
Llangeitho, Cardiganshire
Sire: Ceitho Welsh Flyer 1080 (*chapter 27.12*)
Dam: Coedmawr Polly (roan, height: 14 hands 2 in,
foaled 1904)
by King Flyer 35 (*chapter 25.8*)

30

Tyngwndwn Mathrafal Lady (foaled 1958)
Nebo Black Magic (foaled 1962)
Derwen Rosina (foaled 1962)
Derwen Rosina's Last (foaled 1970)

1 Derwen Rosina's Last 9736	2 Nebo Black Magic 4370	4 Pentre Eiddwen Comet 1796	8 Eiddwen's Image 1703
			9 Dewi Black Bess
		5 12953 Tyngwndwn Mathrafal Lady	10 Mathrafal 1629
			11 9160 Tyngwndwn Beauty
	3 Derwen Rosina	6 Cahn Dafydd 1758	10 Mathrafal 1629
			13 9150 Gwenogwen
		7 Rhandir Black	14 Pentre Eiddwen Comet 1796
			15 Bess

1. Derwen Rosina's Last

Registration number 9736 in the *Welsh Stud Book,*
Vol. LIII
Black, star, two white hind fetlocks, height: 14 hands
3 in, foaled 1970
Breeders: E. R. Lloyd and Sons, Ynyshir Farm,
Pennant, Llanon, Cardiganshire

As his name suggests, Derwen Rosina's Last was an orphan foal, his Champion dam dying when still in her prime, with the foal just four weeks old. Rosina's Last survived this set-back to become one of the best sires of the 'seventies (and hopefully will continue well into the 'eighties).

Rosina's Last soon made his mark at stud topping the 1976 Cob sire ratings with such as Derwen Telynores a yearling filly who swept all before her in 1974 and Derwen Serenllys who was exported to Australia. Rosina's Last was equal top sire (with his own sire) in 1978 and fourth in 1979.

The progeny of Derwen Rosina's Last have been in great demand in the sale rings e.g. at the 1978 Llanarth Sale Derwen Ribbon of Blue

Derwen Rosina's Last.

topped the colt foals at 600 guineas and Derwen Dyma Hi topped the filly foals at 1,300 guineas; at the 1979 Sale, Maesyrafon Tywysog Du a black three-year-old colt fetched 1,500 guineas, the second highest figure of the sale.

Possibly the best of all by Rosina's Last is Derwen King Last, foaled in 1977, out of Derwen Queen (who is half-sister to Rosina's Last being a daughter of Derwen Rosina, a year older than Rosina's Last); this colt as a yearling won the youngstock Championship at Lampeter, Reserve Male Champion at the Royal Welsh Show, Champion of the Ponies of Britain at Peterborough and Reserve Champion at both the United Counties and Brecon Shows.

2. Nebo Black Magic
Registration number 4370 in the *Welsh Stud Book, Vol. XLVII*
Black, star, two white hind fetlocks, height: 15 hands, foaled 1962
Breeders: W. G. and M. E. Jones, Lluest Hen, Nebo, Llanon, Cardiganshire

Nebo Black Magic was sold by his breeders when quite young to Messrs Roscoe Lloyd and Sons who then sold him to

Nebo Black Magic.

Brynymor Welsh Magic, son of Nebo Black Magic. (Photograph courtesy of D. Davies.)

England and Black Magic for a few years did his stint pulling a baker's cart around the streets of London. His next move was to run out with a few mares in Essex but since his owner did not keep enough mares to justify his keeping a stallion, Black Magic was entered for Llanybyther Sale. It is very fortunate for Messrs. Roscoe Lloyd and Sons (and for other breeders within the Principality) that they bought Black Magic and very soon (1971) he was winning the Male Championship at the Royal Welsh Show. Black Magic was Reserve Overall Champion to the winning mare Parc Rachel (*chapter 28.1*) at the 1971 and 1975 Royal Welsh Shows; in 1973 he went one stage better winning the George, Prince of Wales Cup from the winning mare Tyhen Mattie, the seventeen-year-old daughter of Mathrafal (*chapter 28.4*).

Nebo Black Magic has long since been well up in the sire ratings list: third in 1975, and 1976, second in 1977, equal first (with his son Derwen Rosina's Last) in 1978 and second in 1979.

Black Magic's progeny have also made their mark in the sale rings:

491

top of the 1978 Builth Wells Sale was the chesnut two-year-old filly Marchgoed Golden Magic selling for 1,200 guineas whilst the second-highest male on the 1979 Builth Wells Sale was the bay two-year-old colt Brynymor April Magic (at 1,050 guineas) a full-brother to the brilliant young Brynymor Welsh Magic (which is also owned by Derwen Stud). The top-priced female Welsh Cob to be sold at any 1979 Sale was Derwen Romana, a bay filly foal out of Tydi Rosita by Meiarth Royal Eiddwen (*chapter 29*) which fetched 1,350 guineas.

One of Black Magic's best progeny without doubt is the lovely black mare Derwen Rosinda (foaled 1970) a daugther of Derwen Seren who is grand-daughter of the noted Polly of Hercws. Rosinda won the novice brood mare class at the 1979 Royal Welsh Show and ended up Reserve Supreme Champion to Open brood mare class winner Ffoslas Black Lady a daughter of Brenin Dafydd.

3. Derwen Rosina
Registration number 9261 F.S.2 in the appendix of
the *Welsh Stud Book, Vol. XLVI*
Black, small star, height: 14 hands 2 in, foaled 1962
Breeder: E. J. Williams, Rhandir Uchaf,
Llangwyryfon, Cardiganshire

If any Welsh Cob has been missed at the peak of its career then this is

Derwen Rosina.

the case with Derwen Rosina. Purchased as a foal from her breeder, Derwen Rosina was Champion female at the Royal Welsh Show at the remarkably young age of four years, a feat which she repeated again in 1967 and 1968, on the last occasion being also the recipient of the George, Prince of Wales cup, the highest accolade possible for the Welsh Cob breed. Derwen Rosina died in 1970 and during her short life she produced:

1965 Derwen Deryn Du, colt, by Llanarth Braint (*chapter 27.1*), senior Stud stallion at the Redwood Stud of Mr. and Mrs. Davies, Cilcennin, Lampeter.

1966 Barren.

1967 Derwen Llwynog, colt, by Nebo Black Magic. This is a big chesnut stallion who excelled himself in long distance rides when owned by Mrs. J. Beaumont. Bought back by Derwen Stud on a Llanarth Sale, he is now producing some very good stock.

1968 Derwen Seren Teledu, filly, by Pentre Eiddwen Comet (*chapter 25.2*). A lovely mare, producing exceptional stock such as Derwen Telynores (1973) by Derwen Rosina's Last and Mr. Nelson Smith's successful young stallion Derwen Telynor (1972) by Nebo Black Magic (Travallion Stud, Coventry).

1969 Derwen Queen, filly, by Hendy Brenin. A valuable mare for the Derwen Stud, dam of Derwen King Last.

1970 Derwen Rosina's Last (*chapter 30.1*).

4. Pentre Eiddwen Comet (*chapter 25.2*)

5. Tyngwndwn Mathrafal Lady
Registration number 12953 in the *Welsh Stud Book, Vol. XLIII*
Dark chesnut, blaze, four white legs, height:
14 hands 2 in, foaled 1958
Breeder: Idris Jones, Tyngwndwn, Cross Inn, Llanon, Cardiganshire
Owners: W. G. and M. E. Jones, Lluest Hen, Nebo, Llanon, Cardiganshire

Mathrafal Lady was given by Mr. Idris Jones to his son and daughter-in-law on the occasion of their marriage in 1961 along with her filly foal Nebo Fair Lady, sired by Meiarth Royal Eiddwen, (*chapter 29*).

Tyngwndwn Mathrafal Lady.

Mathrafal Lady has a strong dislike to being shown and her claim to fame is through her progeny which have taken the show ring by storm. Appended here is a list of her progeny:

1961 Nebo Fair Lady, filly, by Meiarth Royal Eiddwen. Fair Lady was exported to the U.S.A.

1962 Nebo Black Magic, colt, (*2, this chapter*).

1963 Nebo Welsh Lady, filly, by Meiarth Royal Eiddwen (*chapter 29*). After producing Nebo Rosebud (1968) (by Rhystyd Prince) which is retained at the Nebo Stud, Welsh Lady was sold to Mrs. Cooke of the Nantcol Stud for whom she won the female Championships at the Royal Agricultural Society of England Shows in 1971 and 1972 as well as many other prizes under saddle. At the Nantcol Stud, Welsh Lady produced Nantcol Welsh Poppy (by Llanarth Rhodri) in 1972 and Nantcol Flying Lady (by Llanarth Flying Comet) in 1973. Welsh Lady and these two daughters competed at the 1973 Royal Welsh Show for Mrs. Cooke and were placed in enormous classes; the two fillies were then sold on the 1974 Llanarth Sale (lots 131 and 132). Welsh Lady was also sold to Mr. Smith of the Trevallion Stud and competed at the 1975 Royal Welsh Show for him (with filly foal by Brenin Dafydd at foot).

Nebo Rosebud meanwhile remained at Nebo winning a first prize at the 1971 Royal Welsh Show. However she is best known for her outstanding progeny including the two well-known stallions Nebo Brenin (foaled 1971, by Parc Welsh Flyer, *chapter 28*) and Nebo Magic (foaled 1975, by Nebo Black Magic) both retained at Nebo, then Nebo Joker, foaled 1974 (by Parc Welsh Flyer) sold to Mrs. Williams, Moreton-in-Marsh at the 1974 Llanarth Sale.

Four of the progeny of Mathrafal photographed in 1978. From the left: Tanygroes Susanna (foaled in 1959), Chancerie Ray (foaled in 1956, died in 1979), Tyngwndwn Mathrafal Lady and Cefn Parc Boy (foaled in 1952, died in 1979). (Photograph courtesy of I. J. R. Lloyd.)

Nebo Brenin son of Nebo Rosebud, daughter of Nebo Welsh Lady daughter of Tyngwndwn Mathrafal Lady.

1964 Nebo Cariad, filly (sold as a foal).

1967 Nebo Beauty, filly, by Rhystyd Prince. Beauty has also been retained at Nebo producing Nebo Flyer in 1971 (by Parc Welsh Flyer), Nebo Mark in 1973 (by Rhosfarch Frenin) (sold Llanarth Sale 1974), Nebo Charmer in 1974 (by Nebo Black Magic), Nebo Comet in 1975 by Parc Welsh Flyer.

1968 Nebo Princess, filly, by Rhystyd Prince, sold to Oswestry then bought to Derwen Stud where she bred one or two foals before being sold to Yorkshire.

1969 Nebo Tywysog, colt, by Brenin Dafydd. Tywysog was gelded and was a member of George Bowman's famous driving team.

1970 Nebo Dafydd, colt, by Brenin Dafydd. Nebo Dafydd is a very successful stallion at Mrs. Mary Edwards' Cascob Stud. His progeny have demanded high prices at Sales, such as Craven Highlight a three-year-old filly sold for 850 guineas at the 1978

Builth Wells Sale, Cascob Bitannia a bay filly foal sold for 650 guineas at the 1979 Builth Wells Sale and Cascob Little Princess a five-year-old black mare sold for 720 guineas at the 1979Llanarth Sale.

1973 Nebo Princess Ann, filly, by Hafrena Frenin. This filly was a member of the winning group (three from the same dam) at the1975 Royal Welsh Show. She is dam of the spectacular young stallion Nebo Daniel which is a good winner and also retained at Nebo.

1974 Nebo Brenhines, filly, by her grand-son Nebo Brenin. A good show filly, she won a first prize in a very large class at the 1975 Royal Welsh Show and with Princess Ann and Nebo Black Magic, won the progeny class.

1976 Tyngwndwn Fair Lady, filly, by Nebo Brenin.

1977 Nebo Sportsman, colt, by Nebo Brenin; retained at Nebo but leased to Miss Glynis Rapps in Gloucestershire.

1978 Nebo Mab-y-Brenin, colt, by Nebo Brenin (retained).

1979 Nebo Glyndwr, colt, by Nebo Daniel, sold to Mr. Francis of Llanelly.

This impressive list of progeny shows that Mathrafal Lady has had a considerable influence on the Welsh Cob breed and has proved to be a very valuable wedding present!

6. Cahn Dafydd (*chapter 28.2*)

7. Rhandir Black
Registration number 1490 F.S.1 in the appendix of
the *Welsh Stud Book, Vol. XXXIX*
Black, small star, foaled 1955
Breeder: E. J. Williams, Rhandir Uchaf,
Llangwyryfon, Cardiganshire

Rhandir Black is best known for the three full-sisters she produced by Cahn Dafydd: Derwen Rosina in 1962, Rhandir Rosina in 1963 and Rhandir Margarita in 1965.

Derwen Rosina went to Derwen Stud as a foal; Rhandir Rosina stayed at Rhandir Uchaf producing e.g. Rhandir Gwenogwen (foaled in 1972, sired by Parc Commando); Gwenogwen was a good winner in youngstock classes for Mr. Williams later winning for him a third prize in the adult class at the 1976 Royal Welsh Show then in 1978 and 1979 winning third and fifth prizes for her new owners Mr. and Mrs. Tim

Rhandir Black. (Photograph courtesy of I. J. R. Lloyd.)

Eales; Rhandir Margarita became the property of Messrs. D. D. Jones and Son of Ystrad Dewi, Llanddewi Brefi, producing Brenin Penfarch (foaled in 1969) for them first followed by many other good foals up to Ystrad Dewi Olwen (foaled in 1975) by Parc Welsh Flyer. Rhandir Margarita was then sold by the Messrs. Jones on the 1975 Llanarth Sale (lot 96) when she went to the Derwen Stud, her first foal produced there being Derwen Marlin (foaled in 1976 by Nebo Brenin) a very nice filly sold first to Mr. P. R. Faulkner then re-sold on the 1979 Llanarth Sale for 950 guineas.

The later progeny of Rhandir Black are: Rhandir Marina (foaled in 1967, sired by Farian Prince) who is producing good stock in the ownership of Mr. West of Swansea e.g. her yearling colt Danygraig Diemwnt Du sold on the 1979 Llanarth Sale; Rhandir Rhiannon (foaled in 1970) by Parc Commando and her full-sister (retained) Rhandir Rachel the following year, then Rhandir Rowena (foaled in 1977) by the Welsh Pony (Cob type) stallion Fronarth Welsh Jack.

8. Eiddwen's Image *(chapter 25.4)*

9. Dewi Black Bess *(chapter 25.5)*

10. Mathrafal *(chapter 28.4)*

498

11. Tyngwndwn Beauty

Registration number 9160 in the *Welsh Stud Book,*
Vol. XXXII
Cream, blaze, white hind legs, height: 14 hands 2 in,
foaled 1939
Owner and Breeder: Idris Jones, Tyngwndwn, Cross
Inn, Llanon, Cardiganshire
Sire: Cymro'r Wy 1561
Dam: 8362 Isfryn Bess by Creuddyn
Welsh Flyer 1015
G-dam: 3574 Gelmast Sally by Satisfaction
G-g-dam: 3573 Gelmast Peggy by King Jack

Tyngwndwn Beauty has the rare distinction of being dam and grand-dam to two recipients of the George, Prince of Wales Cup for the Champion Welsh Cob at the Royal Welsh Show.

Tyngwndwn Beauty produced three daughters, all sired by Brenin Gwalia (*chapter 23.1*) namely Tyngwndwn Bess (1943), Dolly (1944), and Malen (1946). Then there was a big gap of eleven years in her breeding programme until she produced another three consecutive foals all sired by Mathrafal (*chapter 28.4*); these were Tyngwndwn Cream Boy (1957), Mathrafal Lady (1958) and Tyngwndwn Prince (1959); her last foal

Tyngwndwn Beauty.

499

Stud card of Cymro'r Wy sire of Tyngwndwn Beauty for 1937.

being Tyngwndwn Llwyd o'r Glyn (1960) sired by Cahn Dafydd (*chapter 28.2*). Tyngwndwn Cream Boy was proclaimed Champion Welsh Cob at the 1963 Royal Welsh Show after beating in his class: Llwynog-y-Garth (winner in 1949, 1950 and 1960), Llangybi Seldom Seen, Pentre Rainbow (winner in 1962), Pentre Eiddwen Comet (winner in 1951, 1953, 1956, 1957, 1958 and 1959), Cymro Lan, Brenin-y-Bryniau and Llanarth Brummel (winner in 1964 and 1965), in that order.

Cymro'r Wy was foaled in 1932 and won a second prize (and reserve for the Championship) at the 1939 Royal Welsh Show. In 1937 he was the Premium stallion for North Cardiganshire and left some very good stock in that area including Cymro'r Ystwyth, (a stallion bred from the noted Cwmhwylog strain) that eventually took the place of his sire for Mr. Tom Wood-Jones.

The dam of Tyngwndwn Beauty was Isfryn Bess by Creuddyn Welsh

500

Flyer. Isfryn Bess was bred in 1918 by Morgan Jones, Isfryn, Llanfarian, father of Idris Jones (Tyngwndwn) and grandfather of Geraint Jones (Lluest Hen, Nebo).

The sire of Isfryn Bess was Creuddyn Welsh Flyer (foaled in 1915) who was a premium stallion for South Cardiganshire for many years in in the ownership of Mr. Tom James, Myrtle Hill; Isfryn Bess being one of his first foals.

Creuddyn Welsh Flyer was a dark bay standing 15 hands 1½ in and was sired by Comet (Maenarthur) by Messenger (Dafydd Evans, Pengelly) by Eiddwen Flyer II (*chapter 21.2*). His dam was Brown by Caridgan Briton (Ceffyl Pregethwr, *chapter 1*) by Briton Comet (Tynfron) by Young Comet by Old Comet (*chapter 18.2*) g-dam: Teify by Young Welsh Flyer (Berthlwyd) by Welsh Flyer (*chapter 18.1*) g-g-dam: Lock by Old Express (ceffyl Pwlli Uchaf).

The dam of Isfryn Bess was Gelmast Sally a cream 13-hand mare bred (in 1909) by William Rowlands, Gelmast, Devil's Bridge, Aberystwyth. She was sired by Satisfaction (Blaengorffen, *chapter 24.14*) and her dam Gelmast Peggy was a 13-hand chesnut roan mare (foaled in 1905) sired by King Jack (*chapter 23*).

13. **Gwenogwen** (*chapter 28.5*)

15. **Bess**
Registration number 1083 F.S. in the appendix of the
Welsh Stud Book, Vol. XXXVI
Black, blaze, two white hind legs, height: 14 hands
2 in, foaled 1943
Owner and Breeder: E. J. Williams, Rhandir Uchaf,
Llangwyryfon, Cardiganshire
Sire: Llethi Valiant 1238 (*chapter 26.12*).

Index

504

505

506

509

512

513